MW01122396

A Domestic Policy-Making Approach to World Market Integration

Christian Robin

A Domestic Policy-Making Approach to World Market Integration

Chile, Argentina, Peru, and Bolivia in Comparison

Südwestdeutscher Verlag für Hochschulschriften

Impressum/Imprint (nur für Deutschland/ only for Germany)

Bibliografische Information der Deutschen Nationalbibliothek: Die Deutsche Nationalbibliothek verzeichnet diese Publikation in der Deutschen Nationalbibliografie; detaillierte bibliografische Daten sind im Internet über http://dnb.d-nb.de abrufbar.

Verlag: Südwestdeutscher Verlag für Hochschulschriften Aktiengesellschaft & Co. KG
Dudweiler Landstr. 99, 66123 Saarbrücken, Deutschland
Telefon +49 681 37 20 271-1, Telefax +49 681 37 20 271-0, Email: info@svh-verlag.de
Zugl.: Zürich, Universität, Diss., 2008

Herstellung in Deutschland:
Schaltungsdienst Lange o.H.G., Berlin
Books on Demand GmbH, Norderstedt
Reha GmbH, Saarbrücken
Amazon Distribution GmbH, Leipzig
ISBN: 978-3-8381-0101-9

Imprint (only for USA, GB)

Bibliographic information published by the Deutsche Nationalbibliothek: The Deutsche Nationalbibliothek lists this publication in the Deutsche Nationalbibliografie; detailed bibliographic data are available in the Internet at http://dnb.d-nb.de.

Publisher:
Südwestdeutscher Verlag für Hochschulschriften Aktiengesellschaft & Co. KG
Dudweiler Landstr. 99, 66123 Saarbrücken, Germany
Phone +49 681 37 20 271-1, Fax +49 681 37 20 271-0, Email: info@svh-verlag.de

Printed in the U.S.A.
Printed in the U.K. by (see last page)
ISBN: 978-3-8381-0101-9

Contents

Boxes, Figures, and Tables

Acknowledgements

Many have contributed to make this thesis possible. First of all, I am very thankful to my supervisor, Thomas Bernauer, for his dedicated support and his open-minded attitude. Although the topic of this study was not related to ongoing projects in the CIS, Thomas Bernauer encouraged me to study a subject of great personal interest, and in which I consider there to be a lack of research. In the same way, I would like to thank to Gabi Hesselbein, a committed senior researcher on African affairs. Especially after finishing my MA thesis on State-Business Relations in Democratic Consolidation Processes, Gabi gave me the impetus necessary to take on such an endeavour. Equally, I appreciated the guidance – sometimes intentional and sometimes not – provided by Roy Suter, former doctoral student of Thomas Bernauer. Furthermore, I would like to thank to the entire Bernauer Group, especially Claudia Jenny, for their support and warm reception during my stay at the CIS office. Finally, to Dieter Ruloff, I am grateful for accepting the job of co-examiner of this extensive study.

In South America, I am heavily indebted to countless people, who improved the content of this thesis by insightful conversations, documents, contacts, and psychological support. Particularly in light of the numerous interviews conducted, one should probably make an analysis on the productivity crunch caused by doctoral students such as myself, who, thirsty of knowledge, do not allow people to complete their duties. In this regard, special heartfelt acknowledgement and thanks goes to the hundreds of state and business officials, entrepreneurs, academic personnel and administrative staff who opened their doors to me and helped me to learn a great deal about how trade policy making in Latin America works. Yet, despite all these valuable perceptions and factional information, mistakes and unwanted biased interpretation on subjects involved in this study cannot be fully avoided and are due to my negligence alone.

In *Argentina*, I am mostly indebted to Adrián Makuc (National Director of Foreign Trade Policy), Luciana Mermet (Trade Policy Advisor in the Ministry of Economy), Jorge Campbell (Ex-State Secretary of Foreign Economic Relations), Rodolfo Rúa Boiero (President of the Centre of Studies on Economic Integration and International Trade), and Christiane De Kojic (Head of the CIPA Foreign Trade Department). All of them are busy, first-class professionals, who explained to me in repeated, time-consuming talks the daily problems faced regarding the inadequacy of IT equipment, the complicated MERCOSUR agenda, the absence of interministerial coordination, and the indifference among local entrepreneurs regarding trade policy, etc. From the world of academia, I am particularly grateful for guidance, valuable advice and feedback from Félix Peña (UNTREF and Bank Boston Foundation), Roberto Bouzas (FLACSO and San Andrés University) and the staff of the Latin American Integration Institute, La Plata. From FUNDES International, a special thank-you goes to Philippe Schneuwly, who encouraged me towards the challenging end of my research due to his rich experiences as a former PhD candidate. Moreover, Philippe, together with Kuno Iten (the most human Swiss banker I've ever met), helped me transport the tons of material collected during my field visits to Europe.

In *Bolivia* and *Peru,* I was able to count on the invaluable patronage of SECO in the scope of the ongoing Trade Cooperation Projects. Aside from the financial support which made the extensive field research in both Andean countries possible, I am very thankful to two Project Managers, Markus Reichmuth (Peru) and Thomas Hentschel (Bolivia), for their extremely collaborative behaviour and openly sharing with me their long lasting field experience in Latin America. In *Bolivia,* a special thank-you also goes to the IBCE team, Gary Rodríguez, Soraya Fernández and Lorgio Arano, who nourished me with abundant written data and sharp analysis on Bolivia's failed trade integration. Furthermore, the professionalism exhibited by this private sector think tank (fairly unique in Latin America) made me believe in a better future for this marvellous country that suffers from tremendously weak institutions. On the state side, special thanks goes to Helen De Rico, Gustavo Invernizzi, Carmen Otalora and Humberto Zambrana, for the time offered to explain to me the current and past problems identified in Bolivia's state executive branch.

In *Peru,* sincere thanks go to Marco Santos (Ex-scholar of World Trade Institute, Berne, and during 2004, Project Assistant at the Pacific University) and Viviana Sanchez (legal advisor in the Ministry of Economy and Finance). Within a short time, Marco and Viviana became close friends, generous hosts, provider of (confidential) documents and open-minded key informants. Moreover, inside the public sector, I would like to thank Victoria Elmore and Ricardo Paredes who took, on several occasions, the time to explain to me the hopeful climb of the Ministry of Foreign Trade and Tourism. In the same way, I appreciated the rich insights provided by Adolfo Lopez (Ex-Vice-Minister of Integration and currently a CAN General Secretariat functionary), lamenting the erratic participation of his country in the Andean Community. Finally, I was very grateful to Ramon Morante, Head of the SNI Foreign Trade Department, for providing me with an unfiltered testimony of the fluid relations he maintains with the official negotiation team on two occasions. In *Chile,* my debts are slightly smaller due to my focus on studies carried out by others. Nonetheless, I became a very lucky witness of the profound case knowledge openly shared by Sebastián Sáez. Being one of the most insightful interviews I've ever conducted, I was able to gather first hand information regarding the very revealing Chilean case. I would also like to say a especially thank you to Pedro Reuss, as representative of Latin America's most efficient business interlocutor, SOFOFA, and Adrian Buvinic, the dynamic and self-confident Director of Legal Affairs of the DIRECON office for valuable case facts.

Without support from my family, this work would not have come about. Heartfelt thanks goes to my wife, Macarena, for her infinite assistance, comprehension, encouragement and joy of life; to my son, Mateo, for making clear that there is life besides a PhD; to my sister, Catherine, for providing sound administrative support during my stays overseas. Also, I owe very much to my parents, Marie-Therese and Peter, who have guided and supported me throughout my whole life, and who have left me the needed space and confidence to find my own answers. Finally, a huge thank-you goes to Therese Robin, my godmother, for her immeasurable sympathy and generosity, and Klaus Robin, my godfather, PhD in Zoology and the country's most accomplished "bird expert." Undoubtedly, Klaus' audacious way of being a professional and his go-ahead spirit has inspired me and worked as a great remedy against doubts and insecurities.

***

Financial Support for this study was provided by the Academic Trainee Fund (FAN) and the Ecoscientia-Foundation. It is very gratefully acknowledged. I am especially thankful to Dr. Ulrich E. Gut, Managing Director of FAN, for his reliable attention and confidence in my work. As mentioned, the Swiss State Secretariat for Economic Affairs (SECO) strongly contributed to this thesis in financing the cost of field research in Bolivia and Peru. Here, a special thank goes to Hans-Peter Egler, Head of the Environment and Trade Cooperation Division. Finally, notable "sympathy contributions" were granted by the Foundations AVINA and Reiser-Siemssen.

Abbreviations

Introduction, Analytical Framework and Conclusions

ACE	Economic Complementary Agreements
ALADI	Latin American Integration Association (Asociación Latinoamericana de Integración)
ALALC	Latin American Free Trade Association (Asociación Latinoamericana de Libre Comercio)
APEC	Asia Pacific Economic Forum
ATPDEA	Andean Trade Promotion and Drug Eradication Act
CAN	Andean Community of Nations (Comunidad Andina de Naciones)
CEPAL	Comisión Económica para América Latina y el Caribe
CET	Common External Tariff
COECE	Entrepreneurial Coordinator of Foreign Trade (Coordinadora de Organismos Empresariales de Comercio Exterior)
CUSTFA	Canada-US Free Trade Agreement
DBLA	Dresdner Bank Lateinamerika
ECLAC	Economic Commission for Latin America and the Caribbean
EU	European Union
EFTA	European Free Trade Association
EPB	Economic Planning Board
FDI	Foreign Direct Investment
FOB	Free on Board
FTAA	Free Trade Area of the Americas
FTA	Free Trade Agreements
GATT	General Agreement on Tariffs and Trade
GATS	General Agreement on Trade in Services
GDP	Gross Domestic Product
GSP	General System of Preferences
IDB	Inter-American Development Bank
IMF	International Monetary Fund
ISI	Import Substitution Industrialization
ITN	International Trade Negotiations
ITO	International Trade Organisation
NAFTA	North American Free Trade Agreement
MERCOSUR	Common Market of the South (Mercado Común del Sur)
MFN	Most Favored Nation
MM	Multipolar Model
NGO	Non-Governmental Organization
OECD	Organization for Economic Co-operation and Development
PCC	Trade Cooperation Programme
PICE	Program for Integration and Economic Cooperation
PTA	Preferential Trade Agreement
SECO	Swiss State Secretary of Economic Affairs
SME	Small and Medium Sized Enterprise
SM	Springboard Model
US	United States
USTR	United States Trade Representative
TRIPS	Agreement on Trade-Related Aspects of Intellectual Property Rights
WEF	World Economic Forum
WTO	World Trade Organization

Chile

ABIF	Association of Banking and Financial Institutes (Asociación de Bancos e Instituciones Financieras)
ALADI	Latin American Integration Association (Asociación Latinoamericana de Integración)
ALALC	Latin American Free Trade Association (Asociación Latinoamericana de Libre Comercio)
APEC	Asia Pacific Economic Forum
ASEXMA	Association of Exporters of Manufactured Goods (Asociación de Exportadores de Manufacturas y Servicios)
ASIMET	Chilean Association of Metall Industry (Asociaciòn Chilena de Industrias Metalúrgicas y Metalmecánicas)
CASE	Entrepreneurial Advisory Committees (Consejo Asesor Empresarial)
CEP	Centre for Public Studies (Centro de Estudios Públicos)
CERA	Argentinean Chamber of Exporters (Cámara Argentina de Exportadores)
CET	Common External Tariff
CNC	National Chamber of Commerce (Cámara Nacional de Comercio)
CPA	Confederation of Agriculture Producers (Confederación de Productores Agrícolas)
CODESSER	Corporation of Social Development of the Rural Sector (Corporación de Desarrollo Social del Sector Rural)
CONAPYME	Council of the Small and Medium Company (Consejo de la Mediana y Pequeña Empresa)
CONICYT	National Commission of Science and Technology (Comisión Nacional de Investigación Científica y Tecnológica)
CNR	National Commission of Irrigation (Comisión Nacional de Riego)
CONUPIA	Confederation of Small and Micro Manufactures and Handicraft Associations (Confederación Gremial Nacional Unida de la Mediana, Pequeña, Microindustria, Servicios y Artesanado)
COPEC	Petroleum Company of Chile (Compañia de Petróleos de Chile)
CORFO	Chilean Development Corporation (Corporación de Fomento de la Producción)
CORMA	Chilean Lumber Corporation (Corporación Chilena de la Madera)
CPC	Confederation of Production and Commerce (Confederación de Producción y Comercio)
CUT	Central Workers Union (Central Unitaria de Trabajadores)
DIRECON	General Directorate of International Economic Relations (Dirección General de Relaciones Económicas Internacionales)
EFTA	European Free Trade Association
FEPACH	Federation of Food Processing Industries of Chile (Federación de Procesadores de Alimentos y Agroindustriales de Chile)
FIA	Foundation for Agrarian Innovation (Fundación para la Innovación Agraria)
FISA	Santiago's International Ferry (Fería Internacional de Santiago)
FOB	Free on Board
FTA	Free Trade Agreement
INDAP	Institute of Rural Development (Instituto de Desarrollo Agropecuario)
ILO	International Labour Organization
ITT	International Telephone and Telegraph
NAFTA	North American Free Trade Agreement
ODEPA	Agrarian Research and Policy Office (Oficina de Estudios y Políticas Agrarias)
PBS	Price Band System
PEPALC	Program for Special Studies (Programa de Estudios para el Acuerdo de Libre Comercio entre Chile y Estados Unidos)
PTA	Preferential Trade Agreement
RUT	Single Tax Register (Registro Único Tributario)
SECOFI	Secretariat of Trade and Industry (Secretaría de Comercio y Fomento Industrial)
SERCOTEC	Service for Technical Cooperation (Servicio de Cooperación Técnica)
SNA	National Agriculture Society (Sociedad Nacional de Agricultura)
SOFOFA	Society of Manufacturing Promotion (Sociedad de Fomento Fabril)
SONAMI	National Mining Society (Sociedad Nacional de Minería)

SONAPESCA	Fisheries Society of Chile (Sociedad Nacional de Pesca)
SPS	Sanitary and Phytosanitary Measures
USTR	United States Trade Representative

Argentina

AIERA	Arg. Association of Importers and Exporters (Asociación de Importadores y Exportadores de la República Argentina)
ABRA	Arg. Banking Association (Asociación de Bancos de la República Argentina)
ACE	Agreement of Economic Complementation (Acuerdo de Complementación Económica)
ACIEL	Coordinated Action of Free Entrepreneurial Institutions (Acción Coordinadora de las Instituciones Empresarias Libres)
ADELCO	Consumer Protection Association (Asociación de Defensa del Consumidor)
ADEFA	Arg. Association of Auto Motor Producers (Asociación de Fábricas de Automotores de Argentina)
ADIMRA	Arg. Association of Metalurchical Industry (Asociación de la Industria Metalúrgica de la República Argentina)
AEA	Arg. Enterpreneurship Association (Asociación Empresaria Argentina)
AFARTE	Arg. Association of Consumer Electronics Industry (Asociación de Fábricas Argentinas Terminales de Electrónica)
ALADI	Latin America Integration Association (Asociación Latinoamericana de Integración)
ALALC	Latin America Free Trade Area (Asociación Latinoamericana de Libre Comercio)
AFCP	Association of Cellulose and Paper Producers (Asociación de Fabricantes de Celuosa y Papel)
AFIP	Federal Administration of State Revenues (Administradora Federal de Ingresos Públicos)
APEGEL	Permanent Assembly of Enterpreneurial Entities (Asamblea Permanente de Entidades Gremiales Empresarias)
APYME	Assembly of Small and Medium Entrepreneurs (Asamblea de Pequeños y Medianos Empresarios)
BICE	Investment and Foreign Trade Bank (Banco de Inversión y Comercio Exterior)
BNDES	National Bank of Economic and Social Development (Banco Nacional de Desarrollo Económico y Social)
BOLSA	Buenos Aires Traders' Union (Bolsa de Comercio de Buenos Aires)
CAA	Arg. Sugar Producers Centre (Centro Argentino Azucarero)
CAC	National Chamber of Commerce (Camara Argentina de Comercio)
CAC	Arg. Chamber of Construction (Cámara Argentina de la Construcción)
CAEME	Arg. Chamber of Farmaceutical Specialities (Cámara Argentina de Especialidades Medicinales)
CAFI	Arg. Chamber of Fruit Producers (Cámara Argentina de Fruticultores Integrados)
CAIP	Arg. Chamber of Plastic Industry (Cámara Argentina de la Industria Plástica)
CAMIMA	Arg. Chamber of SME Metalurchical Industry (Cámara de la Pequeña y Mediana Industria Metalúrgica Argentina)
CACE	Private Sector Advisory Council on Foreign Trade (Consejo Asesor de Comercio Exterior)
CEA	Arg. Entrepreneurial Council (Consejo Empresario Argentino)
CEI	Centre of International Economy (Centro de Economía Internacional)
CENI	Study Centre of International Negotiations (Centro de Estudios para las Negociaciones Internacionales)
CERA	Arg. Export Chamber (Cámara Argentina de Exportadores)
CET	Common External Tariff
CIAI	Arg. Chamber of Clothing Industry (Camara Industrial Argentina de la Indumentaria)
CIARA-CEC	Arg. Chamber of Vegetable Oils Industry-Centre of Cereals Exporters (Cámara de la Industria Aceitera de la República Argentina- Centro de Exportadores de Cereales)
CICA	Arg. Chamber of Footwear Industry (Cámara de la Industria de Calzado Argentina)
CIL	Centre of Dairy Industry (Centro de la Industria Lechera)

CILFA	Chamber of Argentinean Pharmaceutical Laboratories (Cámara Industrial de Laboratorios Farmaceuticos Argentinos)
CIPA	Chamber of Foodstuffs Industry (Cámara de Industriales de Productos Alimenticios)
CIQIP	Chamber of Chemical and Petrochemical Industry (Cámara de la Industria Química y Petroquímica)
CIS	Centre of Steel Industry (Centro de Industriales Siderúrgicos)
CGE	General Confederation of Economy (Confederación General Económica)
CGT	General Confederation of Labor (Confederación General del Trabajo)
CNCE	National Foreign Trade Commission (Comisión Nacional de Comercio Exterior)
CONIAGRO	Confederation of Rural Cooperatives (Confederación Intercooperativa Agropecuaria)
COOPERALA	Enterpreneurial Chamber of Pharmaceutical Laboratories (Cámara Empresaria de Laboratorios Farmacéuticos)
COPAL	Coordinator for Food and Beverage Industry (Coordinadora de las Industrias de Productos Alimenticios)
CORFO	Chilean Development Corporation (Corporación de Fomento de la Producción)
CRA	Arg. Rural Confederations (Confederación Rural Argentina)
FAA	Arg. Agrarian Federation (Federación Agraria Argentina)
FAIGA	Arg. Federation of Grafic Industry (Federación Argentina de la Industria Gráfica y Afines)
FCES	MERCOSUR Economic and Social Consultative Forum (Foro Económico y Social del MERCOSUR)
FITA	Arg. Federation of Textiles Industries (Federación Argentina de Industrias Textiles)
FTA	Free Trade Area
FTAA	Free Trade Area of the America
GMC	Common Market Group (Grupo del Mercado Común)
IDI	Institute for Industrial Development (Instituto para el Desarrollo Industrial)
INAI	Institute of International Agriculture Negotiations (Instituto de Negociaciones Agrícolas Internacionales)
INDEC	National Statistics Institute (Instituto Nacional de Estadísticas y Censos)
INTI	National Institute of Industrial Technology (Instituto Nacional de Tecnología Industrial)
ISEN	National Foreign Service Institute (Instituto del Servicio Exterior de la Nación)
MENA	National Entrepreneurial Round Table (Mesa Empresarial Nacional)
MERCOSUR	Common Market of the South (Mercado Común del Sur)
MEP	Ministry of Economy and Production (Ministerio de Economía y Producción)
MIA	Argentinean Industrial Movement (Movimento Industrial Argentino)
MIN	National Industrial Movement (Movimiento Industrial Nacional)
MRECIC	Ministry of Foreign Relations, International Trade and Worship (Ministerio de Relaciones Exteriores, Comercio Internacional y Culto)
MOI	Manufactures of Industrial Origin (Manufacturas de Origen Industrial)
PICE	Argentinean-Brazilian Program for Integration and Economic Cooperation (Programa de Integración y Cooperación Económica)
SEBRAE	Brazilian Service for Micro y Small Firm Support (Servicio Brasilero de Apoyo de Micro y Pequeñas Empresas)
SICE	Secretariat of Industry and Foreign Trade (Secretaría de Industria y Comercio Exterior)
SINAPA	National System of Administrative Profession (Sistema Nacional de la Profesión Administrativa)
SRA	Argentinean Rural Society (Sociedad Rural Argentina)
UIA	Argentinean Industrialists Union (Unión Industrial Argentina)
UGT	General Union of Milk Producers (Unión General de Tamberos)
YPF	State Petroleum Company (Yacimientos Petrolíferos Fiscales)

Peru

ACE	Economic Complementary Agreement (Acuerdo de Complementación Económica)
ADEX	Exporters Association (Asociación de Exportadores)

ADIFAN	Association of Pharmaceutical Industries of National Origin (Asociación de Industrias Farmacéuticas de Origen y Capital Nacionales)
AGAP	Association of Agro Exporter Entities (Asociación de Gremios Productores Agroexportadores)
ALADI	Latin American Integration Association (Asociación Latinoamericana de Integración)
ALAFARPE	National Association of Pharmaceutical Laboratories of Peru (Asociación Nacional de Laboratorios Farmaceúticos de Perú
APEC	Asia-Pacific Economic Cooperation
APESEG	Peruvian Association of Assurance Companies (Asociación Peruana de Empresas de Seguros)
ATPA	Andean Trade Promotion Act
ATPDEA	Andean Trade Promotion and Drug Eradication Act
CADE	Annual Business Executives Conferences (Conferencia Anual de Ejecutivos)
CAF	Andean Development Corporation (Corporación Andina de Fomento)
CAN	Andean Community of Nations (Comunidad Andina de Naciones)
CCL	Lima Chamber of Commerce (Cámara de Comercio de Lima)
CENI	Entrepreneurial Council of International Negotiations (Consejo Empresarial de Negociones Internaciones)
CEPES	Peruvian Centre of Social Studies (Centro Peruano de Estudios Sociales)
CERTEX	Certificate of Tax Return on Non-Traditional Exports (Certificado de Reintegro a la Exportación No Tradicional)
CET	Common External Tariff
CNC	National Council for Competitiveness
COMEXPERU	Foreign Trade Society of Peru
COMPYMEP	Peruvian Council of Micro, Small, Medium Scale Firms Organizations (Consejo de Organizaciones de la Micro, Pequeña y Mediana Empresa del Perú)
CONFIEP	National Confederation of Private Entrepreneurship Institutions (Confederación Nacional de Instituciones Empresariales Privadas)
CONVEAGRO	National Agrarian Convention (Convención Nacional Del Agro)
COPEI	Committee of Small Industry (Comité de la Pequeña Industria)
FAO	Food and Agriculture Organization
FONGAL	National Fund of Dairy Livestock (Fondo Nacional de Ganadería Lechera)
FOPEX	Fund for Non-Traditional Export Promotion
FTA	Free Trade Area
GSP	General System of Preferences
ICE	Foreign Trade Institute (Instituto de Comercio Exterior)
IDB	Inter-American Development Bank
INDECOPI	National Institute of Intellectual Property and Competition Defense (Instituto Nacional de Defensa del Consumidor)
IPAE	Peruvian Institute of Business Administration (IPAE)
IPE	National Planning Institute
IPR	Intellectual Properties Rights
MICITI	Ministry of Industry, Domestic Trade, Tourism and Integration (Ministerio de Industria, Comercio Interno, Turismo e Integración)
MINAG	Ministry of Agriculture (Ministerio de Agricultura)
MITI	Ministry of Industry, Tourism, Integration (Ministerio de Industria, Turismo, Integración)
MITINCI	Ministry of Industry, Tourism, Integration and International Trade Negotiations (Ministerio de Industria, Turismo, Integración y Negociaciones Comerciales Internacionales)
MEF	Ministry of Economy and Finance (Ministerio de Economía y Finanzas)
MINCETUR	Ministry of Foreign Trade and Tourism (Ministerio de Comercio Exterior y Turismo)
ONIT	National Integration Office (Oficina Nacional de Integración)
PBS	Price Band System
PENX	National Export Plan (Plan Nacional de Exportación)
PeruCámeras	National Chamber of Commerce, Production & Services (Cámara Nacional de Commercio, Producción y Servicios)

PROMPEX	Export Promotion Commission (Comisión para la Promoción de Exportaciones)
SADA	Arequipa Rural Society (Sociedad Agrícola de Arequipa)
SENASA	National Servico of Agrarian Sanity (Servicio Nacional de Sanidad Agraria)
SNMPE	National Society of Mining, Petroleum & Energy (Sociedad Nacional de Minería, Petroleo y Energía)
SNI	National Industry Society (Sociedad Nacional de Industrias)
SNP	National Fishery Society (Sociedad Nacional de Pesquería)
UP	Pacific University (Universidad del Pacífico)
US-AFTA	United States-Andean Free Trade Agreement
USTR	United States Trade Representative
VMCE	Vice-Ministry of Foreign Trade (Vice-Ministerio de Comercio Exterior)

Bolivia

ABA	Bolivian Association of Insurances (Asociación Boliviana de Aseguradoras)
ACE	Economic Complementary Agreement (Acuerdo de Complementación Económica)
ACAP	Central Storehouse of Farming Equipments (Almacen Central Agricola y Pecuario)
ADN	Democratic Nationalist Action (Acción Democrática Nacionalista)
ALADI	Latin American Integration Association (Asociación Latinoamericana de Integración)
ALALC	Latin American Association for Free Trade (Asociación Latinoamericana de Libre Comercio)
ANAPO	National Association of Oleaginous and Wheat Producers (Asociación de Productores de Oleaginosas y Trigo)
ATPA	Andean Trade Preference Act
ATPDEA	Andean Trade Promotion and Drug Eradication Act
ASOBAN	Bolivian Association of Private Banks (Asociación de Bancos Privados de Bolivia)
CABOFACE	National Brewery Chamber (Cámara Boliviana de Fabricantes de Cerveza)
CADEPIA	Departamental Chamber of Small Scale Industry (Cámara Departamental de la Pequeña Industria y Artesanía)
CADEX	Santa Cruz Export Chamber (Cámara de Exportadores de Santa Cruz)
CAF	Andean Development Coporation (Corporación Andina de Fomento)
CAINCO	Santa Cruz Chamber of Industry, Commerce, Services and Tourism (Cámara de Industria, Comercio, Servicios y Turismo de Santa Cruz)
CAMEX	La Paz Chamber of Exporters (Cámara de Exportadores de La Paz)
CAN	Andean Community of Nations (Comunidad Andina de Naciones)
CANEB	National Chamber of Exporters (Cámara Nacional de Exportadores)
CAO	Eastern Chamber of Agriculture (Cámara Oriental de Agricultura)
CBC	National Chamber Construction (Cámara Nacional de la Construcción)
CBF	Bolivian Development Corporation (Corporación Boliviana de Fomento)
CEDEIM	Tax Refund Certificates (Certificados de Devolución Impositiva)
CEDLA	Study Centre of Labor and Rural Development (Centro de Estudios para el Desarrollo Laboral y Agrario)
CEPB	Bolivian Confederation of Private Entrepreneurship (CEPB)
CEPROBOL	Promotion Centre of Bolivia (Centro de Promoción Bolivia)
CERTEX	Certificates of Tax Reimbursments (Certificados de Reintegro Tributarios)
CIFABOL	Bolivian Chamber of Pharmaceutical Industry (Cámara de la Industria Farmacéutica de Bolivia)
CIOEC	Coordinator of Small Scale Farming Unit Organizations of Bolivia (Comité Integrador de Organizaciones Económicas Campesinas)
CNC	National Chamber of Commerce (Cámara Nacional de Comercio)
CNI	National Chamber of Industry (Cámara Nacional de Industria)
COB	Central Workers Union (Central Obrera Boliviana)
CODEPLAN	National Council of Economy and Planning (Consejo Nacional de Economía y Planificación)
COMIBOL	Bolivian Mining Corporation (Corporación Minera de Bolivia)

CONAPE	National Council of Economic Policy (Consejo Nacional de Planificación Económica)
CONEX	National Export Council (Consejo Nacional de Exportaciones)
CORDECRUZ	Santa Cruz Development Corporation (Corporación de Desarrollo de Santa Cruz)
ENEX	National Export Strategy (Estrategia Nacional de Exportaciones)
FEBOPI	Bolivian Federation of Small Industry (Federación Boliviana de la Pequeña Industria)
FEGASACRUZ	Santa Cruz Federation of Livestock Farming (Federación de Ganaderos de Santa Cruz)
GSP	Generalised System of Preferences
IBCE	Bolivian Institute of Foreign Trade (Instituto Boliviano de Comercio Exterior)
INE	National Institute for Statistics (Instituto Nacional de Estadística)
ITC	International Trade Centre UNCTAD/WTO
INPEX	National Institute of Export Promotion (Instituto Nacional de Promoción de Exportaciones)
LOPE	Ministerial Law of the Executive Power (Ley de Organización del Poder Ejecutivo)
MAS	Movement towards Socialism (Movimiento al Socialismo)
MBL	Free Bolivian Movement (Moviemiento Bolivia Libre)
MDE	Ministry of Economic Development (Ministerio de Desarrollo Económico)
MCEI	Minister of Foreign Trade and Investment (Ministerio de Comercio Exterior e Inversiones)
MECE	Ministry of Exports and Economic Competitiveness (Ministerio de Exportaciones y Competitividad Económica)
MIR	Leftist Revolution Movement (Movimiento de Izquierda Revolucionaria)
MNR	Nationalist Revolution Movement (Movimiento Nacionalista Revolucionario)
RITEX	Temporary Import Regime for Export Promotion (Régimen de Internación Temporal para Perfeccionamiento Activo).
SAFCO	System of Financial Administration and Governmental Control (Sistema de Administración Financiera y Control Gubernamental)
SAT	Technical Assistance Service (Servicio de Asistencia Técnica)
SBPC	Bolivian System of Productivity and Competitiveness (Sistema Boliviano de Productividad y Competitividad)
SEGIN	General Secretariat of Integration (Secretaría General de Integración)
SENASA	National Service of Agriculture Sanity (Servicio Nacional de Sanidad Agroalimentaria)
SENAPI	National Service of Intelectual Property (Servicio Nacional de Propiedad Intelectual)
SICOMEX	Service of Foreign Trade Information (Servicio de Información para Comercio Exterior)
SLDC	Small and Less Developed Country
UDAPE	Analyzing Unit for Economic and Social Policy (Unidad de Análisis de Políticas Sociales y Económicas)
UMSA	Mayor University of San Andrés (Universidad Mayor de San Andrés)
UNCI	Unit for International Trade Negotiation (Unidad de Negociaciones Comerciales Internacionales)
UPC	Productivity and Competitiveness Unit (Unidad de Productividad y Competitividad)
US-AFTA	United States - Andean Free Trade Talks
USAID	United States Development Agency
USTR	United States Trade Representative
VAT	Value Added Tax
VICE	Vice-Ministry of Industry, Commerce and Exports (Vice-Ministerio de Industria, Comercio y Exportaciones)
VREI	Vice-Ministry of International Economic Relations (Vice-Ministerio de Relaciones Economicas Internacionales)

1   Introduction

If we are to understand the modern challenges of world market integration, there are few better examples than those found in South America. More than in any other region, countries in this region have experienced drastic changes during the last two decades concerning the way their economies are integrated into global markets. In the 1980s, these changes were mainly a result of external shocks, in terms of debt crises and the consequent balance of payment problems which forced governments to abandon the remaining features of the state-led import substitution industrialisation strategies practiced since the 1930s. Consequently, these countries began shifting towards a widespread disengagement of the State in national economies, and the liberalisation of trade regimes in particular (Edwards 1995). These initial reform steps, aimed at further economic openness, were largely based on unilateral measures and, in the case of trade reforms, implied a substantial reduction of external tariffs – from a annual regional average of over 40 percent to just 12 percent (Devlin/Estevadeordal 2001: 1).

On more stable macroeconomic grounds, trade policy took on a new meaning during the 1990s. The adjustment approach (Williamson 1990), with the principal goal of correcting relative prices, was no longer the central pillar, instead, national governments set forth active world market integration plans, and fostered the development of exports as a means to lower their dependency on a narrow range of mostly unprocessed commodities; which until this point had been one of the main causes of the balance of payment problems experienced by most countries in the region (Loser/Guerguil 1999).

A strategic and indispensable policy tool in this process constituted the search for market access and foreign investments, by means of reciprocal forms of liberalisation. On the *multilateral level,* the Uruguay Round (1986-1994) was South America's first significant experience within the multilateral trading system. While almost entirely absent within the former system of the General Agreement of Trade and Tariffs (GATT), from 1995 the World Trade Organization (WTO) evolved into a vital reference framework for policy-makers in the region, i.e. South American countries not only incorporated the WTO agreements into national law, but undertook far-reaching commitments in most areas involved. On the *regional and extra-regional level,* the countries' involvement became even more widespread than with multilateral initiatives. In this respect, the customs union agreements of the Common Market of the South, or "MERCOSUR" (Brazil, Argentina, Paraguay, and Uruguay), and the Andean Group (Colombia, Peru, Venezuela, Bolivia, and Ecuador) stand out, as do numerous bilateral preferential trade agreements, both between Latin American countries, and with trading partners in Europe, North America, and Asia.

With this agenda, Latin America became a paradigmatic case of modern trade policies. Rather than being based merely on unilateral measures, trade policy has increasingly been implemented by reciprocal forms of liberalisation on the multilateral and (extra-) regional level. Furthermore, the notion of "trade" has become much broader. Rather than the traditional focus on abolishing tariff and non-tariff barriers, the WTO, MERCOSUR and North American Free Trade Agreement (NAFTA) all moved towards a wide set of "behind-the-border-measures" affecting foreign business transactions, such as regulating services, investment, state procurement, intellectual property rights and subsidies.

This shift in the trade policy agenda was accompanied by changing views on what constitutes a successful strategy for world market integration. Discussions no longer focussed only on whether or not openness to trade – low tariffs, absent non-tariff barriers (NTB's) and export taxes – proves beneficial to developing countries, but on how, when and under what rules and background conditions trade liberalisation is to be carried out. For example, Dani Rodrik, a prominent critic of the WTO, does not question the positive effects of free trade on economic growth, productivity and poverty reduction in the long-term, but suggests that WTO institutions – being, to a wide extent, the reference schemes for regional initiatives – do not adequately meet the necessities of developing nations, and argues in favour of a more gradualist approach based on "local experimentation" (Rodrik 1999; 2000b).

On the other hand, in recent years the World Bank – often criticised for its "one-size-fits-all" approach to trade reform when advising bank clients – has been urged to expand its focus. According to "Assessing WB support for trade 1987-2004" by the World Bank Independent Evaluation Group (IEG 2006), the Bank traditionally placed too much emphasis on import liberalisation, especially during the initial period of reform, having been overly optimistic for growth in the short run. Accordingly (IEG 2006: xvi), *"it underestimated the complexity and sequencing of complementary policies (e.g. competition, labour, fiscal policies); the role of the external environment (investment climate), the interaction among trade, growth, and distributional outcomes; and the country-specific context (such as initial conditions and institutions) in which these policies interacted".*

Studying experiences in South America, we find strong empirical arguments that suggest that "trade openness" plays a secondary role when explaining the success of world market integration processes. For instance, in 1985 Bolivia opted for a liberal, outward-oriented model, abandoning tariff ceilings, NTBs and other regulations that distorted domestic prices, and in the process becoming one of the earliest reformers in Latin America. Moreover, in the 1990s the country signed a broad range of multilateral and regional trade agreements to consolidate and enhance the "modern economy" image. However, after twenty years, tangible benefits for the Bolivian people were negligible, and the once visionary New Economic Policy turned into a symbol of social exclusion that, for many sectors of Bolivian society, embodied the "disruptive forces" of globalisation.[1] Therefore, in this case low tariffs and a high number of trade agreements can be viewed as a failure, rather than a policy success, thus favouring the arguments put forward by free trade critics convinced that protectionist, state-led development strategies offer the best chances for developing countries.

Nevertheless, explanations must not be over simplified. For instance, Chile, with currently the lowest tariff levels in the region, can indeed be seen as a successful case, as this thesis will show in Chapter Three. But in Chile, the application of low uniformed, or "flat rate", tariffs was just one of several features crucial to the country's policy success.[2] Contrary to experiences in other South American countries over the last 20 years, Chile has managed to implement a coherent mixture of unilateral, regional and extra-regional trade policy measures, underlining its capacity to make simultaneous use of each level in favour of national export development. The cornerstone of the applied Multipolar Model embraced, aside from the flat rate concept, active trade policy on the regional and extra-regional level, and wide-reaching export promotion schemes for non-traditional exports. Finally, "heterodox", state-led policies were employed to accompany and prepare the relatively threatened segments of the local agriculture and small business sectors for the impacts of liberalised trade.

---

[1] In January 2006, a socialist government was elected with Evo Morales, the first State President with indigenous origins, at the helm. Consequently, the new Government Development Plan put in force has sought so far to rid itself of every element that composed the former NEP approach.

[2] In the following chapter, "Analytical Framework", I divide "policy success" into three possible categories; policy outcome (trade performance), policy impact (economic growth/poverty reduction) and policy output (the result of policy-making processes, e.g. trade reforms). For the purpose of this thesis, the policy success is output oriented.

Thus, it is natural to ask ourselves whether Chile's strategy could be implemented by any other country. Indeed, given the widespread problems regarding the development of national world market integration strategies, reliable policy advice in this area is strongly needed. However, attempts to transfer successful "blueprints" from one economy to another commonly fail, due to domestic background conditions that widely differ from those of model cases. Peru and Bolivia, and later also Argentina, faced harsh difficulties in adopting Chile's approach to integration, as this thesis exposes in chapters four, five and six. Thus, the key objective of this thesis is not primarily to question "what" strategy is required for successful world market integration, but to "how" and "under what background conditions" such strategies are acquired and maintained over time.

In Peru, for example, when far-reaching economic reforms were implemented in 1991, key economic policy-makers decided to undergo a world market integration strategy very similar in design to the Chilean example. But in the aftermath, major incoherencies were identified both regarding time inconsistency and contradictions between unilateral trade liberalisation, regional integration initiatives and export promotion schemes. Thus, Peru's example highlights the essence of today's trade policy-making, which particularly stresses the capabilities of developing countries: Trade policy is not about singular reform steps concerning the level of national tariffs, but rather is a set of policy areas, covering both border and behind-the-border-measures, parallel negotiations on different international levels, and the complex incorporation of trade agreements into national laws.

Nevertheless, existing theories on trade policy mainly focus on the preferences of domestic actors, and refer to the redistributive character of trade policies that are manifested at given moments. Literature on International Political Economy conceives trade decisions as conflict management among economic sectors that face dramatic changes in the rules and institutions that govern their markets (Milner 1988; Hillman 1989; Frieden 1991; Rodrik 1995; Hiscox 2002). Based on a sectoral approach, whereby production factors are understood to be immobile between industries, the outcome of such processes can be explained by analysing the political behaviour of export-oriented industries that favour liberalisation, and respectively, the import-competing sector being affected by reform steps. But this traditional view on the "politics of trade reforms" must be complemented in light of the current challenges of world market integration. For example, the analysis of actor preferences might explain why Chile adopted more outward-oriented policies than Brazil, where influential domestic market-oriented industrialists effectively inhibit far-reaching trade liberalisations. But it is harder to explain why Peru, which likewise undertook far-reaching trade reforms, failed to implement integration policies with the same success as Chile.

Therefore, to fill this explanatory gap, in this thesis I examine the effects of institutions involved in domestic policy-making processes, that is, formal and informal rules which shape the behaviour of collective actors, analysing to what extent these factors favour, or hinder, the success of world market integration strategies. The relevance of institutional variables, ranging from coordination among public and private actors, parliament procedures, state bureaucracy structures, and forms of business participation, to the resources and analytical capacities of civil society actors, has been highlighted by several working papers published by international organisations concerned with positive economic integration scenarios for Latin American States, such as the Inter-American Development Bank (Jordana/Ramió 2002; Ostry 2002) and the UN Economic Commission for Latin America and the Caribbean (Porras 2003; Sáez 2005). These papers provide a good overview of the institutional topics involved in the process of trade policy-making. But in order to reveal the causal relationship between particular institutional features and the success of world market integrations strategies, the work to be undertaken requires a stronger delimitation of key variables, the systematisation of empirical data, and the analysis of cause-effects links within determined time periods.

Drawing on neo-institutionalism literature by Schmitter and Streeck (1999) and Peter Evans (1995), in this thesis I thus systematise the analysis of the institutional factors of state bureaucracies and business associations, enlightening the cause-effects links between them and the success of world market integrations strategies. The analysis of the complex internal structures of state bureaucracy - defined as the executive branch in charge of trade policy - becomes particularly revealing due to its central position in the conduction of international trade policy affairs, considering that in developing countries the involvement of the legislative branch is often very limited. Indeed, although practically all South American countries have returned to democracy since the 1980s, democratic achievements to date appear to have been limited only to the right to vote and to express opinions freely.

On the other hand, business associations, i.e. trade and industrial chambers, and peak and sectoral organisations, are not only expected to assume the task of intermediating among the economic sectors affected by trade policy rules, but should also have key trade data at their disposal, such as growth perspectives, consumer trends, technological innovations, fiscal and labour regulations, sanitary rules and technical obstacles. In the light of these institutional imperatives, this book has sought to find answers to the following research question:

How, and to what extent, does the success of world market integration strategies in developing countries depend on the institutional strength of state bureaucracies and business associations?

This research question is relevant for both practical and theoretical reasons. As noted, the challenge faced by developing nations to integrate into world markets has changed in such a way that it has become necessary to highlight the close relationship between national and international trade policies. But while the participation of developing countries within the world trading system has widely been discussed, little systematised work has been done on the domestic perspectives in developing countries, that is, how domestic actors are facing the challenges of international trade policy tendencies. A better understanding of domestic policy-making processes is crucial if we are to understand results achieved at the international level, and draw insights on how to take best advantage of opportunities provided by the current system, and how to change international trade rules to favour developing states.

Therefore, this study will analyse the success of *world market integration strategies*, whereby such strategies are conceptualised as a particular set of trade related policies that developing countries adopt within the context of a gradual liberalisation of the global economy, and a shift of trade policy-making towards regional and multilateral levels.[3] For the purpose of this study, *success* is defined as a high degree of coherence by implementing a world market integration strategy, considering to what extent essential principals, policies, and objectives of the selected strategy have been put into practice and maintained over the period of analysis. Furthermore, it is assumed that coherently implemented, or "successful", world market integration strategies will contribute to a successful trade performance, such as high export growth and export diversification, and finally, to achieve the goal of poverty reduction in two ways - by contributing to economic growth, and by creating jobs. Chapter two, the analytical framework, will deepen the discussion on key concepts, and also shed light on the control

---

[3] As the analytical framework exposes in detail, the world market integration strategies pursued thus far by South American countries have ranged between: The Multipolar Model based on the creation of a dense network of bilateral free trade agreements in- and outside the region; and the Springboard Model, which focuses on deeper forms of regional integration by establishing a common regional market and a customs union.

variables used in this thesis, i.e. the factors with possible influences on the success/failure of world market integration strategies, which must be observed during the empirical research.

Methodology and Case Studies

For the empirical examination of the theoretical propositions developed in the theory framework, I adhere to a research strategy that focuses on qualitative case studies. According to Robert Yin (1998: 233) the more that research questions seek to explain how, and why, something occurs – as in this study – the more relevant the case study method will be, mainly due to a profound examination of causal chains, which is considered to be more important than a broad analytical focus. Furthermore, the case study method is more adequate than quantitative research when the number of potential cases is limited, and aggregate data absent. Even when including the smallest independent country in the region, there are no more than ten adequate cases available in South America; which is too limited a basis for a larger analysis. Furthermore, with respect to the data structure, it is clear that very little aggregate information and/or empirical studies exist. Particularly, with respect to the independent variables – "institutional strength of state bureaucracies" and "business associations" – it was unrealistic to expect well prepared data-sets. Instead, I was compelled to search for primary information in an individual, explorative way, as I show later in this chapter.

In this study a "case" is conceptualised as the process of domestic trade policy-making from 1985 to 2004. Each case firstly involves the examination of the country's world market integration strategy (section one), encompassing unilateral trade policies, (extra) integration endeavours, and sector- and export-oriented promotion schemes. In sections two and three, the independent variables – the institutional strength of state bureaucracy and business associations, respectively – are separately analysed. Finally, an assessment, in section four, discusses the causal pathways between independent and dependent variables, i.e. when, and how, the two selected explanatory variables caused the success/failure of world market integration strategies, and to what extent other (control) variables disturbed the effects on the dependent variable. Therein, I adhere to the *"process tracing"* method, whereby the researcher examines the chain of events through which initial case conditions are translated into case outcomes. In this manner: "the cause-effect link that connects independent variables and outcomes is disentangled and divided into smaller steps; then the researcher looks for observable evidence in each step" (Van Evera 1997: 64).

The propositions of the analytical framework are investigated by means of four country studies, considering different experiences in South America. As indicated at the outset of this paper, South American countries have become excellent examples of the changed pattern of world market integration. Moreover, I narrowed down the focus of the study to just one developing region in order to have *similar background conditions* between the cases, thus avoiding the impact of possible varying influences such as economy, culture, geography and politics (Van Evera 1997: 52). For instance, even by selecting culturally proximate countries in Central America or Mexico, one faces the problem of adequately assessing the enormous influence of the US market on trade policy related decisions. Nevertheless, it is unlikely to expect general background conditions to be identical amongst any group of countries. Therefore, with respect to the countries selected – Argentina, Bolivia, Chile and Peru – there are irrefutable differences concerning geographic extension, size and structure of the population, industrial development, GDP size, etc. However, several important similarities among the four countries over the last two decades provide a comparable playing field for the study of world market integration strategies.

First, in the aftermath of the debt crisis of the 1980s, each country moved towards far-reaching market reforms in order to counter inflationary pressures and balance of payment deficits. Although Bolivian and Peruvian trade reforms took place from 1985 and 1990 respectively, in Chile and Argentina the first reform wave took place in the 1970s. However, the debt crisis of the 1980s led to a serious economic backlash, explaining why the world market integration strategies currently in force did not emerge before 1985 in Chile and 1990 in Argentina.

Second, prior to 1985, traditional exports depended, without exceptions, on a narrow range of industrial and agricultural commodities: cereals and meat (Argentina), mining (Peru, Chile, and Bolivia), fish and fish meal (Peru, Chile) and hydrocarbons (Bolivia, Argentina). Given their oscillating world market prices, and mainly limited labour demand, the four countries thus had clear incentives to foster the diversification of national exports.

Third, it was during the 1980s that Latin American countries made the transition from authoritarian to democratic regimes; Argentina in 1983, Bolivia in 1982, Chile in 1989, and Peru in 1980. Aside from free elections, democratic rule implied more checks and balances, and more transparency and openness towards society. It should be noted, however, that these new democracies are still marked by widespread presidentialism, as well as distinctive forms of populism, both considered serious obstacles to the consolidation of democratic regimes (Diamond/ Hartlyn/Linz/Lipset 1997; Mainwaring/Shugart/Soberg 1997; Merkel/Puhle 1999).

As well as similar background conditions, Van Evera (1997: 77-88) recommends the selection of cases *with extreme (high or low) variable values*, and the existence of *strong variances on the study variable* (both between and within cases) in order to control the effect of disturbing third variables, and to facilitate the isolation of causal relations between the independent and dependent variable. Therefore, in the following section I briefly summarise the extremes and variances identified in each case with respect to the study variable (the dependent variable).

Case Study 1: Chile passed through different stages during the process of adopting an exemplary Multipolar Model. The Southern cone state maintained an authoritarian regime from 1973 to 1989, and it is these military leaders who can take credit for putting in practice the so-called "flat rate" regime and the wide-reaching export promotion schemes, which were initiated as of 1985. Nevertheless the cornerstone of the current trade policy was launched under democratic ruling, and it was in the 1990s that Chile evolved into a world-wide pioneer of New Regionalism. Inside Latin America, Chile's world market integration advanced further than in any other country, by consolidating bilateral Free Trade Agreements (FTAs) with practically every Latin American State. Later, from 1996 emphasis was placed on strengthening extra-regional ties. Through so-called "latest generation" FTAs - involving a broad range of new trade topics - with North American, European and Asian countries, the small emerging economy became an attractive partner in trade and investments for the big players of the world economy. As a result of these combined efforts, Chile registered impressive export growth rates and a significant export diversification based on non-traditional export champions, such as lumber, cellulose products, fruits, vegetables, salmon, wines and various manufactured goods.

Case Study 2: Argentina's strategy for world market integration was far less successful than that of its neighbouring country, although it was initially responsible for an innovative, proactive approach to integration; the Integration Programme for Economic Cooperation (PICE) with Brazil. From 1986, the PICE aimed at searching for industrial complementarities between the leading South American economies, and combined trade issues with other areas such as defence, research and development, culture, and industrial promotion. The underlying principle was gradualism and experimentation, wherein small liberalisation steps in specific sectors would allow sensible industrial sectors to prepare themselves before foreign competitors. However, this "springboard logic" received major revision from 1990 onwards. Aside from far-reaching unilateral trade reforms, the MERCOSUR, founded in March 1991, took on a universal and automatic liberalisation approach (rather than a gradual, sector-specific one), aiming to reach full liberalisation within four years. This new initiative thus favoured the fast expansion of intra-zone trade in sectors where Argentina enjoyed comparative advantages, such as petrochemicals and food processing. In the aftermath, nevertheless, a coherent implementation of this strategy became undermined by several factors.

First, the goal of establishing a common regional market and customs union, which demanded common external trade policies and the harmonisation of behind-the-border measures (in line with the Springboard Model), stood in contradiction to Argentina's economic policy. Hence, the implementation of the regional integration objectives stagnated, as member states did not view the MERCOSUR as a reference scheme for unilateral policy-making. In general, the observable lack of intra-MERCOSUR cohesion, and a loss of international credibility, hindered the group's ability to act as a powerful trading block both inside, and outside, Latin America. For example, virtually all external negotiations launched became deadlocked. *Second,* several permanent and temporary exceptions from the liberal trade regime persisted. But the fact that these protectionist measures were applied in an uncoordinated, ad-hoc manner, underlined the high unpredictability of domestic trade policies, and the lack of clarity related to the strategy for each sectors' world market integration. *Third,* while sector-specific policies were absent (except for the automotive regime), official export promotion facilities suffered from the combination of frequent modifications, modest resources and a high degree of institutional fragmentation.

Case Study 3: In 1991, Peru implemented far-reaching market reforms, in which trade liberalisation was a cornerstone. In a strategy that reflected the Chilean example, the country sought to adopt a "modern" flat rate tariff, and to define individual forms of world market integration by leaving the Andean Group (later Andean Community of Nations-CAN) where members pursued a Common External Tariff (CET) based on a four-tier structure. Nevertheless, the original policy goals failed to appear. Instead of setting forth vigorous bilateral trade diplomacy, in 1997 Peru returned to the CAN without a clear commitment to the ongoing Andean integration process. In fact, the controversies of the Common External Tariff (CET) could not be resolved within the period of analysis. However, the flat rate model originally sought has yet to be reached, and from 2002 Peru has been applying seven different tariff lines.

In the ongoing decade, Peru attained certain policy success nonetheless, discerning significant progress in assuming a Multipolar Model. By this point, the country had set forth a rather active trade policy, involving the strengthening of trade relations with the US, the Pacific Area, and MERCOSUR, and the implementation of the National Export Strategy 2003-2013. Though the pursued model had yet to be consolidated at the time of writing, the trade policy applied in the last years notably differed from the passive and incoherent trade policy sustained throughout the 1990s.

Case Study 4: The Bolivian experience can be considered an outright failure. The poor, landlocked Andean country opened up its economy in 1985, abandoning such policies as tariff ceilings, price regulations and subsidies, and became one of the earliest reformers in Latin America. Later, during the 1990s, Bolivia signed several far-reaching trade arrangements in the multilateral, and above all regional, spheres. The FTAs signed with the CAN (itself being a CAN member), MERCOSUR, and Mexico particularly stand out.

But since no significant support schemes for exporters were put into practice, such as market assistance, fiscal incentives or sector-specific measures, the enhanced market access opportunities were poorly exploited. In light of the massive structural shortcomings faced by the local entrepreneurship (market size, infrastructure, technology, etc.), the distinctive liberal trade regime primarily caused large trade deficits. As a result, the market-led, outward-looking strategy has, in recent years, become heavily opposed to by civil society actors, such as indigenous groups, workers, NGO's and state universities. Above all, the government's intention to strengthen trade relations with the US caused major social unrest domestically. In this way, the blind search for "trade openness" was responsible, among others factors, for the increasing destabilisation of the political system observed in the ongoing decade.

Data Collection

A simple, but important, case selection criterion has been *data richness and data access*, since the "process tracing" procedure requires a great deal of data to detangle policy-making chains.

Thus, privileged access to public and private sector organisations was essential, given that the required data was disperse and often rather confidential. Moreover, the availability of written data was often hindered by poor documentation and a widespread reluctance among state and business entities to disseminate information. Therefore, Bolivia, Argentina, Chile and Peru provided good opportunities for field research. In Argentina and Chile, I had already gathered vast information, case knowledge, and contacts during the field research for my MA Thesis (Robin 2001). Moreover, in Chile several working papers, related to the topics involved, provided a useful analytical background. Argentina had the additional benefit of being my country of residence in 2003-2004. In the case of Bolivia and Peru, contacts were facilitated as a result of collaboration in the 2003-2006 Trade Cooperation Project conducted by the State Secretary of Economic Affairs (SECO).

Principally, field research focused on the conduction of interviews with people who possessed first-hand knowledge on topics of interest. Thus, interviewing key actors or experts became the centre piece of empirical research, with a total of 311 interviews eventually conducted with state officials, special advisers, employees of business associations, university professors, entrepreneurs, etc. I carried out two types of interview techniques during this process, dividing them into semi-structured and open-end expert interviews (Atteslander 1995; Flick 1999).

Open-end expert interviews were minimally structured, explorative talks, aimed at the collection of factual information and the interpretation of different variables involved in the analysis, and often sought to gather this information in an historical perspective, i.e. how the variable evolved within the period of analysis. In total, 109 interviews of this type were carried out, involving state officials (39), business representatives (33) and outside experts (37) (category definitions follow later). Considering their practical use, nonetheless, most of these conversations were used to provide a better understanding of the case, helping to corroborate opinions and to narrow down topics and events involved in each case. In the end only a limited number of verbal reports, approximately five to six in each case, were utilised to explain key facts.

To ensure the high validity of these reports, the risk of biased or incomplete information was mitigated by considering the following criteria when defining "selected interview partners": (1) university graduate; (2) More than 10 years of professional experience in the trade policy fields; and (3) open minded and helpful behaviour (evaluated by my subjective impression and the time of the interview - i.e. more than one hour). Naturally, objective case facts could not be guaranteed merely by these criteria, therefore, it was necessary to examine the independence of assessments (considering past and present professional obligations, for example), and to confirm the statements made through other expert interviews, and with existing written information.

Semi-structured interviews, or "Leitfadengespräche", are widely used by social scientists, since they offer something in between open, explorative talks and standardised surveys. Such interviews usually consist of previously determined "core questions," linked to defined variable (dimensions), and flexible "detailed questions", wherein the interviewer gathers additional case facts, exploring new ground and exchanging ideas. In this study, semi-structured interviews were applied to combine both the standardisation of data collection and to explore the research field through an open-end interview style.

In summary, three questionnaires composed of "core questions" were employed to gather perceptions, according to three categories of interview partners; (1) business representatives, (2) state officials, and (3) outside experts. The survey carried out among *business representatives (BR)* was the most exhaustive (123 interviews), principally addressing management staff or trade policy advisors. To a lesser extent, board of directors and external consultants were consulted. The survey did not rely on a strict sample, but rather the selection of entities was adapted to each country's characteristics. A core group was maintained, however, over the four cases, embracing multisectoral, or "umbrella", organisations, and the sector peak entities of agriculture, industry, commerce, and exports (for a detailed selection, see Appendix 1).

Surveys with *state officials* (41 interviews) and *outside experts* (38) were considerably more limited than the business surveys, for the following reasons: In the case of state officials, functionaries generally focus on just a few agencies such as the Ministries of Foreign Affairs, Foreign Trade, Economy, Industry and Agriculture. Thus, it often appeared far more valuable to hold in-depth discussions on specific topics and to explore their career paths, rather than to pose questions on a broad range of rather superficial questions, especially when taking into account difficulties in obtaining an interview with accomplished senior officials (deputies, special advisors, and heads of areas). The conversations with *outside experts* (academics, former state officials and consultants) similarly had a rather open-end character (nevertheless, approximately 50% were held in a semi-structured way). In particular, academics were often reluctant to give structured answers to a broad range of topics, and instead, tended to provide interpretations on specific issues of interest. For these reasons, on several occasions it was not possible to cover all the core questions, causing missing data as a consequence.

The questionnaires were structured in the following way: Depending on the category, the questionnaires were composed of 14 to 18 questions, using an ordinal scale with four possible answers (e.g. very close coordination, rather close coordination, rather sporadic, very sporadic or absent coordination). The survey with business associations was the most exhaustive, as detailed organisational data on business associations had to be collected (staff size, revenues, membership data, etc). Otherwise, the questionnaires were rather similar along the three categories, and referred to the division of responsibilities and inter-ministerial coordination in trade policy formulations, especially regarding the conduction of international trade negotiations, the size and technical capacities of the trade policy staff, transparency maintained during the conduction of international negotiations, state-business coordination and the intermediation of business interests.

With regards to the period of field research, interviews were conducted between September 2003 and March 2005. Wherever possible, semi-structured interviews were set forth within a shorter timeframe, i.e. between February and October 2004, in order to avoid strong time distortions that could potentially weaken comparison between cases. As is shown in Table 1, the duration, and number, of interviews varied notably between countries, especially between Argentina and Chile. In this regard, it is necessary to emphasise that Argentina was my country of residence during the time when field activities took place. Therefore, during my stay in Argentina I worked on document analysis, the preparation of field visits, transcription of interviews, data searches on the Internet, the methodological development in general and the attendance of post-graduate courses on the topic of research. In Chile, conversely, data collection was based heavily on secondary literature and a limited number of interviews, taking into account that existing studies on research related topics provided a solid base, allowing for only selected primary data collection.

Table 1.1: Interviews

	Open-End Expert Interviews	Semi-Structured Interviews
Business Representatives	33	123
Argentina	14	58
Chile	4	-
Bolivia	5	36
Peru	10	29
State Officials	39	41
Argentina	12	12
Chile	6	-
Bolivia	12	14
Peru	9	15
Outside Experts	37	38
Argentina	10	12
Chile	2	-
Bolivia	15	15
Peru	10	11
Total	109	202
Argentina	36	82
Chile	12	-
Bolivia	32	65
Peru	29	55
Time	**September 2003 - March 2005**	**February 2004 – October 2004**
Argentina	30 weeks	20 weeks
Chile	2 weeks (2 stays)	-
Bolivia	3 weeks (2 stays)	5 weeks (2 stays)
Peru	3 weeks (2 stays)	5 weeks (3 stays)

The methodological strength of case study interviews, according to Robert Yin (1998: 231-232), is that these interviews are "targeted", in the sense that they focus directly on topics of interest for the interviewer; furthermore, they are "insightful", considering that causal inter-ferences perceived by the key informant can be provided. Weak aspects of this data collection method are related, nevertheless, to poorly constructed, or suggestive, questions that lead to misguided answers. Moreover, in most cases responses are strongly subjective, representing only one particular point of view in relation to the case. Conversely, outside experts have a broader focus, but often do not know the contextual details of the case. Finally, the supply of faulty information is rather common, since interviewees often feel the need to transmit merely half truths, do not remember the case well (but do not admit or recognise that fact), and/or answers tend to be too reflexive, in the sense that interviewees usually say what the interviewer wants to hear.

Hence, to corroborate verbal reports with other types of evidence, so as to determine robust "case facts", I conducted not only a high number of interviews, but also made extensive use of written data whenever reliable information was available, and data analysis could be carried out within a reasonable time. In this sense, working papers, text of laws, resolutions, meeting minutes, newspaper articles, annual reports of business associations, trade statistics, budget data, organisational charts and other official data were incorporated. Nonetheless, apart from the Chilean case, where secondary literature provided useful empirical data and interpretation, the conduction of interviews became the key method for data collection. Moreover, it should be noted that field visits in Bolivia, Peru and Chile were far too short to prepare a comprehensive research of archives, and the widespread problems of secrecy, overbearing administrative procedures and a lack of documentation of local organisations further limited research.

This book is structured along the following lines. Chapter 2 develops the analytical framework that is designed to evaluate the success of world market integration strategies in developing countries. Chapters 3 to 6 form the core of the book: They contain detailed case studies on the world market integration steps underwent by the four selected countries. Finally, the results of the four in-depth case studies are summarised and compared in chapter 7.

2   Analytical Framework

The analytical framework that guides the empirical research conducted in this study is structured as follows. In the *first section* I define the key concepts used in this thesis, discuss the theoretical and practical relevance of the research question, and review the state of art on world market integration and domestic trade policy-making in developing countries. In the *second section,* I explore the evolution of the international trade system, as seem from a development perspective, placing particular emphasis on the dynamic interrelation between unilateralism, multilateralism, and regionalism, accentuated since the mid-1980s by the initiation of the Uruguay Round. It is from this standpoint that the two most common modes of world market integration in South America have been conceptualised: the Multipolar and Springboard Models. In the *third section,* I enlighten, from a theoretical perspective, the process of trade policy-making on the domestic level, and develop the two explanatory variables used in this study: the institutional strength of state bureaucracies and business associations. In the *forth and final section* of this chapter, the test hypothesis is exposed and its logical structure discussed in detail.

2.1 Key Concepts, Relevance of the Research Question and State of the Art

Research Question and Key Concepts

This study aims to enhance our theoretical and practical knowledge of the causal relationship between the institutions involved in domestic policy-making, and the way developing countries achieve the integration of their economies into world markets. Specifically, I address the following research question: *How, and to what extent, does the success of world market integration strategies in developing countries depend on the institutional strength of state bureaucracies and business associations?* The research question contains several key concepts that are outlined below.

From the 1950s to 1980s, the concept of developing countries' *world market integration strategies* was commonly associated with a set of unilateral trade and economic policies, including tariffs and non-tariff barriers, and subsidies for exports and industrial transformation. As a result, distinctive approaches to world market integration emerged. On the one hand, Import-Substituting Industrialisation (ISI) strategies, widely applied in Latin

America, and on the other hand, Export-Led Growth (ELG) strategies, implemented by several states in East Asia. In both approaches the widespread state support granted to local industries was a common factor. But ISI experiences were more protectionist in nature than their ELG counterparts, as industries were permanently shielded from international competition through high tariff and non-tariff barriers, and a monetary policy that kept the domestic currency overvalued (Bulmer-Thomas 1994: 276-323). Conversely, ELG strategies, in line with the infant industry concept developed in the 19th century by Friedrich List (1856), consisted of selective protection and support schemes in order to enhance the international competitiveness of domestic manufactures within a determined time frame (Amsden 1989).

From the 1980s, the connotation of world market integration strategies adapted to the changing international context, assimilating with the general tendency towards trade liberalisation, and the inclusion of developing nations into the world trading system. In particular, discussion on adequate world market integration strategies began to consider the adoption of "market-led" institutions in the scope of GATT, and from 1995, within the WTO framework. The debate on China is paradigmatic here. While scholars in favour of gradualism and local experimentation (Rodrik 1999) put emphasis on the evolutionary, experimental, and incremental nature of the successful reforms in China, and thus the need to combine non-capitalist institutions with market-led institutions, the convergence school (Sachs/ Woo 2000) urges China towards institutional harmonisation with the WTO, rather than institutional innovation, suggesting that the ingredients for a dynamic market economy are already well-known.

In Latin America, the trend towards institutional harmonisation in general advanced more rapidly than in Asia, since local experimentation with ISI was drastically abolished as a consequence of the balance of payments crisis in the 1980s. Originally based on unilateral reforms to control inflationary pressure, since the 1990s the adoption of market-led institutions has taken place increasingly within the WTO scope, and by means of regional integration endeavours, as the next section of this chapter outlines in detail.

For the purpose of this study, the notion of world market integration strategies adopts this altered international context. It is thus conceptualised as: *a particular set of trade related policies that developing countries adopt within a context of gradual liberalisation of the global economy and a shift of trade policy-making towards regional and multilateral levels.*

With respect to the *success* of world market integration strategies, definitions are generally related to the policy outcome (trade performance), policy impact (economic growth and/or poverty reduction) or policy output (such as trade reforms). In general, economic assessments consider the first two definitions. While policy outcome usually refers to improvements in a country's trade performance - for instance export growth, greater export diversification, higher firm-level productivity or increased marked shares - most economic studies seek to measure broader economic and social impacts, and assess the benefits of trade in fostering economic growth (Sachs/Warner 1995), productivity (Edwards 1998), and reducing poverty (Wood 1997; Dollar/Kray 2003).

From a political science perspective, success is often associated with policy outputs, that is, particular policy reforms originating from the policy-making processes. In this regard, "success" can be taken to be WTO adherence, implemented trade liberalisations or signed regional trade agreements. In this study, conversely, success does not refer to a single policy event or action, but considers the evolution of a set of trade related policies over a certain time period. Specifically, successful world market strategies are defined as *a high degree of coherence by implementing a world market integration strategy, considering to what extent essential principals, policies, and objectives of the selected strategy have been put into practice and maintained over the period of analysis (1985 to 2004)*. The measurement of the degree of coherence is herein related to two idealistic modes of world market integration, which have been pursued within the revised international context: the Multipolar and Springboard Models (further explained in section 2.2).

It is further assumed – but not analysed in this study – that coherently implemented, or "successful", world market integration strategies will help to improve the trade performance of a country, and finally, to achieve the goals of economic growth, job creation and poverty reduction.

Box 2.1: The Success of World Market Integration Strategies

Policy Output	Coherent implementation of the world market integration strategy over the period of analysis (1985 to 2004).
Policy Outcome	Improved trade performance (increase in exports, greater export diversification, increased market shares, higher firm-level productivity)
Policy Impact	Economic growth, job creation and poverty reduction

As is often indicated, the broad adoption of market institutions in Latin America from the 1980s onwards did not meet most of the initially set expectations. In particular, the limited "trickle down" effects of economic growth received broad criticism towards the end of the 1990s, an aspect used by globalisation adversaries as evidence of the disruptive forces of trade liberalisations and other adjustment policies that made up the so called 'Washington Consensus'. To counter these critical voices, arguments have since been put forward stressing the necessity of strong development institutions as a precondition for successful market reforms (Burki/Perry 1998; Graham/Naím 1998, World Bank Development Report 2002). In essence, the herein demanded second generation reforms particularly embrace the judiciary system, public administration and legislative powers, and thus aim to provide answers to problems of widespread corruption, legal certainty and overbearing bureaucratic procedures affecting business transactions.

These insights often rely upon a rational choice approach, conceptualising *institutions* in accordance to North (1990: 3) as *"the rules of the game of society or, more formally, the humanly devised constraints that shape human integration."* Accordingly, the *strength of institutions* becomes an equivalent to high social acceptance of societal norms and regulatory systems among individuals in a particular community. The more that rules, both informal and formal, affecting business operations are broadly accepted and openly transparent, the more transactions take place within a predictable, trustful environment, thus allowing an efficient pursuit of economic interests (see also Arrow 1974; Putnam 1993b; Fukuyama 1995).

Institutional strength applied to state bureaucracies and business associations also draws on stable and predictable rules and norms which govern interactions among actors. But unlike individuals acting in particular social contexts, the behaviour of collective actors is determined further by the internal structural constraints of organisations. Hence, the outcome of collective action cannot be seen as the simple aggregate of individual preferences, but instead as a result of several factors influencing, or filtering, collective actors' interests, such as internal decision making procedures, the number of involved actors, common resources and principals.

Regarding the collective action of entrepreneurs, the institutional strength of business associations is related to the complicated, intermediary, position between two independent and resourceful actors – firms on one side, and state authorities on the other. If a business association is to be taken into account, it is obliged to insert itself into the direct exchange of market actors and state authorities, by offering a service at a beneficial price or quality, according to the neocorporatist logic sustained by Schmitter and Streeck (1999: 19). Therefore, the *institutional strength of business associations* is defined as the capacity of organisations representing private sectors interests – i.e. trade and industrial chambers, business councils, peak entities, farmers' organisations, entities representing specific sectors or branches – to effectively intermediate the often opposing preferences within the private sector, and simultaneously, to maintain close relations with state authorities. Section 2.3 further enlightens the complexity of associative business action by placing emphasis on four different, and often opposing, logics affecting business associations in their search to become strong interlocutors (or intermediary agents) of private sector interests.

In the case of state bureaucracies, institutional strength concerns the structures and norms determining the work inside the executive branch, and the way in which other non-state actors, especially business agents, are incorporated into the development of trade policy. In this way, it is understood that the behaviour of bureaucrats is not simply guided by an obvious, clearly defined "public interest", but by the outcome of multifaceted interaction patterns with other state and non-state actors.

Bearing in mind the rampant corruption and rent-seeking behaviour common to developing countries, Peter Evans' concept of Embedded Autonomy (1995) combines the strength of bureaucratic structures with two seemingly opposing features: *First,* a high degree of autonomy, or insulation, of policy-makers from societal pressure, in order to reduce rent-seeking opportunities. *Second,* bureaucrats require the capacity to maintain fluent relations with the business sector, through channels which allow the permanent negotiation and monitoring of economic goals and policies, in order to fine-tune and adapt public policies to the possibilities of economic sectors responsible for efficient strategy/policy implementation.

In this study, the notion of Embedded Autonomy was adapted to the underlying context and objectives of the research conducted. Hence, *the institutional strength of state bureaucracy* has been conceptualised as an executive branch wherein the responsibilities for the conduction of international trade policy affairs are clearly perceived, the trade policy staff are adequately doted, and finally, a degree of openness is sustained towards business and non-business regarding their incorporation into the trade policy-making process.

Relevance of Research Questions and State of the Art

Analysing the influence of business and state related institutions on the success of world market integration strategies is relevant both from a practical and theoretical point of view.

On the practical side, the need for institutional reforms as a quasi precondition for successful economic policy reforms has been increasingly recognised by both local governments and international organisations that support such reform steps. As is briefly described in the following paragraphs, initial analysis has been conducted by organisations, such as the Inter-American Development Bank (IDB) and the UN Economic Commission for Latin America and the Caribbean (ECLAC), concerned with sound economic integration scenarios in Latin America, indicating the weight of institutional factors in successful trade policy-making. Consequently, in most countries in the region, IDB loans have been aimed at the "Institutional Strengthening of Foreign Trade". However, support is often rather unspecific, ranging from facilitating trade policy advisors, to impact assessments, IT solutions, and the organisation of seminars and workshops on trade related topics. To date, these support schemes have generally been insufficient to foster the institutional framework necessary to adequately face the challenges of current world market integration forces. Thus, it is of no surprise that debate has arisen on whether the rules of the world trading system are really beneficial for developing countries, or conversely, whether they simply overstrain local capacities within these countries.

Although any "cookbook-style" advice can be provided, this study aims to generate to practical solutions, as it discusses and systematises institutional factors weighing on the domestic level, where the essential problems of world market integration often arise. Being very rich in empirical details, I explore the effects of these institutional features on the way a country integrates into world markets by means of four country studies. As a consequence, useful guidelines can be offered as regards how, and under what conditions, countries and donor agencies should work on the institutional strengthening of national trade policy-making.

This study is also relevant from a theoretical point of view, since the existing literature on trade policy and world market integration generally fails to systematically explore the conditions under which institutional factors on the domestic level determine the success of such policy endeavours over a long period of time, taking into account the changing pattern of world market integration which has taken place in the last two decades.

Focussing on the explanatory variables set forth in this study, nevertheless, much valuable theoretical and practical work has already been carried out. Numerous studies have indicated that trade policy is the substance of domestic politics. Tariffs, non-tariff barriers and quotas are common issues for a broad range of interest groups, from farmers and retailers to manufacturers and trade unions. Dani Rodrik aptly describes the perspective of policy-makers when pursuing trade policy reforms (2000b: 1-2):

> *"For them, the changes in tariff schedules are typically only a small part of the process. What is at stake is a deeper transformation of the patterns of behaviour within the public sector, and of the government's relationship with the private sector and the rest of the world. The reform goes beyond particular levels of tariffs and quantitative restrictions; it sets new rules and expectations regarding how these policy choices are made and implemented, establishes new constraints and opportunities for economic policy more broadly, creates a new set of stakeholders while disenfranchising the previous ones, and gives rise to a new philosophy on what development policy is all about. Hence, trade reform ends up being much more than a change in relative prices; it becomes an institutional reform of a major kind."*

Frequently, the United States has served as a paradigmatic case to illustrate the importance of domestic politics, where internal political conflicts are accentuated by the Congress' power to levy tariffs and regulate foreign trade, strongly restricting the President's international trade policy actions. For example, Milner (1997: 135-158) and Jackson (1997: 31-44) show how protectionist voices within the US Congress were responsible for the failure of establishing the International Trade Organisation in the post war period. Rather than a powerful supranational institution fostering and enforcing free trade, the contracting parties agreed upon the GATT Secretariat, which was allotted scarce legal and economic resources, thus demonstrating the unwillingness to guarantee free trade.

Inspired by the "two-level games" notion (Evans/Jacobson/Putnam 1993) and worried about the lack of knowledge regarding "level one" in those games, the domestic trade policy-making level in Latin America has been enlightened by several studies and working papers published in recent years. Directed by Sylvia Ostry (2002), a project on trade policy-making in eight Western Hemisphere nations focused on the question of how best to accommodate the participation on non-state actors in the formulation of national trade policies and negotiations strategies.[1] This Occasional Paper provides an overview of the considerable diversity in the policy-making process among these countries (Argentina, Brazil, Canada, Chile, Colombia, United States, Mexico, and Uruguay) regarding, among other aspects, the procedures for consultations, the actors involved, scheduling, and institutional arrangements.

---

[1] The project was jointly conducted by the Inter-American Development Bank and the University of Toronto's Munk Centre for International Studies.

Although the country studies were not structured along identical lines, two important findings can be mentioned: *First,* there is a clear dividing line between the two North American countries, representing the industrialised world, and the six Latin American countries. While in the former countries the participation of legislators and other non-business actors is strongly anchored, in Latin America only business actors are actively involved in these processes. *Second,* two strategic resources for participating in trade policy are identified: money and analytical knowledge. Thus, Ostry infers that the superior financial and technical capabilities of business actors explain their leading role in consultation procedures, while non-business actors are generally short of such means.

Other works draw similarly structured conclusions. For both Lengyel and Ventura-Dias in *Trade Policy Reforms in Latin America - Multilateral Rules and Domestic Institutions* and Sáez (2005) in *Trade Policy-making in Latin America – A Compared Analysis,* the participation of civil society and congress is described as incipient in Latin America compared to the consolidated role of business representatives.[2] Together with the widespread absence of formal and transparent forms of consultation, the authors observe that this limited participation hinders the construction of a firm consensus, thus undermining the legitimacy of trade policy initiatives. Above all, the findings of Lengyel and Ventura-Dias sustain a very critical tone, stating that:

> *"well-entrenched habits and rules of the game in the domestic political-institutional context have conspired against the emergence of more open and transparent patterns of participation in that they only tend to integrate that part of society structured along corporatist lines or patronage webs, condemning the rest to exclusion"* (2004: 203; see also Prats 2000).

Likewise, the two previously mentioned studies make useful observations about the central position of the state's executive powers. As involvement of the legislative is limited and the approval of international trade agreements often a mere formality, international trade policy actions depend on the internal features of the executive branch. Therefore, so called "institutional deficits", such as the high rotation of state officials, untrained staff, jurisdictional struggles, and the failure to establish stable consultation with non-state actors all impact negatively on the development of trade policy. The most noteworthy efforts that stress the institutional aspects of the executive branch have been made by Jordana and Ramió in *Institutional Design and Foreign Trade Policy Management in Latin America* (2002). The

---

[2] Lengyel and Ventura-Dias compare eight Latin American countries, Sáez collects data from nine.

paper examines the most common organisational models for trade policy-making, underscoring the fact that different institutional arrangements generally reflect variations in how the political systems are structured, what role the State assumes in the economy, and how government bodies engage in consultations with interest groups. Each of the four models developed (for instance the *Foreign Affairs Model,* where international trade policy is centralised inside the Ministry of Foreign Affairs), possesses its pros and cons with respect to the way trade policy is developed, as section 2.3 explains in detail.

In general, most of the institutional factors involved in trade policy-making have been considered in the aforementioned papers. Nevertheless, three factors particular to this study differentiate it from the rest: *First,* the contributions made so far have brought together different country experiences in a rather flexible, unstructured way. Rather than defining variables and methodologies in a systematic manner, country studies have relied mostly on the impressions and data collection of the authors in charge, being, in general, economists rather than political scientists.

Second, no empirical puzzle is explained in the corresponding works, that is, no causal pathways are developed in order to explain a defined outcome (e.g. number of agreements signed) by a specific explanatory variable (e.g. formality of consultation channels). Therefore, only a sketchy idea is transmitted to the reader of the true importance of institutions.

Third, discussions on the role of business are still weakly developed. The papers give the impression, especially Ostry (2002) and Lengyel and Ventura-Dias (2004), that institutional deficits in Latin America basically concern the common exclusion of non-business actors from policy-making, while the participation of business agents is guaranteed by their superior financial and technical capabilities. But this view would appear to be overly simplified. Although I fully agree with the need for a strong, formal inclusion of broad parts of the society in order to obtain a higher legitimacy and stability of policy reforms, I argue against a dichotomic view on business and non-business actors. Numerous works on the collective action of entrepreneurs have shown that business is by no means a homogenous actor. Different firm sizes, opposing sectoral interests, intra-sectoral competition, political allies, idiosyncrasy, short-term thinking, and lack of information, are all factors which underline the difficulty of bringing capitalists together (Offe/ Wiesenthal 1980; Maxfield/ Schneider 1997). Therefore, this thesis will shed further light on how institutional features of collective business actions, further developed in section 2.3, can become determining factors in explaining the outcome of policy reforms.

2.2 The International Trade System from a Development Perspective

The following section is structured as follows. In the first part, I stress the shift of trade policy, on both multilateral and regional levels, that has taken place since the mid-1980s, when the Uruguay Round was initiated, particularly discussing its relevance for developing countries. On these grounds, in the second part I develop two idealistic modes of world market integration which have been pursued in Latin America within the international context outlined in the previous section: the Multipolar and Springboard Models.

The Uruguay Round - the Watershed for the Multilateral Trading System

Although the creation of the General Agreement on Tariffs and Trade (GATT) in 1947 supported international trade as a means to decrease reliance on unilateral measures, the reciprocal tariff concessions made in the scope of GATT were only gradual, and became widely criticised by domestic lobbyist. Additionally, numerous institutional provisions beyond trade served as "safety valves" in terms of protectionist measures adapted to domestic needs, i.e. Article XIX (general safeguard), Article XX (safeguard human, animal and live plants), Article XI (a safeguard for security purposes), Article XVIII (safeguard the protection of the balance of payments and infant industries), Article XI (quantitative controls on exports and imports of agricultural products and fisheries). Also, the GATT's basic principle of fostering trade liberalisation became undermined by the failure to establish the International Trade Organisation (ITO). With the GATT Secretariat, conversely, the contracting parties agreed upon an institution with modest legal and economic resources, implying limits to the enforcement of the free trade rules embodied in GATT norms.

On these grounds, the advances made since the 1980s are rather noteworthy. It was with the conclusion of the Tokyo Round in 1979 that the administration of multilateral trade began to receive increasing criticism, leading industrial nations to begin pushing forward new trade issues. Therefore, the eighth negotiation round of GATT, launched in 1986 in Punta del Este, Uruguay, began with ambitious goals that went well beyond the traditional focus on border issues. After this round ended eight years later in Marrakech, Morocco, John Jackson expressed his surprise (1997: 46) about how much of the original agenda had been completed. In fact, even though only half this agenda had been fulfilled, the Uruguay Round would become the largest ever.

The introduction of new complex regulatory issues such as trade in services, intellectual property rights and trade related investment measures, represented a turning point in the nature of trade policy, considering the broadened focus on behind-the-border policies. These "new" trade topics arose as a result of new claims, mainly originating from multinational companies which had changed their patterns of production and trade in light of technical innovations, mostly in areas such as telecommunications and transportation.

Beyond these new areas, other innovations agreed upon concerned comprehensive agreements on agricultural trade, subsidies and textiles. Finally, the strengthening of the institutional framework for international trade through the creation of the World Trade Organization, and the permanent dispute settlement system, in force since 1995, enabled an enhanced monitoring and enforcement of the multilateral rules agreed upon by the member states.

Uruguay came to be a watershed for all WTO members, above all for developing nations. In the 1980s, the participation of third world countries was marginal, with discussions focusing merely on the definition of provisions for Special and Differential Treatment for developing countries.[3] Effective participation, in terms of comprehensively falling under GATT norms, and the ability to influence on the negotiations' outcome, did not take place before the Uruguay Round (Srinivasan 1999). Therefore, and as a result of the following three factors, the Marrakech agreements changed the developing nations' *modus vivendi* within the multilateral trading system.

1) *Single Undertaking*: Eventually introduced, the "single undertaking" mechanism implied that all countries had to adhere to the major agreements concerning the WTO. Therefore, new areas embodied in the General Agreement on Trade in Services (GATS) and the Agreement on Trade-Related Aspects of Intellectual Property Rights

---

[3] Of note here is the Enabling Clause enacted by the end of the Tokyo Round in 1979, entitling the "Differential and More Favorable Treatment, Reciprocity and Fuller Participation of Developing Countries." Thereafter, the practice of extending preferential tariffs by developed to developing countries in the scope of the General System of Preferences (GSP) and the implementation of preferential agreements among developing contracting parties, obtained legal status. Today, special treatment provisions can be classified in five main groups: provisions aimed at increasing trade opportunities through market access; norms requiring WTO members to safeguard the interest of developing countries; norms allowing flexibility to developing countries on rules and disciplines governing trade measures; norms allowing longer transitional periods to developing countries; and provisions for technical assistance; see WTO 1999.

(TRIPS), as well as former plurilateral agreements concerning trade in goods, had to be adopted in a comprehensive manner.[4]

2) *Depth of Commitments*: In light of the unilateral economic liberalisation undertaken since the 1980s, developing States (and South American States in particular) undertook important specific commitments. While in the areas of goods, many countries bound almost all agricultural and industrial tariffs, as regards trade in services, the main commitments focused on sectors such as financial services, telecommunications, tourism and professional services.[5]

3) *Agriculture*: An area that had been practically excluded in previous decades, specific commitments by developed countries were included, by means of the Agreement on Agriculture, to improve market access and reduce market distorting subsidies. Member states, moreover, agreed to initiate talks to continue the reform process one year before the end of the implementation period, i.e. by the end of 1999.

In assessing the benefits of this increased involvement, being moreover manifested by the large number of developing nations adhering to the WTO, standpoints are ambiguous. On the one hand, it seems unclear whether the agreement on agriculture, which for many developing countries represented the principal "offensive interest", implied a milestone for liberalisation or not. The mandate agreed upon in Marrakech to deepen liberalisation in agricultural trade is, in any case, a pending issue thus far.

Furthermore, in light of the many new topics such as intellectual property rights and trade-related investment measures that emerged in multilateral trade discussions, developing countries have, to date, largely remained "rule takers". This adoption of rules made in industrialised countries can be assessed from two perspectives. The first rationale deals with the fact that "importing" new rules or regulatory systems might often be easier than building them on their own, as those systems have already been tested at the international level (Lawrence 1996: 17). Also Rodrik, generally critical of WTO institutions, (1999, 2000b: 12) underlines the fact that disciplines imposed by the WTO in the areas of tariff binding, quantitative restrictions, subsidies, services, trade-related investment measures and property

---

[4] For example, the plurilateral agreement on non-tariff measures negotiated in the Tokyo Round, where developing countries originally stayed out, are now part of single undertaking, and are thus applicable to all members. Currently, only two existing agreements in the area of goods - the Agreement on Trade in Civil Aircraft and the Agreement on Government Procurement - remain plurilateral.

[5] In the range of services, the overwhelming majority of commitments made by developing countries (and also developed countries) were actually binding existing situations rather than undertaking new liberalisation efforts.

rights can provide predictability, transparency, rule bound behaviour, and non-discrimination in areas often subject to discretion and rent-seeking.

A second perspective, which has been prominently put forward by Rodrik, considers that such gains from institutional harmonisation cannot substitute each country's efforts to build its own institutions based on local experimentation, given that imported rules often do not precisely match local conditions. With striking empirical evidence, Rodrik, and other voices critical of rigid multilateral rules, argue that industrialised countries likewise implemented far-reaching industrial subsidy schemes and selective forms of protection in order to reach the required levels of competitiveness. Therefore, successful institutional reforms typically combine imported blueprints with a set of country-specific, heterodox-style policies aimed at the gradual integration of domestic industries into world markets.

The Rise of (New-) Regionalism

Trade policies that were influenced by the trend towards internationalisation were not limited to strengthening multilateral rules, but also strongly encompassed the rise of regional integration forces. Heated debates took place regarding whether such regional cooperation would favour or hinder the development of the multilateral trading system; i.e. if they were "building on stumbling blocks" (Bhagwati 1992; Lawrence 1996; Winters 1996) [6]. However, challenging the multilateral system or not, preferential trade agreements among two or more countries have evolved into extremely popular policy choices; indeed, by July 2003, only three member countries – Macau China, Mongolia and Chinese Taipei – were not party to a regional trade agreement. Hence, over 265 of these agreements have been registered by the WTO with respect to the GATT Article 24, which allows regional trade arrangements to be established if certain criteria are met. [7]

Although the most prominent regional economic agreements were realised by the leading GATT members – CUSFTA in 1988 between Canada and the US, EU-Maastricht

---

[6] To this discussion, the WTO points out that in case a member enters into a regional trade arrangement by which it allows more favourable conditions to its trade with other parties in that arrangement, than to other WTO members' trade, it departs from the guiding principle of non-discrimination defined in Article I of the GATT, and Article I of GATS, among others. On the other hand, the WTO (WTO 2004; Regionalism - Friends or Rivals?) considers regional integration as a possible complementary force because agreements between neighbouring countries contemplate free trade among them with no need to increase barriers on trade with the outside world. When profound commitments were made in new topics, moreover, such as competition policies, investment and trade facilitation measures, state procurement and environmental rules (issues launched at the first ministerial meeting in Singapore in December 1996) regional agreements became the cutting edge of trade policy development paving the way for further arrangement inside the WTO.

[7] According to GATT Article 24: "If a free trade area or customs union is created, duties and other trade barriers should be reduced or removed on virtually all sectors of trade in the group. Non-members should not find trade with the group any more restrictive than before the group was established."

Treaty in 1992, and NAFTA between the US, Mexico and Canada in 1994 – the involvement of developing nations in regional endeavours was also widespread; especially when considering the regional integration treaties launched in South America in the 1990s. The principal endeavours were the creation of the Common Market of the South (MERCOSUR) in 1991 between Argentina, Brazil, Uruguay and Paraguay, and from 1989, the "re-launching" of the Andean Group, created twenty years previously by Venezuela, Colombia, Peru, Ecuador and Bolivia. These countries set high targets as they strove for common regional markets that included the establishment of customs unions. Furthermore, the so far quasi dormant Latin American Integration Association (ALADI as it is known by its Spanish acronym) created in 1980, became, in the 1990s, a functional framework for numerous bilateral Economic Complementary Agreements (or ACEs), providing reciprocal trade preferences among the twelve member states.[8]

Beyond the regional level, the trade policy agenda of the 1990s became increasingly influenced by the United States, which began to seek furthering trade relations with Latin America. During the first Presidential Summit Meeting of the Americas in 1995, four years after the US administration announced the Initiative for the Enterprise of the Americas, 34 Heads of State from the Western Hemisphere set the goal of establishing a Free Trade Area for the Americas (FTAA). Nonetheless, the far-reaching, NAFTA inspired, project became more and more controversial and had finally stalled by the end of 2003. As a consequence, the US government began emphasising bilateral strategies as a means to achieve Free Trade Agreements (FTAs); for example, it negotiated such strategies with Chile, Central American countries, Colombia, and Peru. As well as deepening relations with the US, most States set forth attempts to integrate their economies with Asian and European partners.

Against this background of bustling regionalism, debates emerged concerning the question of whether (extra-) regional endeavours left more room for local experimentation and heterodox policies, in the sense developed by Rodrik. For Devlin and Estevadeordal (2001) the conclusions are clear. Comparing the "New Regionalism" in the scope of ALADI, MERCOSUR, CAN and FTAA, with the "Old Regionalism" embodied by the inward-looking, "protectionist" integration schemes pursued in Latin America during the 1960s and 1970s, they conclude that current regional developments should, by no means, be qualified as

---

[8] Through the Montevideo treaty, ALADI became in 1980 the successor of the Latin American Free Trade Area (ALALC) founded in 1960. Even though ALADI did not stand up to very many immediate substantial concessions, its open nature *vis-à-vis* the rigid ALALC scheme enabled the signing of agreements between a small group of members, with no obligation to reach multilateral scope at the regional level. To date, most of the approximately 60 agreements encompass a bilateral trade exchange of preferences for specific products.

opposing forces to Multilateralism, but instead as, generally, complementary. Compared to the Old Regionalism, three evidently contrasting properties of the New Regionalism stand out:

1) *Lock-In Effect:* The agreements signed in the last two decades have become integral parts of the economic reforms underway since the 1980s. Consequently, governments fostered regional integration to underline their commitment to further liberalisation in times of arduous multilateral talks and difficult political conditions for unilateral opening.

2) *Scope and Modalities:* Although the earliest ALADI agreements were simply structured and based on a limited exchange of only temporary preferences on trade for specific products, more recent regional trade agreements have defined comprehensive liberalisation schemes, become broader in scope and set forth detailed enforcement mechanism.

3) *Attraction of FDIs:* Given the global competition for FDIs, the creation of regional consumer markets such as MERCOSUR became strongly associated to the attraction of foreign capital, abolishing entry restrictions applied in previous decades.

Therefore, a significant portion of local trade policy-making has been transferred to levels where rule making responds to the trend for institutional harmonisation, largely driven by the NAFTA and EU experience. In this scenario, developing nations have been moving within a rather small room for autonomous unilateral policy development, being challenged to use this remaining space in order to bring international market trends best in line with the realities of domestic economic sectors.

Springboard versus Multipolar Model

Up until the mid-1990s, economic integration within South America took place as a strong reaction to the rise of regionalism in Europe and North America. Understood as a "pragmatic intermediate step to world market integration" (Sangmeister 1999: 78-92), the *Springboard Model,* based on distinct regional coordination on trade and economic policies, can be seen as an expression of this regional response. The main projects in this regard have become the MERCOSUR and the lesser known Andean Community of Nations (CAN).

Both integration projects place emphasis on the establishment of common regional markets and customs unions. As stated by Devlin and Estevadeordal, the leitmotifs of these in-depth modes of economic integration, which go beyond the removal of border barriers by requiring the intra-regional harmonisation of economic policies, did not concern the insulation from international markets but rather the attraction of foreign investors. Beyond this, the Springboard Model is aimed at the expansion of limited domestic markets.[9] Hence, local manufacturers can adapt their production schemes to the requirements of world markets within a "familiar" market space, reflecting more symmetric competition than that found on the international level. The application of an escalated tariff structure provides certain protection to local industries, while it reduces import costs for required inputs. Furthermore, productive complementarities and increased economies of scale on the regional level are likely to prosper due to enhanced intra-industrial trade and business alliances between neighbouring countries.

Based on common external tariffs, a final but crucial element of the Springboard Model is the implementation of common trade policies, which implies the conduction of international negotiations as a trading block. The main idea behind such a policy is that the bargaining power of developing countries could potentially increase, through south-south cooperation schemes, in the scope of regional and multilateral trade negotiations, such as the WTO Development Round of Doha, the FTAA talks encompassing the Western Hemisphere and the bi-regional trade negotiations between MERCOSUR and the European Union.

Nonetheless, the *Multipolar Model*, paradigmatically pursued by Chile since the 1990s (Silva 2001; ECLAC 2002) has turned into a powerful alternative to the Springboard Model.[10] Contrary to the building of regional trading blocks, the Multipolar Model foresees the application of a very open, non-discriminatory regionalism, involving the country in a dense network of regional, extra-regional and multilateral free trade arrangements.

Essential to this strategy is the definition of "non-traditional export champions", such as processed goods, which differ from traditional commodity exports, for which local diplomacy negotiates preferential market access all over the globe. To take advantage of the broad external market options, export industries receive active state support through

---

[9] Lawrence (1996: 7-8) has drawn a distinction between deeper integration, that is, integration that moves beyond the removal of border barriers, and shallow integration, which is trade liberalisation. Regarding this approach, in-depth integration does not mean better or more efficient integration. For instance, the adoption of a common standard might discriminate against external imports and increase internal costs. Alternatively, in-depth integration could put in place measures that enhance efficiency such as the international enforcement of competitive policies or the international implementation of policies to deal with global greenhouse gases.

[10] The denomination "Multipolar" strategy has been used previously by Martin Redrado, former chief negotiator of Argentina; see Redrado 2003; Redrado/ Lacunza 2004.

marketing assistance, fiscal incentives, and other promotion schemes, sometimes exceeding the margins of the WTO regulatory framework.

Furthermore, through the adoption of Free Trade Agreements (FTA) of the "latest generation" that cover new trade disciplines such as intellectual property, services, investment rules, competitive policies, state procurement, and labour and environmental protection, the country opts for institutional harmonisation with developed nations rather than local experimentation, promoting the image of a reliable, modern economy that is thus attractive to foreign investors. The adoption of a low and uniform tariff structure, or "flat rate", can be considered similar, as it manifests the openness, predictability, and neutrality of the trade regime. In Table 2.1 the crucial features of both models are shown for comparative purposes.

Table 2.1: Springboard versus Multipolar Model

	Springboard Model	Multipolar Model
Geographic Orientation	World market integration based on previous regional integration	Open regionalism simultaneously using all possible venues in (extra) regional and multilateral spheres
Negotiation Strategy	Increasing international leverage by conducting negotiations as country blocks based on the customs union concept	Flexible for bilateral negotiations; pursuing FTA of the latest generation to underline the reliability of market oriented policies (lock-in effect)
Tariff Policy	Multiple or "escalated" tariff structure promoting manufacturing sectors by providing cheaper inputs and higher protection for value added products	Low uniform tariff or "flat rate" emphasising the predictability, transparency and neutrality of the trade regime
Industrial policy	Focus on value added chains and intra-industrial cooperation schemes on the regional level	Selective policies favouring a small range of non-traditional export champions
Trade Promotion	Important, but less explicit than in the Multipolar Model	Essential to take advantage of market access opportunities

Source: own elaboration based on Sangmeister (1999); Devlin and Estevadeordal (2001); Redrado/Lacunza 2004

2.3 World Market Integration – A Domestic Policy-Making Approach

In this *third section,* I start by discussing the development of world market integration strategies from a domestic policy-making perspective. Next, the two explanatory variables used in this study are explored in detail: the institutional strength of state bureaucracies and business associations.

World Market Integration - A Domestic Policy-Making Approach

As conceptualised in the previous section, today's world market integration strategies can be seen as a broad set of trade related policies that countries adopt within the context of the gradual liberalisation of the global economy, and a general shift of trade policy-making towards regional and multilateral levels. Hence, exogenous factors clearly influence strategic trade policy decisions; indeed, both the Springboard and Multipolar Models represent the prevailing policy options in South America that adapt regional economies to the current challenges of global markets.

Despite the driving forces of Multilateralism and, particularly, of Regionalism (being exogenous factors), the analysis of domestic politics (endogenous factor) remains crucial to explain why, how, when, and to what extent countries integrate their economies into world markets. In general, trade policy outputs can be analysed as domestic responses to a particular international setting, such as high commodity prices, debt crisis, recession or world war. For example, important works by Peter Gourevitch in *Politics in Hard Times* (1986) and Ronald Rogowski in *Commerce and Coalition* (1989) expose, from a historical perspective, the close relationship between the evolution of international trade and domestic politics.

Aside from the historical context, all works dealing with trade policy reforms consider, at least implicitly, the "firmness of domestic coalitions" as a key factor if reforms are to be successful, considering the necessity to respond to the strongly unequal impacts on domestic sectors usually caused by trade reforms. From a two-level game perspective, linking international and national politics, high-ranking officials are urged to take into account domestic concerns. According to Putnam (1993a), interaction patterns between domestic and international policies are divided into a first phase of negotiations among state officials (Level I) and a second phase in which international agreements must be ratified by domestic actors (Level II).

As this separation is rather vague in practice, the definition of negotiation strategies on Level I requires prior consultation at the domestic Level II, and moreover, before any agreement is signed negotiators must try out preliminary versions to test the views of constituents. Therefore, the process of ratification goes well beyond formal institutions, i.e. the voting procedure within the legislative power, and refers to any domestic policy-making characteristic required to endorse or implement a Level I agreement, whether formally or informally (1993a: 438).[11]

Table 2.2: Two-Level Game according to Putnam

	Level	Function	Win-Set Determinants	Actors
Negotiation Phase	I	Bargaining between States, leading to an agreement	Negotiators' strategies	State officials
Ratification Phase	II	Bargaining among domestic constituents on whether to ratify the agreement	Preferences and coalitions Institutions	Organised business, state agencies, trade unions, parties, "public opinion," civil society, etc.

Source: Putnam 1993a: 438.

In describing this two-level game, Putnam (1993: 439) uses the notion of "win-sets", defined as: *"the set of all possible international agreements (Level I) that would "win" (that is, gain the necessary support among the domestic constituents) when simply voted up or down."* For Putnam, both the size and certainty of win-sets must be taken into account. While the size depends on the configuration of domestic preferences at a specific time, defining the negotiation room for state officials involved at Level I (larger win-sets make agreements more likely), certainty goes beyond the preferences of actors and concerns the credibility of the proposals submitted (1993a: 441). With respect to the latter, Putnam argues (1993a: 453) that a high degree of uncertainty regarding the win-set presented by the opponent increases the risk of involuntary defection, in terms of the inability to deliver what was previously agreed,

---

[11] Although the ratification of international agreements is commonly linked to formal mechanisms inside Parliament, in this study informal means are considered, bearing in mind that legislative powers had become rather irrelevant in the trade policy-making examined. Therefore, it seems useful to work with a broad ratification model that consists of informal and formal actions of interests groups inclined to support the official trade integration strategy. For example, indicative behaviour can be publications, favourable media or active participation in the scope of formal and non-formal consultation channels. Besides, ratification goes beyond (pre-) negotiation phases and also embraces post-negotiation phases where agreements are embodied in national laws and procedures, and thus, guarantee their effective implementation. In this phase, affected interest groups can avoid forms of defection (voluntary or involuntary) through the sound application of norms and through helping the executive to perfect the correspondence between negotiated content and domestic regulation.

and, hence, causes the failure of negotiations or the necessity to compensate "wobbly win-sets" through more generous side-payments than would be needed under conditions of certainty.

Although this study is not based on the analysis of international negotiations leading to specific trade agreements, Putnam's notion of "win-sets" points at the determinants and actors which affect the domestic policy-making processes. Regarding the determinants of "win-sets" that define their size and certainty, literature on trade politics mainly focuses on preferences, rather than institutions. Specifically, there is a wide range of Political Economy literature that focusses on sectorally determined interests, leading to coalition formation, conflict, and influence over policy-making outcomes.

For example, Gourevitch (1986) outlines different production profiles – determined by international competitiveness, labour intensity, etc. – which are responsible for particular sectoral coalitions that influence the development model adopted by a country at any given moment, ranging from classical liberalism to neo-mercantilism. Sectoral interests are at stake also in Rogowski's *Commerce and Coalition* (1989). Drawing on the Stolper-Samuelson theorem, which states that abundant factors in an economy gain from trade, whilst scarce factors loose out, Rogowski argues that the dominant cleavages defining the degree of trade openness are determined by a country's endowment with capital, land, and labour. Accordingly, "capital" is assumed as a homogenous unit which compete – depending on the specific circumstances within international trade - with the labour class and land owners.

For many, Stolper-Samuelson's assumptions fail to analyse intra-class conflicts, and are seen as unrealistic because factor mobility is taken for granted (Frieden 1991; Hillman 1982, 1989; Rodrik 1995; Milner 1988). Conversely, many authors stress the high adjustment costs involved in shifting assets (machinery, skilled labour, etc.) between industries. While labour or tax regulation normally implies classical class conflicts between the united labour and capital, trade policy options can provoke internal divisions inside the business sector. Specifically, according to the Ricardo-Viner model that assumes the immobility of production factors, business consensus is often hindered by the division among import-competing industries lobbying for the preservation of their domestic market, and export industries seeking improved access to overseas markets. Whether exporting or not, further conflicts arise from different demands regarding imported inputs and external service suppliers (e.g. distributors, banks, courier companies, etc.) that lower production costs, and hence, raise competitiveness.

Nevertheless, such sectoral approaches, whether general or specific, normally discount the key role of institutions in forming and transmitting interests. Indeed, common interests within determined sectors do not necessarily lead to collective actions, and as a further consequence, into policy outcomes. As a result, for this study, which is not concerned with single reform steps, but rather with the level of coherence achieved by implementing a country's world market integration strategy over the period of analysis, it does not suffice to rely on a simple pluralism in which policy favours are exchanged on the political market for various forms of support. Instead, it is necessary to analyse the institutional mechanisms inside the state and business sectors that are responsible for filtering, preparing and analysing trade policy options available within the increasingly complex pattern of world market integration.

The State Bureaucracy

Defining "national interests" is not only a process challenged by competing interests among economic sectors, but also by state officials representing their countries at the international level. More so than in industrialised countries, "bureaucratic politics" in developing nations are associated with weak state structures that permit rent-seeking behaviour and overbearing "hyper-legalism". These weak, inefficient forms of state organisation have been outlined in detail by public choice theorists since the 1970s (Krueger 1974, Buchanan/ Tollison/ Tullock 1980), who began to systematise the widespread common suspicions with regard to the unfair distribution of public rents, such as import licences, soft loans and industrial subsidies. In this way, business factions tend to form "distributional coalitions" that put pressure on state officials to divert resources – or rents – towards them, and away from their most efficient and collectively optimal uses. For this reason, the management of state-led development strategies in Latin America have been condemned to failure, as is highlighted in a wide range of literature (e.g. Hirschmann 1971; O'Donnell 1973; Bulmer-Thomas 1994). The rampant rent-seeking responsible for fiscal debts lead to unambiguous policy prescriptions in the 1980s: thus, only through a wide-ranging economic disengagement of the State, can rents be reduced and entrepreneurs compelled to respond to market forces.

However, a different perspective has been put forward by neo-institutionalists (Johnson 1982; Amsden 1989, 2001; Wade 1990; Evans 1995; Fields 1995). Since the 1980s, these scholars identified, mainly in Japan, Taiwan and Korea, an efficient development State in charge of planning, coordinating and monitoring the process of industrial transformation.

Accordingly, theorists argued that the genesis of internationally competitive industries such as electronics, steel, shipbuilding, automotive, textiles and clothing, had not been carried out by individual firms but grew out of joint projects which the State shared with business groups. Based on this theory, Peter Evans' notion of Embedded Autonomy (1995) identified a combination of three elements:

1) *Embeddedness*: One of the factors crucial to any transformation project that demands policy planning is a close interaction pattern between state and business that provides channels for the permanent negotiation, renegotiation, and monitoring of economic goals and policies. Relations can be formal, in the scope of advisory bodies, as well as informal, in societal networking spheres. While the State plans, coordinates, and monitors, the private sector implements strategies and contributes with its "decentralised intelligence" from markets.

2) *State Autonomy:* So as not to convert embedded state-business relations into squandering rent seeking networks, state bureaucracies need to be organised along the lines laid out by Max Weber.[12] In this way, bureaucracy is not associated with hyper-legalism, paternalism or bribery, but with loyal public servants who recognise the pursuit of collective objectives as the best way to maximise individual interests. As a precondition, Evans names (1) the implementation of meritocratic systems of recruitment, (2) the promotion of public careers as a reliable career path, (3) competitive remuneration compared to the private sector; and finally, (4) high social prestige for public servants.

3) *Pilot Agency:* Coherent economic policy demands an "institutionalised brain" in charge of policy planning and overall coordination, that is, intra-governmental

---

[12] The role of bureaucratic authority structures in facilitating economic growth has been a sociological concern since Max Weber's classic contributions almost 100 years ago. Recently, Evans and Rauch (1999) used original data sets to examine the characteristics of core state economic agencies and the growth records of a sample of 35 developing countries between 1970 and 1990. They found that Weberian characteristics significantly enhance prospects for economic growth, even when they initially controlled levels of GDP per capita and human capital. Considering their results, Evans and Rauch suggest that Weberianness should be included as a factor in general models for economic growth. However, they highlight the need for more attention by policymakers to build better bureaucracies and more research by social scientists on variations in how state bureaucracies are organised; see Evans/ Rauch 1999. However, the difference among the concepts of Weber and Evans is related to the fact that Weber saw the state bureaucracy as an insulated institution from the private sector, while for Evans the government needs the business sector as a source of decentralised intelligence which provides information on possibilities and limitations.

leadership is to be assumed by one clearly identifiable economic department instead of dividing responsibilities among a large number of state departments.[13]

The notion of embedded autonomy offers rich theoretical insights, even though this study does not focussed on explaining the success of industrial transformation in authoritarian development States in East Asia during the 1960s and 1970s, but rather analyses state structures in South America from the 1980s, when democracy and market reforms emerged as prevailing policy options.

When analysing trade policy-making, several institutional features need to be considered, however. The concentration of resources and responsibilities inside the executive branch is often hindered, as trade policy comprises a vast ensemble of ministries and agencies in charge of defining, setting, and implementing policies. The agencies frequently involved here are the Ministries of Trade, Foreign Affairs, Economy and Industry. Moreover, international trade policy has become very broad in scope, thus requiring specialised agencies dealing with agriculture, technical standards, intellectual property, telecommunications, transportation, construction, labour, justice, education, and others.

Coordination problems between various state departments are therefore common, bearing in mind their varying functional logics. For example, the finance department might oppose liberalisation, or a particular tariff structure, in light of falling, or less predictable, revenues. In part, this conservative fiscal perspective is often sustained by sectoral ministries such as those involved with agriculture and industry, which seek to protect import-competing branches. Conversely, these ministries can be in conflict with the Finance Ministry, seeking lower tariffs for inputs. Finally, the Ministry of Foreign Affairs might support the outward-oriented strategy developed inside the Ministry of Economy, yet set other geographical priorities due to political reasons.

---

[13] Obviously, Evans behaved inductively here by analysing, for example, the centric role of the Economic Planning Board (EPB) in Korea, where responsibilities and the most talented officials were concentrated inside a single department (1995: 51–55).

Jordana and Ramió (2002: 5) examined the most common models for trade policy-making, underlining the fact that different institutional arrangements generally reflect variations in how the political systems are structured, what role the State assumes in the economy, and how government bodies engage in consultations with interest groups. Therein, each model possesses its pros and cons concerning the aim of conducting trade policy efficiently, and adequately linked to economic policy-making in general.

Table 2.3: Organisational Models in International Trade Policy

Foreign Affairs Model	Economy/Industry Model	Foreign Trade Model
Frequent Pros		
o Coherence of foreign policies by having only one interlocutor abroad o Institutional link with foreign networks (market information, trade promotion) o Maintains traditional governance style; and low risk related to business capture	o Coherence between economic/industrial policies and trade polices o Maintains traditional governance style	o Autonomous trade policy o Prominent presidential incidence
Frequent Cons		
o Mixed policy objectives o Political motivations often prevail o Weak presidential incidence	o Duality regarding trade and foreign policies o Diversified policy goals (subordinating trade) o High risk related to business capture o Weak presidential incidence	o Strong need for coordination o Weak linkages with long-term economic policies o Weakly enrooted style of governance o Inter-ministerial struggles

With respect to the notion of embedded autonomy, each institutional arrangement includes elements that might resemble the idealistic construction, and others that appear to be dysfunctional. In the *Foreign Affairs Model*, for example, the organisational deficit is supposed to lie in its separation from the economic policy planning, and the tendency for outward-oriented diplomacy to be somewhat "detached" from the realities of domestic economic sectors. Thus, embeddedness in terms of efficient interaction patterns with business is somewhat unlikely. Conversely, in most foreign affairs ministries, civil service is institutionalised, contrasting remarkably with other public agencies. This is so because the recruitment systems are more sophisticated and career perspectives are more stable.

The *Economy or Industry Model* has been assessed rather negatively, although the unified handling of domestic and foreign economic policies greatly resembles the pilot agency concept. The critical aspects mentioned by Jordana and Ramió, such as the subordination of trade policies, risks related to business capture, and the duality of trade and foreign policies, are not necessarily given, and depend very much on the prevailing policy orientation and the coordination pattern upheld inside the executive branch, and with the private sector. Moreover, the traditional ties between Ministries of Economy and business factions can be crucial in precisely matching the realities of the domestic sector with the available policy options within international trade policy spheres.

Finally, the *Foreign Trade Model* is a relatively new institutional phenomenon in Latin America, strongly inspired by the US Trade Representative. In obtaining ministerial rank, such a "pilot agency" in trade policy affairs receives special political attention. Yet, concerning the concept established by Evans, a specific Foreign Trade Ministry does not work as an economic policy core agency, but is focused on coordinating trade policy concerns among the different economic policy related ministries. In any case, the implementation of such a model seems a challenging task, given that this style of governance is still weakly enrooted, and often causes inter-ministerial struggles.

Adapted to the purpose of this study, it should be considered the often widespread limitations public administrations suffer from in developing countries in general, and in Latin America in particular (Mendez 1999; Nef 2003). Therefore, the bureaucracy ideal, in a Weberian sense, cannot be taken as an absolute reference, as first approximations might entail positive effects already. Furthermore, the discussion on the adequacy of each of the models outlined also encounters empirical constraints. For example, while in Australia the Foreign Trade Model has worked very effectively to date; in Malaysia the Industry Model has become a broadly acknowledged solution, and in Chile, the Foreign Affairs approach has converted into a model case inside South America, as I shall elucidate in Chapter Three.

Despite such variances, for the purpose of this study I identified three general aspects, which have been used as variable dimensions for the purpose of empirical research, related to the institutional strength of state bureaucracies, all of which are also greatly foreseen in the embedded autonomy concept. Box 2.2 provides an overview:

Box 2.2: Institutional Strength of State Bureaucracies

Responsibilities	o Clear division of labour in the conduction of international trade policy affairs.
	o Close inter-ministerial coordination among the different sectoral departments involved in international trade policy affairs.
Resources	o Organisational strength of the trade policy team with respect to staff size, technical expertise, and the application of civil service models inclined to meritocracy and continuity.
Openness	o Transparent conduction of international trade policy affairs.
	o Permanent consultation mechanism aimed at domestic businesses, enabling close coordination of sectoral interests and related technical concerns.

The Organisation of Business Interests

Following the trade liberalisation of the 1980s, the newly outward-oriented South American nations began to emphasise the virtue of entrepreneurship. Thus, governments became more prone to accept private business inputs on trade policy-making. Martin Redrado, Argentina's chief negotiator from 2002 to 2004, points out (Redrado 2003: 66-67): *"If we make concessions in order to "unblock" external markets and carry out export promotion activities, the idea is for firms to take advantage of these market opportunities. Otherwise our market access strategy will be incoherent; spending thereby scarce public resources."*

Notwithstanding the foregoing statement, the participation of business in policy-making still faces many negative connotations. In public spheres, local entrepreneurs are often seen as risk adverse, preferring personal channels to state officials in order to avoid public scrutiny, and as a result, causing subornment and discretional decisions. Likewise, literature on rent-seeking points exclusively at negative aspects, without stressing the useful contributions of sound business advocacy behaviour. For Schmitter and Streeck (1999: 9), the dilemma of the limited amount of attention paid to political business actions is wide-reaching, and can be explained, at least in part, by the absence of systematised data, thus leaving space to impressionist judgments of this issue. They advert (ibid.) that *"reliable information on, not to speak of analysis of, the resources, organizational characteristics, activities, and strategies of formal associations specialized in the promotion and protectionism of trade or employer interests is rare."* Furthermore, they conclude (ibid.) *"some of the lack of attention may be attributed to the secrecy and confidentiality which tends to surround the operation of business associations and, hence, to greater problems of accessibility by scholars to the data necessary to evaluate the role of such associations in political lives."*

The empirical analysis of formal business organisations in developing countries is also limited, and generally depicts a certain institutional fragility (Merkel/Sandschneider 1999). From a more practical view, Kostecki (2002: 2) identified a range of advocacy problems in the WTO scope, adverting that *"business advocacy is a reality of the trading system and there is no reason why managers and the business community in developing countries should remain inactive when needs arise."* As principal activities, he mentioned the monitoring of trade talks by a certain interest group, building a case in favour of that interest, presenting it to policy-makers for their acceptance and support, assisting the authorities in negotiations abroad and controlling the advocacy process, evaluating the benefits obtained and communicating the results to associated sectors. For Kostecki (2002: 9), past experience clearly suggests that lobbyists from the developing world spend a relatively smaller share of their resources on advocacy than their developed country counterparts, outlining the following six aspects as causes:

1) *Lack of Awareness.* Industry leaders in developing countries are often unaware of the potential benefits of advocacy.

2) *Short-Sightedness.* Returns on business advocacy in trade policy have to be considered in a long-term perspective, whereas industry leaders in the developing world have a shorter decision horizon.

3) *High Cost/Benefit Ratio.* The relative costs of business advocacy for many newcomers may be higher in developing countries, due to the *modus operandi* of the local administration, such as a lack of transparency or accountability, higher information costs, and the economic distance from the negotiation forum (Geneva in the WTO case).

4) *High Risk.* Returns on business advocacy are more risky in developing countries, due to political instability and the unpredictability of trade policy-making.

5) *Resistance to Change.* Related to cost/benefit issues is the resistance to change. Resistance to change in the trade policy of developing countries is partly due to the feeling of insecurity and threat, encouraged in many quarters by the process of globalisation in low-income countries.

6) *Lack of Economies of Scale.* Given the lack of economies of scale, the potential benefits of lobbying in trade policy tend to be lower for the developing country industries, especially for Small and Medium Size Enterprises (SME).

From a political science perspective, it was Maxfield and Schneider et al. (1997) who highlighted that in several countries, any efforts towards encompassing business organisation, i.e. the capacity of multisectoral associations to control and monitor each other's performance and assure compliance to collectively agreed strategies, entailed growth enhancing effects. Also Mancur Olson (1982) acknowledged that multisectoral organisations tend to assume a state like perspective due to their broad functional scope, and thus, support policies favourable to economy wide efficiency.

In Colombia, for example, Thorp and Durand underlined (1997: 216-237) that the valuable encompassing properties of the National Coffee Federation facilitated not only efficient collaboration with the government in designing and administrating efficient export promotion schemes, but also provided outstanding collective goods in the range of warehousing, quality controls, marketing, and technical innovation. In the Mexican case, Ben Ross Schneider (1997: 191-216) showed that the presence of the Entrepreneurial Coordinator of Foreign Trade (COECE), created in 1990 by the national business council CCE, was crucial for a sound integration into the NAFTA, since it allowed the official negotiators to interact permanently with a technically competent and encompassing interlocutor within the (pre-) negotiation periods. In so doing, the concentration in multiple topic forums contributed to the consolidation of trade reform, by building support in the private sector, increasing the flow of information between business and government, and allowing business to propose complementary and compensatory policies.

Identifying major organisational requirements for sound business associations, Schmitter and Streeck (1999) draw from the neocorporatistic premise that interest groups do not only pressure governments in order to influence policy outcome, but are also interested in engaging in a stable and cooperative exchange with state authorities (see also Czada 1994; Schubert 1995). In this manner, Schmitter and Streeck (1999: 19) point to the complicated, intermediary, position between two independent and resourceful actors – firms on the one hand, and state agencies on the other. Accordingly, in order not to be overlooked within the intermediation of interests, a business association is obliged to insert itself into the direct exchange of market actors and state authorities, by offering a service at a beneficial price or quality. In Figure 2.1, Schmitter and Streeck (1999: 20) illustrate the complexity of associative business action, by emphasising four different, and often opposing, logics affecting the organisational properties of any voluntaristic, free association that aims to be a strong interlocutor of business interests.

■ **Figure 2.1: The Competing Logics of Associative Business Action**

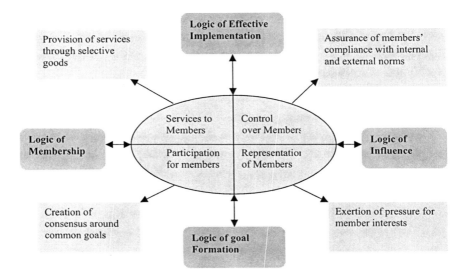

For a better understanding of these four logics, Figure 2.1 outlines four types of activities that each refers to two different logics, due to the fact that the logics are mutually linked. In order to achieve the essence of the neocorporatistic approach, I first stress the required capacities of business associations to align the Logic of Membership with the Logic of Influence.

The Logic of Membership makes reference to the demanding task of defining common positions and providing useful services to (potential) members. The more an association knows how to deal with diverse member profiles, the larger the membership, and consequently the more resources can be extracted. As regards the creation of consensus around trade policy affairs, however, any coordination by associations representing a broad array of products and branches can become problematic, since factions pursue opposing interests, as was indicated in the previous section.

The *Logic of Influence* is orientated towards the imperative to interact steadily with policy-makers, influencing policy outputs, and consolidating the association's institutional status. In this instance, associations search for public resources such as concessions, subsidies and official recognition. To achieve these goals, two apparently contradictory activities are required. In "control over members" the compliance of both internal and external obligations stands out, such as the sound payment of affiliation rates, and the fulfilment of agreements signed with the government, respectively (e.g. price controls, investment goals or distribution of export quotas). Under "representation of members" a wide range of lobbying activities could be enlisted, e.g. fiscal incentives for exports or lower tariffs for inputs.

Therefore, the main difficulty of interest intermediation consists in respecting both logics simultaneously.[14] The government has obvious interests in maintaining a permanent dialogue with associations that exhibit a degree of representation. However, it is also logical that the creation of internal consensus and the assurance of members' behaviour are more demanding among a broad membership than a narrow group of capitalists. On the other hand, entrepreneurs will only bet their resources on their sectoral representative if, and when, privileged access to decision making is guaranteed, otherwise they will choose another, more informal option. Beyond the Logics of Membership and Influence, Schmitter and Streeck also stress two other sets of challenging imperatives that have to be considered by business organisations; the Logic of Effective Implementation and the Logic of Goal Formation.

The Logic of Effective Implementation refers, in general terms, to the way in which (1999: 19) "specified tasks or outcomes are attained with certainty and efficiency", and is focussed on features such as the "routinization of operation, specializations of functions, directness of communication and speed in decision making." In other words, the authors are concerned with the quality of administrative structures, as well as the usefulness of the services provided to members (such as technical advisory, market surveys, trade data, custom procedures, business rounds and trade missions). According to Figure 1, this logic also discerns the ability to assure member compliance in internal and external affairs.

The Logic of Goal Formation, finally, points to the democratic characteristics of internal decision making and questions whether associational goals are formed by inclusive, deliberative member participation rather than by oligarchic domination "from above" (1999: 20). Thus, democratically inclined modes require the provision of checks and balances, deliberative institutions, and in general, active member participation. Even though such

---

[14] Schmitter and Streeck apply this notion particularly in the context of labour relations, and for compliance with collective labour agreements.

"democratisation of business representation" might hamper external negotiations, since opposing views need to be taken into account, in the end, the broad and active participation of entrepreneurs increases the pressure of collective concerns with regard to the involvement in official policy-making.

For the purpose of this study, the notion of the institutional strength of business associations draws on Schmitter and Streeck's insights, being defined as the capacity of private sector organisations to effectively intermediate the often opposing trade policy preferences within the private sector, and simultaneously, to maintain close relations with state authorities. The variable dimension relevant to the empirical research has been divided into two areas – leadership and organisational strength - as Box 2.3 exposes in detail.

Box 2.3: Institutional Strength of Business Associations

Leadership	o Existence of widely recognised peak, or "umbrella", associations, capable of coordinating economic policies between the leading sectoral and regional representatives o Existence of widely recognised institutional mechanisms (e.g. commission, council) ensuring an effective intermediation of trade interests between sectoral and regional representatives.
Organi-sational Strength	o Regular payment of the membership dues o High diversification of the entity's revenues o Active participation by entrepreneurs in the scope of internal (business) and external (government) coordination channels on international trade policy affairs o Large size of permanent staff o High in-house expertise, i.e. professionals monitoring and analysing international trade policy affairs

2.4 The Hypothesis and its Logical Structure

In light of the theoretical assumptions and concepts presented in sections 2.1 to 2.3, in this section I define the hypothesis, and later discuss its logical structure. *The success of world market integration strategies in developing countries (Dependent Variable B) depends on the institutional strength of state bureaucracies (Independent Variable A1) and business associations (Independent Variable A2).*

■ **Figure 2.2: Arrow Diagram**

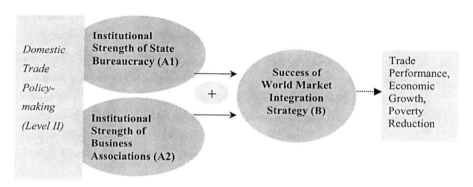

As shown in section 2.1., *a successful world market integration strategy* is conceptualised as a "high degree of coherence reached by implementing a particular set of trade related policies that developing countries adopt within a context of gradual liberalisation of the global economy and a shift of trade policy-making towards regional and multilateral levels, considering to what extent essential principals, policies, and objectives of the selected strategy have been put into practice and maintained over the period of analysis (1985 to 2004)." The measurement of the degree of coherence is, herein, related to two idealistic modes of world market integration, which have been pursued within the enlightened international context: the Multipolar and Springboard Models. These are further outlined in section 2.2. It is further assumed – but not analysed in this study – that coherently implemented world market integration strategies will contribute to the improvement of a country's trade performance, and finally, to the achievement of economic growth and poverty reduction.

Regarding the explanatory part of the hypothesis, *the institutional strength of state bureaucracy* has been defined as an executive branch, wherein the responsibilities as regards the conduction of international trade policy affairs are clearly perceived, the trade policy staff is adequately doted, and finally, a degree of openness is sustained towards business and non-business as regards their incorporation into the trade policy-making process. On the other hand, *the institutional strength of business associations* is defined as the capacity of organisations representing private sectors interests – i.e. trade and industrial chambers, business councils, peak associations, farmers organisations, and entities representing specific sectors or branches – to effectively intermediate the often opposing trade policy preferences within the private sector, and simultaneously, to maintain close relations with state authorities.

When discussing the logical structure of the hypothesis, I use Zetterberg's theory to distinguish five potential relationships between the independent and dependent variables:

1. *Reversible or irreversible (if A1+2, then B and if B then A1+2/ if A1+2 then B, but if B not A1+2):* The hypothesis is <u>reversible</u> because it is conceivable that the success of a world market integration strategy (high value of B) strengthens the country's state bureaucracy and business associations (high value of A1+2), rather than vice versa. For example, an important trade agreement, which might be an integral part of the country's policy success, can spur domestic actors to prepare themselves for upcoming trade policy challenges, through the creation of an inter-sectoral coordination pattern or the strengthening of trade policy advisory units inside the state and business sector.

2. *Deterministic or probabilistic (if A1+2, then always B/ if A1+2, then probably B):* The hypothesis is <u>probabilistic</u> because whilst it is likely that A1+2 cause B, it is by no means certain, i.e. several disturbing effects might hinder the influence from A1+2 on B (see point 5).

3. *Successive or coexistent (if A1+2, then later B/ if A1+2, then at the same time B):* The hypothesis is <u>successive</u> because A1+2 must operate for a certain period of time before strong effects on the B-value can be observed. Therefore, strengthening domestic institutions, both inside the state and business sector, can be conceived as an investment that at a given moment causes a cohesive whole of trade policies, spurring economic growth and reducing poverty.

4. *Sufficient or conditional (if A1+2, then B, without considering other influences/ if A1+2, then B, but only if D is present):* The hypothesis is <u>sufficient</u> because no condition variable is required.

5. *Necessary or subsidiary (if A1+2, then and only then B/ if A1+2, then B, but also if C then B):* The hypothesis is subsidiary because it is possible that other variables may influence the value of B.

Point five indicates that the value of B cannot be attributed to A1+2 without first analysing other potential influences on the dependent variable. To mitigate the disturbing influences of economy, culture, geography and politics, among others, I narrowed down the focus of this study to South American countries, thus ensuring *similar background conditions* between the cases (Van Evera 1997: 52). Nevertheless, it was unlikely to expect general background conditions to be identical among the countries selected. With respect to these countries – Argentina, Bolivia, Chile and Peru – there are irrefutable differences concerning geographic extension, size and structure of the population, industrial development, GDP size, etc. Conversely, several important similarities among the four countries provided, in the last two decades, a comparable playing field for trade integration strategies.

First, in the aftermath of the debt crisis at the outset of the 1980s, the countries moved towards far-reaching market reforms so as to encounter inflationary pressures, and balance of payment deficits. While the Bolivian and Peruvian trade reforms took place from 1985 to 1990, respectively, in Chile and Argentina the first reform wave had already taken place by the end of the 1970s. However, the debt crisis in the 1980s led to a serious backlash, thus accounting for the fact that the world market integration strategies currently in force were not implemented before 1985 in Chile and 1989 in Argentina.

Second, before 1985, traditional exports depended, without exception, on a narrow range of industrial and agricultural commodities, like cereals and meat (Argentina), mining (Peru, Chile, and Bolivia), fish and fish meal (Peru, Chile) and hydrocarbons (Bolivia, Argentina). Due to their oscillating world market prices, and mainly limited demand for labour, the four countries had clear incentives to foster the diversification of national exports.

Third, it was in the 1980s when, in Latin America, countries made the transition from authoritarian to democratic regimes; Argentina in 1983, Bolivia in 1982, Chile in 1989, and Peru in 1980. Apart from free elections, democratic rule implied more checks and balances, and more transparency and openness towards society. It should be noted, however, that these new democracies in Latin America are still marked by widespread presidentialism and distinctive forms of populism, which are serious obstacles to the consolidation of democratic regimes (Diamond/Hartlyn/Linz/Lipset 1997; Mainwaring/Shugart/Soberg 1997; Merkel/Puhle 1999).

Despite this, to ensure that the value of B does not result from a factor other than A1+2, I defined four so called *control variables*:

C1 - Heterogeneity of Sectoral Preferences: As outlined in section 2.3, heterogeneous interests have often been used to explain the outcome of trade policy, considering the distributive implications of trade reforms. Accordingly, the institutional requirements to filter and coordinate diverging sectoral interests might be lower in countries with a homogenous business sector, than in countries where there is strong competition between the views of farmers, industrialists and traders. For example, in Brazil, the coherent implementation of a world market integration strategy over a certain period, where regional, rural and industrial factions often maintain opposing interests, demands a higher value of A1+2 than in small and medium sized countries where business interest are generally more homogenous.

C2 - Heterogeneity of Foreign Preferences: As indicated in section 2.1, a domestic policy-making approach to world market integration strategies encounters limits when exogenous factors determine policy options. Particularly, the preferences of other countries must be taken into account as integration steps necessarily depend on the policy coordination of two or more countries. For example, the coherent implementation of the Springboard Model, requiring a far-reaching south-south coordination of economic policies, can be inhibited by the absent will of neighbour countries to liberalise their home market and to harmonise technical and sanitarian measures. In this study, Argentina's trade policy was affected by strong heterogeneous foreign preferences, which required adequate assessement. For example, the protectionist behaviour of the US and European governments regarding the further liberalising of agriculture trade stands out, being a major obstacle to the conclusion of the FTAA and MERCOSUR-EU free trade talks.

C3 - Political Instability (C3): A general interference on policy-making processes which affects, among others, the development of trade policy, concerns political crisis features, such as the compulsory resignation of the head or chief, mass riots, corruption scandals, or other governance crisis. Such incidences, rather common in developing countries, often entail negative impacts on long-term oriented policies. Therefore, the strong populist attitudes of political leaders in responding exclusively to specific popular demands to increase governmental legitimacy in the short-term, can undermine prior achievements, or accentuate failures in other policy areas. For instance, analysing the Bolivian case, I faced the problem of assessing the effects of political crisis features such as mass riots and compulsory resignations of state presidents, observed from 2000 to 2004, strongly interfering in the causal relationship I sought to elucidate.

C4 – Macroeconomic Instability: As well as high political instability, another general interference on long-term oriented policy-making is macroeconomic turmoil. Indeed, inflationary pressure, balance of payments problems, fiscal deficits and volatile exchange rates, have often hindered, especially in Latin America countries, the maintenance of development policies over a longer period of time. Even though the economic instability registered during the 1980s was considerably decreased in the 1990s throughout the region, the potential impacts of exceptional macroeconomic features ought to be discussed. Specifically, Argentina during 2001-02 (debt crisis, volatile exchange rates, fiscal deficits), and Bolivia from 1998 to 2004 (fiscal deficits), required detailed analyses regarding the corresponding impacts on the B value. Finally, I illustrate below a variety of case scenarios which confirm or falsify the hypothesis.

Table 2.4: Falsification and Confirmation of Hypothesis

	Falsification of Hypothesis	Confirmation of Hypothesis
Success of World Market Integration Strategies	Low A1+A2 Low influence of C1-C4	High A1+A2 Low influence of C1-C4
Failure of World Market Integration Strategies	High A1+A2 Low influence of C1-C4	Low A1+A2 Low influence of C1-C4

It is important to note, however, that in practice the values of variables change over the period of analysis, and often range somewhere between high and low. For example in Chile, the most successful case in this study, a very high B value was not reached before 1995. Before this, the Multipolar Model had yet to be consolidated. In Argentina, the B value had been rather high in the second half of the 1980s, when the country was pursuing innovative integration initiatives with Brazil, but came down in the course of the 1990s, when incoherencies between unilateral and regional policies became increasingly apparent. A1 or A2 often behaved unequally, moreover, entailing different impacts on the value of B. For example, Peru's trade policy expertise inside the public sector was strengthened from 2002, while responses inside the private sector turned out to be rather more modest. Hence, trade policy endeavours initiated at this time can be traced back more to the newly created Ministry of Foreign Trade and Tourism rather than to the leading trade and industrial chambers.

3   Chile

The world market integration strategy pursued by Chile from 1985 appears comprehensible to any observer. As the domestic market is small, with just 15 million inhabitants and a per capita income of about US$4,500, local policy makers opted for an export-led growth strategy rather than an inward-looking solution. Moreover, considering the fact that ongoing South American integration endeavors provided few predictable options, Chile set forth an exhaustive worldwide search so as to further market access. As a result of the undertaken efforts, the country registered, in the last two decades, an impressive quantitative export growth coupled with almost constant trade surpluses. Furthermore, local exports attained a steady process of sectoral diversification, involving clearly outward oriented industries from the forestry (pulp, timber), fishery (salmon, fish meal) and agriculture (vines, vegetables, fresh fruits) and various manufactures.

With this record, Chile became a model case for policy makers both inside and out with the region, even though critics claim that the export structure is still overly dependent on minimally processed natural resources. But perhaps the most remarkable feature is not primarily referred to the countries export figures – which are more impressive in East Asian countries – but concerns the high degree of coherence reached in implementing trade policies over the last 20 years. Instead of altering principals and objectives, as usually occurred in neighbouring countries, in Chile the export-oriented model developed gradually, constantly improving and enhancing previous efforts, rather than abolishing them. In this regard, the democratic government that took office in 1990 did not aim to rupture the trade policy of its authoritarian predecessor (e.g. in maintaining the "flat rate regime") but to complement efforts in extending market access opportunities through preferential trade agreements.

Therefore, this chapter describes the outstanding properties of the outward oriented Multipolar Model pursued from 1985 and 2004, and provides explanations for its success. Accordingly, this chapter is structured along the following lines. The *first section* outlines the different policy areas that make up the world market integration strategy (Dependent Variable B), i.e. unilateral trade regime, regional and extra-regional integration, sectoral and trade promotion policies. *Section two* enlightens the organisation of Chile's public sector in the trade policy area (Independent Variable A1), thus showing how the local bureaucracies responded to the emerging challenges of the international trading system. Then, *section three* outlines the institutional responses of the business sector on the same issue (Independent Variable A2).

Based on section one to three, *section four* provides an assessment of the case by means of exploring the links between the independent and dependent variables during the period of analysis, and controls the possible influences of other variables (C1-4) on the B value.

3.1 The Successful Development of the Multipolar Model

This first section is structured in accordance with the different policy areas that make up the world market integration strategy (Dependent Variable B), i.e. unilateral trade regime, regional and extra-regional integration, and sectoral and trade promotion policies. The final subsection summarises the results and provides an overview of the trade performance from 1985 to 2004.

Unilateral Trade Regime

Placing trust on the forces of liberal trade, one of the first steps towards reform announced by the military government after the coup-d'état in September 1973 was the reduction of border tariffs and the unification of the exchange rate (French-Davis 2002). The most radical liberalisation concerning the nominal protection of local industry took place in April 1975, however, when the military government declared the aim to remove all non-tariff barriers and to abolish tariff walls of up to 120 percent (220 percent before 1973), progressively establishing a new tariff range of 10 to 35 percent by 1978. In 1979, the government finally decided to reach a flat rate structure of 10 percent for all imports. Furthermore, international competition for domestic industries was further accentuated by the decrease of the exchange rate from 34 to 17.8 percent between 1975 and 1982 (French-Davis et al 2000: 137). As a consequence, at the outset of the 1980s the country suffered from devastating trade deficits which forced the government to raise the flat rate to 35 percent in September 1984. From 1985, on more stable economic grounds, the uniform tariff was gradually reduced once more, reaching 15 percent in 1988.

The process of unilateral liberalisation was not altered when the democratic centre-left government *Concertación* took office in 1990. Indeed, the uniform tariff rate was further lowered in 1991 to 11 percent by the new economic team in the Ministry of Finance. In this regard, Sebastian Sáez remarks (2002: 37) that this: "reflects the philosophical legacy of those economists who where responsible for the country's commercial strategy during the military regime, in the sense that trade opening and economic deregulation in general would provide welfare benefits for the whole of society irrespective of what happened in the rest of the world." Seven years later, in 1998, the Ministry of Finance once again proposed a uniform cut from 11 to

6 percent. Additionally, in the context of the Asian financial crisis that negatively affected the trade balance as well as the exchange rate, the new tariff reduction became more politically sensible, given that it was linked to policies to offset any predictable increase in imports that might be detrimental to domestic production, i.e. small annual tariff reductions reaching 6 percent in 2003 and a legislation on safeguard measures (Sáez 2002: 38). In any case, the unilateral trade reforms implemented as of 1985, outlined below, can be seen as the most ambitious within the region.

Table 3.1: Unilateral Tariff Reforms from 1985

1985	1988	1991	1999	2000	2001	2002	2003
20 (from 35)	15	11	10	9	8	7	6

On these grounds, the WTO considers Chile's trade policy an exemplary model. The Secretariat Report states that (Trade Policy Review 2003: vii): "since its last review in 1997, Chile has continued to reform and liberalize its already open trade and investment regimes. It has thus unilaterally reduced tariffs, streamlined customs procedures, ceased to apply capital controls, and floated the exchange rate. Inter-sectoral neutrality has remained a key feature of Chile's policies, as witnessed by an almost uniform applied MFN tariff, the absence of significant programmes to assist specific activities, and the granting of national treatment in government procurement and to foreign investors, in all but a few cases."

Nevertheless, Trade Policy Reviews from 1997 and 2003 objected to several policies, even though efforts made in between were recognised. The major distortions probably arose as a result of the use of the Price Band System (PBS), maintained since 1985, for various edible vegetable oils, sugar, wheat, and wheat flour. Comparable to the Andean Price Band System, the PBS was intended to reduce the impact of international price fluctuations on the domestic prices of these goods, i.e. specific duties based on previously calculated reference prices were added to the *ad valorem* rate to bring the import price up to the reference price.[1] However, this system stands in contrast with the recent gradual reduction of Chile's tariffs, since specific obligations can effectively maintain tariffs on these agricultural products quite high, as pointed out by the WTO (2003: 35). For example, the effective tariff rates applied for sugar moved in 1999 and 2000 between 60-70 percent in the context of low world market prices, well above the country's

---

[1] If the import price exceeds the reference price, rebates lead to a reduction of the tariffs applied. Price bands are established once a year, through Presidential Decree, taking into account average international prices of the respective goods at major commodity marketplaces; for more details, see Law No. 18.525.

WTO bound rate of 31.5 percent. In 2003, Chile was finally obliged to revise the system due to Argentina's successful intervention in the WTO scope.[2]

Other concerns mentioned by the WTO are related to the export support schemes kept in place. In total, Chile notified six support schemes involving subsidies. While three were related to regional measures focusing on the extreme northern and southern provinces (generally accepted by the WTO), since 1997 Chile has modified the simplified drawback system, the deferred payment of customs duties and tax benefits, and the Motor Vehicle Statute in order to bring them in line with the WTO Agreement on Subsidies and Countervailing Measures (2.1.4). Lastly, with certain suspicion, the WTO noted Chile's vigorous involvement in preferential trade agreements. As observed in the latest review (2003: vii), the increasing number of such agreements "has reduced the share of Chilean trade conducted under MFN conditions, is injecting complexity into its trade regime, may undermine the neutrality of economic policies, and may result in trade and investment diversion."

Regional Integration

Chile's trade diplomacy has been clearly seen as a pragmatic instrument to extend market access in times of sluggish multilateral liberalisation. Accordingly, by 2004 over 70 percent of national exports took place in the scope of preferential trade agreements signed since 1990. But beyond the multilateral scope, the options for advanced trade integration in Latin America also became overly pretentious for the southern Andean state, even though the region political and economic situation had clearly been altered. While Chile's abrupt withdrawal from the Andean Group in 1976 was compliant with clear doctrinaire reasons in a protectionist environment, in contrast MERCOSUR, launched in 1991, seemed to be a natural partner, due to both physical and conceptual reasons, bearing in mind the neoliberal scenario visualised by the dynamic reform administrations of Carlos Menem (Argentina) and Fernando Collor de Mello (Brazil).

In the end, though, Chile sustained different preferences as the country was reluctant to fully integrate into the emerging trading block. The sudden decision of the Chilean government in November 2000 to initiate talks on free trade with the United States interrupted the previous

---

[2] In October 2000, Argentina requested consultations with Chile regarding the PBS; these were held with no success. Mutually satisfactory solutions were not achieved, thus, giving headway to a WTO dispute settlement panel; the panel concluded that the PBS was inconsistent with Chile's obligations under Article II of GATT 1994 (on import tax limits; yet later reversed by the Appellate Body) and with Article 4.2 of the Agreement on Agriculture (on market access). In November 2001, Chile amended Article 12 of Law No. 18.525 to prevent those rates resulting from the application of the PBS from exceeding Chile's bound rates; see WTO documents WT/DS207/R, 3 May 2002 and WT/DS207/AB/R 23 September 2002. Notwithstanding, the solution found by Chile was not recognised as satisfactory by Argentina, leading to other still ongoing consultations by 2004.

discussions held with MERCOSUR countries which sought to define the modalities of Chile's full admission into the Southern Cone block. To understand Chile's conduct (which jeopardised a full MERCOSUR commitment) a summary is provided in the article "MERCOSUR: Problems and Interrogation Marks," published in August 2000 by the conservative think-tank Liberty and Development:

> *The Common External Tariff (CET):* Chile refused to reverse the successive reduction of its flat rate, sustaining its orientation to the EU and NAFTA with average tariffs of roughly 3 percent rather than MERCOSUR with 14 percent. Moreover, the CET was considered as functional only for Brazil's industrial policy.

> *Common Distrust:* Among local entrepreneurs widespread distrust prevailed regarding Brazil's commitment toward trade openness. Hence, the country had no interest in tying its booming economy too closely to that of its neighbour's, who had just started the long and painful process of economic restructuring; Chile had taken the lead as a pioneer in the region in previous decades.

> *United States:* From the outset of the 1990s, Chile was highly tempted to become a full NAFTA member, and therefore rejected invitations to enter into a regional customs union, considering that it would hinder its bilateral discussions on free trade with the US.

> *Agriculture:* Local farmers, above all wheat, sugar, beef, and oleaginous crops producers, strongly opposed full integration as a result of the threatening competing sectors in Argentina and Brazil.

Nonetheless, the refusal to become a full MERCOSUR member was by no means a signal of disregard to trade relations with other Latin American countries. In June 1996, Chile was the first non-member signatory state of a comprehensive agreement with the newly created trading block, including full reciprocal liberalisation for the trading of goods until 2014, participation in common MERCOSUR bodies as an Associate Member, and substantial commitments related to transport means towards the Pacific.[3] In addition, as shown in Table 3.2, during the 1990s Chile intensified its reciprocal liberalisations in the region more than any other country. While the main focus was based on the fostering of intra-regional trade in goods, applying ALADI-based norms in connection with rules of origin, safeguard measures, customs valuation, dispute settlement, SPS measures, etc., in recent years Chile pursued the application of Free Trade

---

[3] Other provisions covered unfair business practices, safeguard measures, dispute settlement, customs valuation, technical regulations, SPS measures, export promotion measures, investment and intellectual property rights.

Agreements (FTAs) of the "latest generation" which set forth detailed norms and included new disciplines, such as services, competition policy and state procurement.

Table 3.2: Preferential Trade Agreements in Latin America

Agreement	Tariff Reduction Program	Coverage and Status
Mexico 01/01/1992 FTA since 01/08/1999	2 tariff reduction programs in 4 and 6 years, respectively	Latest generation FTAs including services, state procurement, competition policy and intellectual property rights
Venezuela 01/07/1993	2 tariff reduction programs in 4 and 6 years, respectively	Trade in goods, investment, transport Foreseen: Services
Bolivia 06/04/1993	Partial Scope Agreement covering a limited number of products	Trade in goods Failed attempt in 2003 to negotiate a latest generation FTA
Colombia 01/01/1994	2 tariff reduction programs in 4 and 5 years, respectively	Trade in goods, investment, transport Foreseen: services, state procurement
Ecuador 01/01/1994	2 tariff reduction programs in 3 and 5 years, respectively	Trade in goods, investment, transport Foreseen: services
MERCOSUR 10/09/1996	2 tariff reduction programs started in 1997 will expire in 2014	Trade in goods, investment, physical infrastructure, energy; Planning: services and state procurement
Peru 01/07/1998	4 tariff reduction programs with a term of 5, 10, 15, and 18 years; 5 special tariff reduction programs for the textile sector with a term of 3, 6 and 8 years.	Trade in goods, investment, transport; Foreseen: Latest generation FTA
Cuba 01/12/1999	Partial Scope Agreement covering a limited number of products	Trade in goods
Central America 14/02/2002 Costa Rica 06/03/2002 El Salvador	Gradual elimination of bilateral tariffs until 2015 using different phase-out schemes.	Latest generation FTA

Source: own elaboration, based on ECLAC 2002: 16.

Even though Chile distrusted the regional integration forces in Latin America, it held strong reasons for furthering regional trade relations. From a foreign policy perspective, the trade area appeared to be a sound tool for good neighbour policies after often hostile relations during the military regime (1973-1989). Besides, compared to other destinations, exports going to Latin American markets have generally consisted of manufactured goods such as lumber, processed foods, paper, textiles, metal mechanics, software, etc. Last but not least, since the 1990s Chile has evolved into a salient investor in South America, and hence, has become interested in stable economic relations. For example, in 2004, Chile was the second largest foreign direct investor in Argentina (after Spain) holding major assets in forestry, energy, and shopping malls (ADI 2005).

Extra-Regional Integration

With the onset of the 1990s, Chile began to show signs of its ambition to go beyond the regional scope. In this regard, the general incentives related to the diversified structure of exports, where roughly 80 percent of foreign sales used to go beyond Latin American markets, and the fact that the private sector was searching for foreign investments and low-price capital goods from industrialised countries. Therefore, I will briefly present the most significant endeavours which targeted North American, European, and Asian markets.

United States: The Initiative for the Enterprise of the Americas launched in 1991 by the Bush administration and the later US attempts to expand the NAFTA model steadily southward was received with unparalleled enthusiasm in Chile, due to two fundamental reasons. First, the increase in agricultural exports (mainly fruit) towards the US market (since the mid-1980s) encountered numerous market entry barriers which demanded appropriate solutions. Second, the government was convinced that through trade agreements with the United States, Chile could best "cement" the unilateral reforms previously implemented, thus becoming more attractive for foreign investors.

Therefore, Chile quickly began to put in place wide-reaching measures to demonstrate the country's high degree of "preparedness" to sign a broad FTA that consisted, among others, in assessing topics decisive to the US government such as the protection of investments, intellectual property rights and environmental standards. Nonetheless, in the aftermath of a formal invitation in 1994 to join the NAFTA, the process of deepening economic relations was suspended in the light of the Clinton administration's inability to obtain the fast-track authority from Congress, and an antidumping and countervailing duty petition filed in 1997 in the United States which affected the imports of Chilean salmon. Notwithstanding, after 12 years of persevered lobbying, in June 2003 Chile was able to reach its objective and become the first South American country to sign a FTA of this magnitude with the US, embodied in 24 chapters, covering 19 negotiation issues.[4] In the traditional area of trade, the duty-free bilateral trade of goods and products was established until 2016; hence, a 12-year liberalisation period for the most sensitive agricultural products, such as wheat on the part of Chile, was granted.

Canada: The US's tardiness had the effect that the FTA signed in 2003 became a sort of climax after intense, previously conducted negotiations. The FTA signed with Canada in November 1996 proved to be the first technical test for Chile's negotiators, coming on the back of the recently concluded and politically demanding MERCOSUR negotiations. For the first time, the agreement based on NAFTA principles included provisions for trade in services, competition, labour and environmental issues, and efficient dispute settlement mechanisms. However, contrary to the NAFTA treaty, the agreement foresaw reciprocal exemption from anti-dumping measures, set forth less restrictive rules of origin in general, and identified exemptions or included longer phasing-out terms for sensitive products.[5] Chile's principal interests involved an improved legal framework for Canada's investment in the mining sector and enhanced market access for non-traditional exports like fruits, salmon, and wines.

Europe: A comprehensive package was further signed in November 2002 with the European Union. Although similar in technical aspects, the additional provisions on political, scientific, and cultural cooperation stand out, underlining the wide-ranging "association" approach put forward by the EU.[6] Furthermore, the Europeans placed emphasis on two side-agreements on trade in wines and on alcoholic and flavoured beverages, including provisions on the protection of geographical indications and denominations, traditional expressions, and complementary quality indications, trade marks, and labels.

Moreover, the fact that the EU signed a trade agreement with a relatively small South American country can be considered as a "coup" for local diplomacy, since the EU initially sought a broad, strategic partnership with the MERCOSUR. Chile had essential interests in the

---

[4] Chapters in the US-Chile FTA: I. Initial Provisions, II. General Definitions, III. National Treatment and Market Access for Goods, IV. Rules of Origin and Origin Procedures, V. Customs Administration, VI. Sanitary and Phytosanitary Measures, VII. Technical Barriers to Trade, VIII. Trade Remedies, IX. Government Procurement, X. Investment, XI. Cross-Border Trade in Services, XII. Financial Services, XIII. Telecommunications, XIV. Temporary Entry for Business Persons, XV. Electronic Commerce, XVI. Competition Policy, Designated Monopolies, and State Enterprises, XVII. Intellectual Property Rights, XVIII. Labor, XIX. Environment, XX. Transparency, XXI. Administration of the Agreement, XXII. Dispute Settlement XXIII. Exceptions, XXIV. Final Provisions.

[5] Most tariff lines were phased-out by January 2003. Special phasing-out terms (up to 17 years) were set for pork and beef meat, vegetable oils, potato products, corn and wheat flour, sugar products and milling wheat. Chile retained its duties on dairy, poultry, and egg products, and Canada retained its out-of quota tariffs on the same products. Rules of origin were based mainly on the principle of substantial transformation. Since the agreement entered into force, its dispute settlement mechanism was used on two occasions: concerning the imports of Chilean salmon into Canada, and Chile's safeguard measures on wheat and wheat flour, sugar, and edible vegetable oils.

[6] For more details, *see http://europa.eu.int/comm/external_relations/chile/assoc_agr/.*

agreement since Europe has traditionally been its biggest trading partner, main source of FDI's, and finally, principal donor for technical cooperation projects. The accord established a FTA covering the reciprocal liberalisation of trade in goods that entered into effect in March 2003, offered a maximum transitional period of 10 years, and aimed to reach a full liberalisation for 97.1 percent of bilateral trade, per sector, with 100 percent full liberalisation of industrial trade, 81 percent of agricultural trade and 91 percent of trade in fisheries. Furthermore, with the remaining Western European partners organised under the Free Trade Association EFTA a similarly structured agreement was signed in March 2003.

Asia: Since the 1980s, exports towards the Asian Pacific have continually increased, accounting for 30 percent of national overseas sales by 2004. On these dynamic grounds, the distinctive trade diplomacy efforts regarding both negotiations and promotion were unquestionable at the domestic level. Therefore, in 1994 Chile was the first Latin American country to become a full member of the Asia Pacific Economic Forum (APEC); furthermore, Chile hosted two APEC summits in 1997 and 2004, consolidating its role as the "gateway" to South America, based on its reliability, flexibility, and commitment as a negotiation partner. Additionally, in February 2003 Chile and South Korea reached the conclusion of the first transpacific FTA. Apart from the exempted rules on labour and environmental standards, the coverage of the agreement and its modalities resemble a latest generation treaty based on NAFTA principles.[7] Moreover, pioneer negotiations with China, India, New Zealand, Singapore and Brunei Darussalam were launched in 2003 and completed during 2005. By the time all these agreements have entered into force, more than 90 percent of Chile's exports will operate under reciprocal preference regimes.

Export and Sector Promotion

Concerning the promotion of exports, state support schemes are more widespread compared to those of other countries in the region (Alvarez 1993; Pietrobelli 1998; Macario 1998; 2000), though Chile is often said to be an example of a marked driven economy. Since 1985, a series of initiatives have been undertaken to stimulate non-traditional exports, i.e. fruits, vegetables, timber, salmon, wines and other manufactured products. Thus, I briefly present the official export promotion instruments that have been applied.

---

[7] Chile granted immediate tariff-free access to 67 percent of its tariff lines, while South Korea introduced immediate duty-free treatment on 87 percent of its tariff lines. The other goods obtained tariff-free access within five, seven, ten, or thirteen years. Chile was allowed to permanently exclude refrigerators, washing machines, sugar, wheat, and oilseeds and Korea reserved rice, apples and pears.

Fiscal Incentives: To "offset" the harm to exports created by tariffs on imported inputs and other taxes, both a general and a specific drawback system were introduced in 1988 and 1985, respectively. While the former is still available for all exporters, refunding the import duties paid on goods incorporated into the production process, the specific refund regime came to be perceived as a clear export subsidy for non-traditional exports, since it provided new export firms a simplified refund of up to 10 percent on the FOB value (WTO 1997). Thus, by 1998 the original law had to be modified in-keeping with the WTO Agreement on Subsidies and Countervailing Measures, reducing refunds progressively to a single rate of 3 percent. Therefore, the total amount of costs refunded decreased from US$210 million in 1996 to US$86 million in 2002 (WTO 2003).[8] Moreover, the WTO considered the deferred payment of tariffs on imported capital goods enacted in 1987 as an export subsidy. In order to encourage investments in productive capacity, the payment of duties on imported capital goods could be deferred for seven years and exempted altogether if a firm's exports exceed 60 percent of sales. Whilst this was also modified in 1998, the amount paid by this instrument was still US$178 million by 2000.[9]

Marketing Assistance: The promotion agency *Prochile* created in 1974 has gained an outstanding reputation. Both state officials and entrepreneurs from neighbouring countries are usually fascinated by the high budget and the market studies available on the agency's functional web page; www.prochile.cl (For example, to obtain data Argentinean exporters often seek R.U.T. figures from Chilean firms that allow free access). Since 1979, the agency depends on the Ministry of Foreign Affairs and has a dense global network of about 60 commercial offices and trade representations. Focusing on non-traditional exports, *Prochile* provides data on foreign markets, country image promotion by generic publicity and targeted missions, marketing strategies support and the identification of administrative problems encountered by exporters. Furthermore, the promotion agency has been aimed at stimulating coordination between SME's in their production, design, marketing and promotion activities, together with private sector institutions, such as the Association of Exporters of Manufactured Goods (ASEXMA).

Although local promotion resources have generally been higher than in neighbouring countries, from 2000 annual budgets have decreased remarkably compared to the 1990s, when

---

[8] In the case of the general drawback system, above all large firms in the chemical and mining industry benefited from the annual refunds of US$30-45 million; see Boston Consulting Group 2004 and WTO 2003.
[9] Law No. 19.589 of November 1998 gradually eliminated the debt reductions for deferred payments initially granted. However, under a transitional article the law withheld the possibility of debt reductions for companies that requested deferred payment of tariffs and taxes before November 1998. Further transitional provisions allowed companies to take advantage of deferred payment of tariffs or tax credits until December 2002. Under this regime, only instalments with expiration dates up to December 2005 are eligible for debt reduction; see WTO 2003.

the budget was well above US$20 million.[10] To a certain extent, the gradual decline can be seen as a result of the increasingly critical voices regarding *Prochile's* management style. A benchmark assessment by the Boston Consulting Group (2004; see also Macario 2000) concluded that since the agency's climax in the 1980s, no additional promotional services have been developed, and current services do not surpass the basic programs provided by other export promotion agencies. As the principal reasons for the standstill, the analysis mentioned the omission of management reforms, low operational autonomy inside the Ministry of Foreign Affairs, absent independent revenues, and constraints on how to allocate resources; for example 75 percent of the budget is linked to the promotion of agricultural exports.

In addition to *Prochile*, a very successful account in the promotion of non-traditional exports has been ascribed to *Fundación Chile*, a joint venture between the government and the US multinational ITT which has been in force since 1976 (Cordua 1994). Particularly in the 1980s, the organisation was responsible for a flourishing development of exports with added value towards the US market. In this regard, the principal idea has been the introduction of innovative new technologies from abroad and then selling those businesses based on these new technologies, thus, becoming the main catalyst for new export trade in gourmet mini-vegetables, prestige brand timber products, and salmon.

Enhancing Competitiveness of SME's: During the 1990s, Chile strengthened its framework dedicated to improve the competitiveness of SME's, increasing expenditures from 0.34 to 0.93 percent of the GDP between 1990 and 1999 (Ministry of Economy 2000). In so doing, the democratic government sought to overcome the strong dependence on a limited number of large-scale companies exporting minimally processed natural resources. Above all, towards the end of the decade, resources became increasingly earmarked for horizontal promotion instruments, without contravening WTO norms. Hence, practically all resources were channelled and coordinated through the Chilean Development Corporation (CORFO) aimed at promoting economic development by encouraging investment and competitiveness (Esser 1999: 33-46). Founded in 1939, CORFO operated until the 1970s as a holding company for state owned firms, assuming the responsibility for the creation of the vast majority of large industrial firms from the 1940s. Furthermore, a study carried out by Alvarez (1993) revealed that of the 20 top private export companies, at least thirteen had been created by CORFO, including prominent companies from the mining and forestry sectors. Nonetheless, after being downgraded by the

---

[10] The budget of *Prochile* is integrated by different sources such as international donor programs, agriculture export funds and direct resources from the national treasury; see the Boston Consulting Group 2004 for further information. In 2005 the resources were increased again from US$15.4 to US$17.4 million according to the newspaper *Diario PyMEs* dated 17/11/04.

military regime, CORFO was reborn in the 1990s and currently acts as a second-tier bank, managing credit programs in the area of technology transfer, investments for SME's, technical assistance, vocational training and the development of supply chains.[11]

Summary Dependent Variable B

During the study period, Chile attained a successful trade integration strategy. Contrary to occurrences in other South American countries over the last 20 years, Chile managed to implement a coherent blend of unilateral, regional and extra regional trade policy measures, and hence, underlined its capacity to make simultaneous use of each level in favour of national export development. Resuming this section, the following box highlights the cornerstones of the local Multipolar Model: the application of the flat rate concept, active trade policy on the regional and extra-regional level and wide-reaching export promotion schemes for non-traditional exports. Furthermore, "heterodox", state-led policies were employed to accompany and prepare the relatively threatened segments of the local agriculture and small scales firms from the impacts of liberalised trade.

Box 3.1: Summary Dependent Variable B

Unilateral Trade Regime	Regional Integration	Extra-Regional Integration	Export Promotion	Sector Promotion
1985-2003: gradual reduction of "flat rate" tariff from 35 to 6 percent Exceptions: Price Band System maintained for wheat, sugar and vegetable oils	Since 1990, active trade policy in the regional sphere by means of reciprocal trade liberalisations favouring exports of manufactures; Full MERCOSUR membership was refused due to disagreements on the customs union.	From 1996, pioneer in the signing of bilateral FTAs of the "latest generation" with North American, European and Asian partners.	Until recently, Chile maintained substantial fiscal incentives that supported exports beyond the WTO margin. Strong foreign presence of the export promotion agency *Prochile*.	Agriculture and SME benefited from a broad range of technical assistance and credit facilities to enhance productivity and economy of scale.

---

[11] Regarding the promotion of exports, two CORFO credit lines were related to export finance; WTO 2003. While the B.21 line allowed Chilean producers of capital goods, durable consumer goods, and engineering, consulting, and other services to provide foreign buyers long-term financing, the B.22 line allowed non-traditional Chilean exporters with annual sales of less than US$30 million long-term financing for the purchase of production supplies, as well as investments necessary for the installation of commercialisation infrastructure facilities in foreign countries. In 2002, disbursements under these credit lines amounted to US$5.9 million and US$2.4 million, respectively.

The coherent pursuit of the Multipolar Model contributed to the impressive quantitative export increases of roughly 840 percent and the practically constant trade surpluses between 1985 and 2004. From a qualitative perspective, improvements can be noted with regard to the steady expansion of outward oriented industries from the forestry (pulp, lumber), fishery (salmon, fish meal) and agriculture (vines, fresh fruits, vegetables) and diverse manufactures, therefore reducing the share of mining exports from 62 to 44 percent. Objections are made regarding the remaining dependence on natural resources and natural resourced-based manufactures which still account for roughly 90 percent of current exports. Although some added value could be incorporated into commodities from mining, forestry, fishery and agriculture, the major challenge for future policy making concerns is to enhance the sustainability of world market integration by making local exports more "brain oriented," and thus, lowering the dependence on volatile commodity prices and increasing the potential of generating jobs.

3.2. State Bureaucracy: Towards the Foreign Affairs Model

This section is structured along the following lines. The first subsection, *responsibilities,* exposes the division of labour in the conduction of international trade policy affairs, involving the inter-ministerial coordination among the different sectoral departments involved. Subsequently, in *resources,* there is a description of how the trade policy team evolved in the last two decades with respect to staff size, technical expertise, and the application of civil service models. Finally, the subsection *openness* discusses the consultation mechanism towards the business and civil society.

Responsibilities

For a greater understanding of local policy making, the extraordinary powers of the President of the Republic that date back to 1980 when the military leaders defined the constitutional norms must be mentioned. As regards the area of foreign affairs, the President's office used to have the responsibility of negotiating, concluding, signing and ratifying international agreements; therefore, the role of Congress was limited to granting approval (article 50; 1). If the President demanded, the discussions of international matters were highly confidential (article 32; 17). Lastly, the President held the exclusive initiative to propose bills on matters concerning changes in the country's political or administrative organisation, annual budgets, taxes, and tariffs, leaving hardly any space for parliamentarian initiatives.

As regards the executive branch, since 1979 the international trade policy area depends on the General Directorate of Foreign Economic Affairs (DIRECON) in the Foreign Affairs Ministry (Decree Law 53/1979). Given that none of the state officials, outside experts and business representatives consulted in 2004 questioned the DIRECON's competencies in directing the negotiations and representation in international economic forums, the promotion of exports and the proposal for regulatory measures, a continuance of this subsection seems unnecessary. Moreover, its institutional stability is underscored by its organisational chart that remained unaltered over the last two decades; disregarding some functional amendments. Although the predominant agency in this crucial policy area had, surprisingly, not even been granted the rank of Undersecretariat, DIRECON's officials convincingly highlighted the wide-reaching autonomy regarding the appointment of officials and the use of budgetary resources, indicating thus their merely formal dependence on the widely unknown Undersecretariat of International Affairs.[12]

Nonetheless, the outstanding status that DIRECON currently enjoys appears to be anything but natural if its historical roots are examined. In 1979, when DIRECON was created, it could have been considered the pragmatic merger of three weak entities, composed of the independent Chilean Institute of Export Promotion (*Prochile*), the Executive Secretariat for the Latin American Free Trade Association (ALALC), and the General Directorate of Economic Affairs; the latter two areas depended on the Ministry of Foreign Affairs (*State Officials (SO)* Buvinic and Campos 17/02/05). In any event, the institutional strength of DIRECON was limited through the 1980s due mainly to three reasons,:

1) *Regional Integration*: In 1976, Chile decided to withdraw its membership from the Andean Group. Therefore, the military regime underlined its ideological differences from the inward oriented integration endeavours in Latin America, which have been demonstrated by its widespread absence in the scope of the ALALC (1960-1980) and ALADI since 1980.

2) *Discarded Diplomacy*: Not only had the regional integration been considered of little importance, the diplomatic cadre was also perceived as an inefficient, conservative ambit spoiled by party politics, and hence, incapable of managing foreign affairs with serious economic implications. In this context, the status of the Ministry of Foreign Affairs in the government was quite low (Fernandois/Wilhelmy 1989).

3) *"Chicago Boys"*: Conversely, the Ministry of Finance assumed the protagonist role in the principal areas of the country's economy which involved trade policies. The best example of the Ministry's central role was the incorporation of roughly 25 young economists in 1975 to accelerate the structural adjustment reforms. In the following years, this group of orthodox-liberal technocrats became commonly known as the *Chicago Boys*, as they had been largely educated in the University of Chicago by scholars such as Milton Friedman and Arnold Harberger.[13] Under the direction of Sergio de Castro (1974 – 1982), the

---

[12] See interview with the Chief of the Legal Department, Alejandro Buvinic (17/02/05). At that time, Mr. Buvinic presented the guidelines for the current reform project, "The Ministry of Foreign Affairs in the 21st Century," whereby the trade policy area was supposed to be institutionally upgraded to the level of Undersecretariat.

[13] The Chicago Boys were graduates of the Catholic University of Chile. After their graduation, they went to the Economics Departments of the University of Chicago through a scholarship program for Chilean post-graduates in the late 1950s. The influence of the Chicago Boys was very strong indeed; roughly 100 students attended the University of Chicago between 1957 and 1970. These graduates achieved positions of great prominence in large scale companies and/or in heading the Ministries of Finance (Sergio de Castro, Hernán Búchi), Economy (Jorge Cauas, Rolf Lauders, and Pablo Baraona), Labor (Jose Pinker), the Central Bank (Miguel Kast, Sergio de Castro) and the Ministries of Planning, among others; see Valdes/ Goodwin 1995.

Ministry of Finance became the ruling government agency in charge of the economic reforms designed to disengage the State from the economy. Concurrently, the Finance Department absorbed (from the Ministry of Economy) attributions in crucial areas, such as public investment and tax policies (including tariffs).

Within this institutional context, regional integration, as well as multilateral discussions in the scope of the Uruguay Round negotiations, were barely monitored by anybody, considering that the economic branch inside the Ministry of Foreign Affairs suffered from serious weaknesses (the Mission to Geneva continued to be a part of this Ministry), and the powerful Ministry of Finance perceived trade policies as mere unilateral instruments for structural adjustments, neglecting the participation in international trade policy forums (*Outside Expert (OE)* Sáez 27/09/04).

At the outset of the 1990s, during the first democratic government of Patricio Aylwin (1990-1994), the state executive began responding to the forces of regional and multilateral trade policy. However, the main factors for this change had not been released by the Uruguay Round, but were related to the emerging New Regionalism embodied in the US Initiative for the Enterprise for the Americas (1991), the creation of MERCOSUR (1991), and the entering into force of NAFTA (1994). Despite an increasing domestic interest, reports pointed to a disorganised and conflictive environment inside the state bureaucracy (SO Buvinic 17/02/05; Silva 2000; Porras 2003). Table 3.3 provides an overview of the main objectives and rationale put forward in the different governmental departments.

Table 3.3: Trade Integration Priorities inside the Government from 1990 to 1994

	Ministries of Finance	Ministry of Economy	Foreign Affairs Ministry
Priority	NAFTA	Latin America; Asian-Pacific; Europe	MERCOSUR; Andean Group (later CAN)
Rationale	Lock-In Effect	Second Stage of Exports	"Good Neighbourhood"

The *Ministry of Finance* responded most enthusiastically to the Initiative for the Enterprise for the Americas and the possible adherence to the NAFTA. The team that surrounded Alejandro Foxley, whose policy orientation strongly resembled that of its authoritarian predecessor, perceived the possible US expansion towards the south as an historical chance to cement the unilateral economic reforms implemented since the mid-1970s. Consequently, the

Ministry took up the initiative to prepare Chile's trade policy assimilation toward North America by making comprehensive assessments related to the preparedness of the economic sectors and the domestic legal framework. In addition, the Ministry could rely upon a business sector that showed clear signs of support for a possible hemispheric integration (3.3).

The staff inside the *Ministry of Economy* held clear interests (after being in the "shadow" of the *Chicago Boys* for 15 years) to be in charge of the promotion and regulation of economic sectors. After the fast expansion of the commodity sector in the 1980s, the "Second Stage of Exports" had to set forth the guidelines for the incorporation of higher added value in the products being sold abroad (Diaz/Ramos 1998; Silva 2000). In light of this perspective, the Ministry of Economy argued in favour of the disregarded regional markets and the steady expansion of promotion facilities in the scope of the Chilean Development Corporation (CORFO). This belief led to the creation of negotiation expertise and the assumption of leadership in the trade discussions with Venezuela and Colombia that took place in 1992-93. Simultaneously, the department began absorbing responsibility for the European and Asian-Pacific negotiations, though without immediate results.

The principal reason for the fairly uncontrolled regional division of trade responsibilities was evidently associated with the still weak position of the *Ministry of Foreign Affairs* concerning economic affairs. In any case, in this first stage of trade integration, the local diplomacy argued in favour of furthering economic links within Latin America, this being the Ministry's main area of influence. The prevailing policy rationale among the leading diplomats perceived the MERCOSUR and the revival of the Andean Group as excellent opportunities to re-establish the strained relations during the military regime (see Insulza 1998). Moreover, during the first half of the 1990s, the role of DIRECON in international trade policy affairs remained modest, considering the key position of the Finance Ministry in trade related aspects. Indeed, it wasn't until the presidency of Eduardo Frey (1994-2000), the second term of the centre-left coalition *Concertación*, that an institutional strengthening of DIRECON took place, due to the following factors:

1) Increasing Pragmatism: By the end of the Aylwin administration, there was a growing consensus among key officials that the "institutional disorder" previously notable could no longer be maintained in light of the international challenges to be faced. Sebastian Sáez, by that time trade policy advisor in the Ministry of Finance, stated (OE 27/09/04): "For a small developing country like Chile there is not much sense interfering in discussions related to global warming or arms proliferation issues; what is really at stake, is to make use of international affairs as a tool for its economic development." To some extent, the increasing pragmatism in the domestic deliberations was related to the decision adopted by the US Congress in October 1994 to postpone the fast-track authority for an indefinite time. Though a backlash, this exogenous factor allowed other integration options to receive more attention. As a result, the Ministry of Finance (heading the North America area) initiated permanent coordination activities with DIRECON during and after the free trade talks with Canada in 1995-96.

2) MERCOSUR: The Chile-MERCOSUR talks, initiated in September 1994, became crucial to the DIRECON staff because international trade policies generated controversies at the domestic level as never before. Most significantly, the domestic farming lobby, fearing competition from the large scale agriculture in Argentina and Brazil, took the topic to Parliament and to mass media. In this heated phase, DIRECON officials carried out highly effective work, managing to not only squeeze everything possible out of MERCOSUR, as a key Argentinean official lamented (SO Cañellas 09/12/04), but also to gain ample support from the governmental coalition for the painful liberalisation process (Goméz 1998; Aninat et al. 2004: 22-26).

3) Rotation of Senior Officials: As in other Latin American countries, inter-agency rotation of key officials is fairly common in Chile. By the mid-1990s, this practice favoured DIRECON's institutional rise as well as its coordination with the Ministries of Economy, Agriculture and Finance (SO Buvinic 17/02/05; Silva 2000: 315). Hence, Carlos Mladinic entered as DIRECON's head of office in 1994 as a highly doted Undersecretary of Economy and left DIRECON in 1996 as Minister of Agriculture. His successor was Juan Gabriel Valdes, an internationally recognised academic who worked from 1994 to 1996 as head of the International Division of the Ministry of Finance, and therefore, acted as chief negotiator in the trade talks with Canada. As Valdes left DIRECON in 1999, he was appointed Minister of Foreign Affairs. On these grounds, DIRECON consolidated its role as a dynamic agency pushing forward Chile's integration into world markets. After Juan Gabriel Valdes left office, it was, above all, Osvaldo Rosales (2000 - 2004) who fostered the role of DIRECON in the striking negotiations with the EU, US, EFTA, and South Korea.[14]

Based on this clear institutional leadership of the Foreign Affairs Ministry, the existing inter-ministerial coordination mechanisms began to work effectively. After an initial failed attempt to establish an Interministerial Committee for International Economic Negotiations in

---

[14] Osvaldo Rosales served from 1990 to 1999 as Regional Adviser at the ECLAC headquarters in Santiago de Chile.

1992, a second version, in effect since 1995, enjoyed broad recognition inside the government.[15] Chaired by the Minister of Foreign Affairs and attended by the heads of Finance, Economy and Agriculture, the Committee became the institutionalised advisory board in charge of counselling the presidency and concerting policy guidelines within the cabinet at ministerial level. The assistance from the General Secretary of the Presidency facilitated the link between trade policies and the official presidential agenda. Furthermore, the core technical coordination in negotiations, as well as in trade disputes (e.g. salmon exports to the US), had been operating inside the Committee of Negotiators, lead by the head of DIRECON. The coordination body convened the office holders of the different sectoral divisions more frequently than the more formal Interministerial Committee for International Economic Negotiations, where political representatives met. Nonetheless, (former) key officials commented that the formal provisions of inter-ministerial coordination have been increasingly replaced by informal interaction patterns (OE Sáez 27/09/04; SO Buvinic 17/02/05). Table 3.4 sums up the negotiation responsibilities in governmental areas outside DIRECON.[16]

Table 3.4: Negotiations Responsibilities outside DIRECON

	Ministry of Finance	Ministry of Agriculture	Ministry of Economy
Department in Charge	Division of International Affairs	ODEPA	Undersecretariat of Economy
Responsibilities	Financial Services Investment Facilities	Agriculture, (Phyto-) sanitary issues	Intellectual Property, Technical Trade Obstacles
Prominent Features	High negotiation leverage in general due to the ministry's institutional weight (e.g. taxes and tariffs)	"Backed" by strong rural constituency; central role of agricultural concerns in trade talks	Weak role in the area of market access for industrial goods

Source: own elaboration based on Silva 2001; Porras 2003

---

[15] According to the report by Sáez (OE 27/09/04), in the first phase the advisory board suffered from an extremely broad institutional environment, considering that agencies outside the areas of economy participated in the meetings, and as a result, the rhythm of these meetings was not dynamic and the results slowed down remarkably.

[16] Beyond the below enlisted core agencies, numerous other state entities influenced the course of trade policy actions. For example, during the US-FTA talks including 19 negotiation issues, the official team had been integrated by 22 governmental departments in total, covering the National Customs, Ministries of Internal Affairs, Education, Labour, Central Bank, National Copper Council, National Commission for the Environment, Undersecretariats of Telecommunications and Fishery, Superintendence of Banks and Insurance Entities, among others.

Despite DIRECON's broadly acknowledged role in trade policy affairs, Table 6 underscores the crucial roles of other sectoral entities in trade talks. Thus, the Ministry of Finance is a salient institution in light of its duties in the areas of financial services and investments affairs. In addition, the team monitors all trade issues, bearing in mind the Ministry's key competencies in fiscal policies. The incidence of the Ministry of Agriculture is due to the controversies surrounding agricultural issues, both in the regional and in the multilateral spheres, and the fact that the agency maintained strategic relations with powerful agriculture advocates inside and outside Congress. Conversely, the Ministry of Economy became, in a sense, a "victim" of DIRECON's strong role in negotiations. Apart from the intellectual property area, the presence of the Ministry of Economy in recent trade rounds has been rather weak, as Sebastian Sáez, the former chief of area lamented (OE 27/09/04). In consideration of the Economy/Foreign Trade Model (2.3), Sáez remarked that in order to assure consistency between foreign and national economic policies, a more distinctive participation of the Ministry of Economy would be essential, considering the agency's responsibility for economic promotion and sectoral regulation.

Resources

It is common to hear foreign officials talking respectfully about Chile's negotiation team (for example M. Cañellas from Argentina 09/12/04; Z. Rodriguez from Bolivia 17/12/04). However, as I previously mentioned, this local strength remains a somewhat new phenomena, dating back to the mid-1990s. The completion of the Uruguay Round and the first trade talks with Mexico, Bolivia, and Venezuela had been run by a rather small and inexperienced team (SO Paz 28/09/04; Porras 2003: 41-42), as Carmen Paz (28/09/2004) serving from 1992 in the area of market access recalled: "for us, the breakthrough definitely came with the MERCOSUR negotiations; thereafter we started growing continuously. A skilled group of 50 negotiators was created inside DIRECON where initially we had only 10 to 15 persons."

To enhance professionalism within the agency, DIRECON was inspired by the USTR and Mexico's Secretariat of Trade and Industry (SECOFI), and in the mid-1990s, introduced a matrix organisation based on geographic and issue areas that intersected in the different stages of negotiations and in the coordination of dispute settlements. As a result, the two divisions in charge of negotiations, the Multilateral and Bilateral Directorates, were closely linked with small offices responsible for either areas or topics, as shown below.

Table 3.5: Trade Divisions inside DIRECON

	Directorates of Bilateral Affairs	**Directorates of Multilateral Affairs**
Geographic Areas	North America	APEC
	MERCOSUR	WTO
	Andean Community	Asia
	Central America	OECD
Topics	Market Access	Intellectual Property
	Trade Defence	Services, Investment/
	Implementation and Administration of Agreements	Air Transport
		Trade and Sustainable Development
		Cooperation, Science and Technology

Source: DIRECON 2005; see www.direcon.cl.

Each small office has approximately three to four employees on average. The negotiation team is further composed by the head office, holding an advisory board, with two to three special advisors and the Trade Analysis Unit where six to seven economists carry out studies related to the impact of these agreements and the evolution of trade flows in general. Against the background of the numerous trade agreements currently in force, in recent years a trend to transfer personnel to post-negotiation areas involving the implementation, administration, and the evaluation of international trade agreements has become apparent. By October 2004, internal discussions were considering the creation of a Directorate to be exclusively in charge of implementation and administration (SO's Paz 28/09/04; Ruis 18/02/05).

In total, DIRECON employed around 500 persons in 2004, involving several divisions or offices which did not participate formally in negotiations, such as the Directorate for Export Promotion (*Prochile*), the Departments of Administration and Legal Affairs, and the recently created Office for Trade Disputes (SO's Buvinic and Campos 17/02/05). The staff can be divided into three distinct labour regimes, as shown below:

1) *Permanent Civil Servants*: This category includes permanent employees covered by social security and other security benefits for public servants. To increase the number of personnel, modifications to the annual budget law must be approved. Nonetheless, since 1990 the possibility to increase the number of public servants (112) proved to be impossible in compliance with the dispositions of Decree Law 280/1990, considering that powers in Congress rejected an expansion of stable bureaucratic staff despite firm lobby

efforts displayed by DIRECON's office holders. The wage structure implies rather modest salaries not exceeding the US$2,000 ceiling.

2) *Temporary Employees*: As a result of the rising importance of the policy area, the number of temporarily hired employees increased significantly, reaching 206 persons in 2004 *vis-à-vis* 86 in 2001 (DIRECON 2001; 2004a). In general, labour conditions are relatively poor since contracts have to be renewed on a yearly basis and do not consider social security benefits. The wage structure is similar to the previous category.

3) *Consultant or "honoured functionary"*: This category was the most popular as salaries were often double those of permanent staff. Due to a lack of transparency related to the modalities of these specific consulting services, recent efforts sought to decrease the number of professionals hired under this category. Nonetheless, at the end of 2004, the number of consultants was still close to 200.

In light of this combination of unrewarding, unstable and rather non-transparent posts which did not pass civil service exams, the task that has yet to be accomplished is the harmonisation of the prevailing labour regimes and the improvement of labour conditions for permanent civil servants. These institutional reforms are aimed to complement and strengthen the widespread public administration reforms implemented as of the transition to democracy.[17] Nonetheless, despite the absence of stability in the labour force, DIRECON achieved the enhancement of trade policy skills through several provisions set forth. Hence, Juan Puig (SO 18/02/2005) from Human Resources stated that DIRECON worked closely with local universities and international organisations, such as the WTO, UNCTAD or IDB, to provide training programs (commonly referred to as "expertise") for every single negotiator. Also, Puig mentioned that a university degree is required prior to entering office and many of the young professionals, averaging 35 years, hold a MA degree or are about to be granted this degree.

In general, all departments involved in trade policy affairs improved their expertise in the course of the 1990s. In this regard, the *Ministry of Finance* was awakened by Chile's possible NAFTA adherence, and thus carried out the first local efforts. Sebastian Sáez, at that time special advisor to Alejandro Foxley's team (OE 27/09/04), recollected that in order to be considered by

---

[17] The Chilean government has undertaken considerable efforts in recent years to reform the public administration and the legal framework. In June 2000, the President created a Project for the Reform and Modernisation of the State. Subsequently in January 2003, the political parties were represented in Congress and the government signed an Agreement for the Modernisation of the State, Transparency, and Promotion of Growth. This Agreement provided 49 individual legal and administrative initiatives in areas such as: simplifying procedures in the public service, increasing fiscal transparency, decentralisation, creation of one-stop offices, and increasing the use of new technologies in the public administration, such as electronic signatures. As part of these reform efforts, new legislation on public procurement has already entered into effect. Additional information is available at MINSEGPRES online information, http://www.modernizacion.cl/.

the US, Chile was asked to first carry out exhaustive assessments of domestic sectors so as to be well informed with respect to the legal issues of the GATT regulations, particularly property rights. Sáez concluded that even the well trained economists working in the prestige laden agency had been faced with a widespread lack of preparedness; thereafter, ad-hoc forms or in-house training were put forward. Subsequently, the training of professionals was systematised; in 1994 an entire negotiation team was created in the Division of International Affairs under Juan Gabriel Valdes (head of area 1994-96) and Eduardo Aninat (Minister of Finance 1994-99). Although this team was partially transferred to DIRECON when the negotiations of the agreement with Canada concluded, the number of personnel currently working in the finance department is still considerable, equipped with seven to eight well trained economists.

For the *Ministry of Agriculture* the turning point came into view with the MERCOSUR negotiations. The in-house capacity was first strengthened in an informal advisory unit that depended on the Ministerial Office, which in 1996 was transferred as a trade policy branch to the Agrarian Research and Policy Office (ODEPA). Created in 1992, ODEPA enjoys widespread operational autonomy from the Ministry and is responsible for monitoring and assessing the developments that affect domestic rural sectors. Out of the approximately 100 employees working in ODEPA, seven trade policy experts assigned to the Division for International Affairs monitor agricultural trade discussions and provide assistance in coordination with DIRECON (SO Cerda 17/02/2005). With regard to the *Ministry of Economy*, finally, its Trade Department has been modestly involved in recent negotiations. Sebastian Sáez (OE 27/09/04), head of the Department from 2001 to 2004 reported that the six professionals serving in this department worked on a broad range of trade-related topics but often could not assist in negotiation rounds, partly due to the low travel budget,.

Openness

From the outset of the 1990s, the trade policy experts inside the different government departments sought dialogue with the leading private sector entities in order to define economy wide and sectoral interests. State-business relations registered a noteworthy change before the democratic transition and concerned the intense policy coordination in the aftermath of the debt crisis in the 1980s. Eduardo Silva observed (1997: 156-172) that after the radical liberal adjustment policies implemented since 1975 entered into a deep legitimacy crisis against the numerous bankruptcies and huge trade and balance of payment deficits, the military regime opted to establish a close state-business collaboration pattern, in which the following features stood out (see also Imbusch 1995: 324-378):

1) *Consultation*: Economic policy related departments created communication channels toward business in the policy formulation stage, requiring each sector to propose measures that could stimulate investments. Beyond the predominantly informal interaction patterns, the Council for Economic and Social Affairs in the scope of the Ministry of Economy organised the first institutionalised forum in 1984, where business representatives were able to submit proposals to the state executive.

2) *Appointment of Policy Makers*: The mostly inexperienced and orthodox liberal *Chicago Boys,* who presided over the first wave of economic reforms, lost influence inside the government. Top economic policy makers, especially inside sectoral ministries, such as economy, agriculture and mining, were now drawn from the entrepreneurship or from experienced civil service officers who where familiar which the concerns of local economic sectors.

3) *Selection of Interlocutors*: The only ties that the *Chicago Boys* maintained before the debt crisis were informal and basically limited to the two principal holding companies closely interconnected with the banking sector. As *Cruzat-Larraín* and *Vial* collapsed in 1982, business associations began to be seriously considered as more viable options. Above all, the Confederation of Production and Commerce (CPC) composed of large-scale sectors from industry, agriculture, mining, commerce, banking and construction evolved into the government's strategic partner.

The democratic government that took office in December 1989 did not change this close state-business collaboration pattern. Silva (1997: 173-179) and Imbusch (1995: 391-445) pointed at a marked "open door policy" applied by the top deputies since exhibiting credibility was considered crucial to settle the fears of investors. Therefore, office holders in the areas of economic matters collaborated directly with the umbrella organization CPC in the formulation of business wide issues like the tax and labour reform and with sector associations on specific policies (e.g. promotion schemes, infrastructure, regulations).

Whilst the trade policy area had not been exempted from these close state-business interactions, it was transformed into the model case in the course of the 1990s; indeed the vigorous international trade diplomacy became a joint endeavour exclusively created under democratic ruling. Establishing the close network of bilateral, regional and multilateral arrangements required an intensive policy learning process by both the state and business, however. As exposed in the previous subsection, on the public side efforts had to first of all be made to define each agency's role in international trade policy affairs. Conversely, for local business, which had scarce knowledge about the properties of emerging regionalism, the deepening of trade relations through bilateral treaties initially aroused only suspicion. Particularly in the case of South American countries, the past experience of protectionism and financial turmoil were not considered solid grounds for deeper bilateral engagements in economic affairs.

On the government side, consultation mechanisms testified to the state's willingness to attract business enterprises to be its associates (Montero/Federici 1997; V. Silva 2000; 2001; Porras 2003; WTO 2003; Sáez 2002). For example, *the Committee for Private Sector Participation,* created in 1995 and chaired by the Minister of Economy, provided a means to inform the private sector of advances attained in negotiations and to learn the exporters' view points in general. Aside from business factions represented by the CPC, the Central Workers Union (CUT) and academic scholars were also invited to join the policy debate. Subsequently, DIRECON established a special *Council for Export Consultation* in order to maintain direct relations with private sector entities regarding technical concerns.

In practice though, the modus operandi of these formally established forums should be questioned to a certain extent. Data drawn from Montero/Federici 1997, Silva 2001, Porras 2003 and Sáez 2002 provided only very brief descriptions. Conversely, verbal reports gathered from state officials and business representatives proved to be misleading or incomplete as regards the accurate denominations and responsibilities of the established channels (SO Paz 28/09/04; BR Font 27/09/04; BR Reus 27/09/04; OE Sáez 27/09/04). Therefore, we can infer that the concept of strongly institutionalised consultation procedures appears inappropriate appropriate. Rather, the mentioned verbal reports revealed that DIRECON officials began to establish close ties with business entities that went beyond the formal sphere; or as it was described by a representative of SOFOFA, the national industry chamber, "formal mechanisms were replaced by informal ones as reciprocal trust increased" (BR Reus 27/09/2004).

This tendency towards close, informal channels between DIRECON and a rather limited group of business representatives was also criticised since important decisions on international trade policy affairs had been taken within rather exclusive circles. According to a confidential ex-state official report (September 2004), the *Committee for Private Sector Participation* (later denominated *Public-Private Committee on International Economic Relations)* has not convened since the year 2000, and thus, has increased business complaints as regards the somewhat non-transparent official coordination. Hence, the public sector responded by launching the *Public-Private Council for Export Development* in April 2003. Thereafter, debates have been structured by four working groups on trade facilitation, international integration, export support schemes, and on promotion of exports and tourism. By July 2005, the Council had convened on five occasions, typically integrating the top functionaries from the Ministries of Foreign Affairs, Economy, Finance, and Agriculture, National Customs, CORFO, Prochile, ODEPA and the Foreign Investment Committee. Business participation was also widespread, and covered about 40 of the leading entities (SOFOFA Annual Reports 2003-05).

Controversial views were also gathered regarding the lack of transparency towards non-business actors. On one hand, there is an official view sustained by Osvaldo Rosales (head of DIRECON 2001-2004), which pointed at the widespread dialogue forums provided for civil society within the scope of the free trade talks with the United States (CIPMA Seminar; October 2001). Rosales mentioned that the Advisory Council, composed of 35 personalities from society, served as a permanent link to the government throughout the negotiations. Furthermore, numerous meetings were organised in order to consult with NGO's, universities, and labour unions. Lastly, Rosales highlighted the survey data provided by the Foundation *Futuro* in which 70 percent of Chileans considered a FTA as beneficial.

On the other hand, a representative of the Chilean Alliance for Fair and Responsible Trade (OE 28/09/04) – a leading umbrella NGO comprised of environmental and human rights groups, unions and academic bodies – expressed its incongruity with the way trade talks with the US were conducted, as they "suffered from a gigantic democratic deficit since we did not know the legal text before it was signed," and hence, advocated for the opening of real channels for citizen participation on trade issues, to ensure the legitimacy of commitments assumed by trade agreements. Instead, for the NGO "the dialogue organized by the government was somewhat hypocritical as the topics mentioned by us were disregarded at the negotiation table."

Finally, Porras (2003) observed that civil society participation has visibly increased in recent years. For example, since the trade talks with the EU the Central Workers Union (CUT) is usually present in the "room next door" with a special advisor. Moreover, the Chilean Alliance for Fair and Responsible Trade received a special mention from Porras (2003: 59-60), given its outstanding networking capacity with US organisations, such as Public Citizen, Sierra Club or Earth Friends. Despite these efforts, in line with Sikkink (*1998*), he concluded that achievements have not been enough to place topics such as environment, trade and gender, labour rights firmly on the public agenda.

Summary Independent Variable A1

According to the three variable dimensions observed, the institutional strength of Chile's state bureaucracy in the area of international trade policy affairs is rather high. As resumed in Box 3.2, from 1995 the government was able to define an organisational model recognised among key domestic actors, and build up an adequate trade policy staff that became increasingly familiar with state-of-the-art negotiation techniques and new trade issues. Furthermore, the democratic government maintained the distinctive state-business collaboration patterns already initiated during the authoritarian regime.

Box 3.2: Summary Independent Variable A1

Responsibilities	Resources	Openness
Neglected by the military leaders, international trade policy affairs received strong attention by government departments as of 1990. After struggle for competences in 1990-94, since the mid-1990s the challenging new regional forces have convinced domestic actors to opt for a strong, autonomous trade policy branch inside the Foreign Affairs Ministry.	In the course of the 1990s, there was a permanent increase of the trade policy advisory staff. In addition, the vast negotiation experiences gave Chile's negotiation team international recognition; enhancing the stability of the bureaucratic cadre remains a pending task.	Though rather informal, close ties towards business maintained by the DIRECON office point at the continuance of the business-state collaboration pattern initiated in the 1980s. However, free trade critical NGO's resisted governmental efforts to gain broader support from society for the local trade policies.

3.3. The Institutional Strength of Business Associations

This section is structured in accordance with the variable dimensions of the Independent Variable A2. The first subsection, Institutional Leadership, analyses the establishment of a widely recognised peak, or "umbrella", association capable of coordinating economic policies between the leading sectoral and regional representatives. It further describes the institutional mechanism that ensures the effective intermediation of trade interests among leading sectoral and regional representatives. The second subsection, Organisational Strength, makes an assessment of the professionalism involved in business advocacy, stressing the domestic pattern of financing, participatory behaviour, and in-house trade policy expertise. The final subsection summarises the results and provides an overview of the business representation pattern throughout the period of 1985-2004.

Institutional Leadership

Today's strong influence of business associations in national politics has its origin in the debt crisis of 1982 when the Confederation of Production and Commerce (CPS), a national umbrella organisation, became the privileged "civilian" associate of the authoritarian regime. In just a few years, the CPC gained broad internal and external recognition as a firm advocate of the pragmatic liberal model set forth in the mid-1980s.

With the country's transformation into a democratic regime, the behaviour of the leading private sector entities altered little. For local entrepreneurs it was clear that "development" was not primarily related to the established political system, but to a business friendly environment. Therefore, the capitalist's mission went beyond simple lobbying by embracing broad activities aimed at convincing society of the appropriate direction to be taken. "It does not suffice to struggle for the increase of the GDP if the key stakeholders of the free enterprise do not share these results with the people," were the words of the former CPC President, Manuel Feliú (1986-90) in his book *Free Entrepreneurship* (Imbusch 1995: 367).[18]

Given the marked institutional leadership of the national peak associations, the first democratic government of the centre-left coalition could introduce only small modifications in

---

[18] In spreading this notion, the democratic regime did not mean to become an obstacle for the conservative business elites as they maintained, or even expanded, their areas of influence by controlling the major media companies, financing of political parties, closing links with universities and influential think-tanks, such as the Centre for Public Studies (CEP) and the Institute of Liberty and Development. For political party financing, see expert interview with Miguel Landeros Perkic, 10/11/2000. The control over the media is described in Robin 2001b; for links between business and think tanks see *Qué Pasa* from 11/06/01.

the tax and labour regulations, the two major reforms endeavours of the Aylwin administration.[19] Among other factors, the advocacy power of the CPC is explained by its membership, consisting of the six main sector associations that can generally be considered as the singular representatives in each of their corresponding sectors.[20]

Table 3.6: Business Representation Structure in Chile

Scale	Industry/ Construction	Agriculture/ Mining	Trade/ Banking
CPC *1933 *Large-Scale Firms*	Society of Manufacturing Promotion (SOFOFA) *1883 Chamber of Construction *1951	National Society of Agriculture (SNA)*1838 National Society of Mining (SONAMI)*1883	National Chamber of Commerce (CNC) *1858 Association of Banks and Financial Entities (ABIF) *1943
CONAPYME *1999 *Small-Scale Firms*	Confederation of Small and Micro Manufactures and Handicraft Associations (CONUPIA) *1966	Confederation of Agriculture Producers (CPA) *1973 (not CONAPYME member)	Confederation of Commerce, Retailers and Tourism *1938 Confederation of Truck Drivers *1953

Source: own elaboration based on Imbusch 1995: 216-229.

Table 3.6 indicates the marked segmentation between small and large scale representatives. In general terms, the influence of small-scale firms' associations was weaker than that of large company representatives, due to the following three main reasons:

1) *Competitiveness Gap*: The most competitive, outward oriented sectors are predominantly based on large firms (Castillo/Álvarez 1998). Also, the competitive range of small and medium size exporters are associated to large enterprise organisations (see later on in this section).

2) *Trajectory:* Small firms' organisations are much younger than large scale representatives in the area of agriculture (SNA), commerce (CNC), mining (SONAMI) and industry (SOFOFA) created in the years 1838 and 1883. Furthermore, CONAPYME, the peak association established in 1999, has encountered a strongly fragmented membership considering the high number of firms and sectors (Robin 2001a; González Gil 18/11/00).

---

[19] While labour relations could not be improved in favour of trade unions (for example, collective bargaining, strike breaker), the tax reform meant only a temporary increase (during 3 years) of the corporate tax from 10 to 15 percent. For further details; see Imbusch 1995: 410-428; Silva 1997: 173-178.
[20] Nevertheless, the internal structure of associate members varies remarkably since the associations held affiliates in the rank of regional and sector chambers and individual firms. As a result, many firms and chambers are affiliated in different associations, thus representation structures are more complex than was first thought. For a detailed analysis of local association structures; see Campero 1988.

3) *Financing:* Small-scale firms' associations suffer from scarce resources due to the fact that when it comes to paying dues, members are notoriously absent. CONUPIA (BR 18/02/05), as the peak entity of small manufactures, reported that less than 25 percent of members meet payment deadlines regularly. As a result, CONUPIA and other associations have been dependent on subsidies provided by the Service for Technical Cooperation (SERCOTEC) to strengthen the organisational development of the highly fragmented segment of small and micro enterprises, and hence, to give counterbalance to the large-scale sectors that were evidently facing financial problems to a lesser degree.

The leadership of CPC also faced a declining tendency towards the end of the 1990s. As was elucidate in greater detail in the MA thesis "Entrepreneurial Behaviour within the Process of Democratic Consolidation in Chile and Argentina (Robin, 2001: 52-61), increasing rivalry stemmed mainly from the Society of Manufacturing Promotion. From 1998, SOFOFA's President, Felipe Lamarca, (1997-2001) provoked an open conflict with the umbrella organisation headed by Walter Riesco (1996-2000). Lamarca, an idiosyncratic, impulsive leader, and manager of the *Compañía de Petróleos de Chile S.A.* (COPEC) – Chile's largest private company – undermined the CPC's leadership through multiple activities, such as criticising official CPC positions, holding direct dialogue with the government with respect to labour policies, abstaining from the Executive Committee, refusing to pay dues as an affiliate member, and finally, in March 2000, by the temporary suspension of its CPC membership. Evidently, such conflicts were mainly based on personal rivalry between Lamarca and Riesco, best illustrated by the opposing points of view related to the trial of Augusto Pinochet; Riesco defended the former dictator whereas Lamarca did not (*El Metropolitano* 11/08/2000).

Nonetheless, the Lamarca Chairmanship marked a dividing-line in the intermediation of local business interests. Although the CPC kept up an important "coordination force" during 2001-2005 (the time when Juan Claro assumed both the chair of SOFOFA and the CPC), SOFOFA consolidated its leading role in areas such as trade, energy, education and state procurement, symbolised herein by the Pro-Growth Agenda I and II, where the industrialists' organisation manifested its strategic relation toward the government. Two features accentuated the entity's increased leverage:

1) *Multisectoral Approach*: From 1990 to 2004, SOFOFA increased its membership from 28 to 36 sector associations, further including 2,500 corporate affiliates and eight regional chambers (BR Reus 27/09/04; Robin 2001a). Moreover, the membership in 2004 accounted for 90 percent of industrial production and 30 percent of the GDP (BR Reus

27/09/04), and also represented industry sectors, i.e. energy, telecommunications, water and sewage, and information technology for port services, as well as air, maritime and rail transport. The pursued multisectoral approach was underscored by the presidencies of Juan Claro (2001-2005) and Bruno Philippi (from 2005), who preside the Board of Directors of *Emel SA* (Energy distribution) and *Telefónica,* respectively.

2) *Export Champions:* The most dynamic export branches are affiliated, without exception, to SOFOFA, i.e. the Salmon and Trout Producers Association, the Winery Association of Chile, the Federation of Food Processing Industries of Chile (FEPACH), the Chilean Lumber Corporation (CORMA), and the Fisheries Association of Chile (SONAPESCA). Several of these became affiliated as of 1997 when Felipe Lamarca assumed the Chairmanship. Moreover, SME exporters are also associate members through the Association of Exporters of Manufactures (ASEXMA), the major private export promotion agency.

The Intermediation of Trade Interests and Organisational Strength

As indicated, at the outset of the 1990s doubts prevailed among the Chilean entrepreneurship in relation to regional trade arrangements, perceiving them as somehow heterodox instruments that could undermine the achievements of unilateral trade liberalisation implemented under the authoritarian regime. But faced by the emerging regional initiatives of the MERCOSUR and NAFTA, the leading business entities began to respond to the changing international scenario as I outline subsequently in the case of CPC (peak association), SOFOFA (industry), SNA (agriculture), and the Santiago Chamber of Commerce (trade and services).

Confederation of Production and Commerce (CPC): Supported by the Ministry of Finance, the prospect of becoming a member of NAFTA caused, at the beginning of the 1990s, strong reactions among the large-scale firms associated inside the CPC. For this reason, the umbrella organisation took over control and put into practice the so-called Program for Special Studies (PEPALC). Thereafter, acknowledged economists from the Catholic University carried out exhaustive impact assessment studies in order to measure the possible effects of a NAFTA membership on different economic sectors (Coeymans/Larraín 1992). Furthermore, the peak entity began to harmonise the prevailing private sector views within the Commission for International Affairs, where members would deliberate over the available integration options. By the mid-1990s, the CPC performed as an effective multisectoral coordination force in the scope of the controversial negotiations with the MERCOSUR states. While the industrial and service sectors held strong offensive interests, the CPC authorities placed special emphasis on the concerns of the local agriculture sector to balance inter-sectoral views. Supporting the agreement in general terms, the umbrella organisation underscored the potential liberalisation costs for farmers, and thus, supported the claims of the National Agriculture Society (SNA) for effective compensation measures (Silva 2000: 327-323).

After the negotiations with MERCOSUR, the CPC, as a forum for deliberation and multisectoral coordination efforts, underwent significant modifications. Since other sectoral entities, such as the SNA, SOFOFA, and the Santiago Chamber of Commerce, increased their protagonism in the trade policy area; the CPC's coordination function began to decrease and become overshadowed by an increased focus on dissemination activities. For example, in 2001, when the "historical" opportunity to negotiate an FTA with the US finally became feasible, the CPC became a salient promoter of the trade agreement through awareness campaigns carried out inside and outside the country.[21] With respect to the internal structure of the multisectoral organisation, Box 3.3 provides an overview of financing, internal trade policy making, trade policy expertise, and staff. Data was collected in 2001 and corroborated in 2004.

Box 3.3: Organisational Properties of the Confederation of Production and Commerce

Financing	Revenues originate exclusively from associate sectors; no supply of services
Trade Policy Making	Commission for International Affairs; monthly meetings are said to be attended regularly, totalling approximately 15 persons, including CPC staff
Staff	Approximately 10 officials, including administrative staff
Trade Experts	There is one economic policy advisors who dedicates 50 percent of time to the monitoring and coordination on trade policy concerns

Sources: BR García Aspillaga 02/11/00; BR Font 27/09/04, CPC Annual Report 2003-04

In general, the CPC was not prominent for its excellence in technical analysis due to the modest professional level of its staff. Instead, CPC has been characterised as a place where sectors can meet to coordinate business positions, underlining the umbrella organisation's capacity to unite business, and to submit harmonised proposals to the authorities, or as Carlos Urenda, CPC's Managing Director, stated (*El Diario* 18/12/01), "the government shall know our

---

[21] For example, the CPC organised the campaign "Half Day for Chile" aimed at convincing key actors in the United States regarding the interest and the readiness of Chile to sign a free trade agreement. Therefore, every businessman travelling to the US informed the CPC and the CPC scheduled meetings with important members of Congress; see Font 27/09/04.

worries..., we contribute our experience and the government has the power to bring it to law." Such matters were manifested by the active participation of CPC members in no less than 30 private-public commissions, encompassing areas such as the environment, labour, energy, statistics, taxes, etc. However, as previously stated, in the trade policy area the ability to intermediate interests among business passed over, step-by-step, to the large sectoral associations.

Society of Manufacturing Promotion (SOFOFA): At the time Chile entered into negotiations with MERCOSUR, the internal structure of the umbrella organisation appeared inadequate for the coordination of technical tasks, such as setting schedules, defining rules of origin, and identifying technical trade barriers. SOFOFA, as a professional industrial entity, assumed the CPC's Technical Secretariat as of 1995, thus holding consultations at the level of associate sectors and serving as a permanent channel with state authorities.[22] Despite the high degree of technical readiness, SOFOFA's institutional leadership was undermined for several years due to quarrels with the National Corporation of Exporters. Since its creation in 1988, this entity sought to perform as an alternative forum for the emerging non-traditional sectors of agriculture and industrial manufactures by responding exclusively to their needs. However, this aspiration failed to establish clear advocacy structures because many firms and associations in the area of non-traditional products (e.g. fruits, wines, metal mechanics, food processing, wine industry, and salmon production) were associates of both the National Corporation of Exporters and SOFOFA.

In recent years, SOFOFA was able, nevertheless, to consolidate its leadership far beyond the traditional industry. Notably, manufacturing exporters throughout the sectors began to rely on SOFOFA's intermediation capacities, including SME organisations, such as ASEXMA and ASIMET from the metal working industry. Finally, in December 2004 previous struggles officially came to an end, as the National Corporation of Exporters became a member of SOFOFA, paving the way for the establishment of the *National Council of Exporters – SOFOFA* which would represent all business export associations.[23] Reviewing the activities displayed by SOFOFA during the crucial negotiations with the US, the EU, EFTA and South Korea, several different elements underline its outstanding role as a business interlocutor:

---

[22] The attempts undertaken by CPC to rotate the Technical Secretariat among sector associations in subsequent negotiations – EU trade talks should have been coordinated by the National Chamber of Commerce – were restated by SOFOFA authorities (though written and verbal data gathered do not provide a full picture). For further information; see Silva V. 2000; 2001; Porras 2003; BR Reuss 27/09/2004.

[23] The President of the National Corporation of Exporters, Ronald Brown, mentioned in May 2004 that he was working with SOFOFA to overcome the fragmentation inside the exporter's sector. Ronald Brown used to head the National Association of Exporters, an entity which is also under SOFOFA, representing mainly fruit exporters; see Journal LyDTech 25/05/04. For the National Council of Exporters-SOFOFA; see Annual Report 2004-2005, 28-29.

1) *Deliberation and Coordination Forum*: Since 1995, SOFOFA has organised the Council of International Relations, which serves as a deliberation body to inform on current trade policy topics and to define strategies. Meetings take places three to four times per year and working groups are put together as and when specific topics require in-depth solutions. The number of participating business officials and entrepreneurs has grown progressively, reaching a membership of 80 persons by 2004. Hence, the Council became a popular public-private consultation forum where official negotiators stated their points of view on current talks and export issues in general. Furthermore, since September 2003 SOFOFA premises have been the venue for the Public-Private Council for Export Development, initially driven by the public sector (2.2.3). With regard to overseas contacts, SOFOFA was the seat of the Technical Secretariat for the Entrepreneurial Advisory Committees (CASE) which provided a formalised bilateral business exchange in-keeping with the existing ALADI agreements (Annual Reports 2001-2005; Reus 27/09/2004; Robin 2001a).

2) *Capacity Building and Monitoring*: SOFOFA has been the leading entity in familiarising entrepreneurs with the upcoming challenges of new regulations and promotion schemes through the organisation of seminars and workshops. Often the events have been organised in cooperation with DIRECON and other state agencies. Also, SOFOFA carries out permanent monitoring and evaluation of trade flows, tariffs and obstacles to Chile's exports in foreign markets (Annual Reports 1997-2005).

3) *Collaborative Behaviour*: Related to the features previously mentioned, SOFOFA acted in a proactive manner, formulating initiatives and proposals aimed at improving the administration of agreements and enhancing the access to new markets for local products. Due to these evident reasons, state authorities learned to appreciate this collaborative behaviour; thus, DIRECON officials began to maintain a more privileged relationship with SOFOFAthan with the National Cooperation of Exporters, which frequently stayed out of these activities due to its hostile behaviour and lack of interest to submit new proposals, as a confidential ex-state official report indicated (OE September 2004).

Finally, Box 3.4 underscores the institutional strength of SOFOFA in pointing at the entity's organisational grounds.

Box 3.4: Organisational Properties of the Society of Manufacturing Promotion

Financing	The yearly budget of approximately US$ 1.5 million is covered up to 70 percent by "predictable" revenues from its members. The remaining 30 percent is funded through services (e.g. event management). Since 1990, the budget has steadily increased.
Trade Policy Making	The Council for International Relations brings together 70-80 business persons from foreign trade related sectors. Aside from the plenary meetings that take place three-four times a year; specialists of each branch contribute in the scope of ad-hoc working groups by submitting proposals for specific problems faced by exporters. The Committee of International Negotiations, which existed until 2001, was integrated into the Council for International Affairs and the ad-hoc working groups. In this regard, the most active branches are usually fruits, forestry, fishery, metal working and the chemical industry.
Staff	Approximately 50 officials, including administrative staff
Trade Experts	Area of Foreign Trade and International Economic Relations composed of two former trade diplomats and five-six assistants.

Sources: Annual Report 2003-04; BR Pedro Reuss 27/09/04; Robin 2001a; Porras 2003: 25

The apparent internal professionalism began to be constructed with the negotiations conducted with MERCOSUR and Canada, when SOFOFA authorities saw the need to incorporate state-of-the-art trade policy advisory skills. Thus, in 1995 SOFOFA hired Hugo Baierlein and Pedro Reuss, former trade diplomats from DIRECON. It was Hugo Baierlein who strengthened the Foreign Trade and International Economic Relations branch, placing emphasis on key issues involved in international trade policy affairs (e.g. specific rules of origin, schedules). Pedro Reuss, on the other hand, started to deal with the operational aspects involved in export business (customs procedures, market assistance, etc.). Moreover, Andres Concha, SOFOFA's General Secretary since 1997, is said to have the capacity to bring together first class specialists from inside and outside SOFOFA, which proved crucial for the internal private sector organisation in preparation for the "mega talks" with the US, the EU and the Asian countries.[24]

National Society of Agriculture (SNA): What SOFOFA represents for the local industry, the SNA represents for agricultural elites. Chile's oldest business entity (1838) is considered as the most influential member inside the CPC aside from SOFOFA. But contrary to SOFOFA, the

---

[24] For example, Andres Concha in past negotiations was responsible for selecting the coordinators of the Technical Commissions created for the specific purpose of exchanging information permanently with state authorities; see BR Reuss 27/9/04; OE Sáez 27/09/04.

SNA membership behaved with strong reluctance regarding the world market integration strategy set forth. Therefore, SNA authorities faced the challenge of advocating both producers oriented principally towards the domestic market (such as cereals, vegetable oils, sugar, livestock), as well as outward oriented producers of fruits and wines. In the end, however, the defensive interests prevailed, given the fact that the concerns of exporters were dealt with inside SOFOFA.

Certainly, the SNA's main intervention during the 1990s took place in the different stages of the MERCOSUR talks, heading the domestic opposition against profound liberalisation commitments on varying policy levels (Gomez 1998). Highlighting the potentially enormous economic and social cost for traditional agriculture, the SNA was able to gain the support of the umbrella organisation CPC. Furthermore, the agrarian entity mobilised a broad movement by organising powerful demonstrations and marches in August 1995. In these demonstrations approximately 30,000 farmers throughout the regions and organisations demanded the consideration of agrarian concerns (Porras 2003: 52). These manifestations brought the issue into the public sphere and, above all, into Congress, where the agrarian sector enjoyed an important constituency (representatives of the Upper and Lower Houses) composed mainly by representatives from the rural areas in central and southern Chile. Also on subsequent occasions, such as the US free trade talks in 2001-02, negotiations with New Zealand in 2004, and in discussions addressing how and when to abolish the local Price Band System, the SNA authorities coordinated the protectionist interests in wheat, vegetable oils, and sugar producing sectors.

Even though the trend towards liberalism could not, evidently, be halted, the SNA's lobby achievements are rather impressive. In the field of agriculture, the usually liberal Chilean government upheld a wide range of supporting schemes, ranging from technological innovation, irrigation systems, technical and market assistance, investment and credit lines.[25] Moreover, the long phasing-out modalities for the elimination of tariffs on sensitive products stand out. In the Chile-MERCOSUR agreement of 1996, the phasing-outs applicable to wheat, vegetable oils and sugar were not scheduled to begin prior to 2007, and thus reach their conclusions by 2014. In the US-Chile FTA, these sensitive products will be liberalised within a 12-year period. Box 3.5 gives a brief outline of the organisational properties of the top rural association.

---

[25] The state institutions involved are CORFO, FIA, Prochile, CONICYT, INDAP, and CNR. For an overview, see "Governmental Agriculture Programs" on the SNA webpage, http://www.sna.upsystem.cl/. According to the WTO (2003), the majority of these support schemes are horizontal in nature, and thus, do not contravene WTO norms.

Box 3.5: Organisational Properties of the National Society of Agriculture

Financing	The SNA revenues are strongly diversified and based on member dues, the organisation of Santiago's International Fair (FISA), and the running of vocational schools (CODESSER), and a rural radio and research centre, among others. Aside from SOFOFA and the National Chamber of Construction, the SNA is the country's most solvent business organisation.
Trade Policy Making	Working groups derive from the Board Council, composed of 11 members.
Staff	Approximately 30 employees work in Santiago's head office.
Trade Experts	The Department of Studies monitors international trade policies. The Department is directed by a Commercial Engineer with a MA Degree from Harvard in Public Administration. Assistance is further provided by an Economist and an Agricultural Engineer, respectively.

Source: BR Gana Errazuriz 28/09/04; Imbusch 1995: 220.

Although the SNA has recently enhanced its trade policy expertise through well trained professionals, the key for the entity's leverage in domestic policy making has been based on its broad societal network (embracing numerous activities and services provided in rural areas), its strong constituency inside the Congress, and an outstanding presence in the mass media and in public spheres in general. Similar to rural organisations in Europe, the SNA therefore offers local farmers considerably more than mere lobbying, and thus, exhibits a high degree of social cohesion among the Chilean farming community.

Santiago Chamber of Commerce: In connection with the new area of trade in services, the Santiago Chamber of Commerce was able to become the main business interlocutor. In 1996, when the service issue was addressed in the scope of the negotiations with Canada, the Santiago Chamber of Commerce met the challenge of systematising and promoting domestic interests related to this intangible and extremely wide-reaching topic of services. Consequently, the Chamber hired a specialist, Claudio Ortiz, who had previously been responsible for negotiations in the scope of GATS in the mission to Geneva. The Committee of Service Exporting Companies was composed of approximately 30 associations and enterprises, and in recent talks with Mexico, Central America, the United States and the European Union, it sought to drive forward the liberalisation of service sectors, focusing mainly on software diverse engineering services, printing, energy distribution, maritime transports, etc. Nevertheless, progress in these fields remains modest, both as regards market access conditions and export volumes. However, the fact that at this early stage advocacy was promoted is a signal of the distinctive proactive performance of the local business community (OE Sáez 27/09/04; Silva 2001: 59-61).

Summary Independent Variable A2

This section indicates a rather high institutional strength of business associations. Regarding the variable dimension Institutional Leadership, the coordination (intermediation) capacity of the multisectoral "umbrella" organisation CPC and the sectoral entities SOFOFA (industry), SNA (agriculture), and the Santiago Chamber of Commerce (trade in services) stand out. The *organisation strength* of those key business associations can be explained largely by the strong diversification of revenues, the members' paying habits, the participatory behaviour of entrepreneurs and business entities, the large size of permanent staff, and the strengthening of in-house trade expertise.

Box 3.6: Summary Independent Variable A2

Leadership	Organisational Strength
The six leading sector associations from mining, industry, trade, finance, construction, and agriculture are represented inside the broadly recognised peak entity, CPC. Towards the end of the 1990s, the CPC's intermediation capacity was lowered to a certain degree by SOFOFA, which assumed a multisectoral representation approach in several policy fields. Specifically, SOFOFA became the clear business interlocutor by convening and representing export related interests and cooperating steadily with DIRECON officials. The SNA achieved different policy making levels to ensure the effective representation of defensive rural concerns. Since 1996, services have been organised inside the Santiago Chamber of Commerce, systematising the interests in this often confusing negotiation issue.	Aside from the widespread financial and administrative solidity of the Chilean business associations, they responded to the increasing technical requirements of international trade policy as of the 1990s. Therefore, the sectoral entities in industry, agriculture, and commerce all exhibited well prepared trade policy advisory units. SOFOFA and the Santiago Chamber of Commerce, for example, decided as of the mid-1990s to hire former trade diplomats to prepare members for upcoming foreign challenges and to guarantee efficient relations with state agencies.

3.4 Assessment

After examining the evolution of the dependent and independent variables individually, in this final section I assess how, and to what extent, Chile's success in implementing a coherent world market integration strategy has been caused by these two variables, or whether third variable influences became responsible for the observed policy output. However, before stressing the established causal relationship, it is important to point at what is so successful about the way Chile sought to integrate its economy into world markets. Two aspects should be mentioned.

First, Chile's export-led growth strategy has been developed gradually over the last 20 years, and thus, has been sheltered from radical policy changes implying altering objectives and instruments, a common policy-making pattern in South America. *Second,* in light of shifting trade policy towards regional and multilateral spheres, Chile has made use, more than any other South America country, of international trade policy affairs as a tool for economic development. Hence, Chile has managed to implement a cohesive and all inclusive package of unilateral, regional, and extra-regional trade policy measures aimed at the favourable development of national exports.

To explain the economic success registered from 1985, one must look at the key role of economic reforms implemented during the authoritarian regime (1973-1989). And indeed, most of the cornerstones of Chile's economic policy currently in force date back to reforms implemented by the *Chicago Boys* who took control of the Finance Ministry during the dictatorship of Augusto Pinochet, setting in motion the wave of privatisations and labour market reforms, and building a business-friendly tax environment. As these policies enjoyed broad acceptance among the local business sector, the transition to democracy was characterised by the strong disposition of the newly elected policy-makers to continue key economic policies, signalling predictability both inside and outside the country.

On the contrary, the "authoritarian legacy" in the trade policy area is more ambiguous. The Multipolar Model, which at present exemplifies the country, is much broader than the trade reforms implemented under the military regime. Though the "success story" was launched in February 1985, when under the leadership of finance minister *Hernán Buchi* an export-oriented strategy was set forth, based on continuous unilateral tariff reductions and far-reaching export promotion schemes, the *Chicago Boys* conceived trade policy as a mere unilateral tool, and thus, did not take advantage of possible forms of reciprocal liberalisation that provide local industry with improved market access conditions in overseas markets.

Thus, putting an end to this orthodox, "ivory-tower" attitude can be seen as the real achievement of democratic policy makers. They understood that successful world market integration goes beyond coherent, predictable, business-friendly domestic policies, but demands an accurate analysis of what is needed domestically and what can be obtained externally. In this regard, the democratic government that took office in 1990 did not only aim to preserve the trade policy of its authoritarian predecessor (e.g. in maintaining the "flat rate regime") but to complement efforts in extending market access opportunities through preferential trade agreements all over the global, thus attaining a paradigmatic Multipolar Model.

Aside from this clarification, which is particularly necessary due to the commonly claimed effects of the authoritarian policy reforms, Box 3.7 sums up the value of the observed variables and the explaining power each one possesses. Consequently, I will next explain when, and how, the values of variables changed over time and how they influenced the value of B.

Box 3.7: Explaining Chile's Successful World Market Integration Strategy

Variable	Variable Dimension	Value (Variance 1985-2004)	Explaining Power for Policy Success (B)
A1: Institutional Strength of State Bureaucracy	Responsibilities	1985-1994: rather low 1995-2004: very high	1995-2004: **very high**
	Resources	1985-1994: rather low 1995-2004: very high	1995-2004: rather high
	Openness	1985-2004: very high	1985-2004: **very high**
A2: Institutional Strength of Business Associations	Leadership	1985-2004: very high	1985-2004: **very high**
	Organisational Strength	1985-1994: rather high 1995-2004: very high	1985-1994: rather high 1995-2004: **very high**
C1: Heterogeneity Sectoral Preferences		1985-2004: rather high	1985-2004: rather low
C2: Heterogeneity Foreign Preferences		1985-2004: rather low	1985-2004: rather low
C3: Political Instability		1985-2004: very low	1985-2004: very low
C4: Macroeconomic Instability		1985-2004: very low	1985-2004: very low

Institutional Strength of State Bureaucracy

According to Box 3.7, the explaining power of Variable A1 is mostly high. Principally, the emergence of a broadly accepted Foreign Affairs Model (*responsibilities*) as of 1995, based on the institutional strengthening of the General Directorate of International Economic Affairs

(DIRECON), was decisive for the successful Multipolar approach to world market integration. Prior to this, policies in the area of international trade policy affairs lacked coherence. As previously noted, during the military regime the DIRECON – created in 1979 – was only theoretically in charge of international trade policy affairs, since in practice trade policy had been dealt with merely as a unilateral issue ruled by the Ministry of Finance. During the first democratic government (1990-94), international trade policy was increasingly perceived as crucial for export development, but the Ministries of Finance, Economy, and Foreign Affairs sustained different priorities, and thus, caused a struggle for competencies. While the Ministry of Economy pursued the development of value-added exports by strengthening relations with Latin American markets (above all with the emerging MERCOSUR), the finance department focused its attention on the possible adherence to the NAFTA, as this option was seen as an opportunity to "cement" previous unilateral liberalisation. Finally, the Foreign Affairs Department, still rather weak, considered deepening trade relations with the Andean and Southern Cone states as an appropriate way to restore good border relations in the region.

Due to a range of factors (explained in 3.2), from 1995 the different state departments involved decided to strengthen the DIRECON office, making it the leading international trade policy branch in order to take on the rising challenges of regional and multilateral forces. In the aftermath, inter-ministerial coordination improved as the division of labour was clearly set, i.e. the Ministry of Finance remained in charge of tariff policy, investment measures, and financial services; the Ministry of Agriculture was responsible for negotiations on agricultural trade; and the Ministry of Economy served as an advisory unit in intellectual property rights, sector-oriented regulatory issues and technical trade obstacles.

Inside the Ministry of Foreign Affairs, the DIRECON enjoyed a distinct autonomous status, for example regarding budget spending and the appointment of officials. Without significant interference from the political branch, the engagement of this economic policy agency could be exclusively focussed on improving market access conditions for export industries, both by means of negotiating preferential trade agreements within and out with the region, and through market assistance activities within the scope of the export promotion authority *Prochile* (also part of the DIRECON office). Due to this institutional setting and a continuous increase of its trade policy staff, from 1995 DIRECON was able to spur international trade talks all over the globe, becoming a pioneer in South America by signing comprehensive free trade agreements with Canada, the United States, the European Union, South Korea, Singapore, and China.

While the strengthened DIRECON largely accounts for this vigorous trade policy, it could be observed, conversely, that the increasingly successful trade policy caused a further strengthening of the DIRECON. Therefore, the policy success consolidated the purpose of the international trade policy branch, and made it much less dependent on inferences of changing policy-makers sustaining altered priorities (a common pattern in South America). Moreover, since these agreements embraced a broad range of policy areas beyond border measures (for example involving the regulation of property rights, state procurement and investment related measures), the DIRECON has become more than a mere trade policy branch in charge of international negotiations, but can be conceptualised as a sort of pilot agency where important decisions for all economic policy areas are adopted.

Another crucial factor of A1 that had a strong influence on the Dependent Variable B was the high degree of openness to business. Indeed, the establishment of close working relations with business entities, above all with the Society of Manufacturing Promotion (SOFOFA), is essential to appropriately understand why, and how, Chile pursued the Multipolar approach to world market integration. In the tradition of the military regime, which in the aftermath of the debt crisis in 1982-83 opened steady participation channels to organised business sectors, the systematic incorporation of business views has been a key element, particularly for DIRECON. There are two main reasons for this: First, the ambitious trade agenda set forth required the private sector to contribute with its "decentralised intelligence" from markets through the provision of information on trade obstacles, investment perspectives, and market trends. Second, SOFOFA became a strategic partner for the DIRECON inside the business sector, as it shared the principals and objective of the Multipolar Model, thus providing firm domestic coalitions and disseminating the properties of trade policy among local sectors.

Institutional Strength of Business Associations

The explaining power of A1 is strongly linked to the effects of A2. In fact, inviting business to participate actively in the development of the Multipolar Model without relying on strong interlocutors inside the private sector would have entailed only limited effects. In this regard, both variable dimensions - *Leadership and Organisational Strength* – became relevant.

Specifically, the leadership of the multisectoral organisation CPC, a business-wide recognised entity, in the coordination of sectoral positions was crucial for Chile's international trade policy until the mid-1990s. By then, the CPC had become responsible for organising the private sector before the possible adherence to the NAFTA treaty. For instance, in carrying out exhaustive impact assessments as regards such an integration step, the CPC managed to channel and articulate the strong interest among the local entrepreneurship, and herewith, signalled to the Chilean and US governments the marked preposition to face this challenge. Thus, the CPC played a similar role to the one adopted by the Mexican business council, CCE, which Schneider (1997) qualified as decisive when accounting for Mexico's entrance into the NAFTA.[26]

From 1994 to 1996, moreover, the leadership of CPC was crucial in the harmonisation of opposing sectoral views within the controversial negotiations with the MERCOSUR. While the industrial and services related sectors favoured far-reaching economic integration (albeit a full membership was rejected due to the customs union concept), the CPC authorities placed special emphasis on the defensive concerns of local farmers in order to balance the inter-sectoral interests. Supporting the free trade agreement in general terms, the umbrella organisation stressed the potential liberalisation costs for farmers, and thus, supported the claims of the National Society of Agriculture (SNA) for far-reaching compensation measures and long phasing-out schemes. As a result, the agreement with MERCOSUR became viable despite strong heterogeneous interests among domestic sectors.

In the second and more dynamic stage from the mid-1990s, the schemes of business intermediation underwent significant changes. The variable dimension *organisation strength* attained more relevance because sectoral associations increased their protagonism. As was pointed out previously, SOFOFA became the privileged interlocutor of the DIRECON office, not only because of its leadership among export-oriented branches, but especially due to its collaborative behaviour in supporting trade policy officials through the permanent monitoring of foreign markets and accomplished technical proposals. For this purpose, SOFOFA hired two former trade diplomats to build up an Area of Foreign Trade and International Economic Relations as of 1995, when negotiations with MERCOSUR and Canada where underway, attaining herewith state-of-the-art trade policy advisory skills. Aside from SOFOFA, other sectoral entities from agriculture (SNA) and services (Santiago Chamber of Commerce) likewise increased their trade policy skills in order to facilitate an efficient exchange with state authorities.

In sum, the manner in which Chile pursued its integration into world markets assumed a neocorporatistic flavour, considering the close state-business collaboration pattern. Aimed at improving the capacity to coordinate public policies – in this case international trade policies – the Chilean government was interested in establishing close and stable relations with particular

---

[26] But contrary to Mexico, the US government however decided later to leave Chile and other Latin American countries out of the NAFTA, and to launch to FTAA initiative embracing the whole Western Hemisphere.

business associations, wherein strong leadership and organisation strength were the most important selection criteria. In general, such policy-making patterns are criticised for their lack of inclusiveness because they imply "representation monopoly", leaving little room for minority actors or groups facing collective action problems.

In Chile's trade policy, indeed, several actors' preferences have been reflected scarcely. One clear exclusion is the segment of import-competing small-scale manufacturers, workers and other members of the civil society, all of which suffer from the widespread fragmentation of their interests. In parts, the centre-left coalition *Concertación,* in power since the transition to democracy in 1990, sought to compensate such asymmetries, for instance by providing technical assistance and subsidised loans to small manufacturers so as to enhance their competitiveness[27]. Regarding the participation of civil society, the government made widespread efforts to foster dialogue with a broad range of society actors on international trade policy affairs. To date, however, the free trade critical civil society organisations have largely felt excluded from the world market integration strategy in force.

Control Variables C1-C4

Assessing the influence of selected control variables C1-C4, disturbing effects could be mostly controlled in the case of Chile. Studying the *sectoral preferences (C1)* involved, one is tempted to argue that the successful development of the export-oriented strategy has been made possible by the small and homogenous private sector that survived the drastic reforms undertaken from the 1970s (see Bartell 1995; Montero 1990). But this argument losses validity when the large number of signed free trade agreements is sought to bring in line with the marked protectionist attitude of the influential farming elite organised inside the National Society of Agriculture (SNA). Hence, the coherent implementation of particular trade policies might be favoured by rather homogenous, export-oriented preferences for local manufacturers (e.g. compared to the more heterogeneous industry in Argentina), but strongly opposed to by farming sectors vulnerable to free trade (e.g. compared to the homogenous, export-oriented preferences of Argentinean farmers).

Regarding the *preferences of other countries (C2),* only once was Chile strongly restricted in its pursuit of a Multipolar Model. In the 1990s, Chile was ready to undertake a comprehensive NAFTA-style agreement with the United States. But for reasons not related to

---

[27] Chile strengthened its framework dedicated to improve the competitiveness of SMEs, increasing expenditures from 0.34 to 0.93 percent of the GDP between 1990 and 1999 (Ministry of Economy 2000).

Chile, this step could not be accomplished until 2003. Thus, the course of action was influenced, but not the essence of Chile's approach to world market integration.

Finally, Chile has not suffer from any *political (C3) or macroeconomic (C4) crisis features* in the last 20 years, strongly differing from most South American countries. As mentioned, during the period of analysis, Chile passed from authoritarian to democratic rule. But the concerted way of administering this process avoided the emergence of political crisis and drastic changes in the making of economic policy.

3.5 References

Literature

Álvarez, Carlos (1993). "La CORFO y la Transformación de la Industria Manufacturera" Pp. 275-372 in *La Transformación de la Producción en Chile*. Santiago de Chile: CEPAL/ ECLAC No. 84.

Aninat, Cristóbal et. al (2004).*Political Institutions, Policy Making Processes and Policy Outcomes in Chile*. Working Paper. Santiago de Chile: Universidad Adolfo Ibáñez.

Bartell, Ernst (1995). "Perceptions by Business Leaders and the Transition to Democracy in Chile" Pp.49-104 in *Business and Democracy in Latin America,* edited by Bartell, E. and Payne, L. Pittsburgh: University of Pittsburgh Press.

Boston Consulting Group (2004). *Export Development and Promotion.Lessons from Four Benchmark Countries.* New Zeeland / Denmark / Malaysia / Chile.

Campero, Guillermo (1988). *Los Gremios Empresariales en Chile*. Santiago de Chile: ILET.

Castillo, Mario and Raúl Álvarez (1998) "El Liderazgo en las Grandes Empresas en Chile" Pp. 85-332 in *Grandes Empresas y Grupos Industriales Latinoamericanos*, edited by Peres, W. Mexico D.F.: Siglo Ventiuno Editores/Economic Commission for Latin America.

Coeymans, Juan Eduardo and Felipe Larraín (1992). "Impacto de un Acuerdo de Libre Comercio entre Chile y los Estado Unidos: Un Enfoque de Equilibrio General" in *Cuadernos de Economía Año 31*. Confederación de la Producción y del Comercio. No 94: 357-399.

Cordua, Joaquín (1994). "Innovación en la Transferencia de Tecnología: La Experiencia de la Fundación Chile" in *Espacios* Review. Caracas, Venezuela. Vol. 15: 147-162.

Díaz, Alvaro and Joseph Ramos (1998). "Apertura y Competitividad" in *Construyendo Opciones. Propuestas Económicas y Sociales para el Cambio de Siglo*, edited by Cortázar, R. and Vial, J. Santiago de Chile: Dolmen.

ECLAC (2002). *The Chilean Strategy of Trade Liberalization and Market Access.* Santiago de Chile: International Trade and Integration Division.

Esser, Klaus (1999). *Institutioneller Wandel unter Globalisierungsdruck Überlegungen zu Aufbau und Koppelung von Nationalstaat und Marktwirtschaft in Chile.* Berlin: Deutsches Institut für Entwicklungspolitik.

Fernandois, Joaquín and Manfred Wilhelmy (1989). "La Cancillería en la Futura Política Exterior de Chile" Pp. 105-120 in *Chile: Política Exterior para la Democracia,* edited by Muñoz, H. Santiago de Chile: Pehuén.

Ffrench-Davis, Ricardo (2000). *Entre el Neoliberalismo y el Crecimiento con Equidad.* Centro de Investigación Económica y Planificación. Santiago de Chile: Dolmen.

Ffrench-Davis, Ricardo (2002). *Economic Reforms in Chile: From Dictatorship to Democracy.* Ann Arbour: University of Michigan Press.

Gomez, Sergio (1998). "Novedades en la Agricultura Chilena. Nuevos Actores Sociales y Escenarios: Negociaciones y Confrontaciones" Chapter III in *Las Agriculturas del Mercosur. El Papel de los Actores Sociales*, edited by Giarraca N. and Cloquell S. Buenos Aires: Edición La Colmena/ CLACSO.

Imbusch, Peter (1995). *Unternehmer und Politik in Chile. Eine Studie zum politischen Verhalten der Unternehmer und ihrer Verbände.* Vervuert Verlag: Frankfurt am Main.

Insulza, José Miguel (1998). *Ensayos sobre Política Exterior de Chile.* Santiago de Chile: Los Andes Editorial.

Liberty and Development (2000). "MERCOSUR: Problemas e Interrogantes" Pp. 2-4 in *Revista Libertad y Desarrollo.* No. 100. Santiago de Chile.

Macario, Carla (1998). *Why and How Do Manufacturing Firms Export Evidence from Successful Exporting Firms in Chile, Colombia and Mexico.* Ph.D. Dissertation. Columbia: University of Missouri.

Macario, Carla (2000). *Export Growth in Latin America, Policies and Performance.* Boulder, Colorado: Lynne Rienner Publishers.

Montero, Cecilia and Jimena Federici (1997). *La Inserción Comercial de Chile en el Mundo: un Caso de Cooperación entre Empresarios y Gobierno.* Working Paper. Santiago de Chile.

Montero, Casassus (1990). "La Evolución del Empresariado Chileno. Surge un Nuevo Actor ?" Pp. 91-122 in *Colección Estudios CIEPLAN.* No. 30. Santiago de Chile.

Pietrobelli, Carlo (1998). *Industry, Competitiveness and Technological Capabilities in Chile. A New Tiger from Latin America?.* London and New York: Macmillan and St. Martin's.

Porras, José Ignacio (2003). *La Estrategia Chilena de Acuerdos Comerciales: Un Análisis Político.* Santiago de Chile: CEPAL/ECLAC.

Robin, Christian (2001a). *Kollektives Unternehmerhandeln im Prozess der demokratischen Konsolidierung Lateinamerikas vor dem Hintergrund einer liberalen Wirtschaftsordnung Eine vergleichende Fallstudie der politischen Regime Argentiniens und Chile in den 90er Jahren.* MA Thesis in Political Science. University of Zurich.

Robin, Christian (2001b). *Pressekonzentration in Chile: Implikationen auf die demokratische Konsolidierung 12 Jahre nach Pinochet.* Institute of Media Research. University of Zurich.

Sáez, Sebastián (2002). "Making Trade Policy: An Assessment." Pp.35-44 in *The Trade Policy Making Process. Level One of the Two Levels Game.* Occasional Paper 13, edited by Ostry, S. Buenos Aires: IDB/Munk Center.

Sikkink, Kathryn (1998). "Transnational Politics, International Relations Theory and Human Rights" in *PS: Political Science and Politics.* Washington, DC. Vol. 31: 516-523.

Silva, Eduardo (1997). "Business Elites, the State, and Economic Change in Chile" Pp. 152-191 in *Business and the State in Developing Countries,* edited by Schneider, B.R. and Maxfield, S.Ithaca, NY: Cornell University Press.

Silva, Verónica (2000). "Política Comercial y la Relación Público-Privada en Chile durante los Años Noventa" Pp.303-333 in *El Estado y el Sector Privado,* edited by Muñoz Gomá, O. Santiago de Chile: FLACSO.

Silva, Verónica (2001). *Estrategia y Agenda Comercial Chilena en los Años Noventa.* Santiago de Chile: CEPAL/ECLAC.

Valenzuela, Arturo (1989). "Origins, Consolidation and Breakdown of a Democratic Regime" Pp. 159-205 in *Democracy in Developing Countries: Latin America,* edited by Diamond, L., Linz, J. and Lipset S.M. Boulder, Colorado: Lynne Rienner Publishers.

Valdes, Juan Gabriel and Craufurd Goodwin (1995). *Pinochet's Economists: The Chicago School in Chile.* Cambridge University Press.

WTO (1997). *Trade Policy Review Chile.* Report by the Secretariat. Body of the WTO. WT/TPR/124.

WTO (2002). *Chile-Price Band System and Safeguard Measures Relating to Certain Agricultural Products.* Report of the Panel. WT/DS207/R; Report of the Appellate Body. WT/DS207/AB/R.

WTO (2003). *Trade Policy Review Chile.* Report by the Secretariat. Body of the WTO. WT/TPR/S/124.

Other Documents

ADI (2005). El Año 2004, *La Consolidación del Despegue Inversor.* Investment Promotion Agency, Argentinean Republic.

CIPMA/ Centro de Investigación y Planificación del Medio Ambiente (2/10/2001). Seminar "Acuerdo de Libre Comercio Chile-Estados Unidos: ¿Qué Preguntas surgen desde la Perspectiva del Desarrollo Sustentable?" Pp. 59-67 in *Ambiente y Desarrollo* Journal. Vol 1. XVII No. 4.

CPC (2003-2004). *Annual Report.*

DBLA (2005). *Economic Research. Latin American Database. Country Indicators from 1980 to 2004.*

Diario Pyme Newspaper (17/11/2004). "Prochile da a conocer Presupuesto 2005: Reforzarán Apoyo a la PYME Exportadora."

DIRECON (2001). *Balance de Gestión Integral.*

DIRECON (2004a). *Balance de Gestión Integral.*

DIRECON (2004b). *Comercio Exterior de Chile 2003.*

DIRECON (2005a). *Informe Comercio Exterior de Chile 1er. Trimestre 2005.*

DIRECON (2005b). *Evolución de las Exportaciones No Tradicionales Chilenas 1998 - 2004.*

El Diario Newspaper (18/12/2001). "Sector Privado participa en más de 30 Comisiones con el Gobierno."

El Mercurio Newspaper (12/02/2005). "¿Cuánto Gasta Chile en Negociar? TLC "con Rebaja."

El Metropolitano Newspaper (11/08/2000). Opinions by Felipe Lamarca and Walter Riesco on the Pinochet Trial.

Journal LyDTech (25/05/04). "Sector Exportador Necesita Mayor Unidad." Interview with Ronald Brown, President of National Corporation of Exporters.

Ministry of Economy (2000). *Comité Público-Privado de la Pequeña Empresa. Balance del Período Junio – Diciembre 1999.*

Qué Pasa Journal (11/06/2001). Business Elite Circles: CEP and Institute of Liberty and Development.

Rosales, Osvaldo (06/10/2005). *Desafíos Económicos de la Inserción Internacional.* Public Speech at *Foros de Política Exterior de Chile 2006-2010*, organized by FLACSO-Chile.

SOFOFA (1997-2005). *Annual Reports.*

Interviews

Date	Name	Organization	Function
27.09.2004	*Sáez, Sebastián (Selected Interview Partner)*	*ECLAC; International Trade and Integration Division*	*Consultant; Ex-Trade Policy Advisor*
27.09.2004	Reus, Pedro	Society of Manufacturing Promotion (SOFOFA)	Corporate Manager; Ex-DIRECON Official
27.09.2004	Font, Barbara	Confederation of Production and Commerce (CPC)	Economic Policy Advisor
28.09.2004	Gana Erraruiz, Francisco	National Society of Agriculture (SNA)	Head of Study Department
28.09.2004	Paz Cortez, Carmen	Ministry of Foreign Affairs/ DIRECON	Trade Policy Advisor; Market Access Affairs
28.09.2004	Confidential	Chilean Alliance for Fair and Responsible Trade	Monitoring International Trade Negotiations
September 2004	Confidential	-	Ex-DIRECON Official
9.12.2004	Cañellas, Marcelo	Ministry of Economy and Production; Argentina	Director of Regional Trade Policy;

			Market Access and ALADI affairs
17.12.2004	Rodriguez, Zandra	Ministry of Foreign Affairs; Bolivia	Director of South American Integration
17.02.2005	Buvinic, Alejandro	DIRECON	Director of Legal Affairs; since 1995 involved in trade talks
17.02.2005	Campos, Jaime	DIRECON	Legal Advisor
17.02.2005	Cerda, Andrea	ODEPA; Foreign Trade Department	Agriculture Trade Policy Advisor
18.02.2005	Puig, Juan	DIRECON	Director Human Ressources
18.02.2005	Ruis, Carlos	DIRECON	Sub-Director of Administrative Department
18.02.2005	Ingrid	CONUPIA	Administrative Assistant
Previous Conversations			
2.11.2000	Macarena García Aspillaga	CPC	Economic Policy Advisor
10.11.2000	Miguel Landeros Perkic	Congress	Legal Advisor
18.11.2000	Verónica González Gil	University Mayor; CPC	Professor of Economics; Member of CPC Board of Directors

Selected Interview Partner

Sáez, Sebastián: Economist; by 2005 Consultant to the International Trade and Integration Division of ECLAC of the United Nations. He published two papers on trade policy making in Chile (2002) and in Latin America (2005). Between 1990 and 1994, Sebastián Sáez worked inside the Ministry of Finance as trade policy advisor. Afterwards, he served inside DIRECON as coordinator of the FTAA talks, and was further engaged in negotiations on services in the scope of the WTO. Finally, in the period of 2000-04, Sebastián Sáez directed the Foreign Trade Division inside the Ministry of Economy and became a member of the Advisory Council within the US-Chile FTA talks.

4 Argentina

"To follow Chile's example is the simple answer for Argentina" commented Chilenean economist Sebastian Edwards in the middle of Argentina's economic, social and political crisis in January 2002 (Wall Street Journal 25/01/2002). Accordingly, rather than raising import tariffs and strengthening ties with Brazil in the scope of MERCOSUR, the transitory administration of Eduardo Duhalde (01/2002-04/2003) could have adopted a pragmatic reform program similar to the one Chile had pursued in early 1985, by cutting import tariffs, fiscal expenditures and corporate taxes. Nevertheless, these foreign recommendations would not have been welcomed by many of the 35 million Argentineans, since for them it was clear that the economic downturn of the 2,736,690 km2 Southern Cone state had nothing to do with a lack of liberal commitment, but rather an overdose of it. To a large extent, these controversial views about the "Argentinean Case" underline the dilemma that to date there has been no firm domestic consensus on which economic model to pursue, i.e. whether structural adjustment policies implemented as of 1989 by the Carlos Menem presidency (1989-1999) represented only the first step of reforms towards sound integration into world markets, or a new failed endeavour in the country's economic policy.

Focussed on trade policy, this chapter discusses the principal features of the world market integration strategy pursued from 1986 and 2004, and provides explanations for the principle shortcomings observed herein. Accordingly, it is structured along the following lines. The *first section* outlines the different policy areas that made up the world market integration strategy (Dependent Variable B), i.e. unilateral trade regime, regional and extra-regional integration, sector and export promotion. *Section two* enlightens the organisation of Argentina's public sector in the trade policy area (Independent Variable A1), thus showing how the local bureaucracy was organised regarding the conduction of international trade policy affairs along the period of analysis. Subsequently, *section three* elucidates the institutional responses of the business sector on the same issue (Independent Variable A2). Based on section one to three, *section four* provides an assessment of the case, and explores the links between the independent and dependent variables, and controls the possible influences of other variables (C1-4) on the B value.

4.1 World Market Integration between the Springboard and Multipolar Model

This first section is structured in accordance with the different policy areas making up the world market integration strategy (Dependent Variable B), i.e. unilateral trade regime, regional and extra-regional integration, sectoral and export promotion policies. The final subsection summarises the results and provides an overview of the trade performance from 1985 to 2004.

Unilateral Trade Regime

As with other states affected by hyperinflation during the 1980s, trade liberalisation in Argentina was transformed by the end of the decade into a tool for macroeconomic adjustment, leaving little space for proactive export promotion policies. Therefore, in August 1989 the new administration of Carlos Menem announced a significant reduction of tariffs in order to reduce domestic prices. On a par with earlier reform efforts, during the period of 1989-90 the inflationary pressure remained high. Against this turbulent background, three Ministers of Economy set forth distinct reform approaches. While the first team of Nestor Rapanelli (July-December 1989) planned to reach a simplified tariff structure ranging from 5 to 25 percent within four years, the second team of Ermán Gonzalez (1990) sought a reduction of tariff dispersion by setting a flat rate of 22 percent by January 1991. Later, the uniform tariff structure was abandoned by Domingo Cavallo in March 1991, who replaced it with a three-level tariff structure of zero percent for raw materials and capital goods not produced locally, 11 percent for intermediate products and 22 percent for nationally manufactured consumer and capital goods. Through these reform measures, average import tariffs were lowered within two years from 30 to 10 percent and NTB's, such as import quotas and licences, were eliminated (Chudnovsky/Porta 1991; Casaburi 1998; Viguera 1998).

As a result of the implemented reform measures, the previously protected industrial sector began to operate within an increasingly more competitive environment.[1] Nonetheless, the turning point for the local industry first came into view as of mid-1991, when Domingo Cavallo's team defined methods to bring the rampant inflation under control. Indeed, after a fixed exchange rate regime, or *currency board*, was introduced in April 1991, inflation rates sharply decreased within a few months and remained close to zero until the drastic currency devaluation in 2002. This stable economic climate – combined with the simultaneous pursuit of

---

[1] It should be noted that Argentina implemented a trade liberalisation program in the late 1970s, but it was abandoned after the financial crisis in the early 1980s.

ambitious privatisations and the deregulation of foreign investments – enabled high economic growth in the 1990s, leading Argentina to become an attractive destination for FDIs, above all for telecommunications, finance, and other services and commodity related sectors (Chudnovsky/Lopez 2001). However, beyond the macroeconomic achievements, the currency board implied a strong currency appreciation and enhanced the pressure on local industry to lower costs compared with those of foreign competitors. In this respect, Domingo Cavallo's economic team (1991-96) was less susceptible to the protectionist claims from threatened sectors than in the past, even though several important permanent and temporary exceptions were conceded, as exposed below:

> *Automotive Regime*: Since 1991, the automotive sector maintained privileged protectionist measures due to a high peak tariff for fully manufactured vehicles (quotas at the onset; later 35 percent in the scope of MERCOSUR), broad fiscal incentives, local content and export performance requirements and the administration of trade volumes in the scope of MERCOSUR.

> *Price Band for Sugar:* Since 1992, Argentina has levied variable import duties on sugar according to price band mechanisms. Consequently, imports from Brazil – the world's largest producer – have been effectively controlled.

> *Statistical Tax:* In the GATT, Argentina bound a statistical tax of 3 percent designed to finance the collection of statistical information relating to imports and exports. In 1998, the tax (temporally increased to 10 percent) had to be reduced to 0.5 percent in view of the fact that a WTO panel concluded that duties were by no means limited in amount to the approximate cost of services rendered. Afterwards, the MERCOSUR block increased the nominal external tariff by 3 percent, compensating for the loss of customs revenues.

> *Safeguard and Antidumping Measures:* Diverse measures such as quotas, additional tariffs and license requirements temporarily affected imports of sensitive products such as paper, consumer electronics, steel, textiles, clothing and footwear. Furthermore, Argentina evolved into one of the most prominent users of anti-dumping measures inside the WTO, mainly against imports from Brazil, China, and the EU. Similar to the safeguard measures applied, the application of antidumping duties varied according to the evolution of relative prices and were often used by large companies from the paper, steel, textiles and chemical industries to temporarily lower competition from abroad (Viguera 1998).

As of 1999, the application of protectionist measures became increasingly common as the country entered into a four-year recession. By the time Brazil decided to enforce a drastic unilateral devaluation of its currency in January 1999, Argentina began to impose numerous ad-hoc restrictions that hindered Brazilian imports in the area of textiles, steel, footwear, consumer electronics, plastics, cleansing products, pork meat, etc. Although some sectors, such as plastic, footwear, paper and the petrochemical industry, reached private agreements aimed at the self-restriction of sales from Brazil, most of the actions lacked a legal fundament and caused severe intra-MERCOSUR conflicts. An alleged "solution" for those disputes emerged in January 2002 as Argentina (against severe fiscal and foreign debt constrains) could no longer maintain the previously "sacrosanct" currency board regime.[2] Therefore, the values of the Argentinean Peso and the Brazilian Real converged during 2002, approximating anew (at least in a macroeconomic perspective) the playing field among the competing sectors. Due to the Peso devaluation, local exports registered remarkable growth rates as of 2003 while imports sharply declined in 2002-03.[3]

Nevertheless, as Brazil's manufacturers slowly but surely began to recover their previous market presence in the course of 2003, protectionist voices from consumer electronics, textiles and footwear industry again began calling for import restrictions. As a result of these lobby actions and Brazil's reluctance to include safeguard provisions in the scope of MERCOSUR, in September 2004 Argentina increased tensions through quantitative import restrictions and licenses for sensitive goods such as washing machines, televisions and footwear. In sum, the recurrent trade disputes, especially with Brazil, point to the fact that intra-regional trade is still susceptible to discretionary policies and prevailing asymmetries on the regional level, thus suggesting unresolved issues, as will be shown in the next subsection.

Regional Integration

In the context of inflation and debt restructuring throughout the region, the Argentinean-Brazilian Program for Integration and Economic Cooperation (PICE) signed in July 1986 suggested a new beginning between the contracting parties. Moreover, for the democratically elected governments of Raúl Alfonsín (1983-1989) and José Sarney (1994-1990), the PICE provided appropriate grounds for good neighbour policies, after the tense relations during previous military regimes (Hirst 1998; Campbell et al. 2000). Hence, the bilateral agreement

---

[2] The deterioration of the economic environment led the government to implement (in 2001) a two-tiered foreign exchange system which would lower the cost of local exports compared with import prices.
[3] While most of the previous NTB's applied in the MERCOSUR framework were abolished in the aftermath of the currency crisis, import operations were hampered by exchange controls imposed during the 2002 crisis. In the course of 2003 these controls were made more flexible or abolished.

covered 23 so called *sector protocols* aimed at fostering trade, and cooperation in science, defence, nuclear waste, infrastructure, and energy, among others.

Compared with the rigid multilateral method applied in the 1960s and 1970s in the scope of the Latin American Free Trade Area (ALALC), PICE pursued a flexible bilateral integration approach based on the ALADI treaty signed in 1980.[4] Furthermore, the parties keenly sought to prevent the determination of unrealistic goals and time schedules, aiming to progress first in specific areas where both consensus and implementation were feasible and to deepen the focus of integration step by step.[5] Carlos Bruno, key official of the Ministry of Foreign Affairs commented (OE 04/03/05): "We hoped to create a dynamic integration by selecting specific sectors with high potential for complementarities," and thus, "leave behind the declaration of illusionary projects which only caused unfulfilled hopes and depressed feelings."

While for Brazil, Argentina was crucial to enhance its regional leadership at a time when Latin America was increasingly marginalised in the aftermath of the debt crisis, for Argentina the emphasis was firmly on economic factors. Aside from the physical proximity and Brazil's domestic market roughly quadrupling the Argentinean market, local technocrats perceived integration with Brazil as key for industrial policies since the search for intra-industrial complementarities was seen as the appropriate instrument to enhance productivity, thus overcoming the standstill of previous decades compared with the impressive industrial development from mid-1960s that took place mainly in the areas of Sao Paulo and Rio de Janeiro.

However, Argentina rejected a rapid dismantling of barriers in order to avoid a deepening of the existing industrial asymmetries, which would have confirmed Argentina's role as Brazil's supplier of raw materials and buyer of manufactured products. Thus, at negotiation tables, Argentina, in particular, proceeded gradually, arduously seeking possibilities for intra-industrial exchange and harmonised trade growth by expanding concessions step by step. Paradigmatic to this "exploration and experimentation" concept was the first protocol for capital goods such as

---

[4] ALADI created in 1980 by the Montevideo treaty substituted ALALC and has acted since then as an institutional framework for the economic integration agreement between the 12 member states. The original ALALC treaty defined the creation of a FTA within 12 years. In 1969, the schedule was extended to 20 years, i.e. until 1980. However, the requirement to extend concessions among all members ("multilaterisation") hindered the contracting parties beyond common minimalist versions.
[5] In a first round, twelve protocols were adopted; 10 of them were related to economic and trade affairs; two were based on Aeronautic Cooperation and Nuclear Waste. In the following years (1986-1986) the number of Protocols signed increased to 23. Sectoral agreements were aimed at expanding trade, encouraging bilateral investments, and fostering cooperation in areas such as nuclear energy and biotechnology. Protocols of: Capital Goods; Trade; Binational Enterprises; Financial Issues; Investment Funds; Energy; Economic Studies; Aeronautic Cooperation; Steel Industry; Transportation; Communications; Nuclear; Cultural; Economic Planning; Food; Automotive, etc.

machinery, hand tools, and electronic equipment. These branches appeared to be perfect for the endeavour as growth perspectives were attractive and the potential for substitution of extra-regional imports was high (less than 10 percent originated from each one of these countries in 1986). Moreover, a slow and balanced expansion of trade volumes would have less of an impact on the balance of payment than large scale sectors such as steel, foodstuffs and automobiles. Finally, Argentina considered the development of this diversified sector, which was dominated by small, innovative family enterprises requiring a qualified labour force, as crucial for the country's industrial policy; and expected a high degree of spillovers towards other branches due to its central position within the national innovation system (Chudnovsky/Porta 1989; 1990).

But despite promising exports in which Argentina could take advantage of its diversified industry focused on short production series (compared with the large scale production in Brazil) the PICE approach soon came under pressure. After a first liberalisation period that restored trade flows to pre debt crisis levels, the exchange of concessions slowed down from mid-1987. Nevertheless, to reaffirm political commitments for bilateral integration, Brazil and Argentina signed, in November 1988, the Integration and Economic Cooperation Treaty, committing the States to undertake measures that would culminate in a common regional market within ten years. But since the ambitious goal was not sustained by clear enforcement mechanisms, its implementation was handed over to the forthcoming presidencies (Campbell et al. 101-106).

At the outset of the 1990s, the new administrations of Carlos Menem (Argentina) and Collor de Mello (Brazil) had strong incentives to further economic relations in light of the global trend towards building regional blocks and the trust created among the neighbours during the 1980s. Conversely, the new economic policy makers indicated their determination to abandon any kinds of protectionism. Especially for Argentina, which promoted market oriented reforms to a greater extent than Brazil, integration efforts were required to attract FDI's, so as to expand trade, and consequently, accelerate the transformation of the local economy (Cavallo 2001). This conceptual turn – personalised by Domingo Cavallo who acted first as Minister of Foreign Affairs (1989-90) and then as Minister of Economy (1991-96) – represented a complete break from the PICE ideology, or in the words of Aldo Ferrer: "the model changed from integration to international insertion" (1997: 8; see also Bustos 1992).

The guidelines for this "international insertion" were embodied in the Act of Buenos Aires signed by Argentina and Brazil in July 1990, and later, in March 1991, when commitments were extended to Uruguay and Paraguay in the scope of the Common Market of the South (MERCOSUR) that was founded in *Asunción, Paraguay*. Accordingly, trade liberalisation would no longer be flexible, sectoral and balanced, but would respond to an automatic, linear and universal tariff elimination mechanism through which free intra-trade was to be reached as of January 1, 1995. And indeed, the ambitious 4-year-term (considering that such an objective had not been reached during decades of negotiations) was surprisingly implemented in almost 90 percent of tariff lines. With regards to the remaining sensitive products, the Final Adjustment Regime established a schedule to reach intra-regional free trade by 1999. In the aftermath, the liberalisation efforts led to a rapid expansion of intra-zone trade, increasing sales in the 1990-97 periods from US$4,100 to 20,100 million. Simultaneously, the share of intra-MERCOSUR trade augmented from 8.9 to 26.6 percent of total members' exports (CEI 1998).

Results began to change, nevertheless, as of 1998 when the emerging economies, both within and out with Latin America, started to stumble. By this time, it had become more and more evident that during the "golden age" of MERCOSUR little had been implemented to consolidate the gains of integration (Nofal 1997a and b; Campbell et al. 2000; Bouzas/Da Motta Veiga/Torent 2002; Peña 2003; MERCOSUR 2004). Consequently, mainy failures of the MERCOSUR approach came to light, particularly in the following key areas:

The Circulation of Goods: Despite the nominal removal of intra-zone tariffs, the sugar and automotive sectors resisted the liberalisation and depended on provisional regimes that, although modified on several occasions, were to remain in force until 2005 (sugar) and 2006 (automobiles). However, the Minister of Economy, Roberto Lavagna, indicated on several occasions during 2004, that Argentina would not liberalise these sectors due to the prevailing structural and regulatory asymmetries. Similar arguments were put forward in the case of countless NTBs employed to offset competitive deficits in sensitive sectors. Aside from quantitative restrictions, a vast range of "hidden" NTBs were based on divergent national regulations on technical, sanitary and phytosanitary standards. To date, the will for harmonisation and/or mutual recognitions has been marginal or absent.

Customs Union: The Common External Tariff (CET) planned by the Asunción Treaty for January 1, 1995 contrasted from the outset with Argentina's notion of integration, which was aimed at the expansion of trade and the attraction of FDIs only. Despite widespread unwillingness to develop common external policies, prior to the presidential meeting in *Ouro Preto* in December 1994, Brazilian negotiators left no doubt about their keenness to meet the original deadline set forth in 1991, regardless of the progress on harmonisation in other areas.[6]

---

[6] The period between March 1991 and December 1994 was denominated as the Transition Period, formally concluded by the Ouro Preto Protocol. This agreement defined the institutional framework of MERCOSUR, and thus, ruled the internal decision making structure; see Boldorini/Zalduendo 1995.

However, the trade-off turned out to be somewhat unbalanced. Besides the fact that Brazil was able to impose most of its domestic tariff structure, for Brazil the CET represented the essence of MERCOSUR, considering that only in this event could the economic block face common international relations under Brazil's leadership. Conversely, for Argentina the reasons to agree on the CET were not obvious. Even though transitory exceptions were included in order to adapt to national realities (44 percent of imports did not comply with the CET at the outset) and the country's average tariff rate was lowered only from 15.4 to 13.9 percent, the decision implied a cementation of the dependency on Brazil concerning the way trade integration should be pursued.[7]

In the aftermath, constant discussions on the customs union negatively affected both MERCOSUR's internal and external agenda. By January 2001, when national exception lists were theoretically to be abolished, Argentina continued to maintain considerably higher tariffs for various product lines such as footwear, clothing, textiles, leather, sugar, pork meat and automobiles (Crespo Armengol/Geffner 2001). On the lower tariff side, salient intra-MERCOSUR disputes have repeatedly arisen due to Argentina's reluctance to increase its tariffs on several capital goods and IT equipment in order to guarantee certain protection for Brazil's industry. Aside from the discussions on the widespread perforation of the CET structure, members have been unwilling, until now, to deal with the customs union debate openly, bearing in mind that the goal of achieving a customs union would require not only a perfect CET but also wide-reaching measures, i.e. abolishing intra-zone customs, establishing a common customs authority with harmonised procedures and the unified application of antidumping and contingency measures.

Regulatory and Structural Asymmetries: As indicated, most problems in the perfection of the common regional market are related to the asymmetries in domestic regulations and the degree of competitiveness. Consequently, as of 1992 ten intergovernmental working groups launched negotiations not only to agree on the CET structure but also with regard to the harmonisation of intra-regional asymmetries in the areas of tax, promotion, industrial, energy, labour, customs, technical and sanitary rules. In this regard, the Act of *Las Leñas* signed in June 1992, where a schedule was defined to harmonise regulatory differences in fields where asymmetries jeopardised the creation of a common market, should have represented a mile stone.

---

[7] As a consequence of the CET, Argentina reorganised its tariff scheme by increasing the number of levels from three to eleven, ranging from 0 to 20 percent (later the number of tariff levels was reduced to eight). According to the so-called Final Regime towards a Customs Union, countries were to include sensitive products in their exception list to give these sectors additional time to proceed with the restructuring process. Argentina maintained exceptions for 300 tariff items, mainly chemical and metal products, paper and footwear; see Bouzas/Pagnotta 2003: 57-58.

Nevertheless, more than a decade later efforts have been largely ineffective. In general terms, the fact that Brazil's private sector suffers from higher fiscal burdens than in Argentina, but enjoys more generous and consistent industry and export promotion schemes, such as fiscal incentives, soft loans, research and development activities and market assistance. Conversely, in the MERCOSUR sphere, the powerful Brazilian State carried out largely insignificant efforts to overcome competitivity gaps, for instance by supporting productive chains and intra-industrial cooperation.[8]

New Topics: As progress in traditional areas slowed, Argentina sought to expand intra-zone liberalisation to service and state procurement areas. Nonetheless, by 2004, tangible results were still meagre. Although a protocol for service liberalisation was signed in 1997, and later, members made reciprocal concessions in four negotiation rounds according to the positive list approach (as in the scope of GATS), the protocol had not been put into force. The state procurement area is still very new and is covered by a protocol with only modest concessions signed in 2003. The agreement is still awaiting ratification by some of its members. Above all, Brazil is hesitant to foster these new topics, as important concessions could entail disadvantages within "mega talks" in the extra regional and multilateral sphere (3.1.3).

Macroeconomic Coordination: As the negative effects of currency devaluations questioned the benefits of integration, the enhanced coordination of macroeconomic policies began to be seen as crucial for the consolidation of MERCOSUR. Thus, a "Mini-Maastricht" in December 2000 defined economic convergence targets for the period 2002-2010 between member states. Even so, the measures lacked enforcement provisions and have yet to be put into effect.

Implementation: Contrary to the overambitious goals set forth in the Asunción Treaty, the Heads of State repeatedly announced the implementation of policies already outlined, for example in the "MERCOSUR Agenda" in December 1995, "the Buenos Aires Agenda" in June 2000, and the "Objectives 2006" declared in July 2003. Undeniably, the numerous efforts to re-launch the regional agenda disseminated a picture of ineffective and irrelevant communitarian regulatory and policy frameworks that, consequently, appeared rather futile for business operations. The shaky legal ground was emphasised by the fact that up until 2004, only 550 out of 1,112 norms (Decisions, Resolutions, and Directives) were put into force; i.e. for the rest, incorporation into internal juridical systems was non-existent (MERCOSUR 2004).

---

[8] In 2005, members finally began to be concerned about funding options to establish a MERCOSUR Fund for Reconstruction and Development, inspired by the convergence regimes administered by the UE.

Extra (Sub-) Regional Integration

The customs union was an idea born in Itamaraty, Brazil's powerful Ministry of Foreign Affairs. Brazil's diplomacy aimed at consolidating the country's leadership in South America through common regional trade policies was initiated when the US Initiative for the Enterprise of the Americas was announced in June 1990. Since the offensive of the Bush administration to foster free trade in the hemisphere was warmly received in countries such as Chile and Argentina, for Brazil the moment had come to work on the creation of a regional block to counter the US expansion towards South America. Itamaraty's strategy sustained throughout the presidencies of *Collor de Mello, Franco, Cardoso and Lula da Silva*, consisted of the establishment of the MERCOSUR as a core group aimed to be expanded steadily throughout the rest of the South American states.[9]

As previously mentioned, Argentina's position differed from this strategy since the government of Carlos Menem pursued a structural adjustment policy in line with the Bretton Woods Institutions; moreover, Argentina maintained a foreign policy with the US which had been commonly denominated as "carnose relations" that made Argentina (together with Chile) a strong candidate for entry into the NAFTA. In this context, by mid-1994 it was Brazil who urged Argentina to make a clear commitment in favour of the customs union approach (Campbell et. al 2000: 154-158). The decisions finally taken in *Ouro Preto* in December 1994 hampered Argentina's later attempts to follow a Multipolar Model in the same way that Chile had done. While its neighbour entered into an intensive network of bilateral trade relations inside and outside Latin America as of 1990, MERCOSUR's external negotiations were deadlocked in the regional as well as in the extra regional sphere, as I shall summarise below:

Chile, Bolivia, Andean Community of Nations (CAN), and Mexico: As previously stated, MERCOSUR was expected to become a regional nucleus that would expand towards other ALADI states. Therefore, the trading block sought to agree, under the framework of ALADI, on full FTAs with Chile, Mexico, and the CAN within a 10-year period (Campbell et. al 2000: 156). The idea was to conduct external talks under the "4 + 1" formula through which MERCOSUR negotiate as a block with each individual country.

---

[9] The idea to integrate South (or Latin) American economies has been given different names. After creating ALALC and ALADI in 1960 and 1980, in 1993 Brazil (under Itamar Franco) put forward the concept of the South American Free Trade Area. However, the project later stalled. More recently, in December 2004, the "Lula" administration convinced regional Heads of States to announce the Community of South American Nations. In 2005, the detailed contents and modalities were still not clear.

Chile turned out to be the most challenging case for the new "4+1" scheme. As a bustling and stable economy in the Southern Cone linked to the Pacific area, from the start Chile was invited to join MERCOSUR as a full member. However, the Andean country rejected the customs union and only accepted a status as Associate Member involving the complete dismantling of tariffs and specific dispositions regarding transportation, investment, and energy, among others.[10] During the negotiations that ended in September 1996, key official reports suggested that the Chilean team was better prepared, and thus able to make use of the diverging interests within MERCOSUR (SO Cañellas 9/12/04; Campbell et. al 2000: 181-185). In the end, the agreement signed in the ALADI framework (ACE No. 36) entailed the removal of most tariffs within eight years, and ten year for sensitive products. Argentina's major agricultural exports such as cereals, beef, dairy products and vegetable oils were treated as ultra sensitive goods that would only be liberalised after 15 and 18 years, respectively.

Of less importance were the talks with *Bolivia* that reached their conclusion three months later. As the Bolivia chapter explains, Bolivia sought a far-reaching alliance with the Southern Cone. Therefore, this poor Andean country largely waived the Special Treatment Status embodied in the ALADI Treaty and accepted, for example, fairly rigid rules of origin, harsh restrictions on textile exports – Bolivia's major interest in manufactures – and left out special safeguards for agricultural goods. Similar to the Chile agreement, Argentina's interests such as duty-free imports of wheat, vegetable oils, meat, cheese, chocolate, and biscuits were treated as ultra sensitive products to be liberalised in 15 to 18 years.

After the talks with Chile and Bolivia concluded, MERCOSUR's external agenda became gridlocked for a prolonged period of time. Though negotiations were initiated with *Mexico, and Andean and Central American states*, eight years passed before the next FTA was signed; this time with the CAN members Peru, Ecuador, Colombia, and Venezuela.[11] Nonetheless, these negotiations became an extremely burdensome endeavour. In two occasions, April 1998 and December 2002, the parties announced that an FTA had to be reached within a specific period of time through so-called Framework Agreements. But the deadlines set forth could never be met, underlining the difficulties faced when transforming official rhetoric into tangible outcomes. Hence, the negotiations suffered from heterogeneous blocks on both sides as the Argentinean official, José Lopez Aramburu, summed up (SO 30/11/04): *"To keep the process ongoing, we tested all possible sorts of negotiations; starting in 1997 with the "4+4" method, but as talks*

---

[10] Regarding issues beyond trade, Argentina paid special attention to improved transport ways towards the Pacific Ocean, while Chile had strong interests in Argentina as the main foreign supplier of natural gas; see Chapter II.
[11] Meanwhile, the countries confirmed or extended the existing bilateral Partial Scope Agreements, usually consisting of a limited number of tariff preferences for specific periods called "historical inheritance."

barely advanced, Brazil opted for the bilateral way and renegotiated the existing Partial Scope Agreements with each Andean state; we did the same and ended up in October 1999 with modest preferences for slightly more than 1000 items." In December 2002, the process was initiated once again by Brazil. This time the Framework Agreement enabled the countries to carry out their negotiations in which ever way they saw fit. Peru was the first CAN member to initiate talks with Argentina and Brazil, and subsequently the remaining states entered into bilateral talks, ending up with two Framework Agreements (ACE 58 with Peru; ACE 59 with Venezuela, Colombia, and Ecuador) with a common legal text and bilateral phasing-out lists.

The FTA, finally signed in October 2004, was concluded mainly due to Brazil's firmness to build a strategic partnership between the regional blocks. In order to achieve this Brazil accepted broad concessions, such as maintaining the Andean Price Band System (Chapter IV), a special agriculture safeguard and long phasing-out schemes. Argentina faced an adverse scenario as its agricultural interests were relegated and defensive concerns identified in textiles and apparels were undermined by Brazil's political determination. Moreover, the minor partners Paraguay and Uruguay jeopardised the talks over the years through their lack of interest in negotiating and their claims to compensate the special treatment granted to the CAN (SO's Monti 18/11/03; Aramburu 30/11/04).

Furthermore, in 2004 the FTA with *Mexico* was anticipated to reach a conclusion. After years of delayed negotiations, the parties signed a Framework Agreement in December 2002 in order to enable each member of MERCOSUR to enter into bilateral talks with Mexico. Nonetheless, the most specific result for Argentina was an increase in the annual quota for the duty free import of 50,000 automobiles. In this case, multinational companies reached a prior agreement which the governments homologated thereafter. To date, Mexico has insisted on the exclusion of Chapters 1 to 24 involving all tariff agricultural items. According to Adrian Makuc (SO 22/04/2004), National Director of Foreign Trade Policy, a breakthrough in these arduous talks depended primarily on previous substantial agreements between Mexico and Brazil. Therefore, the local foreign trade agenda once again relied on actions taken by Brazil.

WTO, FTAA, EU-MERCOSUR and ASIA: MERCOSUR's extra regional agenda encountered similar deficiencies to those of its regional agenda, although with varying contexts. Despite this, the actions undertaken in the multilateral agenda can be seen as an exception. Although Argentina's top policy makers were not present at the *WTO* Ministerial Conference in Doha, as of 2002 the country assumed – jointly with Brazil – a protagonist role within the Development Round launched in Doha. For example, after the unsuccessful Cancun Ministerial

Conference in September 2003, Argentina convened the developing coalition G-22 (thereafter known as G-20) to discuss the group's post-Cancun agenda, urging the developed countries to continue agricultural reforms to achieve the full integration of agriculture under the WTO disciplines.[12] Even though pertinent dealings have been onerous and the firmness of the group has not always been upheld, different reports highlighted the effective (though informal) coordination between MERCOSUR and other emerging states, becoming key players within multilateral talks in general, and in agriculture trade in particular (SO Mermet 21/11/03; Narlikar/Tussie 2003).

Of a more conflictive nature than the coordination inside WTO were the activities of the MERCOSUR block in the extra-regional sphere. Although the countries shared significant interests, since 1995 the common representation within the *Free Trade Area of the Americas (FTAA)* and the *EU-MERCOSUR* talks have been marked by a lack of internal cohesion, explaining in part the impossibility to agree on latest generation FTAs that enable steady preferential access to US and EU markets. Moreover, as regards the *Asian* region, the MERCOSUR expansion toward the Pacific was behind schedule compared with regional competitors and bore hardly any fruits compared with the bilateral strategy pursued by Chile as illustrated in Chapter II.[13]

This poor record contrasts with the rhetoric sustained by the Argentinean State since 2002. Directed by Martin Redrado, chief negotiator from February 2002 to September 2004, trade diplomacy pursued a "multipolar strategy" with enthusiasm (Redrado 2003; Redrado/ Lacunza 2004). Therefore, Redrado did not overlook any opportunity to public stress the importance of all possible venues for negotiations. Technically supported by the Centre for International Economy (CEI), a think-tank attached to the Foreign Affairs Ministry, the key official put into evidence the potential benefits of ongoing, planned and insinuated talks through sophisticated impact studies which had never before been conducted domestically (CEI Studies No. 1-8). Accordingly, complete FTAs with the EU, FTAA, CAN, South Africa, and East Asian States would entail more opportunities than risks, and hence, render a significant GDP growth.

To some extent, the ambitious market access strategy put forward by Martin Redrado was shared by his Brazilian colleagues. Nonetheless, their rationale showed significant differences.

---

[12] In the end, twelve countries (including Argentina, Bolivia, Brazil, Chile, China, Cuba, Egypt, India, Mexico, Paraguay, South Africa and Venezuela) signed the final political statement of the Group.

[13] The expansion toward the Pacific had been on the table since 1997; see MERCOSUR/GMC XXV/Acta N° 01/97. Yet despite the interests announced, concrete diplomatic actions only took place as of 2003. A first partial scope agreement was signed with India in March 2005. Nevertheless, coverage was modest, entailing preferential concessions of 10, 20 and 100 percent for 450 products. Agricultural goods had to be excluded in this first round. Nonetheless, the parties are heading towards a comprehensive FTA in the future.

While the CEI Studies sustaining the outward oriented position of Martin Redrado focused on market access opportunities for export champions, Brazil cautiously examined the impact of new topics involved in international trade policy affairs. Hence, the role of Brazil was striking in the FTAA process where the South American leader acted as an adversary to US concerns. By insisting on clear US commitments to improve market access for agriculture, to abolish great subsidies in this sector, and to revise its discretional antidumping legislation, Brazil left no doubt as regards the preconditions to enter into discussions on the issues of services, state procurement, investment and intellectual property rights (OE Nogués 6/10/03). Brazil's firmness on these new topics, combined with the reluctance of both the US and the EU to grant significant concessions in the area of agriculture, hindered the conclusion of negotiations.

Had it not been compelled to coordinate positions with Brazil, Argentina would most likely have signed two bilateral treaties in a similar fashion to Chile. On the political level, the keenness of the Foreign Affairs Ministry, directed by Redrado, to accomplish negotiations was evident, above all in the case of the nearly completed talks with the EU in September 2004. In deed, critical voices from within the Ministry of Economy and the local industrial sector even suggested (in a colloquial manner) that: "Redrado would sign any paper where the media is present." Moreover, from a technical perspective it should be emphasised that Argentina's legal framework provides, in general, wider market access and a more extensive national treatment status to foreign companies than in Brazil. Therefore, an independent Argentina could have submitted more liberal offers on investments and services than was possible in coordination with Brazil.

Export and Sector Promotion

"The best industrial policy is the policy which does not exist," can be taken as the prevailing expert opinion of the 1990s (OE's Bouzas 15/06/04; Chudnovsky 25/06/04). Indeed, in contrast with other states such as Colombia, Brazil or Mexico, key policy-makers in the Ministry of Economy did not define active industrial policies after the previous protectionism system and subsidies were largely abolished as of September 1989.[14] Moreover, the market-led approach was underscored by means of the deregulation of the foreign investment regime and the privatisation of state owned companies during the period 1990-93 (Chudnovsky at al. 1996).

---

[14] The end of the former industrial regimes was embodied in the Economic Emergency Law enacted in September 1989 in the context of the macroeconomic crisis. For example, the Law caused the dissolution of the Argentina Buy Act obliging the state to favour local production. Subsequently, in 2002, Law No. 25,551 introduced this system again, but the preferential margins aimed to favor SME's are marginal in order not to contravene WTO provisions.

As of 1991, when economic openness began to pressure local industrialists due to the over-valued Argentinean Peso, increasing demands to revise the neutral policy approach led to the adoption of numerous ad-hoc alleviation measures, but did not render significant conceptual turns in the way the Cavallo Team managed economic policies.[15] The sectors with permanent border protection and specific fiscal incentives were limited to the automotive and sugar industries, nevertheless. In more recent years, slightly greater emphasis was placed on assistance mechanisms for the development of small-scale firms, for example by opening subsidised credit lines, increased labour flexibility, and technical assistance. However, the most effective "industrial" and "export promotion" policy was implemented as a result of the involuntary breakdown of the Currency Board in January 2002, that is, through a floating exchange rate regime the exchange rate remained high, decreasing production costs significantly and resulting in an export surge as of 2003.

Disregarding this currency impulse, official export promotion instruments were considered insufficient *vis-à-vis* those maintained by competing neighbours. Nonetheless, according to Bouzas/Pagnotta (2003: 69-81), the low effectiveness of national policies was not related primarily to their absence, but to the frequent modifications and erratic implementation of them, as is briefly outlined below.

Fiscal policies: Since 1985, Argentina has applied diverse tax refund systems to refund import duties, value added tax and other local taxes paid during the different processing stages. Traditionally, this system was applied in the form of export subsidies that refunded up to 20 percent on the FOB value for highly elaborated products. But in the second half of the 1990s, these rates were sharply reduced and have recently ranged between 0 to 6 percent. Moreover, since export taxes were broadly introduced after the Peso devaluation in 2002, the average export tax of 5.3 percent was higher than the average export refund (4.2 percent) in 2004, and particularly affected commodities such as cereals, oil seeds and hydrocarbons, by applying duties of up to 20 percent. Finally, the refund mechanisms available were often described as burdensome, causing notorious delays in the reimbursement of paid taxes, such as the value added tax.[16]

---

[15] In the context of vehement import pressure mainly from Brazil, by the end of 1992 Cavallo implemented wide-reaching export subsidies and industrial reconversion regimes. However, no later than 1996, these temporary supporting schemes came to an end and were not replaced afterwards; see Kosacoff/ Ramos 2001: 222-238.

[16] In order to refund or circumvent import duties on inputs, two mechanisms have been applied to date. Large scale exporters of cereals, automobiles, and steel usually take advantage of the Draw Back facility. Exporters have complained since 1991 with respect to delayed refund of duties which in the years 1991-1997 resulted in an estimated debt of US$2.5 billion (WTO 1999); see also *La Nación* 22/04/03. Conversely, SME exporters generally opt for the less bureaucratic Temporary Admission, enabling companies to get the benefit of duty free import of

Export Financing: Since 1992 export (pre-) finance assistance has been made available through the publicly owned Investment and Foreign Trade Bank (BICE). Compared with the facilities provided in Chile by CORFO and Brazil through BNDES and SEBRAE, export financing in Argentina traditionally faced three shortcomings (Bouzas/Pagnotta 2003: 75-79; Iglesias 2002). *Firstly,* BICE served mainly as a second-tier institution, with subsidies for credit lines from commercial banks. As a result, the diffusion of available credit lines depended primarily on the public relations of the banks involved. *Secondly,* the fact that BICE did not assume any responsibility for risky loans prevented interest rates for loans from being set below 10 percent; compared to 5-7 percent in Brazil and Chile. *Thirdly,* the credit volumes offered were modest up until 2003 (US$178 million) as 87 percent of total funding was dedicated to investment facilities.

Market Assistance: Since 1994, the *Export-Ar Foundation* has been in charge of Argentina's official export promotion. The promotion authority is composed of both public and private sector institutions and depends on the Foreign Affairs Ministry. Consequently, the activities are sustained in coordination with 120 official global representations. Aside from offering trade data and market studies, in recent years the Export-Ar Foundation has become a very active player in the organisation of trade missions and assistance at international fairs. Nevertheless, the major limitations of local export promotion have been related to modest resources combined with a high degree of fragmentation (BR Cerquetella 26/09/03; OE Campbell 17/11/04; Redrado 2003). For example, the Export-Ar Foundation's annual budget of around US$3 million is incomparable with foreign agencies such as the Chilean *Prochile*, who manage budgets of US$20-25 million. Nonetheless, López de Carril, former Export-AR director, claimed that official promotion expenditures would also be close to US$25 million when budget provisions for all provinces were considered (*El Clarin* 10/09/01). The dispersion of resources earmarked by the federal system was also emphasised in the central government. By 2004, four Undersecretariats held responsibilities in the area of export promotion.[17] Furthermore, the Export Promotion Guide published in November 2003 by the Undersecretariat of SME and Regional Development enlisted no less than 22 private and public institutions located in Buenos Aires dedicated to trade promotion activities.[18] Since the individual budget of these organisations

inputs.

[17] While the Undersecretariat (US) of International Commerce (Foreign Affairs) was the main executive agency, the US of Foreign Trade (Economy) defined export promotion regimes. Furthermore, the US's of SME and Regional Development and Agricultural Markets (Economy) defined and ran programs for small and agro exporters.

[18] The institutions ranged from central, provincial and city government, public banks and privately organised entities such as the Bank Boston Foundation, Gas Natural BAN, Argentina Export Foundation, the Argentinean Chambers of Export and Commerce, the Association of Importers and Exporters, the Foundation *Banco Credicoop,* etc.

tended to be modest, there was an obvious dissemination of resources, even though target groups and type of services might differ somewhat.

Summary Dependent Variable B

In general, Argentina's approach to world market integration sustained from 1985 to 2004 has been rather unsuccessful, matching the criteria for neither the Multipolar nor the Springboard model. Resuming this section, the following box highlights the observed shortcomings. The principal weakness concerned the radical change of the modes of integration in 1990, and the adoption of the customs union concept which contrasted with the domestic economic policies. Furthermore, the lack of implementation of the regional integration objectives in the scope of MERCOSUR, questioned the credibility of the emerging trading block in external negotiations. Finally, the uncoordinated protectionist measures undermined the liberal achievements without making reference to a clear heterodox strategy of inserting involved industries gradually into world markets.

Box 4.1: Summary Dependent Variable B

Unilateral Trade Regime	Regional Integration	Extra-Regional Integration	Export Promotion	Sector Promotion
1989-91: Abolishing NTBs and reducing average tariff rates from 30 to 10 percent; later 14 percent.

Exceptions: Automotive regime, and Ad-hoc protection for non-competitive sectors | In 1990, radical conceptual change to integration by shifting from the gradual, sectoral PICE to the automatic, horizontal MERCOSUR.

From 1995, problems in accomplishing the regional market and custom union. | From 1995, the lack of collective action capacity of MERCOSUR prevented the trading block from becoming an integration force inside Latin America and from establishing strong extra-regional trade relations. | Official export promotion suffered from the combination of frequent modifications of instruments, modest resources, and institutional fragmentation among promotion agencies. | Apart from the automotive regime, sectoral policies were absent, and thus, pointed at the non-existence of sectoral strategies to enhance international competitiveness. |

Despite the incoherent implementation of world market integration related policies, in quantitative terms, national exports developed rather successfully in augmenting external sales from US$8,400 to 34,500 million between 1985 and 2004. Due to the trade surpluses in 1985-90, and particularly in 2001-04, moreover, the constant trade deficits registered during the Currency Board 1991-2000 could be reverted and resulted in an overall trade surplus. From a qualitative perspective, however, the dependence on natural resources and natural resource-based manufactures persisted during the period of analysis, with only a slight decrease from 80 to 70 percent. Significant modifications of the national export structure concerned the shift from traditional agriculture goods like cereals and meat towards soybeans and its derivates, and a strong increase in hydrocarbon exports. In the area of manufactures of industrial origin, the country is challenged to broaden foreign sales in a qualitative manner because the "export champions" of the 1990s – above all in the scope of MERCOSUR – were the heavily concentrated industries of steel, automotives and petrochemicals. By 2004, the future of the local automotive industry was moreover uncertain in light of a gradual transfer of assembly factories towards the Brazilian market, which has taken place since the end of the 1990s.

4.2 State Bureaucracy: Between the Foreign Affairs and Economy Model

This section is structured along the following lines. The first subsection, *responsibilities*, outlines the division of labour in the conduction of international trade policy affairs, including the inter-ministerial coordination among the different sectoral departments involved. Then, under *resources,* there is a description of how the trade policy team has evolved in the last two decades with respect to staff size, technical expertise, and the application of civil service models. Finally, the subsection *openness* discusses consultation mechanism towards business and civil society.

Responsibilities

As in other countries in the region, trade policy has been a field dealt with mostly inside the executive branch. Even though legislative powers held the responsibility of approving international agreements, and legislating tariff and customs policies, Congress has been described as a passive actor that follows the executive branch and delegates responsibilities to it; except for specific Congress lobby actions that took place to protect the local sugar and pharmaceutical industries (Bouzas/ Avogadro 2002: 1-3).

This "top down" policy making style should not give the impression of a uniform actor who defines trade policy matters in a rather authoritarian way. From an historical perspective, trade policy affairs have been an area affected by frequent personnel changes entailing further modification regarding the ministerial structure. Accordingly, since the Secretariat of Foreign Trade was created in 1968, this area had changed its denomination and attributions no less then eleven times by 1985, sharing its denomination with Industry, Mining, Economic Affairs, Maritime Interests and International Negotiations and holding the status of Secretariat, Secretariat of State, Ministry and Military Delegation. In the same period of time, this area was run by 21 different officials.

Against this record, office holder "No. 22" represented a break through as regards the development of trade policy. In December 1985, Robert Lavagna – a widely recognised economist close to the *Peronist* party – insisted on merging the Secretariats of Foreign Trade and Industry into one "super agency" within the Ministry of Economy, thus being in charge of industrial development, SME assistance, export promotion and trade policy exchange (OE Campbell 17/11/04; 07/03/05).[19] Due to this setting, the new Secretariat of Industry and Foreign

---

[19] Minister of Economy Juan Sourrouille (father of the macroeconomic Plan Austral) at that time ignored political considerations and selected (as new head of the area with Roberto Lavagna) a member of the Peronist party inside

Trade (SICE) assumed a crucial role in the integration with Brazil, bearing in mind that Lavagna's entrance "coincided" with the Declaration of Iguaçu where both states declared the will to foster bilateral relations on a broad range of issues starting with trade, science, energy, defence, culture, etc. To understand negotiations with Brazil from a bureaucratic perspective, Carlos Bruno (OE 4/03/05) – foreign policy advisor and (Under-) Secretary of Foreign Economic Affairs (1983-1989) – divided the PICE negotiation process into three phases:

Table 4.1: Ministerial Organisation in the Negotiations with Brazil (1983-1989)

Phase	Institutional Setting	Personal Leadership
1983-1985 **Foreign Policy Approach after Return to Democracy**	The design and negotiation of furthering relations with Brazil was exclusively carried out by the Ministry of Foreign Affairs. Integration was conceptualised as a political project to overcome the historical bilateral tensions concerning border areas. Nonetheless, for the foreign policy makers it was clear that economic cooperation would be crucial for further integration in other areas.	Dante Caputo, as Minister of Foreign Affairs and Oscar Romero, as Secretary of Foreign Economic Affairs. Romero assumed the overall coordination of the process due to his close relations with Brazil's political and business elites.
1986-1987 **The Rise of the SICE and the Sectoral PICE Approach**	The SICE team was responsible for the design of the PICE. During negotiations, confirming reports mentioned the excellent relations between key officials and effective coordination in the scope of the Interministerial Task Force, where the heads of the SICE, Secretariat of Foreign Economic Affairs and National Directorate of Economic Policy (Ministry of Economy) met regularly.	Roberto Lavagna became the PICE's mastermind. Oscar Romero remained as the political coordinator of the process.
Mid-1987-1989 **The Decline of SICE and PICE**	After Lavagna left office in mid-1987 in disagreement with the anti-inflationary Spring Plan, the PICE team inside the SICE lost political support in the Economy Ministry. Based on these grounds, the MFA took charge of the process.	Carlos Bruno, new Secretary of Foreign Economic Affairs, and Beatriz Nofal, Undersecretary of the Industrial Development area in the SICE.

Source: OE Bruno 4/03/05; others: OE's Campbell 07/03/05, 17/11/04; Chudnovsky 25/06/04; SO Salafia 7/12/04

The decline of SICE as a conceptual force for regional integration was accelerated from mid-1989 when the Peronist government of Carlos Menem entered office. On this occasion, Domingo

the Radical government of Raúl Alfonsín.

Cavallo, as first Minister of Foreign Affairs tried to speed up the power shift towards his department that had begun with Roberto Lavagna's office departure. Jorge Campbell, by then head of the foreign trade division inside the SICE, recalled (OE 8/06/04): "Only 30 days after Cavallo took office, I found a draft project on my desk which sought to transfer the Foreign Trade Service (composed of hundreds of well trained trade diplomats) to Cavallo's Ministry. Considering that this initiative meant an enormous drain of knowledge on foreign markets, I obviously rejected the draft and collected legal arguments against it."[20]

Nevertheless, legal defence strategies in the Ministry of Economy soon lost force and the expansion plans developed by Cavallo were accomplished by the amended Ministerial Law of December 1992 (Law No. 24,190). With this legal base, still in force today, the principal modification was related to the transfer of the primary responsibility for the execution of trade promotion to the now denominated Ministry of Foreign Relations, International Trade and Worship (MRECIC). Through the inclusion of the Foreign Trade Service in the MRECIC, the previously weak economic branch within the ministry was significantly strengthened. Nonetheless, several factors, outlined below, prevented the MRECIC from taking over the effective responsibility for the conduction and coordination of international trade negotiations.

1) *Foreign Trade Service versus Diplomatic Cadre:* At the outset, the incorporation of the Foreign Trade Service turned out to be a laborious process in which the horizontally organised staff had to be integrated into the distinctive hierarchical composition of the diplomatic service, as exposed in the subsection *resources.*

2) *Lack of Political Leadership:* After completing the incorporation of the Foreign Trade Service, the Secretariat of Foreign Economic Affairs (responsible for international trade policy affairs) suffered from weak political leadership during the Fernando de la Rua administration (2000-02). Several verbal reports highlighted the passive behaviour and lack of knowledge on trade policy issues displayed by Horacio Chighizola, chief negotiator in 2000-01.[21] However, as of February 2002 when Martín Redrado began to vehemently seek a Multipolar strategy, the negotiations force inside the Ministry was increasingly utilised.

---

[20] Jorge Campbell's perspective was altered radically when, in 1994, Menem appointed him as new chief negotiator of the MRECIC. Due to evident reasons (ibid.), "I gladly received the team transferred by the amended Ministerial Law since it implied a clear institutional upscale for my area." Cavallo, by then Minister of Economy, conversely encountered the outcome of his ambitions. Nonetheless, Campbell concluded conciliatory, "Cavallo would have possessed the power to bring the area back, but he was coherent in leaving the Service at that point since he was really convinced that the MRECIC required a strong trade policy branch."

[21] For Carlos Bruno (OE 4/03/05), during the De la Rúa presidency, the MRECIC enjoyed the best negotiation cadre ever. But the problems were the heads of the Ministry. Both Minister Rodriguez Giavarini and Secretary Horacio Chighizola did not master this topic and did not have the necessary time to learn the international trade policy logic.

3) *Inter-ministerial Coordination:* The unstable and conflictive coordination pattern between the MRECIC and the Ministry of Economy was common to the entire study period. This was clearly seen, for instance, in the scope of MERCOSUR when officials from the Secretariat of Industry and Trade demanded the exclusive responsibility for the intra-zone regulation of the automotive trade.

Difficulties with regard to inter-ministerial relations have often been linked to the trade policy role of the Ministry of Economy and Public Works, which since May 2003 has been the Ministry of Economy and Production (MEP). Despite the amended Ministerial Law, in the 1990s the MEP remained the key trade policy agency, considering its widespread competencies in every area related to the definition and implementation of trade policies, i.e. tariffs, export promotion regime, customs polices, and trade defence. Consequently, in setting the "red lines" for international negotiations, economic policy makers remained in charge of the definition of "what" the official delegation was supposed to negotiate, while the trade diplomats in the MRECIC determined "how" to proceed in international trade policy affairs.

In practice though, this division of labour has proven far more ambiguous, since the MRECIC began depending less on external expertise due to the Foreign Trade Service. Conversely, the Ministry of Economy faced the costs of Cavallo's endeavours as Minister of Foreign Affairs and sought to compensate the loss of human resources by establishing a special MERCOSUR area. Nonetheless, the team established in May 1993 did not depend on the Secretariat of Industry and Trade, but evolved inside the Secretariat for Economic Programming.[22] As a result, in the following years the Ministry of Economy operated with two distinct teams in the scope of MERCOSUR and the pre-negotiation phase with Chile.[23] Even though officials involved in these processes reported that inter-team relations became increasingly cordial, the superposition caused an evident dissemination of resources (SO's Mosquera 7/12/04; Makuc 14/03/05; Cañellas 9/12/04). However, the Ministry of Economy's decline as a trade policy branch was to be observed principally as of 1996, when the two areas were merged in the scope of the Undersecretariat of Foreign Trade inside the Secretariat of Industry and Trade. In the following subsection, I shall demonstrate that the steady deterioration is best explained by the drastic reduction of budget resources, frequent alternating of office

---

[22] According to a confidential report by a state official, Alejandro Mayoral, former Director of Economic Policy and Central Bank official, gained the confidence of Domingo Cavallo and convinced him to create a new "bureaucratic space" within the Ministry's macroeconomic area.
[23] One team was headed by Mayoral and the other by Carlos Kesmann, the latter at that time Undersecretary of Foreign Trade.

holders and subordination of trade policy concerns against the emerging fiscal and debt crisis.[24]

To wide extents, the unsteady development of the trade policy area within the state bureaucracy was reflected in the survey carried out from March to October 2004 among 82 state officials, business representatives and experts. The survey candidates were asked: *Inside the executive branch, is there a clear division of labour in the conduction of international trade policy affairs? If not, in what areas can ambiguity be identified?* In the case of business representatives and experts, two thirds perceived a rather unclear division of labour. With regard to state officials, it is noteworthy that none of the functionaries consulted qualified the designation of responsibilities as very clear. Conversely, only one third of state officials perceived the division of labour as rather unclear.

Table 4.2: Division of Labour in International Trade Policy Affairs

	Experts (12)	State Officials (12)	Business (58)	Total (82)
very clear	1	0	2	3 (4%)
rather clear	3	7	14	24 (33%)
quite unclear	7	4	32	43 (58%)
very unclear	1	0	3	4 (5%)
No response	0	1	7	8

When asking in what areas ambiguity could be identified, additional comments mostly referred to the unclear role of the Ministry of Economy and Production (MEP) in the international trade policy area. Daniel Chudnovsky points out the following (OE 25/06/04): *"Considering that the MEP had not defined clear industrial policies as of the 1990s, the presence of the Secretary of Industry (and Trade) in international trade negotiations does not make much sense."* These critical remarks were confirmed by experienced MEP officials, commenting that too often they were assigned to participate in talks, but were not given a well defined, clear mandate based on domestic policies.

The alleged "partnership model" was undermined mainly through the manner in which topics and negotiation forums were divided between the two ministries. In fact, the MEP participated in all negotiation forums and was assigned the responsibility for domestic coordination in areas such as market access, rules of origin, state procurement, investment and defence of trade, whereas the MRECIC has been in charge of topics such as intellectual property

---

[24] For example, Jose Machinea, appointed Minister of Economy by the De La Rúa's administration, was entirely absorbed by establishing an IMF coordinated rescue package in the order of US$40 billion.

rights, services and dispute settlement.[25] According to verbal reports, the distribution of responsibilities relied mostly on the personal characteristic of key negotiators, and thus, proved difficult to identify for foreign observers. Particularly inside the MEP, the negotiation power has been in the hands of a small group of stable bureaucrats, in light of constantly changing office holders. For example, Adrián Makuc, as National Director of Foreign Trade Policy, was present in all forums and topics, and held a prominent role in the WTO framework, above all in the area of industrial goods. Furthermore, Marcelo Cañellas, as Director of Regional Trade Policy, assumed a leading position in talks in the scope of ALADI and the area of market access.[26]

Notwithstanding, the MRECIC has become the clear leading force in the major negotiation forums and topics, although certain areas of intervention are still controlled by the MEP. Therefore, the foreign affairs department became the responsible entity for the integration process with Brazil and subsequent MERCOSUR affairs as of the late 1980s, and from 2002 for the efforts undertaken in the extra-regional sphere, for instance the FTAA and EU-MERCOSUR negotiations. Contrary to the MEP, the MRECIC is clearly organised in-line with negotiation forums, and maintains a formal structure. The South American and Hemispheric Integration division is responsible for affairs inside the Western Hemisphere (e.g. MERCOSUR, ALADI, FTAA), and the Bilateral and Multilateral Affairs division is in charge of multilateral trade talks and bilateral negotiations with extra-regional partners. The nation's chief negotiator is the Secretary of Foreign Economic Affairs and Foreign Trade.

Survey results also provided a rather negative picture to the following question: *Is their close inter-ministerial coordination among the departments involved in International trade policy affairs? If not, in what areas can coordination gaps be identified?* Although state officials underlined remarkable improvements as of 2002, when new office holders entered into closer cooperation in light of the forthcoming "mega negotiations" (SO's Lipovetsky 10/05/04; Makuc 4/09/03), the opinions of experts and state officials, respectively, were less conclusive. While 10 out of 12 experts stated that coordination efforts between the MEP and MRECIC were rather or very sporadic, two thirds of the state officials considered the exchange as rather close and stable. This variance might be explained by the fact that the opinions of experts were negatively influenced by conflictive relations held in the past, whereas state functionaries emphasised the ongoing coordination efforts that had been generated since 2002, after a period of institutional turmoil in the trade policy area, as the following subsection outlines.

---

[25] For example, in the FTAA talks, a National (and Alternating) Coordinator was appointed for each topic. These positions held the responsibility for domestic consultation and data gathering from all state agencies involved.
[26] Also, agricultural topics had been in the hands of Gustavo Ideogram, National Director of Agricultural Markets.

Table 4.3: Inter-Ministerial Trade Policy Coordination

	Experts (12)	State Officials (12)	Business (58)	Total (82)
very close	0	0	1	1 (1%)
rather close	2	8	22	32 (46%)
rather sporadic	6	3	19	28 (40%)
very sporadic	4	0	5	9 (13%)
no response	0	1	11	12

The information gathered from verbal and written reports indicated that in recent years no formal body existed to facilitate inter-ministerial coordination. The previous attempts to institutionalise the inter-agency exchange are lengthy however, and embrace among others the Interministerial Council of Foreign Trade during the administration of Raul Alfonsín (1983-89), the Foreign Trade Council in the Carlos Menem administration (1990-99) and the Interministerial Committee of International Trade during the government of Fernando De la Rúa (2000-01). According to observations by Jorge Campbell (OE 7/03/05), key trade policy official in 1986-87, 1989 and 1994-99, "those who govern, normally do not attend reunions of such formal mechanisms," and "*by sending functionaries of third or even fourth rank, these special bodies lost power very fast and disappeared slowly but surely.*" Instead, Campbell concluded, "*interactions merely depend on how key officials get along with each other.*"

Accordingly, during 2003 and 2004 inter-ministerial coordination was improved due to personal efforts undertaken by the Minister of Economy, Robert Lavagna and Martín Redrado, Secretary of Foreign Economic Affairs and Foreign Trade. Together with the Secretaries of Agriculture (Miguel Campos) and Industry and Trade (Alberto Dumont), the key officials typically held coordination meetings on a twice monthly basis, although their version of events after these meetings sometimes differed, as a senior official anecdotally remarked.[27]

The national coordination prior to the sessions held in MERCOSUR's technical and decision making bodies - Working Groups, Trade Commission and MERCOSUR Group – nevertheless was described as insufficient. Ad-hoc reunions held by the so-called National MERCOSUR Section, which is composed of eight regular senior officials (four alternates) from the MEP, MRECIC and the Central Bank, are said to be poorly attended by the principal senior officials (SO Makuc 22/04/04). With regard to these institutional deficits that negatively affect

---

[27] For example, Adrian Makuc commented (SO 22/04/04) after a reunion regarding the ongoing discussion on the Multilateral System of Preferences among developing countries, that Dumont explained to his officials that in the next coordination meeting in Geneva, negotiation modalities shall be discussed. Redrado's interpretation was different, he told his staff that modalities must be defined immediately not waiting for the Geneva meeting.

the national implementation of decisions taken within the intergovernmental bodies (as exposed in the previous section), for the MERCOSUR expert, Félix Peña, the National Section should become an institutionalised body with responsibilities, a regular agenda and a MERCOSUR Directorate open to the public (Peña 2003; *El Cronista* 19/06/03).

Resources

The assignment of human and financial resources correlated with the division of responsibilities throughout the study period. In this sense, the Foreign Trade Service operated for a long time as the technical backbone of the Ministry of Economy, and thus, played a crucial role when Roberto Lavagna assumed leadership in the sectoral negotiations under the PICE framework in 1986-87. Considering that about 70 percent of trade diplomats served abroad, the remaining 50 to 100 servants provided crucial inputs used at the negotiation table, such as information on the amount each sector was able to export each year, major technical obstacles to bilateral trade and items suffering from deficits, etc. On the political and advisory level, Lavagna appointed a well trained group of committed experts who fully shared the policy approach concerning the industrial connotation of trade integration.[28] For example, negotiations on capital goods (the PICE's first and most promising protocol) were directed by Daniel Chudnovsky, a internationally known expert in national innovation systems and supply chain development (OE Rúa Boiero 26/11/04).

Mainly composed of economists and sector specialists, the unit specialising in export promotion enjoyed a special status. Experts remembered that the country's leading negotiators involved in the GATT and MERCSOUR talks emerged out of this agency, naming, for example, Nestor Stancanelli, Ambassador to Australia in 2004, Alberto Dumont as Secretary of Industry and Trade (in 2005 Ambassador to Geneva) and Rodolfo Rodriguez, acting Ambassador to South Korea (OE's Bouzas 15/06/04; Ochoa 9/12/04). Jorge Campbell, who directed the Service on three occasions, summarised (OE 17/11/04): *"The Service, professionalized in the 1970s under the former Foreign Trade Secretary, Leopoldo Tettamanti, was less rigid than the diplomatic career, considering that officials could take up work at any level, often after working for several years in the private sector. Although the recruitment system was less transparent, tending often to amiguismo, in my opinion, the staff was better prepared to participate in trade talks than teams trained in ISEN (the official Diplomatic School)."*

After the Foreign Trade Service was transferred to the MRECIC in 1993, the Ministry of

---

[28] The appointees mostly involved in the Brazil negotiations were Pedro Dudiuk as Chief Advisor, Jorge Campbell as Head of Foreign Trade Exchange and Beatriz Nofal heading the area of Industrial Development.

Economy suffered from a loss of human resources, and demanded compensation so as to manage the far-reaching competencies that the Ministry still held. To face the emerging MERCOSUR, Domingo Cavallo created an advisory team specialised in regional integration and MERCOSUR affairs, as exposed in the previous section. Nonetheless, even though the cadre financed by means of the UNDP until 1997 produced a handful of first class negotiators, from the mid-1990s the foreign trade branch inside the Ministry of Economy continuously deteriorated in the context of permanently changing office holders and sharply declining budget resources. Table 4.4 highlights the frequent personal changes and the drastic reductions of expenditures related to the "Definition of the Trade Policy Program" (50-0-17) that went far beyond budget cuts made in other budget items.[29]

Table 4.4: The Decline of the Trade Policy Branch inside the Ministry of Economy

Year	Budget $ Peso	Minister of Economy	Secretary of Industry and Trade	Undersecretary of Foreign Trade
1996	28,600,000	Domingo Cavallo+ Roque Fernandez	Carlos Sánchez* Alieto Guadagni**	Carlos Kesman Alejandro Mayoral
1997	19,000,000	Roque Fernandez	Alieto Guadagni	Alejandro Mayoral
1998	9,500,000	Roque Fernandez	Alieto Guadagni	Félix Peña
1999	7,300,000	Roque Fernandez Jose Machinea ++	Alieto Guadagni Debora Giorgi***	Félix Peña
2000	5,200,000	Jose Machinea	Debora Giorgi Javier Tizado	Gonzalo Martinez Mosquera°
2001	5,200,000	Jose Machinea R. Lopez Murphy Domingo Cavallo	Debora Giorgi****	Adolfo Ibañez°° Julio Nogues°°° Diana Tussie
2002	4,600,000 (approximately US$2 mn)	Remes Lenicov/ Juan I. Mendiguren +++ Roberto Lavagna/ Aníbal Fernandez	E.Braun Cantilo***** Carlos Leone Dante Sica	Fernando Martinez°°°° Juan Carlos Estévez
2003	7,800,000 (US$2.6 mn)	Roberto Lavagna++++	Alberto Dumont******	Hugo Polverini Guillermo J. Feldman
2004	5,000,000 (US$1.7 mn)	Roberto Lavagna	Alberto Dumont	Guillermo J. Feldman

Source: Secretariat of Finance 1996-2004/ Library Ambassador Leopoldo H. Tettamanti 2005
+ M. of Economy and Public Works   * S. of Trade and Investment   ° U.S of Trade, Industry and Mining
++ M. of Economy   ** S. of Trade, Industry and Mining   °° U.S. of Trade and Investment
+++ M. of Production   *** S. of Trade   °°° U.S. of Trade Policy
++++ M. of Economy/Production   **** S. Trade and Industry   °°°°U.S. of Trade Policy and Administration
                                     *****S. of Trade, Industry, SME and Regional Development

---

[29] Excluded from this item is the National Foreign Trade Commission (CNCE) in charge of antidumping and safeguard analysis. The staff employed in the CNCE (created in 1994) has earned an outstanding reputation and have higher salaries than functionaries from the Secretariat of Industry and Trade.

From the time when Domingo Cavallo left office in mid-1996, the areas of trade and industry have seen several office holders "who poorly defended the area in times of fiscal constraints," according to a confidential state official report from the Ministry of Economy and Production (March 2005). Hence, Alieto Guadani (1996-99) paid little attention to foreign trade policy concerns, and focused exclusively on issues linked to the automotive regime. In addition, the policy areas have been reorganised numerous times, since the change of governmental authorities typically implied modifications in the ministerial structure, as Table 4.4 underscores. Therefore, in the period between 1999 and 2003, the foreign trade area lost not only enormous financial resources, but also credibility both inside and outside the Ministry of Economy.

The survey data collected in 2004 generally replicates this irregular development of the trade policy staff (though responses did not refer only to the economy department). The survey asked: *Is the official team in charge of international trade policy affairs adequately staffed in order to comply with the technical requirements of modern international trade policy affairs (staff size, talent and experience)? If not, in what areas/issues can limitations be found?* From the answers obtained, merely 40 percent considered the official trade policy team to be adequately staffed. Surprisingly, in this regard, business officials perceived the staff to be more adequate than the state officials themselves. Nonetheless, the most negative responses stemmed from the experts since two thirds considered the human resources as rather or very inadequate.

Table 4.5: Trade Policy Staff

	Experts (12)	State Officials (12)	Business (58)	Total (82)
very adequate	0	0	0	0 (0%)
rather adequate	4	4	23	31 (44%)
rather inadequate	4	6	24	34 (48%)
very inadequate	4	1	1	6 (8%)
no response	0	1	10	11

When asking in what areas/issues limitations could be found, the most common comments were, *"the number of negotiators is too small compared with other countries;" "there are no effective civil service provisions guaranteeing a stable cadre;" "we do not enjoy the social prestige that our Brazilian colleagues do;"* and *"the generalist type prevails, while specialists in particular topics are hardly to be found."* According to the ministerial structures in 2004, trade policy expertise could mostly be found in the following agencies:

Ministry of Foreign Affairs, International Trade and Worship (MRECIC 2004a): The "economic branch" of MRECIC has grown considerably since the mid-1980s, when Argentina began to foster integration with Brazil and participated in the Uruguay Round. Today trade policies are dealt with inside the State Secretariat of Trade and Foreign Economic Affairs which accounted for four percent of the annual budget in 2004 (US$8.3 million) and ten percent of personnel (150 officials). This modest share is explained by the fact that the maintenance of foreign offices was responsible for almost 80 percent of the expenditures and 50 percent of the total staff serving in the Secretariat of Foreign Affairs. The trade policy division is composed of the Undersecretariat of International Trade dedicated to export promotion activities, and the negotiation areas are divided into the Undersecretariat of American Economic Integration and MERCOSUR Affairs, and the National Directorate of International Economic Negotiations.[30] Of the geographical divisions – South America, Hemispheric, Bilateral, Multilateral and MERCOSUR Affairs – MERCOSUR has proved to be the key area, accounting for around 25 employees, whilst the remaining offices were composed of just 5 to 13 state officials. Yet, the core team in charge of conducting and coordinating international trade negotiations has not surpassed 30-35 diplomats.

State officials in the MRECIC enjoy a distinct status in the public sector, mainly due to the steadiness of the diplomatic career, the transparent and meritocratic recruitment system and the diplomatic training in the National Foreign Service Institute (ISEN) created in 1963. Although salaries are usually higher than in other ministries, the prevailing remuneration structure renders unrewarding outcomes for those serving at the domestic level for prolonged periods of time. Luis Ariel Castillo (SO 2/12/03) addresses this issue below: *"There are no incentives to become a mastermind in WTO affairs since it simply does not pay. A Minister (the upper three ranks within the diplomatic scale) sitting on those specific topics cannot earn more than US$2,000, whereby in a Consulate in Montreal he would be paid US$8,000. Therefore, nobody wants to become a "specialist;" rather they pretend to be "generalist" like Henry Kissinger, despite the fact that we obviously require only one real Kissinger and not three hundred mediocre copies of him."*[31]

Nevertheless, even if the "generalist" serving abroad has been favoured by prevailing incentives, there is no doubt that trade policy officials in the MRECIC work in a stable environment and exhibit a sound professional background. Furthermore, the dominance of jurists

---

[30] The National Directorate of International Economic Negotiations could be nominated as unofficial Under-secretariat as it is directly under the Secretariat's office.

[31] The critical objection tends to be confirmed by quantitative data since only 17 percent of the "economic branch" belongs to the three upper diplomatic levels, while the share in foreign embassies is 26 percent. In the case of the highest level (Ambassador), the share is three and nine percent, respectively. In qualitative terms it stands out that in 2004 the crucial division of MERCOSUR affairs was headed by a second level Minister having in mind the existence of 224 higher ranking diplomats.

in the diplomatic cadre has been reduced, particularly since sector experts and economists from the Foreign Trade Service were incorporated in 1993.

Ministry of Economy and Production (Legal and Administrative Department/MEP 2004): MEP is traditionally the most powerful government department, holding the areas of Finance, Agriculture and Fishery, Industry and Trade, SME and Regional Development and 22 decentralised agencies such as the Federal Administration of State Revenues (AFIP) and the National Institute of Industrial Technology (INTI). Within this vast organisation, the Undersecretariat of Trade Policy and Administration inside the Secretariat of Industry and Trade is relatively weakly doted and has lately suffered a severe decline, as I previously exposed. Of the two National Directorates that compose the entity – Foreign Trade Policy and Foreign Trade Administration – the former holds competencies for international negotiations, while the latter is in charge of trade defence, export and import regimes. Another decentralised agency, the National Commission of Foreign Trade (CNCE) is exclusively in charge of analysis in the range of antidumping and contingency measures. In 2004, the Undersecretariat as a whole (without CNCE) had 113 employees on its payroll; with roughly 50-60 functionaries in each National Directorate.

However, the principal restriction of the trade policy area goes further than the limited number of functionaries. For Adrian Makuc as Head of Foreign Trade Policy (22/04/04), work became unrewarding in light of the severe budget cuts for travel, IT equipment and the possibility to hire qualified labour. Therefore, the motivations for the handful of experienced negotiators attending a broad range of forums and issues were drastically reduced (SO's Cañellas 9/12/04; Makuc 14/03/05). As regards civil service provisions, since 1998 (when Adrian Makuc was recruited as National Director) no further formal recruitment of executive positions and internal upgrades have taken place. Consequently, the National System for the Administrative Profession (SINAPA) – which in 1991 introduced pertinent norms on recruitment, permanent evaluations of the cadre, and a transparent promotion regime – has been evaded in practice in recent years. Since the Peso devaluation, moreover, salaries have decreased in relative terms. Inside the National Directorate of Foreign Trade Policy, two officials held in 2004 executive functions guaranteeing a monthly income of 4,700and 5,300 Pesos, respectively (US$1,500-1,800). Conversely, general staff do not reach the US$1,000 ceiling. Lastly, the single possibility for an upgrade in salary categories was to accept the new labour regime created in 2002 (Decree 1421/02) that requires the annual renewal of contracts and excludes social security.

Inside the Secretariat of Agriculture, Livestock and Fishery, developments have been slightly different (SO Petri 15/04/04). For a long time, trade policy expertise was not directly linked to the rural sector. Thus, in the aftermath of the Uruguay Round, the Agriculture department undertook serious efforts to construct a team of talented economists who mastered state-of-the-art impact assessments. In close coordination with colleagues from MRECIC, the compact team of 5-6 professionals has been leading technical discussions with Brazil and the WTO regarding formulas that can significantly lessen the distortion in agricultural trade. It should be noted, furthermore, that leading economists like Gerardo Petri and Gustavo Idigoras, who formed part of the Agriculture department, originated from the Governmental Economists cadre, a program initiated by Domingo Cavallo in 1994 and financed by the World Bank (Guidobono/Zuvanic 1997). The polemic policy maker – inspired by his experiences as President of the Central Bank where civil service is widely implemented – maintained the idea of building a stable cadre of economists who had been previously trained through the four most prestigious MA courses at the domestic level. Nevertheless, the idea was not sustained by Cavallo's successors, as after three years of practice the program was suspended.

Openness

Against the background of institutional changes inside the executive branch, the modes of interaction towards business and other society actors also underwent modifications. Concerning the incorporation of business into trade policy affairs, this can be divided into three distinct periods. The *First Phase (1986-90)* encompasses negotiations with Brazil in the PICE program where the official team performed according to the reluctance of local industrialists to open their markets to Brazilian competitors. Consequently, the negotiations on the sectoral protocols involved the permanent exchange of ideas with business entities prior to and at the negotiation reunions. Particularly, the exchange of concessions in the capital goods area implied an exhaustive consultation procedure with the national Association of Metallurgical Industry (ADIMRA), therefore taking into account the widespread defensive concerns regarding the competition from the large-scale Brazilian industry (OE Rúa Boeiro 26/11/04; Chudnovsky/ Porta 1989).

The *Second Phase (1990-95)* was marked by the policy-making style of Domingo Cavallo that implied little comprehension with regard to protectionist attitudes. Therefore, the room for business to correct the unilateral trade reforms undertaken became small (although there was an increased disposition to apply antidumping measures for particular import pressures suffered by large companies from the steel, petrochemical and paper industry, as discussed in

Viguera 1998; Calvo 2001). In the scope of MERCOSUR, the dismantling of intra-zone tariffs between 1991 and 1994 also adopted an automatic, linear and universal approach that left little margin for lobby. Also, the decision to accept the CET responded to a top down policy making pattern. While in Brazil policy evolved from a close coordination among state, business and labour organisations (Da Motta Vega 2002), in Argentina this crucial decision was made inside the executive power (Bouzas/Pagnotta 2003; Botto 2004).

Finally, the *Third Phase* began in 1995 after the *Ouro Preto* Protocol, covering the time when policy makers sought to foster trade integration with enhanced private sector participation, even when key decisions had been taken earlier. Thus, several institutions were established at the intergovernmental level to involve business in the arduous process of perfecting the regional market; i.e. through the submission of proposals to the Working Groups of the Common Market Group (GMC) and the Trade Commission (CMC), and the establishment of the MERCOSUR Economic and Social Consultative Forum that provided a special consultation channel for business and labour as of 1996.

Conversely, domestic consultation mechanisms remained informal. An exception, however, was the Private Sector Advisory Council on Foreign Trade (CACE) established in August 1998 by the Foreign Trade Undersecretary, Felix Peña (1998-99). Peña stated (OE 24/10/03) that *"CACE existed already in earlier administrations but we revived the entity since closer public-private coordination urged us to do so. Above all in 1999 when Brazil devaluated its currency, approximately 30-35 sectoral representatives met regularly (without periodicity) in the Salón Federal of the Secretariat of Industry and Trade. Usually, I started with a briefing and later the sectors commented on their worries and proposals."* Nonetheless, the activities of CACE came to an end when Felix Peña left office in November 1999, and the relation with business again relied on traditional forms of ad-hoc consultations; i.e. while the Secretariats of Industry, Trade and Agriculture in the Ministry of Economy traditionally maintained close ties with sectoral business representatives, the Ministry of Foreign Affairs was often characterised as being somewhat disconnected from domestic business concerns.

In contrast to this general perception, from 2002 Martin Redrado began to display the properties of trade diplomacy towards business and to other society actors (Redrado 2003). As indicated in the previous section, the Secretary of Trade and International Economic Affairs promoted "his" Multipolar strategy through several mechanisms, as outlined below.

Business Consultation Mechanism: From mid-2002, the MRECIC invited business entities to participate in the FTAA process, by reporting on market access negotiations and requesting detailed contributions from business on trade policy affairs. According to Nora Capello (SO 27/11/03), in charge of overall FTAA coordination, about 100 associations were consulted and, after a certain degree of insistence, the vast majority of them provided answers. Other consultations were carried out within the EU-MERCOSUR and CAN-MERCOSUR negotiations. Moreover, in November 2002, Redrado created the *National Council of International Trade,* initially comprised of 35 business and academic entities (2003: 164; afterwards this number strongly increased). Roughly eight times a year, the "makers of trade policy" met to inform on the status of ongoing trade negotiations and to analyse the official presentation with Council members.

Media Presence and CEI: As never before, a State Secretary in charge of trade policies had sufficient media presence to inform on international trade policy and disseminate the proactive Multipolar strategy followed. In order to generate academic support for the new approach, Redrado revitalised the quasi dormant Centre of International Economy (CEI) by bringing forth his former team of economists from the liberal Foundation Invest. The CEI was created in 1986 within the MRECIC scope for the analysis and deliberation of topics that affected Argentina's world market integration. Afterwards the think tank went through numerous ups and downs, and thereafter, came to principally depend on the concerns of current office holders. Accordingly, since 2002 the CEI has applied sophisticated models of general and sectoral equilibrium in order to demonstrate the benefits of deeper integration within the FTAA, MERCOSUR-UE, MERCOSUR-CAN, and with Asia, etc. (CEI Study Nr. 1-8).

Nonetheless, critical voices lamented that Redrado's personal agenda was the centre of attention (OE Nogués 06/10/03). Therefore, the permanent working relations with business did not go beyond previous administrations, for instance compared with the open attitude of the tandem partnership of Guido Di Tella as Minister and Jorge Campbell as Secretary (OE Rúa Boeiro 03/09/04). For example, although the National Council of International Trade was conceptualised as an ambit for consultation as well as to *"nourish official negotiators with concrete business proposals"* (Redrado 2003: 162), the outstanding purpose concerned the diffusion of Redrado's views on the ongoing negotiations (BR De Kojic 15/09/03; SO Makuc 22/04/04; OE Rúa Boeiro 03/09/04). One member commented that rather than meeting among policy advisors from business entities to work on specific topics, the chief negotiator pursued a more political profile by convening the entities' presidents, i.e. powerful people who know little about trade policy. Consequently, when Redrado was appointed President of the Central Bank, the Council's activities ceased.

Studying the survey data, the responses gathered in 2004 indicated that the existing consultation channels facilitated very or rather close relations between state and business. The survey asked: *Does the government closely coordinate with business associations in trade policy affairs, involving the conduction of international trade negotiations and the implementation of trade agreements? If not, in what sectors/issues can coordination gaps be identified?* As can be seen below, only 30 percent of the responses were critical. Several experts pointed at the sporadic nature of interactions and stated that only a few sectors have stable access to authorities (OE's Nogués 06/10/03; Porta 12/04/04; Sanguinetti 25/06/04; Yoguel 05/03/05). Accordingly, the large scale dominated automotive and steel sectors were said to enjoy a privileged status, while small scale manufacturers, farming units and business representatives from outside the capital city were disregarded to a certain extent.

Table 4.6: State-Business Coordination

	Experts (12)	State Officials (12)	Business (58)	Total (82)
very close	0	2	4	6 (8%)
rather close	7	7	33	47 (63%)
rather sporadic	2	3	16	21 (28%
very sporadic	0	0	1	1 (1%)
no response	3	0	4	7

Concerning transparency in trade policy affairs, experts, state officials and business representatives were asked: *In your opinion, does the government take adequate measures to ensure transparency concerning advances and possible impacts of ongoing international trade negotiations? Can improvements be noted in the last ten years as regards such?* In general, the surveyed people indicated a considerable degree of openness, though responses gathered among experts insinuated a lack of transparency regarding the governmental efforts to inform the public on trade policy affairs. Strikingly, 90 percent of consulted business representatives recognised that compared with the 1990s (making reference to the creation of MERCOSUR and the completion of the Uruguay Round) the government improved the way in which the interested public can be informed on advances and impacts of international trade policy affairs.

Table 4.7: Transparency in International Trade Policy Affairs

	Experts (12)	Business (58)	Total (70)
very transparent	0	5	5 (8%)
rather transparent	2	38	40 (62%)
rather non-transparent	6	11	17 (27%)
very non-transparent	1	1	2 (3%)
no response	3	3	6

Viewing transparency measures set forth to inform non-business actors, dialogue forums have been separated from business consultation channels. Exemptions are small business associations such as the Argentinean Agrarian Federation (FAA) representing farming units, and the Assembly of Small and Medium Entrepreneurs (APYME). Both entities explained that they felt better considered in the scope of the Civil Society Consultative Council, a mechanism created in December 2002 by the Ministry of Foreign Affairs to strengthen civil society participation in ongoing mega negotiations of the FTAA and MERCOSUR-EU (BR's Peretti 11/03/05; Del Bono 14/03/05). In part, the Civil Society Consultative Council can be seen as a response to the shortcomings of the MERCOSUR Economic and Social Consultative Forum (FCES), established by the *Ouro Preto* Protocol. The FCES, comprised of agents from the economic and social sectors of the four member states, has been described as a rather ineffective mechanism to raise the legitimacy of the integration process outside governmental spheres, mainly because the information spread was ex-post decisions, and in general, since its influence over decision making was non-existent (Nofal 1997a; Botto 2001).[32] Nonetheless, for Ambassador Hugo Varsky (SO 13/9/04), appointed Special Representative to the Civil Society Dialogue as of August 2003, *"the participation of civil society shall be vital to MERCOSUR because we pursue a different approach to integration than in NAFTA and FTAA where civil society does not really have a voice."*

However, Varsky admitted that the Consultative Council's leverage on policy making has been modest to date, even though the reunions turned out to be extremely positive experiences where pluralism and mutual respect reigned, becoming vital symbols that helped to improve the environment for the actors involved. Indeed, the space provided by the MRECIC since 2003 has been widely used. While at the outset about 30 organisations met to review the development of trade negotiations, by the end of 2004, the Council had already attracted 340 organisations from labour, environment, women's rights, small scale farming and industry, human rights, etc. The activities have been broad in scope and include a daily newsletter, plenary reunions and events in more than a dozen Sectoral Commissions on technology, small business, family farming, transportation, regional development, youth and integration, and gender, etc. (MRECIC 2004b).

---

[32] Argentina's section consists of the UIA, CAC, SRA, the labour organisation CGT, and the Consumer Association ADELCO. The FCES meets twice a year and formulates recommendations for the MERCOSUR Group.

Summary Independent Variable A1

In general, the institutional strength of Argentina's state bureaucracy in the area of international trade policy affairs has been rather low during the period of analysis. As resumed in Box 4.2, the *responsibilities* in the area of international trade policy, in particular, were imprecisely divided between the Ministries of Foreign Affairs and Economy. Regarding the variable dimension *resources*, the Foreign Affairs Ministry was strengthened by the incorporation of the Foreign Trade Service in 1993, while the Ministry of Economy lost this cadre consisting of well-trained trade diplomats. The relations maintained with business associations have, in general, been rather close, even though a stable institutional environment for state-business collaboration has thus far remained absent. From 2002, the executive branch also sought to strengthen ties with civil society actors.

Box 4.2: Summary Independent Variable A1

Responsibilities	Resources	Openness
The "partnership model" in which the Ministry of Economy defines "what has to be negotiated in international trade policy affairs", and the Ministry of Foreign Affairs decides "how" to implement those inputs, was unclear during the period of analysis, except from 1986-87 when the Secretariat of Industry and Foreign Trade became responsible for designing the innovative PICE approach. Given the absence of clear policy guidelines, the foreign affairs department gained weight and defined integration polices based on limited inter-ministerial consensus.	While the Foreign Affairs Ministry was strengthened by the incorporation of the Foreign Trade Service as of 1993, the trade policy branch inside the Economic Ministry has undergone a steady deterioration since 1996.	Since the mid-1990s, the executive branch has made considerable improvements in informing non-state actors on trade integration matters and incorporating business entities in the policy formulation, even though institutionalised coordination has been missing so far.

4.3 The Institutional Weakness of Business Associations

This section is structured in accordance with the variable dimensions of the Independent Variable A2. The first subsection, Institutional Leadership, analyses the domestic attempts to establish a widely recognised peak or "umbrella" association, capable of coordinating economic policies between the leading sectoral and regional representatives. It further describes the institutional mechanism aimed at the intermediation of trade interests among leading sectoral and regional representatives. The subsection two, Organisation Strength, assesses the professionalism involved in business advocacy, stressing the domestic pattern of financing, participatory behaviour, and in-house trade policy expertise. The final subsection summarises the results and provides an overview of the business representation pattern analysed from 1985 to 2004.

Institutional Leadership

In Argentina, business associations assumed, from an early stage, a leading role in the defence of private entrepreneurship interests (Acuña 1995; Birle 1995). The process of creating national sector organisations dates back to the middle of the 19th Century when the agrarian elite and traders in Buenos Aires established the Argentinean Rural Society (SRA) in 1866 and the Buenos Aires Traders' Union (BOLSA) in 1854. Meanwhile, towards the end of the century, farmers became the main suppliers of agrarian products to European markets; furthermore, in 1887 the local manufacturers created a specialised advocate with the Argentinean Industrial Union (UIA). Other sectoral peak entities were founded before 1930 such as the National Chamber of Commerce (CAC 1924) and the Argentinean Banking Association (ABRA 1919).

Nevertheless, serious problems arose when capitalists sought to bring together distinct sectoral perspectives. Table 4.8 below illustrates the main attempts of entrepreneurs to establish multisectoral representation structures since the 1950s.

Table 4.8: Development of Multisectoral Representation Structures since the 1950s

Type	1950	1960	1970	1980	1990	2000
Peak Associations	CGE * __ _____			_____		
Coordination Forums	ACIEL _____(58-73)					
	APEGE __ (75-77)					
	G-11 (including labour)				__(84-85)	
	G-17				__(87-88)	
	MENA (mainly SME associations)				_____(83-89)	
	Grupo Regente (mainly SME associations)				__(88-89)	
	G-8					_____(88-99
	Grupo Productivo					___(99-01)
Business Councils	G-9 or Industry Captains				_____(83-91)	
	CEA (1976-2002)					
	AEA** (2002 -)					

Source: Birle 1995: 201 (data up to 1991); own elaboration from 1991
* dissolved between 55-58 and 1977-1984 ** AEA: merger between the CEA and the Invest Foundation

Table 4.8 indicates a marked fragmentation inside the domestic business sector that could be overcome only temporarily. Since the political and economic environment for collective business actions has varied greatly over the last 50 years, much of this fragmentation can be explained by endogenous business factors. Subsequently, I next summarise the most relevant aspects (Alberti/ Acuña/Golbert 1984; Acuña 1995; Birle 1995; Viguera 1998; Robin 2001).

Ideological Struggles (1952 – 1982): In forming the Coordinated Action of Free Business Institutions (ACIEL) from 1958 to 1973 and the Permanent Assembly of Entrepreneurial Entities (APEGE) from 1975 to 1976, large business entities tried to counteract the General Economic Confederation (CGE) created in 1952. Together with the General Workers Organisations (CGT), the CGE was created as the "civilian partner" of Juan Domingo Perón (President from 1946-1955 and 1973-1974) who put forward a state interventionist model aimed at creating import substitution industries and strengthening organised labour. Therefore, the peak association representing mainly SME's oriented to the domestic market depended heavily on the political support of the Peronist party, and thus, was dissolved twice under military ruling. Conversely, large scale business failed to overcome interest gaps between the exporting landowners, the banking sector, and manufacturers. Consequently, during the "business friendlier" military regime from 1976 to 1983 where market oriented policies were initiated, state-business collaboration took place only in informal spheres through which a limited group of finance and industrial companies prospered at the expense of the rest of the economy.

Return to Democracy (1983-1989): In 1983 collective business attempts continued to be arduous, although the new democratic regime provided space for national consensus. With the end of violent ideological struggles among social movements and military forces, the government of Raul Alfonsín expressed its will to search for broad consensus related to economic reactivation programs and the control of inflation through price and salary agreements, as shown by the Austral and Spring Plans in 1985 and 1987, respectively. Nevertheless, while business factions failed to build reliable multisectoral interlocutors (for example with the G-9, G-11, G-17, MENA, and REGENTE), the leading labour association, CGT, acted as a solid rock throughout the Alfonsín government.

Towards a Business-Led Model (1990-1997): By getting rid of the main principles related to the Peronist administrations, Carlos Menem bet his political resources on the relationship with large-scale business. Indeed, the ambitious privatisation program, the deregulation of foreign investment and the macroeconomic stability achieved provided the grounds for enhanced unity among entrepreneurs. Thus, the G-8 - comprised of the eight leading sector associations from industry, agriculture, banking, trade and construction – reached, in 1991, a broad internal and external recognition as an interlocutor of the economic reforms implemented by the Domingo Cavallo team. The privileged status of the G-8 was based on the fact that the informal alliance embraced all relevant sectors, and on the unconditional political support for the recently initiated structural adjustments. Conversely, opposing voices from domestic market oriented industries were virtually excluded from the decision making process.

Winners and Losers of Economic Reforms (1998-2002): During the second Carlos Menem administration (1995-1999), the inter-sectoral consensus regarding the economic model to follow became increasingly undermined by opposing sector perspectives inside the G-8. Table 4.9 presents the rival factions which emerged, clearly reflecting the winner and loser groups of the prevailing economic policy.

Table 4.9: Winners and Losers of the Economic Reforms of the 1990s

	"Winners"	"Losers"
Sectors	Finance; trading; warehouses; privatised public utilities such as suppliers of water, gas and electricity and telecommunications; industrial commodities	Industry and SME in general; textiles apparel, footwear and metal works in particular
Properties	Mainly transnational companies Large-scale firms	Mainly domestic companies Small, medium and large sized firms
Sectoral Entities	ABA (Banking) BOLSA (Finance, Trading), CAC (Commerce)	UIA (Industry); to a lesser extent: CRA (Agriculture), CAC (Construction)
Forums	Argentinean Entrepreneurial Council CEA (1967)	Productive Group (1999)
Policy Rationale	The currency board regime favoured foreign capital inflows due to international credibility and US$ assets. Moreover, the highly valued currency enabled low-cost imports and high set tariffs for public utility companies. Privatised firms enjoyed flexible labour regimes negotiated on firm levels.	Despite macroeconomic stability, credits for local industry remained scarce and expensive. The highly valued currency decreased competitiveness of local production. Most industrialists still faced rigid labour norms that had been established decades ago at a sectoral level.

In 1999, when the country entered into a four-year recession and Brazil implemented drastic currency devaluation, the opposing factions began pursuing individual means of lobbying. As was highlighted in my MA thesis on business participation in democratic regimes, these advocacy styles differed remarkably (2001). The "winners" sought to defend the achievement of the 1990s increasingly in informal spheres provided by the CEA, a business council sustained by leading executives from about 30 large-scale companies from banking (e.g. Bank Boston, HSBC-Roberts), public utilities (*Telefónica, Aguas Argentinas),* holding groups (IRSA and Excell), food processing (ARCOR, Unilever, Quickfood), petrochemicals (Dow

Chemical, YPF) and the steel giant Techint Group. In this context, the UIA's traditional industrialist voice weakened since its power base originated from the large-scale steel, petrochemical and food processing industries. Hence, the industrial peak entity evolved into the leading advocate of the "loser group" which, in 1999, created the so-called Productive Group, an informal alliance composed of threatened industries, agricultural and construction entities that became the main opponent of the Currency Board.[33] However, the breakdown of the fixed exchange rate regime in January 2002 cannot be ascribed to the influence of this heterogeneous and loosely organised alliance of "loser factions," but rather reflected the advocacy power of large-scale companies associated to the CEA, considering that the currency board endured for eleven years despite sharply increasing foreign debt.

Post Convertibility (2002-2005): The drastic Peso devaluation caused the former conflicts between the "winning banks" and the "losing industry" to vanish somewhat, while the previous intra-industrial heterogeneity came into view again. Therefore, while the Argentinean Entrepreneurship Association (AEA), founded in May 2002, represented the "establishment" formerly associated to the CEA, the UIA moved into the centre of controversies. Instead of bringing industrialists together, the devaluation and debt crisis caused conflicts which were stalled by the entity's presidential elections in April 2003. For the first time in 12 years and for the second time since the institution's reform in 1981, members failed to establish a consensus list between the competing internal movements – the Argentinean Industrial Movement (MIA) composed of large-scale sectors and the National Industrial Movement (MIN) representing SME's.

Nevertheless, more than ever before, conflict lines went beyond divergences between MIN and MIA and were explained by a rather diffuse mix of political allies, personal rivalries and macroeconomic preferences (OE Ochoa 9/10/03; BR's Pons 10/09/03; Pegoraro and Kait 15/09/04; *El Clarín* 20/04/03). After years of passive behaviour in the UIA, the country's main steel company *Techint* interfered in business politics by supporting the "industrialist list" which argued in favour of a new, more state-led development approach after the distinctive market-led concept followed during the 1990s. Therefore, the oppositional group headed by Guillermo Gotelli, a footwear industrialist, represented not only the majority of the MIN but also influential MIA elements, such as the Industrial Union of Buenos Aires and ADIMRA, the peak association

---

[33] The entities associated in the Productive Group (UIA, CAC and CRA) demanded measures to reactivate the threatened sectors by investment in public works, increased access to credits, safeguard measures, etc.; see *Declaración de Tigre* June 23, 2000 signed by Eduardo Baglietto (CAC), Manuel Cabanellas (CRA) and Osvaldo Rial (UIA). Nonetheless, the polemic leader of this opposing movement against the prevailing economic model became José Ignacio de Mendiguren, a medium sized entrepreneur from the clothing industry who acted from 1999 to 2001 first as Vice-President of the UIA and then from April 2001 as formal head of the Industrialist Union.

of the metal industry. On the other hand, the official and finally winning "consensus list" was led by Alvaro Gaiani, President of the food industry entity, COPAL. Other important members of the winning coalition were the associations representing automobiles (ADEFA), the petrochemical industry (CIQIP) from the MIA, and the Association of Paper and Cellulose Producers (AFCP) from the MIN.

UIA elections took place one month before the presidential election where Nestor Kirchner (the left-wing candidate from the Peronist Party) defeated Carlos Menem, who traditionally maintained close political allies with the winning group, for example with Alvaro Gaiani (COPAL) and Hector Massuh (AFCP). In the aftermath, UIA authorities sought to agree with Nestor Kirchner even though the elected State President began putting forward a notably anti-Menem discourse. The losing "industrialist list" supported by the Techint Group and its president Paolo Rocca, on the other hand, held a clear advantage due to their closer political relations and conceptual coincidences with Nestor Kirchner. Thus, to further undermine the UIA's leadership, the opposing group established an independent organisation called the "Industrialists Group" and started to organise several "Federal Industry" events outside of Buenos Aires. As a result, both industrial streams struggled during 2003-04 for acknowledgment as the leading force within national manufacturing. Nevertheless, in April 2005 before the internal elections took place, conflicts were overcome as the opposing factions agreed on the establishment of a consensus list.[34]

Intermediation of Trade Policy Interests

Regarding the trade policy area, the lack of intermediation capacity inside the business sector went beyond the problem of absent multisectoral mechanisms where opposing trade policy interests could have been effectively coordinated. During the period of analysis, distinctive features of intra-sectoral fragmentation hindered the pursuit of coherent business proposals, as I outline below, dividing these into agricultural and manufacturer interests.

Manufacturers' Interests: As of 1981, when the UIA moved away from representing individual firms and adopted a mixed system of regional and sectoral chambers, the industrial entity became the single representative of local manufacturers. But this institutional turn made the UIA an unreliable trade policy interlocutor for the government because internal heterogeneity enhanced, considering that two opposing streams emerged from within the entity (Birle 1995;

---

[34] Since the Industrial Group had no chance to reach the majority and the sectors inside the official coalition maintained their interest to improve relations with Nestor Kirchner, both factions were eager to find a consensus.

Schwarzer 1998). While the "liberal" large-scale branches of the automotive, petrochemical, steel, metal and food industry organised inside the MIA, the MIN movement represented the inward-looking sectors made up of regional associations out with Buenos Aires and SME dominated entities from the apparel, footwear, plastic, paper, graphic, and metallurgic industries, among others. Even though the institutional weight of the MIA had traditionally been superior, since the 1980s the UIA's official position had to take into account the concerns of the MIN faction in order to prevent the drainage of small and medium size manufacturers and regional chambers to other industrial chambers.[35]

Therefore, in 1986 the UIA was unsupportive of the Alfonsín administration's pursuit of deeper integration with Brazil, and from 1987, set forth (encouraged by the Bretton Woods Institutions) a gradual economic opening through unilateral reforms (Calvo 2001). On these heterogeneous grounds, state authorities established a privileged dialogue with the so-called "Industry Captains" where the principal industrial leaders were informally organised.[36] Nonetheless, the majority of these sectors similarly supported the official strategy only faint-heartedly, and defensive points of view emerged from within certain sectors, such as the steel and automotive industry (Campbell et al. 2000: 102). Accordingly, it would be wrong to qualify the large-scale industry associated inside the MIA faction as truly liberal, considering the traditional close ties maintained with state authorities in order to improve access to public contracts, soft loans, subsidies, and to guarantee the preservation of domestic markets (Birle 1995; Calvo 2001; Sidicaro 2003).

In the 1990s, nonetheless, the resistance against trade liberalisation lowered. In particular, the successful control of inflationary pressures from 1991 supported the market-led approach promoted by the economic team of Domingo Cavallo. Consequently, the UIA authorities opted for a strategy of following the official course so as to maintain privileged relations with the Cavallo team.[37] Nevertheless, in light of this conceptual turn, the UIA's intermediation capacity

---

[35] To provide space for concerted action, the factions decided on a majority-minority electoral mechanism that allowed the nominally weaker MIN to be represented in the directing bodies. Due to this arrangement, the big industrialists' movement, MIA, occupied the UIA presidency except during the terms of 1991 – 1993 (Israel Mahler from the metallurgic industry) and 2001 – 2003 (José Ignacio de Mendiguren from the apparel industry).

[36] Industrial Captains were Jorge Haiek (SOCMA), Eduardo Braun (Astarsa), Ricardo Zinn (Sevel), Guillermo Kuhl (Scania), Jaime Nuñez (Bagley), Vittorio Orsi (Sade), Miguel Roig (Bunge y Born), Carlos Tramutola (Propulsora), Carlos Bulgheroni (Bridas), Alberto Hojman (BGH), and Sebastián Bagó (Bagó), among others.

[37] In 1989-91, when unilateral reforms were implemented, the UIA was headed by Gilberto Montagna of COPAL. His liberal orientation was questioned inside the UIA as several branches suffered from lowered border protection. Thus, UIA members voted for Israel Mahler in 1991 as representative of the threatened metal working industry (ADIMRA). But opposition against trade reforms did not last long and practically disappeared when Domingo Cavallo assumed the post of Minister of Economy. Consequently, the following presidencies of Jorge Blanco Villegas (1993-97), Claudio Sebastiani (1997-98), and Alberto Alvarez Gaiani (1998-99) where marked by a pro-governmental attitude.

in trade policy affairs did not significantly improve, and instead, gave place to two tendencies which further undermined the UIA's credibility as an interlocutor of the national industry. On the one hand, several threatened sectors organised inside the MIN such as textiles, apparel, footwear and several metallurgical branches made use of the "outside advocacy" method by carrying out lobby activities through direct, bilateral channels with the government, and thus, distanced themselves from the internal bodies in charge of inter-sectoral coordination (OE Rua Boeiro 26/11/04; BR Martinez 8/03/05). On the other hand, the "inside advocacy" approach was applied by few sectors and served to obtain official support for specific interests. In this case, the often protectionist interests of the entities representing sugar and paper (MIN) and the steel, automotive, food processing and petrochemical industry organised inside the MIA stand out.

Nonetheless, it is crucial to state that all branch associations have been frequent users of direct channels towards the government. In general terms, the UIA has rarely been perceived as an institution where trade policies are debated and coordinated among associate membership, rather it has been seen by both the public and the private sector merely as a temporary option to follow particular interests, depending on who holds power in the UIA Executive Board and which sector maintains close relations with office holders. Principally, for the large-scale automotive and steel industry, the importance of the UIA as a lobby organisation was limited because both sectors maintained fluent relations both at a company level and through their branch organisations CIS (steel industry) and ADEFA (automobiles).

Agribusiness' Interests: The interests of local agribusiness have mostly been represented by individual firms, while collective business action in the process of opening foreign markets was largely absent (OE Campbell 17/11/04). Therefore, the *Coordinator of the Food and Beverage Industry (COPAL)*, founded in 1976 and representative of 20 branch chambers, was the most active entity, although it often faced internal divergences between groups pursuing the preservation of the domestic market, like the sugar producers or the processed food industry, and export-oriented food commodities such as oleaginous, cereals or meat. The profile of the *Argentinean Export Chamber (CERA),* created in 1927, does not resemble that of an entity that unifies sectoral positions and advises official negotiators at the negotiation table. Instead, CERA has played a role as a promoter of general export concerns, for example, in claiming the refund of duties paid, the improvement of customs procedures or the modernisation of local ports, etc. Concerning the allegedly powerful farmers from the Pampa zone, the existence of no less than four peak organisations stands out: *Argentinean Rural Society (SRA), Argentinean Rural Confederations (CRA), Argentinean Agrarian Federation (FAA),* and the *Confederation of Rural Cooperatives (CONIAGRO).* The lack of a common institutional framework hindered in the past the collective representation of agriculture concerns on the national policy level. In addition, the administrative capacity of these traditional rural entities often does not match with the technical requirements of international trade policy affairs (SO Carpinacci 25/11/03; BR Tomás 14/11/04).

Against this background, the creation of the Institute of International Agriculture Negotiations (INAI) in 1999, in the aftermath of the failed WTO Ministerial Conference in Seattle, represented an institutional novelty. Founded by five entities representing cereals and oleaginous crops, in recent years INAI has assumed the leadership in convening rural organisations. For Gerardo Gargiulo (2003: 53), the emergence of this agricultural policy institute is in part explained by the fact that the leading entities such as the SRA and COPAL resisted the adaptation of their policy advisory structures in accordance with the challenges of current agricultural trade controversies. Instead, the booming food commodity sectors were the ones that faced up to the fact that *"the international developments of production, consumption behaviour, prices and the conservation of natural resources and technology were not favouring Argentina,"* as a young INAI professional summed up (BR Tomás 17/11/04). Therefore, directed by Ernesto Liboreiro, the think-tank strengthened its analytical skills in the multilateral sphere, the emerging regional talks, and issues related to transgenic food and bio-safety. Moreover, since 2002, INAI has been responsible for the Agriculture Round Table where private and public sectors deliberate on current issues of agriculture talks, i.e. export subsidies and credits, quota systems and liberalisation formulas discussed within the WTO scope. Even though many rural entities were hesitant in committing to regular participation, the round table evolved into a lively common place that helped to increase the awareness of risks and opportunities in trade talks and to improve public-private coordination (BR's Liboreiro 29/04/04; Tomás 17/11/04; SO's Petri 15/04/04).

Organisational Strength

Based on a survey with 58 business associations (selection), in this subsection I will shed light on aspects related to the organisational strength of private sector representatives, stressing the importance of diversified revenues, reliable payment of membership dues, active member participation, the existence of permanent staff and in-house trade policy expertise.

Diversification of Association Revenues: Business chambers in Argentina rely primarily on the payment of affiliation dues. Only six of the organisations consulted indicated that in 2004 at least 40 percent stemmed from other sources. Even though the majority (56 percent) had extra revenues, the income collected through service providing and events did not surpass 10 percent.

Consequently, it can be assumed that such activities are modest or non-existent and that business associations in Argentina consider themselves to be exclusively lobby organisations (see also OE Rúa Boeiro 26/11/04), disregarding observable exceptions in the case of the associations of milk producers (UGT), fruits (CAFI), small-scale farming (FAA), importers and exporters (AIERA) and books, where service providing is an integral part of the entity's action.

Table 4.10: What share of revenues originates from other than affiliation dues?

More than 40%	11-40%	0-10%	0%	No Response
6 (11%)	2 (4%)	33 (62%)	12 (23%)	5

In the UIA, service supply is largely absent and predominantly based on a few external funding activities such as the SME-Observatory supported by private, public and international donors and the Euro Centre of Enterprises Cooperation within the EUs AL-Invest Program.[38] However, to maintain its administration, more recently the UIA has depended on incomes from the Annual Industrial Conference. Since 1994, Argentina's main industry chamber is responsible for this event, where state presidents, ministers, state secretaries, academia, and leading entrepreneurs present their points of view on current situations faced by local industry. According to data from 2000, the event generated additional revenues in the amount of US$450,000, representing roughly 60 percent of income in that year (*El Clarín* 18/12/2000). However, verbal reports indicated that in recent years only 20-30 percent of total revenues have originated from the Annual Congress (BR's Biglieri 17/09/03; Lafitte 23/09/04).

Predictability of Association Revenues: Most entities benefited from a regularly paying membership, i.e. 50 percent of the answers stated that 80 to 100 percent of members meet the payment deadline regularly. A rather low share (eight chambers) acknowledged serious problems in ensuring that their members comply with the established financial obligations, i.e. less than 50 percent habitually disburse the affiliation dues. Héctor Kolodny from the Argentinean Chamber of Clothing Industry (CIAI; 08/09/04) states somewhat anecdotally that *"the first expenditures that firms stop paying during times of crisis are the free coffee for employees and chamber's affiliation dues."*

---

[38] SME-Observatory is a technical unit created in 1996 to conduct surveys and data gathering on the economic realities of SME's. Founding members are the Techint Group, UIA Foundation, Province of Cordoba, Secretariat of Science and Technology, and several public banks. The Euro Centre of Enterprises Cooperation is an organism co-financed by the European Commission and UIA helping in the internationalisation of Argentinean SME's and industries and creating strategic alliances with European counterparts.

Table 4.11: What share of membership regularly meets the payment deadline?

80-100%	50-79%	20-49%	less than 20%	no response
29 (54%)	17 (31%)	5 (9%)	3 (6%)	4

Other reports confirm Kolodny's observation, indicating that in previous years effective paying habits were considerably worse than the survey results suggest. Above all, traditional industrial associations suffered a severe economic loss during the recession that took place between 1999 and 2002. Most entities like the UIA were obliged to carry out debt rescheduling to regularise economic relations with members.[39] Drastic methods had to be implemented by ADIMRA, the national representative of the metallurgical industry. Since the sector entered into a deep crisis in the 1990s, most members disappeared or refused to pay their dues, as Alejandra Cerquetella from the Trade Department explained (BR 26/09/03). To prevent institutional collapse, in 2001 ADIMRA introduced a "mandatory contribution" of one percent of the salary volume through a collective labour agreement with the sectoral trade union, UOM.[40] Although its implementation has been polemic, many chambers began to consider the cost and benefits of the new financing scheme; i.e. several sectors such as the plastic, graphic and glass industry have since followed suit. Adrian Biglieri, UIA Executive Director, explains (BR 17/9/03); *"in the aftermath of the deep crisis we underwent, our members see the mandatory contributions as a solution to guarantee them sound revenues; it is a matter of fact that many countries such as Brazil, France and Spain use these systems, why should we not follow those successful examples?"*

Participatory Behaviour of Member/Business: When asking about the properties of internal policy making, around 60 percent of the entities qualified their members' participation as rather or very active. Conversely, 24 and 14 percent of chambers consulted assessed the behaviour as rather passive or very passive, respectively. In 32 of a total of 58 entities, responses made reference to activities inside the Foreign Trade Commission, while the remaining quorums concerned the participation in the Board of Directors, since a specialised body was absent. In sum, the results provide a scenario in which members normally attend meetings, which generally take place twice a month, and submit technical proposals.

---

[39] Nevertheless, the most effective method became the polemic internal election in April 2003 where most chambers cancelled their debts to be enabled for voting, as Roberto Pons from the Trade Department stated, BR 10/09/03.
[40] The implementation of the agreement still faced difficulties in 2003-04 since firms inside the fragmented metal industry rejected the mandatory solution and other competing chambers saw the mandatory solution as illegal and/or also claimed part of the income; see *El Cronista* 9/09/03; BR's Romiro 10/11/2003; Ruiz from CAMIMA 28/02/05.

Table 4.12: Business/ member participation in trade policy affairs

	Experts	State Officials	Total Experts/ State Officials (24)	Business* (58)
very active	0	0	0 (0%)	15 (27%)
rather active	2	2	4 (17%)	19 (34%)
rather passive	8	6	14 (61%)	14 (25%)
very passive	2	3	5 (22%)	8 (14%)
no response	0	1	1	2

* Responses refer to the behaviour of members inside the internal bodies of each chamber.

Nonetheless, these rather positive impressions contrast with the impressions gathered from experts and state officials concerning the behaviour of business entities in international trade policy affairs. About 80 percent of the responses suggested a widespread passivity. Several statements underlined that activity prevails merely in a negative sense, i.e. in the search for the preservation of home markets. Indeed, out of the most active chambers mentioned – CIQyP (petrochemicals), CIPA (food brands), COPAL (food processing in general), ADIMRA (metal industry), CIS (steel industry), CILFA (national laboratories), CICA (footwear), and FITA (textiles) - only COPAL and CIQyP represented clearly outward-oriented industries.[41] When analysing the minutes of meetings provided by the MERCOSUR Department of UIA and the Agriculture Round Table organised by INAI – the liveliest common places during the most recent trade talks – the results also indicate a somewhat limited involvement of business factions.

Table 4.13: MERCOSUR Department and Agriculture Round Table 2002-2004

	Average Attendance	Min/Max	Regularly Participating Entities
UIA MERCOSUR Department 2003 – 2004	15 (22 non-attendance)	11/19	As of the 1990s: CIQyP, CIPA, COPAL, ADIMRA, CIS/ Techint More recently: FAIGA, AFARTE, CAIE, CIAI, CICA and CILFA
INAI Agriculture Round Table 2002-2003	14 business 10 state or academia	13/32	80-100% : INAI, CERA, SRA, CIARA-CEC 50-80%: CIL, CERA, CIPA, Cereal Stock markets Buenos Aires/Rosario

Source: UIA - Minutes number 5, 10, 15, 20, 25, 30 out of 33 and 39 meetings held in 2003 and 2004, respectively; INAI – all minutes of the 11 events organized during 2002-03.

---

[41] Specific comments were made by state officials related to business consultation procedures. For example, reports referred to market access talks with the CAN, the adherence of new WTO members and the state procurement negotiations with MERCOSUR and the EU, making it clear that only between 10 and 15 percent out of the universe consulted responded to the deliberations; see Monti for CAN market access 18/11/03; Alonso for state procurement 4/12/03; Mermet for WTO adherences 20/11/03.

Regarding decision making inside the UIA, the MERCOSUR Department has evolved in recent years into the most popular deliberation body.[42] Even so, during 2003 and 2004 the number of non-attendances (22 on average) clearly exceeded the number of attending members. From an intra-temporal perspective, the recent participation by members seemed to nevertheless be higher than during the 1990s, when only five to six representatives from the petrochemical (CIQyP), food processing (CIPA, COPAL) and steel and metal works (ADIMRA, CIS/ Techint) regularly attended weekly meetings, according to Rodolfo Rúa Boeiro (OE 26/11/04), Department Secretary from 1995 to 1999. Accordingly, in 2003-04 regular participation could be expanded, embracing the representatives of graphics (FAIGA), electronics (AFARTE; CAIE), apparel (CIAI), footwear (CICA) and national laboratories (CILFA). Strikingly, the Sugar Producers Centre (CAA) – the only sector excluded from intra-MERCOSUR trade – is represented by Jorge Zorreguieta who chaired the MERCOSUR Department since the late 1990s.

In contrast to the industrial trade policy deliberation, the Agriculture Round Table is still a rather young enterprise. According to INAI's Meeting Minutes, the eleven meetings held in 2002-03 had an average participation of 24 people, of which 14 where from agricultural organisations. Thus, the number of regular participants was rather limited, and mainly included large company representatives of cereals, oleaginous crops, beef and dairy products. Numerous organisations of small and medium sized producers and representatives in the range of fruits, vegetables, meats, food brands, flowers, honey producers, coffee, tea, spices, etc. to date remained reluctant to participate in the Agriculture Round Table.

Strikingly, large companies also exhibited a rather passive trade policy advocacy. In this regard, the assessment of Christiane de Kojic, since 1962 trade policy advisor of the influential Chamber of Food Manufactures (CIPA), can be considered as highly valid. Asked about the members' participation, de Kojic stated (BR 15/09/03), *"As members' collaboration in our Foreign Trade Committee was close to zero, I decided to proceed through e-mail, to inform the companies on official papers, and to consult them only on specific policies where they might be directly affected. As they usually do not reply, I define our chamber's position and send notes to the Ministries of Economy and Foreign Affairs; astonishing as it may be, even our largest companies do not hire trade policy specialists. Only Molinos (food industry giant; www.molinos.com.ar) hired a talented professional with a MA from FLACSO, though their*

---

[42] In theory, the UIA Trade Department is also responsible for the area of International Trade Negotiations. Nonetheless, since the Mercosur Department was established in 1993, the area increasingly passed over to the MERCOSUR Department, for two main reasons. Firstly, external negotiations were no longer conducted unilaterally, but began to be coordinated in the MERCOSUR scope. Secondly, the MERCOSUR Department has been the only body that held plenary sessions and not small issue commissions, and thus, became the place to be to learn about the latest news.

executives do not take her comments really into account."

Size of Staff and Trade Expertise: Obviously, the participatory behaviour is closely associated with the size and professionalism inside business organisations. In this regard, the results generated by the survey present a clear picture. In general, local entities operate with moderate staff bases. Almost 50 percent consisted of five or less employees, usually comprising a Managing Director and one or two assistants. Only ten organisations had more than ten employees on their payroll, and just two had more than 20. In this respect, the UIA headed the group with 44 employees, followed by ADIMRA with roughly 30 workers. Other rather large organisations were the pharmaceutical entities CILFA, CAEME and COOPERALA with 24, 14 and 11 employees, the Chamber of Plastic Industries CAIP (18), the Union of Public Sector Suppliers (18), Chamber of Petrochemical Industries CIQYP (15), Chamber of Books (14) and the Textile Industry Federation FITA (13). Albeit no specific data was provided by COPAL, SRA and the Chamber of Commerce (CAC), their headquarters most probably comprises more than ten employees, but less than in the case of the UIA and ADIMRA, according to what could be observed during visits to their offices.

Table 4.14: What is the size of permanent staff?

more than 20	11-20	5-10	1-5	no response
2 (4%)	8 (14%)	19 (35%)	26 (47%)	3

Verbal reports stated that principally large industrial entities cut down the personnel as of the 1990s. Juan Pablo Laffitte (BR 23/09/04), UIA Administrative Director as of 1990, commented that in the last 14 years total staff was reduced to about 20 percent. As regards technical staff, Rodolfo Rúa Boeiro, recalled his time as head of ADIMRA's Technical Department that coincided with the PICE program (26/11/04): "By 1986-87, I had attended sectoral negotiations as head of the Commission for International Negotiations in the UIA Trade Department (in representation of ADIMRA). We used to hold weekly meetings with close to 30 people, 20 of them were experts like me and Jose Maria Fumagalli (well-known expert from the petrochemical industry); only as far as ADIMRA, my team was made up of 16 persons, 12 of them professionals, i.e. economists and engineers, etc." In 2003-2004, ADIMRA's technical staff in the Departments of MERCOSUR, Foreign Trade and Statistics totalled two persons each, after it had almostceased to exist towards the end of the decade in light of the economic crisis experienced.

In general terms, the number of experts involved in trade policy advocacy correlates with the modest size of the staff shown in Table 4.14. In no less than 57 percent of the entities, none of the employees were specifically assigned to monitor trade policy affairs in 2003-04. While the vast majority of this group (26 organisations) explicitly relied on the Managing Director's knowledge, seven entities reported that no one actively monitored the trade policy area.

Table 4.15: Who within the staff is monitoring and analysing trade policy affairs?

Think-tank (3 officials)	Trade Department (1-2 officials)	Managing Director	none	no response
5 (9%)	17 (31%)	26 (47%)	7 (13%)	3

Out of the 22 chambers with remunerated trade policy advisors, 17 organisations depended upon a Trade Department with one or two employees. Nevertheless, the chambers often hired external advisors in order to keep costs low.[43] Conversely, entities enjoying significant policy advisory units seemed rare, since only five chambers stated that more than two persons were in charge of trade policy affairs; UIA (7; CENI), INAI (4), CERA (ad-hoc paid consultants in the Institute of International Strategies), FITA (3), CIL (3) and CIQyP (3). Furthermore, the SRA's Economic Study Department is believed to possess three economists.

Apart from INAI, the UIA authorities tried to respond to the changing trade policy scenario with the creation of the Study Centre for International Negotiations (CENI) in February 2003. According to Osvaldo Kacef (BR 22/09/03), at that time the senior analyst, CENI aimed to strengthen the industrial sector's analytical capacities related to trade negotiations and to improve coordination with authorities.[44] Consequently, the team initially composed of two senior and six junior analysts began to carry out sectoral analysis to assess the impact of ongoing trade integration scenarios. Nonetheless, CENI faced initial problems due to the lack of internal and external recognition, considering that comments were mostly critical with respect to the quality of documents developed. Some of these could not be published since corresponding chambers were internally divided as regards the conclusions reached. Additionally, the first CENI Director, Alejandro Mayoral, did not attend the meetings of the Trade and MERCOSUR Departments, and hence, no direct technical support was provided. Lastly, personnel were downsized in 2004 and the question of who should be financing what amount of activities became increasingly unclear.

---

[43] According to Rúa Boeiro (15/03/05), close to 50 percent of the experts in the UIA MERCOSUR Department were external advisors. In general, chambers pay low salaries ranging between US$100-500. By the time Rúa Boeiro worked as Department Secretary (1995-99), close to 50 percent of the consultants provided free services due to their interest to obtain contacts and reputation. Conversely, the number of highly doted policy advisors was small, such as Osvaldo D'Imperio, President of COPAL's Foreign Trade Commission, advising numerous companies and chambers in the farming and food processing sectors.

[44] In February 2003, the UIA signed a common understanding with the Ministries of Economy and Foreign Affairs in order to establish permanent exchange of trade policy analysis and sectoral views; see UIA Conventions 2003a; b.

The shaky grounds of CENI point to the lack of professionalism inside the UIA. With respect to the departments aimed at finding intra-sectoral consensus on a technical level, a study carried out by Alberti et al. (1984) elucidated that out of the six areas, two had not been operating in 1983-84 and the remaining four were supported by only one assistant each (OE Alberti 10/01/01). 20 years later, the state of affairs is remarkably similar, albeit the number of departments has increased to ten. Even though all technical areas were sustained by administrative staff, the MERCOSUR Department is the only one supported by a paid expert. Conversely, the once vital Departments of Trade and Economy were no longer supported technically at the beginning of the 1990s (SO Makuc 14/03/05; OE Rúa Boeiro 15/03/05). As of 1993, the UIA compensated for the absent expertise in part by the creation of the Institute for Industrial Development (IDI), a think-tank that analysed economic policies and their effects on local industry. Due to the Techint Group's financial assistance, the UIA maintained a group of half a dozen well-trained economists coordinated by Jose Machinea, Minister of Economy 1999-2001. Even though their publications enjoyed broad recognition, the IDI experience came to an end after only six years. Fernando Martinez from FITA (BR 8/03/05) summed up the intermezzo: "the IDI was sustained by the great idea to install an analytical body to counter short-sighted business politics, ...but mainly the critical papers regarding the economic policies of the 1990s did not insert the executive bodies of the UIA, therefore the IDI started to lose power and finally came to an end in 1999 as Machinea was appointed Minister of Economy."

In the context of the insufficient professional structures of business advocates, impressions gathered from experts and state officials are not surprising; i.e. 90 percent considered the technical level of proposals submitted in the scope of international trade policy affairs as rather low or very low.

Table 4.16: How do you assess the technical level of business proposals submitted in the area of international trade policy?

	Experts	State officials	Total
very high	0	0	0 (0%)
rather high	1	1	2 (9%)
rather low	6	6	12 (52%)
very low	5	4	9 (39%)
no response	0	1	1

In this regard, comments either indicated that most sectors were short of professionals to elaborate sound proposals or that contributions made by large-scale sectors did not go beyond the limited logic of specific companies, instead of projecting the sector-wide development in a long-term perspective.

Summary Independent Variable A2

This section indicates a low institutional strength of business associations. Regarding the variable dimension *leadership*, the lack of multi-sectoral coordination capacity stands out, negatively affecting the intermediation of economy and trade related policies before the government. Beyond the lack of multisectoral coordination, the effective intermediation of trade interests has been hindered by strong forms of intra-sectoral fragmentation on the side of offensive agribusiness interests and among the mostly defensive manufacturing branches. The *organisation strength* of local business associations is largely deficient for various reasons, as exposed in Box 4.3.

Box 4.3: Summary Independent Variable A2

Leadership	Peak Association	In past decades, local business factions were not able to build stable multisectoral coordination mechanisms. The business wide alliances that have been established thus far (such as the G-8 in the 1990s) have been characterised by their informal setting and susceptibility to changing political and economic contexts.
	Trade Policy Coordination	On the sectoral level, the national manufacturer's representative UIA was unable to coordinate sector-wide trade policy proposals during the whole period of analysis. Regarding the export-oriented interests of local agriculture, timid attempts to coordinate agricultural concerns were launched with the creation of the Institute of International Agriculture Negotiations (INAI) in 1999. However, the intra-sectoral fragmentation among the traditional rural entities remains widespread, considering the existence of four peak entities representing local farmers.
Organisational Strength		The maintenance of close coordination patterns with local business factions has been negatively affected by the organisational weakness of business entity structures regarding their composition of revenues, participatory behaviour and trade policy advisory units. On the other hand, the creation of the think-tanks INAI (1999) and CENI (2003) can be seen as promising initiatives as they enabled the permanent analysis of international trade policy affairs by a handful of mainly young professionals. However, the future of CENI appeared uncertain in 2004 due to the lack of financial means and limited exchange with the entity's technical bodies.

4.4 Assessment

After examining the evolution of the dependent and independent variables individually, in this final section, I assess how, and to what extent, Argentina's failure to implement a coherent world market integration strategy has effectively been caused by the two explaining variables, or whether third variable influences became responsible for the observed policy output.

Before analysing the cause-effects links, however, I point out the main aspects that explain the way that Argentina pursued its integration into world markets. In the period from 1985 to 2004, the country's economic policy underwent drastic changes that took place in the context of macroeconomic turmoil, particularly observed in 1988-90 (hyperinflation) and in 2001-02 (debt crisis). These turbulences also influenced the development of the trade policies, which had to adapt to the prevailing constraints and possibilities. Nevertheless, several empirical puzzles related to trade policy demand explanations which exceed the argument of macroeconomic crisis (C4). The following four situations stand out:

First, in 1986-87, with the Integration Programme for Economic Cooperation (PICE) agreed on with Brazil, an innovative integration approach had been developed that adequately took into account the balance of payment constraints and the limited economies of scales of the local industry. The question thus arises: What explains the creation of the PICE, and what limited its advances?

Second, in 1990-94, the establishment of MERCOSUR represented a radical conceptual shift in trade integration, with the adoption of a fast and universal liberalisation approach (rather than a gradual, sector-specific one), and set the goal of building a regional market including a customs union. The question that arises here is thus: Why such a radical policy shift occurred, and why was the customs union approach selected, given that it contradicted Argentina's unilaterally applied economic policy?

Third, from 1995 to 2004, the implementation of the regional integration objectives, related to the establishment of the common market and the customs union, did not proceed as initially foreseen because member states only minimally assumed the MERCOSUR as a reference scheme for unilateral policy-making. Moreover, Argentina's trade and sector-oriented policies were applied in an uncoordinated, ad-hoc manner, underlining the high unpredictability of domestic policies. For what reason, hence, were long-term trade integration strategies not defined that would have taken into account the threats and possibilities of each sector? Why was MERCOSUR not used as the impetus for sectoral development, inline with the springboard logic?

Fourth, from 2002 to 2004, Argentina's trade policy became more active as the government aimed at the implementation of a Multipolar strategy, promoting national exports towards all possible foreign markets. Compared to previous stages, how can this greater attention to export concerns be explained, and why was its coherent implementation still uncertain in 2004?

In the light of these questions, Table 4.17 sums up the value of the observed variables and the explaining power each one possesses. Therefore, I will next explain when and how the values of the variables changed over time and how they influenced on the value of B.

Table 4.17: Explaining Argentina's Rather Failed World Market Integration Strategy

Variable	Variable Dimension	Value (Variance 1985-2004)	Explaining Power for Policy Success/Failure
A1: Institutional Strength of State Bureaucracy	Responsibilities	1985-1987: rather high 1988-2004: rather low	1985-2004: very high
	Resources	1985-2004: rather high*	1985-2004: rather high
	Openness	1985-1989: rather high 1990-1995: very low 1996-2004: rather high	1985-1989: rather low 1990-1995: rather high 1996-2004: rather low
A2: Institutional Strength of Business Associations	Leadership	1985-2004: very low	1985-2004: very high
	Organisational Strength	1985-2004: very low	1985-2004: very high
C1: Heterogeneity Sectoral Preferences		1985-2004: rather high	1985-2004: rather low
C2: Heterogeneity Foreign Preferences		1985-2004: rather high	1995-2004: rather low
C3: Political Instability		2001-2002: very high	2001-2002: rather high
C4: Macroeconomic Instability		1988-1990: very high 2000-2002: very high	1988-1990: very high 2000-2002: very high

* The value refers to the trade policy staff inside the Ministry of Economy from 1985 to 1992, and to the staff of the Ministry of Foreign Affairs since 1993, that is, when the Foreign Trade Service had been incorporated.

Institutional Strength of State Bureaucracy (A1)

According to Table 4.17, the explaining power of the Independent Variable A1 turned out to be high, and was mostly concentrated in the variable dimension *responsibilities*. In fact, the local "partnership model" in which the Ministry of Economy defines "what" has to be negotiated in trade policy affairs, and the Ministry of Foreign Affairs decides "how" to implement those inputs on the international level, was unclear during practically the whole period of analysis, negatively affecting the development of international trade policies.

In 1986-87, the Secretariat of Industry and Foreign Trade (SICE) inside the Ministry of Economy took over the clear responsibility of designing the innovative PICE approach, whilst the Foreign Affairs Ministry launched initial talks and assumed the overall coordination within this first substantial integration step with Brazil after the return to democracy in 1983. The previous merger of the areas of "trade" and "industry" inside a single state secretariat (a precondition set by Roberto Lavagna on taking office) is moreover crucial to explain the sectoral approach to integration that combined export promotion with industrial policies. By then, the technical work inside the SICE was strongly supported by the Foreign Trade Service, a specialised cadre of career trade diplomats inside the Ministry of Economy (*resources*). Furthermore, the staff in charge of the different sectoral negotiations maintained close working relations with the private sector (*openness*). Hence, the state bureaucracy exhibited rather adequate institutional structures for successful trade integration initiatives. On the side of the private sector, however, such conditions were not present, as I later expose.

In the aftermath, the institutional strength of the executive branch declined, explaining to wide extents the posterior failures occurred in the country's world market integration strategy. In particular, effective inter-ministerial coordination could no longer be ensured in the light of an unclear division of labour for the conduction of international trade policy affairs. Instead, the course of action became strongly dependent on personalised decisions and undermined the institutional role of state bureaucracy as a whole (*responsibilities, resources, and openness*).

Specifically, Domingo Cavallo, Minister of Foreign Affairs (1989-90) and Minister of Economy (1991-1996), defined – being advised by a group of personal advisors from the orthodox-liberal think-tank Mediterranean Foundation – the scope of economic reforms that included trade liberalisations. A reflection of the policy style sustained by Cavallo's economic advisory team also became the integration scheme embodied in the MERCOSUR treaty of 1991, which aimed at a fast expansion of intra-regional trade and the attraction of foreign investment. These new rules favoured the industries from the steel, petrochemicals, foods, and automobile sectors, where large companies dominated, whilst small-scale manufacturers, especially in the range of capital goods, shrank due to the lack of industrial policies, increased import competition and overvaluation of the local currency.

Contrary to the PICE, the private sector organisations were widely excluded from the key decisions regarding the institutional set-up of MERCOSUR (*openness*). The adoption of the

Customs Union in December 1994, which contradicted national policies both before and afterwards, had been described as a concession to Brazil in order to avoid deteriorating bilateral relations (the goal of reaching the CET had yet to be defined in 1991). Evidently, the concession made by Carlos Menem was opposed to by the economy minister (who favoured a free trade zone), although Mr. Cavallo (then as foreign affairs minister) supported the decision in March 1991 when the Asunción Treaty was signed and the goal of reaching a CET by 1995 was set, as Jorge Campbell, chief negotiator inside the Ministry of Affairs (1994-99) explained.[45]

From 1995, the ambitious goals set in the scope of MERCOSUR – which required the harmonisation of trade, macroeconomic, sectoral, and fiscal policies – overstrained the institutional capacities of the local bureaucracy. In particular, the trade policy staff inside the Ministry of Economy experienced a steady decline after the Foreign Trade Service transferred to the Ministry of Foreign Affairs in 1993 and with the continued budget cuts that took place from 1996 *(resources)*.

Given the decreasing capacity of the Ministry of Economy to monitor and technically support the international trade policy, the trade policy branch inside the Foreign Affairs Ministry increasingly assumed the role of defining both policy guidelines and the implementation of negotiations strategies on the MERCOSUR and extra-regional level. Effectively, however, these far-reaching *responsibilities* weren't assumed before 2002 because of a range of internal constraints, in particular the difficulties to incorporate the Foreign Trade Service in the traditional diplomatic career scale and the weak leadership of the office holders in charge between 1999 and 2001 *(resources)*.

In the period of 2002-04, under chief negotiator Martin Redrado, the Ministry of Foreign Affairs assumed nearly full responsibility – although opposed to in parts by the Ministry of Economy – to put forward an ambitious Multipolar Model by planning and initiating numerous negotiations in the regional and extra-regional sphere. Moreover, Mr. Redrado insisted on a marked involvement of the private sector and revived the Centre of International Economy (CEI) in order to convince a broad public with technical arguments of the pursued Multipolar strategy *(openness)*.

By the end of 2004, however, it remained in doubt whether the proactive Multipolar strategy could be successfully implemented, for two main reasons: First, a lack of intra-

---

[45] Anecdotically, Campbell reported that Cavallo called only ten days prior to the *Ouro Preto* Protocol for a meeting with Menem and Di Tella in order to put arguments on the table in favour of a simple FTA, which was, by then, too late to retract. Later on, Cavallo remained the Customs Union's major adversary. By March 2001, when he was again appointed Minister of Economy, the dynamic but unpredictable technocrat openly threatened to downgrade MERCOSUR to a FTA.

MERCOSUR cohesion persisted in 2004, and thus, the conclusion of initiated and planned free trade talks was highly uncertain. Between 1995 and 2004, when Chile and Mexico rapidly expanded trade relations towards (extra-) regional areas, the negotiations launched by MERCOSUR mostly deadlocked. Second, although state-business coordination was much more intense in 2004 than in the first half of the 1990s, the business sector still faced similar institutional deficits.

Institutional Strength of Business Associations (A2)

With respect to the explaining power of Independent Variable A2, the institutional deficits of organised business hampered the coherent implementation of trade policies over the whole period of analysis. In 1986-87, significant progress in the sectoral negotiations with Brazil in the PICE scope was avoided due to the lack of intermediation capacity of the national manufacturers associations UIA. Instead of coordinating between export-oriented and import-competing sectors, defining effective compensation measures for threatened sectors, the UIA authorities proved to be an unreliable interlocutor for the government. Therefore, sectors and individual companies pursued their mostly protectionist interests outside the UIA institutions, and in so doing, limited the state officials' room for negotiations.

In the 1990s, the UIA and seven other leading sectoral associations were organised in the scope of the G-8 alliance. Contrary to previous decades, the private sector demonstrated unity and supported the ongoing economic reforms launched by Mr. Cavallo. But beyond a general business consensus, which was largely based on the conviction that liberalisation was needed to control inflationary pressure, the leading business organisations did not develop detailed concerted policy proposals regarding the MERCOSUR. Instead, the attitude towards this regional integration schemes depended on short-term interests affecting the particular sectors.

For example, the behaviour of local business on the CET issue has been described as passive in comparison with Brazil, where the private sector provided permanent advice to its diplomacy during negotiations; indeed, prior to Ouro Preto, no domestic policy debate really took into account the long-term impacts of a common trade policy regime (Botto 2004; Bouzas and Pagnotta 2003; Motta Veiga 2002). Initial criticism expressed against the CET, principally by the powerful industries such as food processing, steel, and chemicals, disappeared in the light of the impressive import growth in Brazil that had taken place since the beginning of 1994 (a consequence of Brazil's macroeconomic stabilisation plan *"Real")*.

From 2002 to 2004, when the Argentinean government began to pursue an ambitious external trade agenda, denominated "Multipolar strategy" by chief negotiator Martin Redrado, the participation of business associations was mostly faint-hearted or disperse. Contrary to the 1990s, a multisectoral coordination mechanism no longer existed. Moreover, the UIA, as the leading industrial entity, suffered as it became divided internally, since several sectors such as the steel, metalworking, and textiles, built up their own "industrialist group", undermining the *leadership of* the "official UIA". At any rate, trade policy efforts set forth by the UIA authorities were focussed almost exclusively on the claim for an institutionalised safeguard mechanism inside the MERCOSUR in order to protect local industries from threatening import surges originating from Brazil.

The business support for Mr. Redrado's Multipolar strategy was limited primarily to the branches related to booming agriculture commodities. From an institutional perspective, the creation of the Institute for International Agriculture Negotiations (INAI) in 1999 can be seen as the first timid attempts by local farmers to overcome the fragmentation among rural representatives and the lack of professional advocacy structures. Backed by chambers representing cereals and oleaginous crops, after the failed WTO Ministerial in Seattle, INAI began to serve as a steady technical counterpart of the Secretariat of Agriculture and the Ministry of Foreign Affairs within the agriculture talks on the regional and multilateral sphere. Although market access conditions were not improved fundamentally within the period of 1999-2004, the enhanced public-private coordination lead to a stronger presence of the Argentinean government in this crucial policy area.

In general, close coordination patterns with local business factions have been negatively affected by the *organisational weakness* of business entities regarding their composition of revenues, participatory behaviour and trade policy advisory units. In this sense, the creation of the think-tanks INAI (1999) and CENI (2003) can be seen as promising initiatives, as they enabled the permanent analysis of international trade policy affairs by a handful of mainly young professionals. However, the future of CENI appeared uncertain in 2004 due to the lack of financial means and limited exchange with the entity's technical bodies.

Control Variables C1-C4

Assessing the influence of selected control variables C1-C4, certain disturbing effects on the value of B were observed regarding C2, C3 and C4.

Heterogeneity of Foreign Preferences (C2): Being, together with Brazil, one of the world's largest foodstuff producers, the sensitive agriculture issue caused notable difficulties in the free trade talks with the US, EU, CAN, and Mexico. On the other hand, problems linked to heterogeneous agriculture interests became, in parts, compensated by the attractive consumer markets offered by the emerging trading blocks; indeed from 1995, North American, European and Asian countries demonstrated clear interests in deepening trade relations with MERCOSUR states. Moreover, other FTAs such as those signed between Chile-Canada, Chile-EU and Australia-US, indicated the possibility of excluding certain tariff items from reciprocal liberalisation or defining special phasing-out schemes for sensitive products.

Therefore, the main factor for the deadlocked talks was the inadequate implementation of the internal agenda of MERCOSUR, especially the harmonisation of economic policies, and opposing interests between Argentina and Brazil. For example, Brazil's defensive concerns in new behind the border issues contrasted with the far-reaching liberalisation commitment of Argentina (key issues in the FTAA and MERCOSUR-EU negotiations).

Inside MERCOSUR, integration progress depended strongly on Brazil assuming a clear agenda setting role. Therefore, failures in regional integration can be largely explained by Brazil's reluctance to limit its national policy-making autonomy, widespread protectionist measures against intra-zone imports, and its unwillingness to provide necessary funds to face structural asymmetries among members. It is important to note, however, that Argentina confirmed the absent commitment among members for deeper regional integration, considering the lack of incorporation of communitarian norms into national law and the repeated entry barriers for intra-zone imports. Chile, on the other hand, from the onset mistrusted the intra-regional liberalisation efforts, and hence, decided to set forth independent forms of trade integration refusing the MERCOSUR's Customs Union.

Macroeconomic instability (C4): Throughout the 1980s, Argentina suffered from strong inflationary pressure, a shortage of foreign capital, and high fiscal deficits, explaining in parts the decline of the sectoral PICE approach in 1988-89. Later, the introduction of the Currency Board in 1991 and the economic stabilisation in Brazil by 1994 provided favourable grounds for the expansion of intra-regional trade and the consolidation of MEROCOSUR. This integration friendly context was again interrupted by Brazil's abrupt currency devaluation in January 1999 and Argentina's breakdown of the Currency Board in January 2002. In the meantime, Argentina faced macroeconomic turbulences due to its growing foreign debt and fiscal deficits ranging from 3.4 to 5.4 percent of GDP. The period from 2003 to 2004 was again encouraging for regional integration in the context of low inflation and a comparable evolution of exchange rates between Argentina and Brazil.

In conclusion, in the last 20 years trade relations in the Southern Cone were largely influenced by macroeconomic factors. On the other hand, it can be argued that successful regional integration policies were not hindered primarily by macroeconomic variables but due to scant advances made during the "golden times" of MERCOSUR (particularly 1994-98 and 2003-04) in which no solid base was built for encountering more unstable circumstances. In these periods, practically no progress was noticeable regarding the harmonisation of trade and economic policies, such as the convergence of the CET, (phyto-) sanitary measures, and liberalisation of services, among others. Also, in times of macroeconomic stability it was largely the development of coherent unilateral policies on export promotion and sectoral development, which would have supported the ongoing world market integration process.

Political instability (C3): In accordance with C4, *political instability* was registered in 1989-1990 and 2001-02. In the latter occasion, the combination of an unemployment rate beyond 20 percent, a four-year recession and rampant fiscal and debt crises caused the compulsory resignation of State President Fernando de la Rúa. Strikingly, the stabilisation of the economy and political system took place within 2002. As indicated under *macroeconomic instability*, the instability registered in 1989-90 and 2001-02 generated a backlash principally for the ongoing trade integration endeavours with Brazil. Conversely, the country's behaviour in the times in between did not provide significant evidence that coherent trade policies had been implemented.

Heterogeneity of Sectoral Preferences (C1): In the past, the private sector often used to be divided into export-oriented agriculture and inward-looking industry. This heterogeneity could explain the failed attempt to create a business-wide coordination pattern, such as the establishment of a strong peak association. But as of 1990, when economic reforms were implemented, this explanation seems no longer valid. *First,* many manufacturing sectors have become export-oriented and peak tariffs came down to 22 percent, disregarding the automotive regime maintained in the MERCOSUR. *Second,* intra-sectoral division became as widespread as inter-sectoral differences. While the rather homogenous rural interests are represented by no less than four peak entities and several branch organisations lobbying outside these institutions, the manufacturers' association UIA was not able to coordinate a wide range of existing common interests among local manufacturers, becoming particularly evident from the economic opening in the 1990s. Therefore, the main problem of domestic business advocacy has institutional roots and is not due to the existence of extremely heterogeneous preferences.

4.5 References

Literature

Acuña, Carlos (1995). "Business Interests, Dictatorship, and Democracy in Argentina" Pp. 3-48 in *Business and Democracy in Latin America,* edited by Bartell, E. and Payne, L. Pittsburgh: University of Pittsburgh Press.

Alberti G., Golbert, L. and Acuña, C. (1984). "Intereses Industriales y Gobernabilidad Democrática en la Argentina" in *Boletín Informativo Techint* No. 235: 77-124.

Birle, Peter (1995). *Argentinien: Unternehmer, Staat und Demokratie.* Frankfurt am Main: Vervuert.

Boldorini, María Cristina y Susana Czar de Zalduendo (1995). "La Estructura Jurídico-Institucional del MERCOSUR después del Protocolo de Ouro Preto" in *Boletín Informativo Techint* No. 283.

Botto, Mercedes (2001). *La Participación de la Sociedad Civil en los Procesos de Integración Comercial: los Casos del TLCAN, MERCOSUR y ALCA.* Buenos Aires: FLACSO/PIEI No. 3.

Botto, Mercedes (2004). *The Impact of New Regionalism on Trade Policy Making: The Case of Mercosur and the FTAA in Southern Countries.* Draft Version. Buenos Aires: FLACSO.

Bouzas, Roberto and Saul Keifman (1992). "Argentinean Export Promotion Policies: an Overview of the 1976-1985 Decade" in *The Dangers of Export Pessimism,* edited by Hughes, H. San Francisco: International Centre for Economic Growth.

Bouzas, Roberto and Enrique Avogadro (2002). "Trade Policy Making and the Private Sector: a Memorandum of Argentina" in *The Trade Policy Making Process. Level One of the Two Levels Game.* Occasional Paper 13, edited by Ostry, S. Buenos Aires: IDB/Munk Center.

Bouzas, R., Da Motta Veiga, P. and Torrent, R. (2002). *In-depth Study of Mercosur Integration, its Prospects and the Effects thereof on the Market Access of EU Goods, Services and Investment.* European Commission.

Bouzas, Roberto and Emiliano Pagnotta (2003). *Dilemas de la Política Comercial Argentina.* Buenos Aires: Universidad de San Andrés/ Siglo XXI Editores/ Fundación OSDE.

Bustos, Pablo (1992). *El Mercosur: Más de lo Mismo?* .Buenos Aires: Fundación Fiedrich Ebert.

Calvo, Ernesto (2001). *Disconcerted Industrialists: The Politics of Trade Reform in Latin America,* Ph.D Dissertation Thesis: North Western University.

Campbell, Jorge et. al (2000). *Mercosur entre la Realidad y la Utopía.* Buenos Aires: Centro de Economía Internacional/ Nuevohacer.

Casaburi, Gabriel (1998). *Políticas Comerciales e Industriales de la Argentina desde la Década del 1960.* ECLAC/CEPAL- Doc.11097, United Nations.

Cavallo, Domingo (2001). *Pasión por Crear*. Buenos Aires: Ed. Planeta.

CEI (1998). *Panorama del MERCOSUR, No. 1*. Buenos Aires.

CEI Study No.1 (2002). *Integration Alternatives for Argentina: A General Equilibrium Analysis*.

CEI Study No.2 (2000). *ALCA Opportunities and Threats for Argentina: An Analysis of its Sectoral Impact*.

CEI Study No.3 (2003). *MERCOSUR – European Union Agreement: Opportunities and Threats for Argentina*.

CEI Study No.5 (2003). *MERCOSUR – Andean Community Agreement: Opportunities and Threats for Argentina and Brazil*.

CEI Study No.6 (2003). *Opportunities and Challenges for Argentina in the East Asian Market*.

CEI Study No.7 (2004). *Effects on the Argentinean Republic of the Enlargement of the European Union*.

CEI Study No. 8 (2004). *Opportunities and Threats for Argentina in the South-South Trade*.

Chudnovsky, Daniel and Fernando Porta (1989). *En Torno a la Integración Económica Argentino-Brasileña*. Santiago de Chile: ECLALC/CEPAL Journal No. 39.

Chudnovsky, Daniel and Fernando Porta (1990). *La Trayectoria del Proceso de Integración Argentino- Brasileño. Tendencias e Incertidumbres*. Buenos Aires: CENIT.

Chudnovsky, Daniel and Fernando Porta (1991). *La Política de Importaciones en Argentina en el Período 1976-1991*. Buenos Aires: ECLAC/CEPAL.

Chudnovsky, Daniel et el. (1996). *Los Límites de la Apertura: Liberalización, Reestructuración Productiva y Medio Ambiente*. Buenos Aires: Ed. Alianza/CENIT.

Chudnovsky, Daniel and Andres López (2001). "El Caso Argentina" in *El Boom de la Inversión Extranjera Directa en el MERCOSUR*, edited by Chudnovsky, D. Buenos Aires: Siglo XXI.

Crespo Armengol, Eugenia and Maximiliano Geffner (2001). *Estructura Arancelaria Argentina. Informe Final*. Buenos Aires: Mimeo.

Da Motta Veiga, Pedro Luis (2002). "Trade Policy Making in Brazil: Transition Path" in *The Trade Policy Making Process. Level One of the Two Levels Game*. Occasional Paper 13, edited by Ostry, S. Buenos Aires: IDB/Munk Centre.

Ferrer, Aldo (1997). "Los Dos Modelos de MERCOSUR" Pp.9-25 in *Encrucijadas Journal*. Universidad de Buenos Aires.

Gargiulo, Gerardo (2003). *Estudios sobre el Sector Agroalimentario. La Cooperación Público-Privada en la Política Agroalimentaria. Situación Actual y Perspectivas*. Buenos Aires: CEPAL/ Ministerio de Economía y Producción.

Guidobono, Graciela and Laura Zuvanic (1997). "Recursos Humanos y Reforma de la Administración Pública" Pp. 123-143 in *Aportes para el Estado y la Administración Gubernamental*. Buenos Aires: Asociación de Administradores Gubernamentales.

Hirst, Mónica (1998). "Security Policies, Democratization, and Regional Integration in the Southern Cone" Pp.159-187 in *Security & Democracy. Latin America and the Caribbean in the Post-Cold War Era*, edited by Dominguez, J. Pittsburgh: University of Pittsburgh Press.

Iglesias, María Valeria (2002). *Análisis Comparativo de las Políticas de Apoyo al Financiamiento de las Exportaciones PyMES*.

Kosacoff, Bernardo and Adrián Ramos (2001). *Cambios Contemporáneos en la Estructura Industrial Argentina (1975-2000)*. Universidad de Quilmes.

MERCOSUR (2004). *Primer Informe Semestral de la Secretaría del MERCOSUR: Un Foco para el Proceso de Integración Regional*. Montevideo.

Narlikar, Amrita and Diana Tussie (2003). *Bargaining Together in Cancun: Developing Countries and Their Evolving Coalitions*. Working Paper published on Internet.

Nofal, Beatriz (1997a). "Obstáculos Institucionales y Económicos para la Consolidación y Profundización del Mercosur: Propuestas" in *Boletín Informativo Techint* No. 294: 41-48.

Nofal, Beatriz (1997b). "Las Grandes Asignaturas Pendientes en el Mercosur. Alternativas. ¿Profundización o Dilución?" in *Boletín Informativo Techint* No. 292: 78-79.

Peña, Felix (2003). *Concertación de Intereses, Efectividad de las Reglas de Juego y Calidad Institucional en el MERCOSUR*. Programa de Estado de Derecho. Buenos Aires: Honrad Adenauer Fundation.

Redrado, Martin (2003). *Exportar para Crecer*. Buenos Aires: Editorial Planeta.

Redrado, M. and Hernán Lacunza (2004). *A New Approach to Trade Development in Latin America*. Occasional Paper. Buenos Aires: INTAL/IDB.

Robin, Christian (2001). *Kollektives Unternehmerhandeln im Prozess der demokratischen Konsolidierung Lateinamerikas vor dem Hintergrund einer liberalen Wirtschaftsordnung. Eine vergleichende Fallstudie der politischen Regime Argentiniens und Chile in den 90er Jahren*. MA Thesis in Political Science: University of Zurich.

Schwarzer, Jorge (1998). *Implantación de un Modelo Económico. La Experiencia Argentina entre 1975 y el 2000*. Buenos Aires: Editorial AZ.

Sidicaro, Ricardo (2003). *La Crisis del Estado y los Actores Políticos y Socioeconómicos en la Argentina*. Buenos Aires: Eudeba/Libros Del Rojas.

Viguera, Aníbal (1998). *La Política de la Apertura Comercial en la Argentina, 1987-1996*. Paper Prepared for delivery at the 1998 meeting of the Latin American Studies Association. Chicago, Illinois, September 24-26.

WTO (1999). *Trade Policy Review Argentina. Report by the Secretariat*. Body of the WTO. WT/TPR/S/47.

Other Documents

DBLA (2005). *Economic Research. Latin American Database. Country Indicators from 1980 to 2004*.

El Clarín Newspaper (18/12/2000). "Las Empresas Tampoco Pueden Pagar la Cuota. Crecen las Mensualidades Impagas que Deben Cubrir para Pertenecer a la UIA."

El Clarín Newspaper (10/09/2001). "La Argentina es uno de los Países con el Nivel más Bajo de Exportaciones."

El Clarín Newspaper (20/04/2003). "Sin Consenso entre los Industriales. La UIA va a las Urnas".

El Cronista Newspaper (09/09/2003). "Una Contribución Necesaria para Fortalecer al Sector Metalúrgico" by *Manfredo Arheit.*

El Clarin Newspaper (29/07/2005). "Proyecciones para la Próxima Campaña. Prognostican otro Récord de la Soja."

El Cronista Newspaper (19/06/2003). "Los Pasos para que el MERCOSUR sea Creíble" by Félix Peña.

Grupo Productivo (23/06/2000). "Estamos en el Mundo y Debemos Cuidar la Nación" in *La Declaración de Tigre.*

INAI (2002-03). *Summaries of Agriculture Round Table between 4 April 2002 and 16 December 2003*.

INDEC (2004a). *Exportaciones según Complejos Exportadores: Año 2004*.

INDEC (2004b). *Exportaciones por Zonas Económicas según Complejos Exportadores: Año 2004*.

Lacunza, Hernan (18/11/2004). *La Influencia de la Investigación en la Formulación de Políticas Comerciales*. Regional Workshop. FLACSO. Argentina: Buenos Aires.

La Nación Newspaper (22/04/2003). "Pedidos para el Próximo Gobierno. Los Exportadores reclaman una Estrategia."

Legal and Administrative Department/MEP (2004). *Planilla de Personal de la Subsecretaria de Política y Gestion Comercial*. General Directorate of Human Resources.

Library Ambassador Leopoldo H. Tettamanti (2005). *History of the Secretary of Industry, Trade and Mining since 1941*. Unpublished List. Buenos Aires.

MRECIC (2004a). *Jurisdiction 35: Ministry of External Relations, International Commerce and Worship.*

MRECIC (2004b). *Consejo Consultivo de la Sociedad Civil (2004). An Overview 2002-04.* Ministry of Foreign Relations, International Trade and Worship.

Secretariat of Finance (1996-2004). *Definición de Políticas de Comercio Exterior. Presupuesto de Gastos por Entidad. Prog. 17.* Ministry of Economy: National Budget Office.

The Wall Street Journal (25/01/2002). "A Simple Answer for Argentina: Follow Chile's Example" by Sebastian Edwards.

UIA Convention (19/02/2003a). *Convenio de Cooperación entre el Ministerio de la Producción y La Unión Industrial Argentina.* Buenos Aires.

UIA Convention (19/02/2003b). *Convenio entre la Unión Industrial Argentina y el Ministerio de Relaciones Exteriores, Comercio Internacional y Culto.* Buenos Aires.

UIA MERCOSUR Department (2003-04). *Minutes of Meetings 2003 and 2004.*

Undersecretariat of SME and Regional Development (2003). *Export Promotion Guide.* Buenos Aires.

Interviews

OUTSIDE EXPERTS (OE)				
Date	Name	Type	Institution	Function
06.10.2003	Nogues, Julio	Survey NEI	Universidad Di Tella/ Economics Department	Professor; Ex-official in Foreign Trade Affairs
06.10.2003 09.12.2004	Ochoa, Raúl	Survey NEI	BID/ Secretariat of Industry and Trade	International Consultant; Ex-Undersecretary of Foreign Trade
24.10.2003	Peña, Félix	NEI	UNTREF; Bank Boston Foundation	MERCOSUR Expert; Ex-Undersecretary of Foreign Trade
21.04.2005	Porta, Fernando	Survey, NEI	REDES/ Center of Studies on Science, Development and Superior Education	Researcher, Expert in MERCOSUR and Industrial Policy
02.06.2004	Rappoport, Luis	Survey	University of Bologna; ECLAC, BID, etc.	Professor; Expert in Foreign Economic Relations, Europe-Latin America
06.06.2004	Restaino, Carlos	Survey	Centre of Studies on Economic Integration and International Trade (INTEGRAL)	Trade Policy Advisor of Business Entities; Expert in Foreign Trade, Economic Integration
08.06.2004 17.11.2004 07.03.2005	Campbell, Jorge (Key Informant)	Survey NEI NEI	IMCG Consulting	Ex-Secretary of Foreign Economic Affairs, and Undersecretary of Foreign Trade
11.06.2004	Rúa Boeiro,	Survey	Centre of Studies on	Trade Policy Advisor of

26.11.2004 *15.03.2005*	*Rodolfo (Key Informant)*	*NEI* *NEI*	*Economic Integration and International Trade (INTEGRAL)*	*Business Entities; Expert in Foreign Trade and Economic Integration*
15.06.2004	Bouzas, Roberto	NEI	FLACSO; University of San Andrés	Professor in Economics; Academic Director of Master in International Relations and Negotiations
22.06.2004	Berensztein, Sergio	Survey	Universidad Di Tella/ Political Science Department	Professor; Expert in Foreign Affairs, Economic Policy Making
25.06.2004	Chudnovsky, Daniel	Survey	University of San Andrés; Research Center on Transformation Affairs (CENIT)	Professor in Economics; Expert in Industrial Policy and National Innovation Systems
25.06.2004	Berlinski, Julio	Survey	Universidad Di Tella/ Economics Department	Professor; Expert in Trade in Services
25.06.2004	Sanguinetti, Pablo	Survey	Universidad Di Tella/ Economics Department	Professor; Expert in International Trade
28.06.2004	Svarzman, Gustavo	Survey	Ex-Annalist of Centre of International Economic (CEI)	Trade Policy Advisor of State Entities/ Foreign Trade and Economic Integration
04.03.2005	Bruno, Carlos	NEI	Research Centre on Transformation Affairs (CENIT)	Economist; Former Trade Diplomat/ Economic Integration
05.03.2005	Yoguel, Gabriel	NEI	National University of General Sarmiento	Professor in Economics; Expert in Industrial Policy and Supply Chains Development

STATE OFFICIALS (SO)

Date	Name	Type	Agency	Function
04.09.2003 *22.04.2004* *04.03.2005*	*Makuc, Adrián (Key Informant)*	*Survey* *NEI* *NEI*	*MEP/ Undersecretariat of Foreign Trade Affairs*	*National Director of Foreign Trade Policy*
04.11.2003	Jordán, Michael	Survey	MRECIC/ Secretariat of Trade and Foreign Economic Relations	Trade Diplomat; MERCOSUR and Services Affairs
11.11.2003 20.11.2003	Mermet, Luciana	Survey NEI	MEP/ Undersecretariat of Foreign Trade Affairs	Trade Policy Advisor; WTO Affairs
18.11.2003	Monti, Fernanda	Survey NEI	MEP/ Undersecretariat of Foreign Trade Affairs	Trade Policy Advisor; Market Access and Regional Affairs
21.11.2003	Niscovulos, Luis	Survey	MRECIC/ Secretariat of Trade and Foreign Economic Relations	Sub-Director Multilateral Affairs; Trade in Services
25.11.2003	Carpinacci, Luciana	Survey NEI	MRECIC/ Secretariat of Trade and Foreign Economic Relations	Trade Policy Advisor; Agriculture Multilateral Affairs
26.11.2003	Surballe, Rossana	Survey	MRECIC/ Secretariat of Trade and Foreign Economic Relations	Trade Diplomat; Hemispheric and State Procurement Affairs
27.11.2003	Capello, Nora	Survey NEI	MRECIC/ Secretariat of Trade and Foreign Economic Relations	Trade Diplomat; National Coordinator of FTAA Affairs

02.12.2003	Castillo, Luis Ariel	Survey NEI	MRECIC/ Secretariat of Trade and Foreign Economic Relations	Trade Diplomat; Multilateral and Trade in Good Affairs
04.12.2003	Alonso, Cristine	Survey NEI	MEP/ Undersecretariat of Foreign Trade Affairs	Sub-Director MERCOSUR Affairs; State Procurement
15.04.2004	Petri, Gerardo	Survey NEI	MEP/ Secretariat of Agriculture	Coordinator of International Agriculture Negotiations
20.04.2004	De la Guardia, Ernesto	Survey	MRECIC/ Secretariat of Trade and Foreign Economic Relations	Trade Diplomat; MERCOSUR, Services and State Procurement Affairs
10.05.2004	Lipovetsky, Daniel	NEI	MEP/ Undersecretariat of Foreign Trade Affairs	Chief of Advisor
13.09.2004	Varsky, Hugo	NEI	MRECIC/ Secretariat of Trade and Foreign Economic Relations	Special Representative for Civil Society Dialogue
30.11.2004	Lopez Aramburu, José	NEI	MRECIC/ Secretariat of Trade and Foreign Economic Relations	Trade Diplomat; ALADI Affairs
02.12.2004	Salafia, Roberto	NEI	MRECIC/ Secretariat of Trade and Foreign Economic Relations	Sub-Director MERCOSUR Division
07.12.2004	Mosquera, Carlos	NEI	MEP/ Undersecretariat of Foreign Trade Affairs	Trade Policy Advisor; MERCOSUR Affairs
09.12.2004	Marcelo Cañellas	NEI	MEP/ Undersecretariat of Foreign Trade Affairs	Director Regional Trade Policy; Market Access Affairs

BUSINESS REPRESENTATIVES (BR)

Date	Name	Type	Entity	Function
10.09.2003	Pons, Roberto	Survey NEI	UIA	Chief of MERCOSUR and Trade Department
17.09.2003	Biglieri, Adrian	NEI	UIA	Managing Director
22.09.2003	Kasef, Osvaldo	NEI	CENI/ UIA	Coordinator Study Area
26.09.2003	Cerquetella, Alejandra	Survey; NEI	ADIMRA (Arg. Association of Metallurgical Industry)	Chief of Foreign Trade Department
21.10.2003 15.09.2003	De Kojic, Christiane	Survey	CIPA (Chamber of Manufactured Foods Industry)	Chief of Foreign Trade Department
23.10.2003	Solari, Rosario	Survey	CERA (Arg. Chamber of Exporters)	Managing Director
10.11.2003	Campos, Jaime	Survey	AEA (Arg. Entrepreneurchip Association)	Managing Director
10.11.2003	Romiro, Myriam	NEI	ADIMRA	Assistant Social Policy Department
27.11.2003	Barabás, Laura	NEI	CICA (Chamber of Industry Footwear)	Chief of Foreign Trade Department
27.04.2004	Caminoa, Raquel	Survey	CEC (Center of Cereals Exporters)	Chief of Economic Study Division
28.04.2004	Miralles, Gustavo	Survey	CAPOC (Chamber of Organic Foods Producers)	President

29.04.2004	Liboreiro, Ernesto	Survey	INAI	Managing Director
29.04.2004	Amigo, Jorge	Survey	FEDECITRUS (Citrus Fruits Federation)	Managing Director
03.05.2004	Caminoa, Raquel	Survey	CIARA (Chamber of Vegetable Oil Industry)	Chief of Economic Study Division
03.05.2004	Laso, Luis	Survey	Argentinean Chamber of Legume Producers	Manging Director
03.05.2004	Confidential	Survey	Chamber of Pneumatic Industry	Managing Director
05.05.2004	Borrel, Eduardo	Survey	CLIMA (Center of Metallurgical Industry)	Managing Director
04.05.2004	Hernández, Gregorio	Survey	CARMAHE (Traders and Producers of Machines and Tools)	Managing Director
05.05.2004	Rusansky, David	Survey	CACIOFA (Traders in Photographs and Optic Goods)	Managing Director
05.05.2004	Cantarella, Juan	Survey	AFAC (Association of Component Producers; Chemical Industry)	Managing Director
06.05.2004	Monica	Survey	CICOMRA (Chamber of Informatics and Telecommunication)	Administrative Assistant
06.05.2004	Claudia Massari	Survey	CAFCCo (Chamber of Cardboard Industry)	Administrative Assistant
06.05.2004	Domenech, Roberto	Survey	CEPA (Center of Poultry Industry)	Executve President
06.05.2004	Quiñones, Victor Hugo	Survey	CAEME (Arg. Chamber of Pharmaceutical Specialities)	Manager of International Relations
07.05.2004	Rodriguez Canedo, Fernando	Survey	ADEFA (Association of Auto Motor Producers)	Managing Director
07.05.2004	Del Carril, José	Survey	FAIM (Arg. Federation of Mill Industry)	Managing Director
07.05.2004	Padilla, Guillermo	Survey	Arg. Chamber of Liqueur Producers	President
10.05.2004	Ackermann, Beatriz	Survey	Arg. Chamber of Peanuts	Managing Director
11.05.2004	Argüello, Daniel	Survey	Arg. Union of Public Sector Providers	Managing Director
11.05.2004	Valenciano, Eugenio	Survey	AFAT (Association of Arg. Farming Equipment Industry)	Managing Director
11.05.2004	Sethson, Jorge	Survey	Arg. Chamber of Books	Institutional Manager
12.05.2004	Mustones, Pertti/ Colombo, Emilio	Survey	FITA (Arg. Federation of Textiles Industries)	Trade Policy Advisors
13.05.2004	Alvarez, Anibal	Survey	Chamber of Glucose and Derivates Producers	Managing Director

13.05.2004	Fonaris, Antonio	Survey	Chamber of Arg. Brewery Industry	Managing Director
13.05.2004	Petersen, Cristina	Survey	CAPDROFAR (Arg. Chamber of Pharmaceutical Drugs)	Trade Policy Advisor
13.05.2004	Martinez Villa, Anibal	Survey	Arg. Association of Cement Industry	Managing Director
13.05.2004	Gataldi, Gustavo	Survey	Chamber of Abrasive Products Industry	Managing Director
13.05.2004	Gataldi, Gustavo	Survey	Chamber of Paint Industry	Managing Director
13.05.2004	Gataldi, Gustavo	Survey	Chamber of Ceramics and Floors Industry	Managing Director
13.05.2004	Gastaldi, Gustavo	Survey	Arg. Federation of Salt Producers	Managing Director
17.05.2004	Miquel, Miguel	Survey	CAFI (Arg. Chamber of Fruits Producers)	Secretary of Board of Directors
17.05.2004	Di Meglio, Victor	Survey	CAEM (Arg. Chamber of Mining Companies)	Managing Director
19.05.2004	Concilio, Andrea	Survey	CAIAMA (Arg. Chamber of Aluminium Industry)	Managing Director
20.05.2004	De Fina, Adriano	Survey	AIERA (Association of Importers and Experts of Argentina)	Managing Director
24.05.2004	Confidential	Survey	CIL (Center of Diary Industry)	Managing Director
27.05.2004	Lopez, Juan Carlo	Survey	COOPERALA (Chamber of Pharmaceutical Laboratories)	Sub-Manging Director
27.05.2004	Salamanco, Héctor	Survey	ABC (Arg. Consortium of Meat Exporters)	Managing Director
28.05.2004	Iglesias, Raúl	Survey	CADIPSA (Arg. Chamber of Beverage Industry)	Administrative Director
31.05.2004	Rúben I. González	Survey	Arg. Union of Meat Industry	Managing Director
31.05.2004	Prato, Ricardo	Survey	Arg. Chamber of Consumer Electronics and Air Conditioners	Policy Advisor
31.05.2004	Pereyra, Homero	Survey	Arg. Chamber of Jewellery and Watches	President
01.06.2004	Sanchez, Oscar	Survey	CAIP (Arg. Chamber of Plastic Industry)	Manging Director
07.06.2004	Greenberg, Enrique	Survey	CASEL (Arg. Chamber of Security Electronics)	President
07.06.2004	Galarce, Rafael	Survey	CAEMA (Arg. Chamber of Electro Mechanics and Components)	General Secretary
07.06.2004	Días, Patricio	Survey	General Confederation Economy; and of Commerce and Services	Public Relations Manager
08.06.2004	Etchemendy, Cesar	Survey	AFCP (Association of Cellulose and Paper Industry)	Director Sectorial Studies

09.06.2004	Fumagalli, Jose Maria	Survey	CIQYP (Chamber of Chemical and Petrochemical Industry)	Managing Director
10.06.2004	Guillermo Draletti	Survey	General Union of Milk Producers	Managing Director
18.06.2004	Maito, Miguel	Survey	CILFA (Chamber of Argentinean Pharmaceutical Laboratories)	Chief of Foreign Trade and Sanitary Regulation Department
03.09.2004	Rúa Boiero, Rodolfo	Survey	CAC (National Chamber of Commerce)	Vice-President of Commission for Trade Negotiations
08.09.2004	Kolodny, Héctor	Survey	CIAI (Argentinean Chamber of Clothing Industry)	Managing Director
09.09.2004	Ibáñez, Alberto	NEI	UIA	President Trade Department
15.09.2004	Pegoraro, Jorge/Kait, Samuel	NEI	Industrialists Group	Managing Director; Institutional Advisor
23.09.2004	Laffitte, Juan Pablo	NEI	UIA	Head of Administration
17.11.2004	Tomás, Aurelio	NEI	INAI	Trade Policy Analist
28.02.2005	Ruiz, Fernando	Survey	CAMIMA (Chamber of SME sized Metalurchical Industry)	Manging Director
08.03.2005	Martinez, Fernando	NEI	FITA (Arg. Federation of Textiles Industries)	Policy Advisor
14.03.2005	Del Bono, Liliana	NEI	APYME (Assembly of Small and Medium Entrepreneurs)	Manager of International Relations
11.03.2005	Peretti, Pedro	NEI	FAA (Arg. Agrarian Federation)	General Secretary

Selected Interview Partners

Campbell, Jorge: Industrial Engineer; currently President of International Media Consulting Group (IMCG); before the mid-1980s, Jorge Campbell worked in several trading companies dedicated to cereal exports; as Undersecretary of Foreign Trade Exchange (1986-87) he acted as one of the principal negotiators in the sectoral PICE talks with Brazil. Later in the government of Carlos Menem, he first assumed the position of Undersecretary of Foreign Trade (1989) inside the Ministry of Economy and later – between 1994 and 1999 – Campbell headed the Secretariat of Foreign Economic Relations inside the Ministry of Foreign Affairs, thus being the country's chief negotiator in international trade policy affairs. Besides, Jorge Campbell has published several articles on foreign trade and integration affairs, with the comprehensive compilation on MERCOSUR's history in 2000 standing out.

Makuc, Adrián: Economist, currently National Director of Foreign Trade Policy and the

Ministry of Economy's highest doted permanent functionary in international trade policy affairs. Before 1993, Makuc worked inside the industrial peak entity UIA as policy advisor inside the Trade Department. Then, he became part of the erected MERCOSUR Division inside the Ministry of Economy which later merged into the Foreign Trade Division inside the Secretariat of Industry and Trade. In 1998, Adrián Makuc was appointed through formal recruitment procedure as National Director of Foreign Trade Policy. Against the steady decline of the Ministry's trade policy branch and the continuous alternation of office holders of the Undersecretariat in charge, as one of the few career bureaucrats and accomplished negotiator he acted somehow as a solid rock in hard times.

Rúa Boeiro, Rodolfo: Economist, currently President of the Centre of Studies on Economic Integration and International Trade. Since the 1980s, Rúa Boeiro has acquired vast experience as trade policy advisor of business entities and annalist of Argentina's trade integration matters. During the PICE talks in the 1980s and when MERCOSUR was established in 1990-91, he directed the Technical Division of the powerful Association of Metallurgical Industry of the Argentinean Republic (ADIMRA) and acted as President of the UIA Commission of International Trade Negotiations inside the Trade Department. Later, between 1995 and 1995 Rúa Boiero served as General Secretary inside the UIA MERCOSUR Department. Lastly, he has occupied the Vice-Presidency inside the Commission of International Trade Negotiations of the National Chamber of Commerce (CNC).

5   Peru

Five years after Bolivia and simultaneously with Argentina, in 1990 Peru embarked on a development strategy based on economic stabilisation. In this way, the government of Alberto Fujimori sought to recuperate the credibility of Peru's economic policy which had been eroded during previous decades. The outlined "path to recovery" was driven by structural adjustment policies that differed greatly from measures previously in force, particularly the ISI strategy followed under the military ruling of Juan Velasco-Alvarado (1968-75) and the macroeconomic chaos caused during the populist government of Alan García (Paredes/Sachs 1991).

Regarding the pursued world market integration strategy, *section one* outlines the various incoherencies between the unilateral trade regime, (extra-) regional integration, and export and sector promotion policies that persisted throughout the economic policy shift that took place during the 1990s. Indeed, it was not before 2002 that a domestic consensus began to emerge regarding the need to set forth proactive measures in the international trade field in order to overcome the country's modest export performance. *Section two* elucidates the organisation of Peru's public sector in the trade policy area (Independent Variable A1), emphasising the way in which the domestic bureaucracy was organised for the conduction of international trade policy affairs during the period of analysis. Then, *section three* discusses the organisation of the business sector concerning the same issue (Independent Variable A2). Based on sections one to three, *section four* provides an assessment of the case, and explores the links between the independent and dependent variables, and controls the possible influences of other variables (C1-4) on the B value.

5.1 The Late Pursuit of the Multipolar Model

This first section is structured in accordance with the different policy areas that constitute the world market integration strategy (Dependent Variable B), i.e. unilateral trade regime, regional and extra-regional integration, and sectoral and export promotion policies. The final subsection summarises the results and provides an overview of the trade performance from 1985 to 2004.

The Unilateral Trade Regime

A month after taking office, Alberto Fujimori declared that trade policy reform would be a key element for macroeconomic adjustments, so as to overcome the rampant inflation and discretional practices applied to the administration of foreign trade. Above all, trade liberalisation was intensified as of February 1991, when Carlos Boloña became Minister of Economy and Finance. Consequently, in March 1991 the trade regime in force differed greatly from the legal framework applied when Alan Garcia (1985-90) left office (Abusada/Illescas/Taboada 2001). Three main differences can be clearly identified:

1) *Tariff Rates*: Average import tariffs were lowered from 46.5 to 16.8 percent and the maximum rates were reduced from 84 to 25 percent.

2) *Tariff Structure*: The reduction of tariff dispersion became a crucial element for the new economic policy. In total, the former tariff structure composed of 39 tariff levels ranging from 15 to 84 percent was reduced to just 2 levels, of 15 and 25 percent. While the lower level covered inputs, capital goods and consumer goods not produced locally, 25 percent charges were applied to domestic manufactures such as foodstuffs, clothing, footwear, electronics, and pharmaceuticals. Moreover, in December 1990, the government set the goal to gradually achieve a flat rate of 15 percent within four years.

3) *Non-Tariff Barriers (NTBs)*: The efforts to abolish the vast array of NTBs became even more wide-reaching than the tariff liberalisations. Numerous import licenses, which in 539 products such as dairy, chocolates, textiles, yarns, wood furniture and consumer electronics provided a full import protection procedure, were annulled .Furthermore, the reform of NTBs embraced a complex protectionist regime of sanitary and phytosanitary rules, import state monopolies, technical obstacles, import visas and other administrative burdens, which in total accounted for 18 types of restrictions (Abusada/Illescas/Taboada 2001: 69).

As a consequence, since 1992 Peru has become a reliable trading partner applying the tariffs established as a main instrument of border protection (WTO 2000). Trade defence came under the management of a novel decentralised agency (known as INDECOPI) which guaranteed a strict technical analysis of possible anti-dumping and safeguard measures (Camminati/

Thorne/Webb 2005). As a result of this institutional shift, defence measures were applied sparingly.[1]

Conversely, problems in the implementation of a liberal, predictable and neutral trade regime emerged with respect to Peru's plan to reach a uniform tariff structure ("flat rate"), which challenged the Common External Tariff (CET) applied by the Andean Community of Nations (CAN), composed of Peru, Bolivia, Venezuela, Ecuador, and Colombia. When the CET went into effect in January 1995, with four tariff levels, Peru insisted on two levels covering 15 and 25 percent, concentrating on 87 tariff items in the lower category. Subsequently, in April 1997, both levels were lowered by a further five percent down to 12 and 20 percent. Nonetheless, as a tariff surcharge of 5 percent was established for 320 agricultural products such as dairy, vegetables, potatoes, fruits, cereals, wheat, sugar and maize, four levels of 12, 17, 20 and 25 percent were put into effect. Lastly, in April 2001 and March 2002, respectively, Peru opened new tariff lines of four and seven percent for inputs not produced locally that, up to that time, had been in the order of 12 percent. Since 2002, Peru has set forth a tariff structure embracing no less than seven tariff lines.

Table 5.1: Peru's Tariff Structure by December 2002

Tariff lines	4 %	7 %	9 %	12 %	17 %	20 %	25 %
No. Items	1614	1070	1	3165	47	763	331

Source: CAN General Secretariat 2003: 6, based on Central Bank data.

By these measures, Peru moved closer to the escalated tariff concept applied by the CAN, maintaining 5, 10, 15 and 20 percent as the principal tariffs. In the past, Peruvian manufacturers suffered from a competitive disadvantage compared to Colombia, Ecuador and Venezuela, since their industries enjoyed not only generally higher border protection of 20 percent border tariffs, but were also able to buy inputs such as raw materials, and intermediate and capital goods based on a lower, five percent rate. Moreover, numerous CET exceptions allowed CAN members the duty free import of inputs, and extra protection, for example in the automotive regime with up to 40 percent tariffs (González Vigil 2001: 112-152).

[1] Since the institutional reform was launched in 1992, a total of 81 trade protection cases have been presented, of which 57 were followed by a dumping investigation. The application of antidumping duties was approved for 29 of the cases investigated (mainly steel and textiles). Only two cases of safeguard investigations were recorded, one of which was against Chinese textile clothing garments and was still in the negotiation phase in 2004. On December 23, 2003, Peru embarked upon a 200-day-long interim safeguard measure on 106 tariff items.

Conversely, trade in agricultural goods has been ruled under similar conditions to those of its Andean neighbours. In the WTO scope, sensitive agricultural products such as rice, wheat, milk, and maize were set at 68 percent, significantly higher than Peru's general 30 percent bound rate. The rates effectively applied to agricultural products average 14 percent *vis-à-vis* the 16 percent adopted within the CAN, according to FAO data (2003). When surcharge taxes are included, average tariffs are practically equal. Beyond nominal tariffs, Peru faced, jointly with the Andean countries, the uncertainty as to whether the applied Price Band System for sensitive agricultural products is compatible with WTO rules. The main argument sustained by the CAN to maintain this stabilisation mechanism (i.e. allowing import costs to vary freely within a fixed floor and a ceiling price) is related to compensating the distortion in world markets generated by the subsidies paid in developed countries, particularly in the areas of grains, oils, milk, meat, and sugar.[2] Compared with the Andean Price Band System covering 138 items, in Peru only 29 items were subject to variable tariffs, mainly affecting product groups of dairy, maize, sorghum, rice and sugar.[3]

(Sub-)Regional Integration

To a great extent, the trade reforms applied since 1990 coincided with the conceptual shift within the Andean sphere. The liberal reform waves throughout the region encouraged the heads of Andean countries to revitalise the dormant integration process by means of fostering intra-zone trade and marking trade openness towards extra regional partners. Therefore, in December 1991, the State Presidents of Peru, Bolivia, Colombia, Ecuador, and Venezuela agreed, through the Barahona Act, on the creation of the Andean Free Trade Area and on the adoption of a CET by January 1, 1992. With respect to the liberalisation of intra-zone trade between Peru and Ecuador, the abolishment of restricting border measures was set for July 1, 1992.

Nevertheless, the framework defined in December 1991 contrasted with the views of the key policy makers in the Ministry of Economy and Finance (MEF). The team headed by Carlos

---

[2] Beyond the absence of subsidies, in the Peruvian case the fact that the elimination of NTB's from 1991 was not accompanied by a compensatory increase in import tariffs, as occurs in Europe through the "tariffication" option embodied in the WTO agreement for agriculture, stands out.

[3] The Price Band is applied as follows. Every month, a new set of floor-ceiling prices for each relevant commodity are published; if the price of a product under the PBS (e.g. sugar) falls below its floor price, the system is triggered, and a new specific duty is imposed to bring the sugar price back to the floor price level. This additional tariff is valid for all shipments of sugar until the system is revised with the publication of the new set of trigger prices. The experience of the price band scheme applied during 1995-2002 according to FAO data (2003) showed that Peru's total taxes for sugar were as high as 54 percent (without PBS 25 percent) and 59 percent for rice (without PBS 20 percent) at certain periods of the year. Therefore, the FAO report concluded that although Peru maintained the tariffs applied below the bound rates in the scope of the WTO (68 percent), the country may face difficulties in pursuing border protections of these heights in the event tariffs are considerably reduced as a result of further multilateral negotiation rounds.

Boloña, with its distinct orthodox-liberal orientation, opposed the abolishment of the two level structure (15/25) and its conversion into a flat rate of 15 percent in 1995. The Boloña team argued that an escalated, and moreover perforated, CET would cause unpredictable fiscal policies, higher protection and discretional policy making. The MEF team further rejected the notion of the planned free trade area considering that an "even playing field" at the Andean level was hampered by intra-regional trade distortions due to export subsidies, free trade zones and rules of origin (Boloña/Illescas 1997; Abusada/Illescas/Taboada 2001: 136-143).

During 1992, the negotiation arena for Peru's full incorporation into the Andean integration scheme became increasingly small due to Boloña's inflexible position (Boloña 1993: 96). When a deadlock was finally reached by August 1992, the Andean Decision 321 embodied the temporary suspension of Peru's participation in the creation of the four-tiered CET, the intra-regional liberalisation and the less substantial macroeconomic harmonisation policies. So as to better arrange its coexistence with the Andean partners and to move further into the intra-regional liberalisation commitment, Peru negotiated bilateral trade agreements with each CAN member by the end of 1992. But with the exception of the treaty with Bolivia, the signed agreements turned out to be limited in scope, covering a few hundred products which basically reflected the advocacy strength of local sectors, as Gonzalez Vigil observed (2001: 119-120).

In the following years, Peru's relation with the CAN evolved erratically and was marked by a peculiar mix of liberal orthodoxy, foreign policy concerns and discretional policy making. With no specific modalities or deadlines, in 1994 the member states agreed on Decision 353 which defined Peru's gradual reincorporation into the Andean Free Trade Area, the conduction of common foreign affairs and macroeconomic coordination. However, as virtually no advances could be registered in the aftermath, in 1997 the Andean integration stood again at a crossroads. Particularly for the leading CAN countries, Colombia and Venezuela, the cost of maintaining Peru as a formal member seemed to outweigh those of loosing the uncommitted partner (Tello 2004: 108). Therefore, on January 27th the CAN Commission (the main policy making body) defined a 45 day deadline in which the modalities of Peru's participation in the CAN had to be clearly set.

Under this pressure, Peru opted finally to remain within the CAN. The Andean Decision 414 of July 1997, which defined the country's gradual reintegration into regional process, established a tariff reduction schedule to be initiated on August 1, 1997 and concluded on December 31, 2005. As regards the CET, the strategic goal was upheld but modalities had to first be negotiated in the scope of the Andean Commission. From 1997 to 2005, Peru made noteworthy efforts to remove residual border restrictions in intra-regional trade. Although for several products (mainly sugar, cotton, maize, vegetable oils and petroleum) significant tariff and non-tariff burdens remained, as a General Secretariat Report summarised (CAN 2005), 99 percent of Peru's tariff items affecting Andean imports had been cancelled out by August 2005.

The Report's views regarding the plans to reach a customs union implying a perfect CET were less optimistic however. Even though a "breakthrough" took place in January 2002 when the members stipulated the full CET application by December 31, 2003 (and later in October, an agreement was reached for 62 percent of the Andean nomenclature by means of Decision 535), recent years' experiences highlighted the unreliable commitment of Peru's government. Despite the diplomatic insistence to converge the external tariffs, to date Peru has rejected the definitive abolishment of the flat rate ideal.

In 2005, the future of the CAN was uncertain as the planned integration steps aimed at going beyond an Andean FTA generally failed to materialise. The commitment assumed in May 1999 to establish an Andean Common Market by 2005, requiring the creation of conditions for the free movement of goods, services, investments and people, proved to be impossible to reach in light of modest concessions that barely went further than previously implemented unilateral commitments (Niño Tarazona 2003; CAN 2005). Even though all members exhibited limitations in their dedication towards the Andean integration, Peru's unreliable participation has been considered as the most detrimental factor to the harmonisation of trade policies, and thus, prevented the creation of a solid trading block in the challenging regional and multilateral sphere.

Extra- Subregional Integration

Fifteen years of advances and setbacks within the Andean scope entailed negative impacts on Peru's economic integration plans beyond the sub-regional sphere. Cesar Peñaranda, the Chief Advisor in Boloña's team, stated (OE 08/07/04), *"as we left office in December 1992, comprehensive free trade talks were scheduled with Chile and Mexico given the fact that we sought a bilateral strategy outside the Andean Group, in the way that Chile did"*. Whatever the intentions of the Boloña cadre may have been, the subsequent office holders did little, in fact, to make Peru resemble the Chilean case during the 1990s, as I shall briefly summarise below.

ALADI: Inside Latin America, for a long time Peru only pursued so-called Partial Scope Agreements that were based on limited, temporary tariff preferences; for instance with Argentina, Brazil, Chile, Cuba, Mexico and Uruguay. During the 1990s, the only comprehensive

FTA was signed with Chile in June 1998. The bilateral treaty known as ACE No. 38 established the goal of dismantling tariffs by 2016, including immediate liberalisation of one third of tariff items, and a schedule for future liberalisation in 3, 5, 6, 8, 10, 15 and 18 years. Another attempt to negotiate a similarly structured treaty with Mexico became deadlocked as the talks initiated at the end of 1996 came to an end only a few months thereafter. Furthering relations with the MERCOSUR block became a possibility in 1997, when Peru suggested a bilateral approach in the context of its possible departure from the CAN. However, the later reincorporation into the Andean integration scheme put an end to this opportunity. Instead, Peru became part of the free trade talks between MERCOSUR and the CAN launched by the first Framework Agreement in April 1998. After years of frequently interrupted negotiations, in August 2003 Peru agreed with Argentina and Brazil (afterwards also with Uruguay and Paraguay) on the full liberalisation of tariff lines within 15 years. Insofar as sensitive agricultural products, Peru reserved its right to maintain both the Price Band System and residual border duties until 2020.

FTAA – FTA with the United States: Peru's actions directed to North America proved more proactive than its trade diplomacy in South America. During the 1990s, the United States evolved into the prime market for local exports, increasing its share of total exports between 1994 and 2004 from 16 to nearly 30 percent (WTO 2000; MINCETUR 2005a). Between 1991 and 2002, trade relations had been ruled by the Andean Trade Promotion Act (ATPA), a unilateral trade preference scheme enacted by the US Congress. In 2002, ATPA was renewed and expanded by means of the Andean Trade Promotion and Drug Eradication Act (ATPDEA), providing duty-free access for roughly 6,000 non-traditional products in the range of agriculture, jewellery, textiles and clothing.[4]

Against the increasing non-traditional exports, in 2000, Peru set forth a vigorous lobby campaign in the US capital city to promote not only the renovation of ATPA but to expand coverage for textiles and clothing. Simultaneously, the country held strong interests in the FTAA negotiations formally launched in 1998, because the hemispheric project was perceived as a window of opportunity for local manufactures and services (Fairlie 2003). But as the FTAA stalled due to strongly opposing views between MERCOSUR and the US, the Ricardo Toledo administration demonstrated its keenness to negotiate a bilateral FTA as had been signed by Chile and various states in Central America. For example, Peru put into evidence its alignment with the US by its departure from the development faction G-22 in October 2003 in the

---

[4] The ATPA (later APTDEA) offers three main advantages over the US GSP; it covers more tariff categories; imports under ATPA are not subject to GSP competitive-need and country-income restrictions; and qualifying rules for individual products are more liberal in terms of local-content requirements; see www.ustr.org.

aftermath of the WTO Ministerial Conference in Cancún. Therefore, the Bush administration announced on May 3, 2004 that Peru and Ecuador would join the first round of negotiations in the US-Andean Free Trade Agreement (US-AFTA) scheduled for May 18-19, which had originally been planned to be initiated only with Colombia (USTR press releases "AFTA"; www.ustr.gov).

Despite Peru's strong interest, trade talks could not be concluded before December 2005, and thus, the initial goal of concluding negotiations by December 2004 was missed. Disregarding the impact of the US domestic politics, on the Peruvian side two sensitive issues were mainly responsible for hindering the fast conclusion of the negotiations.

1) *Agriculture*: Local agriculture is dominated by subsistence farming located in mountain areas. Sixty percent of productive units are smaller than 0.3 hectares and only 25 percent of cultivated land responds to productive units beyond 15 hectares, mostly found in the coastal areas in the north (MINAG 2004). Hence, peasants felt threatened by the potential "invasion" of subsidised US wheat, maize, sugar, and meat. The US government, moreover, refused to accept the maintenance of the Price Band System as a compensation mechanism for market distortions through domestic support.

2) *Intellectual Property Rights (IPR)*: Under Colombia's leadership, the Andean countries tried to avoid the adoption of US standards of IPR protection and enforcement that went well beyond TRIPS standards. For example, by extending the 20-year patent protection for branded drugs and the limitation of parallel imports and compulsory licensing, the availability of cheap generics becomes increasingly difficult. Furthermore, the Andean negotiators were keen to exclude plants and animals from patentability because of their legal impact on the Andean biodiversity. Patent applicants should, furthermore, be required to disclose the source and country of origin of genetic resources and traditional knowledge used in the invention, thus, enabling fair and equitable benefit sharing.

In general, the Peruvian government maintained, however, less antagonistic positions compared to Colombia, and as a consequence, was able to complete the talks by December 2005, while the negotiations between Colombia and the US continued throughout 2006. While Colombia made numerous objections concerning the new negotiation areas of intellectual property, state procurement, services and investment, for Peru this agreement was considered, above all, as a powerful anchor that would magnify the structural adjustment reforms of the 1990s that were aimed at the attraction of FDIs and the modernisation of domestic economic sectors.

APEC: As of 2002, Peru announced its involvement in several trade policy forums, so as to underline its new proactive course in the search for external markets. For example, through extensive presidential visits throughout the Asian Pacific Area during 2003-04, the government emphasised its will to capitalise Peru's APEC membership as of 1998. The expanding markets in the pacific neighbourhood were to be conquered through mining, fish and non-traditional exports, such as fruits and vegetables. In the aftermath, the free trade talks were nevertheless limited to negotiations launched with Thailand in January 2004, whereby six rounds were concluded by August 2005 with no agreement yet reached (*La Gestión* 16/08/05).

European Union: With respect to the EU, Peru has been seeking to take advantage of its CAN membership, as the Andean block sustains the strategic objective of reaching an Association Agreement with the European countries that would involve, among other aspects a Free Trade Area. Nonetheless, the process has been arduous thus far. After a Political Dialogue and Cooperation Agreement in December 2003 determined that negotiations would be initiated, the parties agreed in January 2004 to carry out a Joint Evaluation of the integration degree attained in the Andean region. Through this previous study on the institutional framework of the CAN and the functioning of the sub-regional market and customs union, the EU expressed evident doubts about the reliability of the CAN as a negotiation partner. In the meantime, Peru's exports benefit from preferential access in the scope of the Andean GSP that was launched in 1990, and renewed at the beginning of 2002 and 2005.

Trade and Sector Promotion

The involvement in regional and hemispheric liberalisation initiatives urged the government to consider accompanying measures that would prepare the local economy for the impact of free trade. Indeed, after the state ceased to be an active promoter and facilitator of sectoral development in the 1990s, the debate on supportive public policies was revitalised, especially in recent years, reaching a peak when Peru decided to participate in the US-AFTA talks. The responses given by the government of Ricardo Toledo (2001-06) embraced the following two programmes:

1) *National Competitiveness Council (CNC).* An attempt to foster economic development came to life in April 2002. According to the WEF Global Competitiveness Report 2004-05 (in which Peru ranked 68 out of 117), the CNC placed priority on ten working streams covering the articulation of supply chains, technical innovation, educational reform, infrastructure, judicial reform, environment and natural resources, among others. The principal method used within the CNC scope was the increase of coordination among

state and private actors involved in the policy area and the definition of policy guidelines and strategies.

2) *National Export Plan 2003-2013 (PENX):* With respect to the development of exports, in 2003 the national government initiated the PENX. As with the CNC, state authorities invited private sector entities to collaborate on several strategic topics affecting the competitiveness of local exports, such as the development of supply chains, research and development, quality standards, trade promotion and intelligence, customs procedures, and transport systems. Accordingly, the sectoral focus considered clothing, jewellery, processed fish, non-traditional agriculture and leather manufactures, among others.

The evaluation made by consulted experts proved to be rather sceptical as regards official efforts to accompany international trade policies, nonetheless. The more heterodox economists stated that attempts rarely went beyond the rhetorical level, and thus, scarcely differed from the structural adjustment policies implemented in the 1990s (OE's Cornejo 4/10/04; González Vigil 15/07/04; Campodónico 14/03/05; Dávila 13/07/04; Rebosio 14/07/04). The more orthodox comments underscored the lack of consistency and clearly stated that the "domestic policy agenda" should not only embrace promotion activities, but that it should also address the modernisation of education, public administration, judicial, transport and tax systems, among others (OE's Garcia 7/07/04; Peñaranda 8/07/04; BR Teullet 7/07/04).

Regarding the promotion of exports, the responsibilities were assumed by the Peruvian Export Promotion Commission (PROMPEX) created in 1996. The work of PROMPEX has been considered as highly effective regarding the promotion of non-traditional exports, especially in developing "clusters" among roughly 40 private organisations in the range of agricultural products, such as asparagus, mangoes, and lemons (Brenes/Emmons/Madrigal 2001). Despite its apparent effectiveness, the activities put forward by PROMPEX have been seriously limited by a modest budget allocation that ranged from US$3 to 5 million (MEF budget data 2004-05; *La Gestión* 20/06/02).

Other facilities offered to exporters were severely reduced in the 1990s. For example, specific programs for export finance or credit guarantees were no longer available in 1994, as private companies, operating under market conditions, took over the supply of such services. Refunds to non-traditional exports of up to 30 percent of the FOB value paid as of the late 1970s (for example through CERTEX) were abolished in the 1990s, moreover. Instead, a reimbursement scheme began operating in 1995 which implied a refund of 5 percent of the FOB value, regardless of the actual amount of duties paid on imported inputs. Nevertheless, this drawback mechanism has only been applied to small scale exporters and limited further to exports that do not incorporate inputs imported under preferential regimes.[5]

Summary Dependent Variable B

In general, Peru's approach to world market integration sustained from 1985 to 2004 has been disappointing, meeting the criteria for neither the Multipolar nor the Springboard models. In summarising this section, Box 5.1 below highlights the main failures observed. Aside from the structural adjustment set forth in 1990, the Peruvian government didn't pursue clear economic integration objectives on the regional and multilateral level. It is only in the present decade that Peru has begun to implement more active international trade policies through noteworthy efforts undertaken in the hemispheric and Pacific area, and predominantly, by fostering non-traditional exports towards the US market.

Box 5.1: Summary Dependent Variable

Unilateral Trade Regime	Regional Integration	Extra-Regional Integration	Export Promotion	Sector Promotion
1990-91: Trade reform that abolished NTBs and lowered average tariffs from 46.5 to 16.8%; later 10.9%. Failed "flat rate" by ending up with 7 tariff lines as of 2002 Exceptions: Price Band System for agriculture products	Uncommitted and erratic CAN membership. In 1992, Peru suspended the membership so as to adopt a flat rate and to define individual forms of trade. But in 1997, Peru returned, though conflicts on the CET issue have yet to be cleared up. Peru signed FTAs with Chile and MERCOSUR.	Since 1998, Peru participated with enthusiasm in the hemispheric FTAA process. As the FTAA stalled, Peru launched bilateral free trade talks with the US as of May 2004 (negotiations were completed in December 2005)	Until PROMPEX was created in 1996, Peru maintained no official export promotion scheme. The National Export Strategy 2003-2013 seeks the development of non-traditional exports, though support schemes have been modest thus far.	As of 1990, the state mostly withdrew as an active promoter and facilitator of sectoral development.

---

[5] In 1998, drawback refunds totaled US$55 million, which represented less than 1 percent of the total value of exports; see WTO 2000. Large scale exporters had the possibility to refund the general tax paid on used inputs. Other measures provided to lower production costs were the temporary admission regime enabling the duty free import of inputs. For a detailed analysis of local trade promotion schemes, see Arbués Pérez Espinoza 2003.

Between 1985 and 2004, Peru registered a considerable export growth, with export sales rising from US$2,977 to 12,486 million, herein overcoming the stagnation of exports observed in the 1970s and 1980s. The overall trade balance was negative, however, with the constant deficits from 1991 to 2001 standing out. In addition, the strong dependence on traditional mining and fishery commodities was not significantly altered, since these tariff items accounted for roughly 70 percent of all exports throughout the period of analysis. The most promising non-traditional exports turned out to be textiles and clothing aimed at the US market, and agriculture and fishery products such as asparagus, mangoes, frozen fish, and calamari, whose exportation was geographically more diversified.

5.2 State Bureaucracy: From the Economy to the Foreign Trade Model?

This section is structured along the following lines. The first subsection, *responsibilities,* exposes the division of labour in the conduction of international trade policy affaires, involving the inter-ministerial coordination among the different sectoral departments involved. Then, *resources* provides a description of how the trade policy team evolved in the last two decades with respect to staff size, technical expertise, and the application of civil service models. Finally, the subsection *openness* discusses the mechanism for consultation with the business and civil society.

Responsibilities

Traditionally, trade policy relied on the executive branch, which operated without significant interference from Congress (OE Araoz 23/02/04; Fairlie 2003). However, the FTA talks with the US made Congress increasingly aware of its role in monitoring and approving international commitments, above all regarding the defence of sensitive areas in agriculture, pharmaceuticals, and textile manufactures; albeit in the latter case the struggles were mainly in the area of imports from China (BR Manzur 26/02/04). Being at loggerheads with the outward oriented MINCETUR, in 2005 the Foreign Trade Commission in Congress put forward a Trade Negotiation Law to urge the executive to regularly inform the legislative on negotiation strategies pursued at the international level (*La Gestión* 16/08/05).

Historically, economic policy in general, and trade policy in particular, were under the exclusive responsibility of the Ministry of Economy and Finance (MEF). In 1969, as the military regime under Juan Velasco opted for the implementation of a distinct ISI model, the regulation and promotion of foreign trade were granted independent status in the state executive. After four years of coexistence with industrial policies, as of 1973 trade concerns received the exclusive attention of the Ministry of Trade. Later, the area of trade policy went through a broad variety of institutional settings as shown in Table 5.2.

Moreover, Table 5.2. clearly indicates that "foreign trade" and "integration" affairs have been divided, although the strengthening of intra-regional trade was central within the scope of the regional integration endeavours of the Andean Group, ALALC and ALADI.

Table 5.2: Foreign Trade and Integration Affairs in the Ministerial Structure 1969-2004

Term/Presidency	Foreign Trade	Integration
1969 – 1973/ Juan Velasco	Ministry of Industry and Trade	National Integration Office (ONIT)
1973 – 1976/ Juan Velasco	Ministry of Trade	
1976 – 1977/ Francisco Morales Bermúdez	Ministry of Trade	Ministry of Integration
1977 – 1980/ Francisco Morales Bermúdez	Ministry of Industry, Trade, Tourism & Integration (MICTI)	ONIT in force until 1981
1980 – 1985/ Fernando Belaunde	Ministry of Economy, Finance and Trade	Ministry of Industry, Tourism and Integration (MITI)
1985 – 1987/ Alan García	Ministry of Industry, Trade, Tourism and Integration	
1987 – 1990/ Alan García	Foreign Trade Institute (ICE)	Ministry of Industry, Domestic Trade, Tourism and Integration (MICITI)
1990 – 2000/ Alberto Fujimori	MEF	Ministry of Industry, Tourism, Integration and International Trade Negotiations (MITINCI)
2000-2001/ Valentín Paniagua	PROMPEX; INDECOPI	
2002 – Ricardo Toledo	MINCETUR; INDECOPI	MINCETUR

Source: General Office of Administration/ MINCETUR 2004a

In the 1970s, Latin American integration affairs were assumed by the National Integration Office (ONIT), a technical department under the presidential office. The interim existence of the Ministry of Integration emphasised the political tone that regional integration enjoyed at that time. As the government of Fernando Belaunde took office in 1980, the area of foreign trade was again transferred into the Ministry of Economy and Finance, whereas integration affairs were placed together with industry and tourism in the MITI area.

Major institutional innovations were introduced during the APRA administration of Alan García (1985-1990). After the creation of the broad-reaching Ministry of Industry, Trade, Tourism and Integration in 1985, in 1987 the populist left-wing government decided to create the Institute of Foreign Trade (ICE), which absorbed the most relevant trade policy competencies, as Enrique Cornejo, the first ICE President (at that time 29 years old), remembered (OE 4/10/04): *"Our idea was to drive forward the development of exports, therefore, a special agency with ministerial rank was established merging the competences in trade related areas of promotion, regulation, and international negotiations."* Verbal reports indicated that the ICE worked rather professionally during its first year of existence, but later began to deteriorate due to excessive bureaucratic procedures, corruption, and political party influences (OE's Cornejo 4/10/04; Lopez 09/02/05; SO Elmore 10/02/05; 4.2.2). Regarding the conduction of international trade policy affairs, the clarity was undermined due to the fact that the ICE covered all areas related to trade policy, while the MICITI remained formally in charge of integration affairs, hence causing inter-ministerial conflicts in the conduction of trade negotiations in the ALADI and Andean Group scope (SO Brandes 15/02/05).

Once again, the institutional setting was strongly modified under the administration of Alberto Fujimori. In times of rationalisation and macroeconomic crisis, the oversized ICE staff disappeared in 1991. But the responsibilities held by ICE were not transferred "neatly" to the Ministry of Industry, Domestic Trade, Tourism and Integration, as Victoria Elmore observed (SO 2/10/05). While the MEF took over the resolute leadership in the definition of new tariff structures and the abolishment non-tariff measures, other areas like trade promotion, contingency measures, and international trade negotiations became virtually unaccounted for, and were later divided among different ministries. In October 1992 regional and multilateral trade affairs were granted legal status when the MICITI was transformed into the Ministry of Industry, Tourism, Integration, and International Trade Negotiations (MITINCI).

During the 1990s, the MITICI operated as a weak agency, since active industrial policies almost vanished. With regard to trade policy, the MEF defined the structure of border measures, and the 1992-created National Institute of Intellectual Property and Defense of the Competition (INDECOPI), became simultaneously in charge of competition policies, protection of intellectual property rights and the application of contingency measures. From 1996, the newly created PROMPEX hosted trade promotion actions in the scope of the office of the Vice-President.

Moreover, the orthodox-liberal economic policy inside the MEF, which lead reform endeavours in the 1990s, left no space for independent policy making as regards international trade policy affairs. Adolfo Lopez (OE 9/02/05), former Vice-Minister of Integration 1990-91 and currently a CAN official, recalled; *"when Peru was about to suspend its participation in 1992, Minister of Economy, Carlos Boloña, invited himself to the meetings of the CAN Commission. Boloña sat next to Peru's formal MITINCI representative and instructed him to sign the documents under his supervision and will."* For Lopez (ibid.), the limitation of MITINCI's negotiation role was t an extent self-inflicted. *"Our negotiators who came over (the CAN headquarter is located in Lima) were never able to negotiate the official position designed by the MEF. Consequently, they did not provide sound technical arguments to the Andean partners indicating why Peru wished to pursue the flat rate, and based on what fiscal reasons Peru could not immediately liberalise intra-regional trade."*

Studying the internal structure of the MITINCI office, this lack of coherent trade policy in the Andean scope is reflected by the two opposing "schools", which prevented, as of 1991, the creation of a concerted position within the ministerial staff.

Table 5.3: The Two Trade Policy "Schools" inside the MITINCI

	"Integration School"	**"Foreign Trade School"**
Policy Rationale	Favoured the Springboard Model in maintaining close relations with the Andean states.	Favoured the Multipolar Model in withdrawing from the CAN and furthering bilateral relations with the US and APEC states.
Leaders and Institutional Scope	Eduardo Brandes; Head of the National Directorate of Integration Affairs	Victoria Elmore; Head of the Foreign Trade Advisory Unit and (from 2000) National Director of Multilateral Affairs
Strategic Partners	Manufacturers (SNI)	Ministry of Economy and Finance (MEF)

Source: SO's Sánchez (9/07/04); Elmore (10/05/05) ; Brandes (15/02/05)

In general terms, the staff inside the National Directorate of Integration Affairs (until 2000 this was the only division of the Vice-Ministry of Integration and International Trade Negotiations) put forward a rather heterodox policy approach in favouring subregional, i.e. Andean, integration schemes and coordinating closely with the local industry associated to the National Society of Industry (SNI). In doing so, Eduardo Brandes, head of this division, veered from the rhetoric sustained by most (Vice-) Ministers in charge during the 1990s, as well by the Foreign Trade Advisory Unit that operated rather informally until 2000 in the Vice-Ministerial Office. This unit, directed by Victoria Elmore, shared the orthodox-liberal policy goals of the MEF in sustaining the flat rate concept and the need to withdraw from the CAN.

According to Victoria Elmore (SO 10/02/05), her point of view first began to be considered at the end of the 1990s, coinciding with Alfredo Ferrero taking office in March 1999. Ferrero, who was invited to become the Vice-Minister of Integration and International Trade Negotiations, began to encourage the hemispheric and pacific forums of FTAA and APEC and argued in favour of a steady expansion toward new markets. To accentuate the new geographical priorities, the National Directorate of Multilateral Affairs was established in 2000. Under

Alfredo Ferrero (who remained in office during four years under the constant changes of office holders and was appointed as Minister of Foreign Trade and Tourism in November 2003) the "foreign trade school" gained rising recognition among state and business actors. Finally, a vigorous lobby undertaken by Ferrero and Raúl Diez Canseco (Minister and Vice-President 07/2001-11/2003) led to the creation of the Ministry of Foreign Trade and Tourism (MINCETUR) in May 2002, which was further backed by an IDB loan of US$5 million (IDB 2002).

Separated from industrial policy, the MINCETUR assumed the responsibility for the formulation and execution of export promotion schemes and the conduction and coordination of trade negotiations in the regional and multilateral spheres. However, as regards the transparency of those responsibilities, the survey carried out from March to October 2004 among 51 experts, state officials and business representatives suggested a somewhat ambiguous picture. The survey candidates were asked: *Inside the executive branch, is there a clear division of labour in the conduction of international trade policy affairs? If not, in what areas can ambiguity be identified?*

Table 5.4: Division of Labour in International Trade Policy Affairs

	Experts (11)	State Officials (15)	Business (25)	Total (51)
very clear	0	0	3	3 (8%)
rather clear	6	5	9	20 (53%)
rather unclear	3	6	6	15 (39%)
very unclear	0	0	0	0 (0%)
no response	2	4	7	13

Although no responses considered the division of labour as very ambiguous, almost 40 percent of respondents had some difficulty in clearly ascribing the ministerial roles in international trade policy affairs. Analysing the answers categorically, it is surprising that state officials tended to perceive responsibilities as less clear than experts and business representatives. As evidence, several officials highlighted the unresolved issue of the division of work between MINCETUR and the Ministry of External Affairs, Peru's official negotiator abroad and coordinator also in foreign economic affairs. For example, regular conflicts arouse in the WTO scope as the mission in Geneva is in the hands of the Ministry of Foreign Affairs. In this regard, a MINCETUR official objected that the Ministry's multilateral competencies were often undermined as the reports from Geneva related to ongoing multilateral talks were often late or incomplete (SO February 2004).

Insofar as business, the vast majority of respondents recognised MINCETUR as a very clear leader in ongoing international negotiations, while the role of the Ministries of Production and Foreign Affairs were described as insignificant. Conversely, the peak entity representing domestic market oriented farmers, CONVEAGRO, considered the Ministry of Agriculture as the main negotiator unit, and hence, tried to minimise the role of the open market-oriented MINCETUR staff. The metal industry still perceived the MEF as the agency that holds the ultimate decision in crucial moments. Above all, the (changing) role of the MEF was discussed by experts stressing the agencies key policy-making position in the 1990s. Thereafter, commentaries portrayed the MEF as a "super agency" where the economic model was developed without interference from other departments. Conversely in 2004, the MEF was still perceived as the most powerful ministry, but other economic policy areas, such as MINCETUR, gained institutional weight inside the government of Ricardo Toledo (2001-2006).

In the 2003-04 period, international trade negotiations took place under the permanent participation of no less than five ministries and numerous specialised bodies, such as INDECOPI and the National Customs Authority who acted as providers of technical support on specific topics (Box 5.2). This organisation model demanded that MINCETUR adopt a distinct role as coordinator, as the contribution of a broad range of policy areas was required. The survey results provided in 2004 indicated, nonetheless, clear shortcomings regarding the pattern of inter-ministerial coordination. In this regard, the questionnaire asked: *Is their close inter-ministerial coordination among the departments involved in International trade policy affairs? If not, in what areas can coordination gaps be identified?*

Table 5.5: Inter-Ministerial Trade Policy Coordination

	Experts (11)	State Officials (15)	Business (25)	Total (51)
very close	0	0	0	0 (0%)
rather close	0	2	6	8 (23%)
rather sporadic	7	8	8	23 (66%)
very sporadic	1	1	2	4 (11%)
no response	3	4	9	16

The results turned out to be fairly identical throughout the categories, given that no sector considered the inter-ministerial coordination pattern as a very close, and only 8 out of the 35 answers rated coordination efforts as rather close. Apart from the usually lamented absence of "the culture of sharing information and of inter-agency teamwork", the most commonly stated shortcomings involved three major aspects:

1) *Competition:* As indicated, competition persisted between the MINCETUR staff, representing the new dynamic trade policy, and the cadre of the Ministry of Foreign Affairs, as Peru's official negotiators abroad.

2) *Policy Approaches:* Each staff followed its own trade integration concept. MINCETUR officials claimed to be the vigorous force in opening markets through bilateral agreements worldwide. The interest of the MEF officials was to maintain uniform tariff rates and to further unilateral liberalisation. The US free trade talks were considered only as a pragmatic tool for the consolidation of the liberal model implemented in the 1990s which would weaken moreover the Andean Community's influence. The Ministry of Agriculture advocated the defensive rural interests and sought to slow down trade liberalisation via international negotiations. Lastly, the Ministry of Foreign Affairs pursued (with little success) the opportunity to foster economic integration in South American integration, considering this to be a useful tool for foreign policies.

3) *Style of Governance:* Despite the fact that the MEF and MINCETUR, as trade policy agencies, shared important policy goals such as the relationship with the US and the consolidation of economic reforms, their style of governance contrasted markedly. In this regard, a young MEF official claimed, significantly, *"MINCETUR fellows are captured by business factions and lack consistent policies"* (October 2004). Conversely, a group of MINCETUR officials lamented *"When MEF officials enter, all good intentions immediately come to an end"*, indicating the orthodoxy upheld by the MEF officials as regards predictable fiscal policies and the flat rate concept (February 2005). Hence, the MEF maintained distant relations with business factions in order to sustain its technocratic style of governance.

As outlined in Box 5.2, despite inter-agency divisions, in the scope of the US-AFTA talks the Peruvian government sustained a formal organisational chart in which inter-ministerial coordination was shown on both the political and the negotiation level through the Multisectoral Commission and the Technical Committee, respectively. On the political level, the US-AFTA talks initiated by MINCETUR enjoyed strong presidential support, given that they were defined as a key project for the enhancement of the limited popularity of Alejandro Toledo's presidency.[6]

---

[6] In 2004-05, the popularity of the Toledo administration oscillated between 5 and 15 percent.

Box 5.2: Peruvian State Organisation in US-AFTA Talks

Political Level: Multisectoral Commission

Head: Minister of Foreign Trade and Tourism - Alfredo Ferrero

Members: Vice-Ministry of Foreign Trade, Ministries of Economy and Finance; Foreign Affairs; Production; Agriculture; Mining and Energy; Justice; Health and Labour; Embassy in Washington

Negotiation Level: Technical Committee

Head and Chief Negotiator: Vice-Minister of Foreign Trade – Pablo De la Flor

Members: MINCETUR and Ministries of Economy and Finance; Foreign Affairs; Agriculture; Production

Area Responsibilities

MINCETUR: Market Access; Customs Procedures; Technical Obstacles; Trade Defence and Competition Policy; Dispute Settlement; Capacity Building; Electronic Trade; Labour and Environment Protection

MEF: Service

PROINVERSION: Investment

MINAG: Agriculture

INDECOPI: Intellectual Property

SENASA: (Phyto-) Sanitary Measures

Source: www.tlcperu-eeuu.gob.pe

On the negotiation level, coordination mechanisms depended mostly on informal links among key bureaucrats. Rather than maintain plenary sessions in the Technical Committee, Chief Negotiator Pablo De la Flor, according to a young MINCETUR negotiator (February 2005), was said to prefer individual meetings with the main negotiators of each area. Proceeding in this manner, Pablo De la Flor possessed a privileged position as he was the only one who accurately knew the possible trade offs among the areas involved. This "bilateral strategy" allowed De la Flor to better control the influence of key officials, above all Eduardo Brandes (MINCETUR), head of the market access area and Javier Illescas (MEF), who directed service negotiations. Nonetheless, by February 2005, during my last field trip in Peru, these talks were still ongoing, pending revealing final stage actions in these historic talks.

Resources

When analysing the human and financial resources involved in trade policy making since 1985, three distinct periods can be highlighted. *The first phase* covers the time prior to 1990 and implies the ISI model that was embodied paradigmatically in the Foreign Trade Institute (ICE) created in 1987. The ICE, in charge of regulating import and export trade, among others, rapidly evolved into a fast expanding bureaucratic space where politics, hyper-legalism and corruption reigned. Although the ICE started with 170 officials in 1987, the number of employees involved in the administration of foreign trade increased to 900 in 1990 (OE Cornejo 4/10/04; SO Elmore 10/02/05). The areas of promotion and negotiation continued to operate in a rather autonomous way however, and remained "technical bodies" with no more than 30 professionals (SO Elmore 10/02/05).

The second phase started with an abrupt decline of resources in 1990-2001, as instructed by the Fujimori government. In particular, agencies coupled with state interventionism, such as the ICE, the National Planning Institute (IPE), and state owned development banks were abolished, as they contravened the initiated market-oriented model. In the case of ICE, only a small number of about 10-15 officials were transferred to the Ministry of Industry, Domestic Trade, Tourism and Integration (MITICI). At first, this group was practically unaccounted for, since the enacted austerity plan prohibited the hiring of new personnel, as Victoria Elmore commented (ibid.). As a result, the small number of ICE officials (who had committed themselves not to work for the public sector during five years) entered MITICI as a part of a "Trade Development Project" that was initially supported by a private sector fund. After roughly one year, the local business entities refused to continue funding trade policy staff, and thus, the payment of salaries came to depend on means provided by the World Bank, and later, the Andean Development Corporation (CAF).

Simultaneously, the integration area in the MITICI (later MITINCI) also suffered from severe budget cuts. Adolfo Lopez, Vice-Minister of Integration (1990-91) reflected (OE 9/10/05): *"The MITINCI was one of the entities most affected by the austerity plans; the state could not dismiss teachers, doctors, or policemen since they were indispensable, but MITICI meant the fullest expression of bureaucratic inefficiency for the sake of producing onerous paperwork involved in the regulation of domestic trade, subsidies, and price controls. During the eight months I stayed in office, I was compelled to reduce the staff in the Vice-Ministry from 100 to 30 employees including chauffeurs, and in the entire Ministry from 2.500 to 800."* In the following years, the MITINCI staff further reduced, ending up with just 180 employees, as Jaime Garcia, Vice-Minister of Integration and International Trade Negotiations in the mid-1990s, reported (OE 07/07/04). On this basis, both the regional and the multilateral areas were relegated during the 1990s, and were covered by no more than a handful of policy experts. While the multilateral area operated as an advisory unit in the Vice-Ministerial Office, regional affairs were dealt with in the National Directorate of Integration Affairs.

Lastly, *the third phase* was developed gradually. For Jaime Garcia (ibid.), the FTAA talks launched at the Santiago Summit in 1998 *"served as a clear dynamic force"* that subsequently entailed a vibrant institutional development during the administration of Alfredo Ferrero. Aware of the domestic shortcomings, as of July 2002 striking efforts were undertaken in the scope of the new MINCETUR to create a team of trade policy advisors capable of handling the demanding international trade policy scenario. In contrast to the 1990s, *"today, the country's best negotiators are convened, though certain areas are not adequately dealt with by the still rather modest team"*, concluded Garcia.

The impression stated by the former MITINCI official was corroborated, to a great extent, by data from the 2004 survey. The following question was posed: *Is the official team in charge of international trade policy affairs adequately staffed in order to comply with the technical requirements of modern international trade policy affairs (staff size, talent and experience)? If not, in what areas/issues can limitations be found?*

Table 5.6: Trade Policy Staff

	Experts (11)	State Officials (15)	Business (25)	Total (51)
absolutely adequate	0	1	0	1 (2%)
rather adequate	3	1	11	15 (34%)
rather inadequate	5	11	9	25 (57%)
very inadequate	1	1	1	3 (7%)
no response	2	1	4	7

Strikingly, it was the business sector that made the most positive assessment of the official negotiation team, perceiving its capacities as even higher than state officials, who considered their own skills in only 2 out of 14 given responses as adequate. In this issue, it stands out that business responses primarily made reference to market access issues, and hence, to areas in which MINCETUR negotiators enjoyed accumulated experience in the scope of ALADI. In contrast to the business sector, both experts and state officials placed emphasis on the lack of specialists in new trade topics, particularly in services, competition policy, state procurement, intellectual property, and environmental measures. However, in all these categories, objections pointed at the rather small team and the fact that the majority of "MINCETUR boys" barely had any field experience. Consequently, the main responsibility in the ongoing talks was still in the hands of a handful of functionaries who had acquired experience since the 1980s. According to ministerial structures in 2004, negotiation expertise could be found in the following agencies.

MINCETUR – Vice-Ministry of Foreign Trade (VMCE): In July 2004, MINCETUR staff totalled 467 employees, involving the Ministerial Office, the Vice-Ministries of Tourism and Foreign Trade, and several decentralised agencies (MINCETUR 2004b). The VMCE had 96 functionaries. Of these, about 40 could be considered a part of the official negotiation team; these were spread through the National Directorates of Integration, Multilateral and Bilateral Affairs. The latter area emerged as a result of the reorganisation that took place in February 2004, in an attempt to respond to trade talks with the US and future bilateral efforts. In December 2003, the VMCE began introducing a matrix organisation based on geographical and issue areas, and thus, mimicked the organisational model applied by Chile, Mexico and the US. Nevertheless, I had difficulties when gathering sound data, due to the fact that the official structure was virtually suspended during the US-AFTA talks which started in May 2004 and involved *"practically the entire VMCE"*, according to comments made by officials during my visits to Lima. In this regard, critical voices remarked that MINCETUR had become a "single issues agency," neglecting other crucial affairs for local export development.

Aside from MINCETUR, who represented the majority of the official team, 20 negotiators originated from other state agencies. Table 5.7 provides an overview of the internal structure of the five main areas outside MINCETUR, involved in the US-AFTA talks.

Table 5.7: The Peruvian Negotiation Team beyond the MINCETUR

	MEF	MINAG	Foreign Affairs	PRODUCE	INDECOPI
Entity in Charge	General Directorate of International Economy	National Office of Agrarian Planning	Undersecretariat of Economic Affairs & International Negotiations	General Directorate of Industry	Intellectual Property Tribunal
Negotiators/ Assistants	3/6	4/8	3/7	2/12	3/6
Areas	Financial services, market access	Agriculture, sanitary rules (SENASA)	Market access, intellectual property	Technical norms, environment	Intellectual property, trade defence
Labour Regime	Temporary Contracts	Temporary contracts	Diplomatic career	Temporary contracts	Private sector regime
Evaluation	Important but small area	Strengthened as of 1999	Small area	Domestic involvement	Important but small area

Source: SO's Sanchez 9/07/04 (MEF); Romero 24/02/04 (MINAG); García 9/07/04 (INDECOPI); Alfaro 12/07/04 (Foreign Affairs); Talavera 13/07/04 (Produce).

Studying Table 5.7, the staff monitoring and analysing international trade negotiations was rather weakly doted. Out with MINCETUR, an organisational strengthening took place only in the Ministry of Agriculture, which had been strongly affected by structural adjustment policies at the beginning of the 1990s. While the Uruguay Round came to an end without the steady participation of the Ministry of Agriculture, since 1999 a team of young economists has been gradually formed in order to carry out professional assessments in this crucial negotiation area.

In general terms, state reforms set forth as of the 1990s did not cover the strengthening of bureaucratic staff in most areas of the central government. Although several well equipped, autonomous, state agencies were established for the administration of taxes, market and banking regulations, the planned wide-reaching public administration reforms could not be carried out due to an insufficient political will to enter into such complex reforms of the so-called second generation. Within the central government, during the 1990s emphasis was placed only on the financial area, above all the MEF and the Central Bank, where bureaucratic quality could be enhanced by generous contracts financed by the World Bank and the UNDP (Wise 2003: 254-166; OE Morón 11/02/2005). In recent years though, labour regimes sustained by international donors have expanded more and more towards other Ministries. Aside from career diplomats in the Ministry of Foreign Affairs, I did not meet a single high-ranking official whose salary was not paid by international donor funds or enjoyed special advisory status – with good reason. For example, in the case of Eduardo Brandes, as chief negotiator in the market access area, it simply did not pay to continue working in the bureaucratic career as salaries barely exceeded US$1,000, vis-à-vis labour regimes applicable to temporary officials who were paid monthly salaries of up to US$5,000 for top positions, including special advisors (BR Brandes 15/02/05).

As of July 2004, only 20 percent of the VMCE staff was permanent, and mainly covered administrative personnel. Another 20 percent corresponded to short-term government contracts, which required renewal every three to six months. The remaining officials worked under contracts supported by the UNDP, and to a lesser extent, by the IDB. In this case, most contracts lasted one year and did not cover social security benefits in the same way as government contracts. Top salaries of US$3,000 and up were allocated under special circumstances for a small number of top officials and special advisors in the Ministry and Vice-Ministry, where transparency was widely absent.[7] Therefore, the bureaucratic staff in the trade policy area was unstable and resembled the common situation in the Peruvian State. The lack of reliable

---

[7] However, the formal salary structure for MINCETUR officials determined monthly earnings from US$900 for assistants and junior Technical Staff, US$1100 for professionals, US$1500 for Assistant Directors, US$1750 for Directors, and US$1900 for General Directors; see SO Franco (14/02/05); MINCETUR (2005b).

employment perspectives is explained by the prevalence of short-term contracts and the dependence of political or personal connections when appointing state officials, thus, rendering the civil service an unrewarding enterprise (OE Morón 11/02/2005). Consequently, a position in the MINCETUR might be an excellent springboard for graduates from national elite schools such as the Catholic, Pacific and Lima Universities to obtain overseas fellowships, or a job offer in a multinational company, an international organisation or a well endowed NGO, but provides virtually no promising long-term career perspectives.

Openness

Until recently, claims for enhanced transparency in the making of trade policies were largely absent. For example, *"the Congress approved in blank the Uruguay agreements, negotiated by a handful of Peruvian officials"* as Alan Fairlie observed (2003: 2), underlining the indifference as regards the evolution of the multilateral trading system. The "closer" Andean integration process faced a similar apathy. *"Unfortunately, our integration endeavours are long-term oriented policies that have not been shared by the societies. Probably most of the limeños (people from Lima) do not even know that the CAN headquarters is located in their city",* lamented a CAN official (OE Larrazabal 24/02/04). For most observers, the FTAA process brought foreign trade affairs into a broader public sphere for the first time. It was the combination of the US involvement and the efforts of top policy makers to emphasise the concerns of exporters in the political arena that made the Peruvian people more aware of the properties of ongoing free trade talks. Therefore, in May 2004 the US-AFTA talks soon became a daily political topic in which most Peruvians held an opinion.

From the official side, a new style of policy making was introduced, especially with the founding of MINCETUR in July 2002. For MINCETUR officials it has become an integral part of their work – in part due to personal political ambitions – to heighten awareness as regards the official trade policy strategy, among civil society, the Legislative and the private sector, and hence, to commit those sectors. Furthermore, the US$5 million loan granted by the IDB in the scope of the Foreign Trade Policy Development Program (IDB 2002) placed special emphasis on the strengthening of dissemination activities and consultative mechanisms. This "new openness" came into view with abundant trade policy information provided by the web page www.tlcperu-eeuu.gob.pe, public lectures before and after negotiation rounds, trade policy reviews and bulletins, dialogue at negotiations inside the "room next door" with congressmen, civil activists, labour and business, and finally, strong media presence (Araoz 2004; OE Araoz 23/02/04).

These efforts were also manifested in the survey data from 2004. Concerning transparency in trade policy affairs, experts and business representatives were asked: *In your opinion, does the government take adequate measures to ensure transparency concerning advances and possible impacts of ongoing international trade negotiations? Can improvements be noted in the last ten years as regards such?* Almost two thirds of answers indicated a very or rather transparent conduction of trade negotiations. Moreover, 17 out of 21 private sector responses indicated that transparency exhibited in 2004 was superior when compared with the 1990s concerning trade policy-making in the sphere of the WTO and CAN. Critical voices against the information provided stemmed from sectors that were threatened by the US-AFTA talks; i.e. the rural sector, national laboratories, and SME companies in general. For example, the concern of these areas was the lack of detailed information on updated draft texts. General objections were expressed by various organisations in Arequipa (Peru's second largest city, located in the south), indicating that regions are largely omitted from centralised trade policy-making processes.

Table 5.8: Transparency in International Trade Policy Affairs

	Experts (11)	Business (25)	Total (36)
very transparent	3	7	10 (31%)
rather transparent	3	9	12 (38%)
rather non-transparent	2	7	9 (28%)
very non-transparent	1	0	1 (3%)
no response	2	2	4

Negative perceptions related to transparency exhibited by official negotiators could be noted also among left-wing representatives opposed to the free trade talks, such as Humberto Campodónico from the State University of San Marcos (OE 14/12/05). In this regard, these voices usually pointed at the intolerable confidential provisions within the trade talks imposed by the US government. However, when compared with the strong opposition emerging in Bolivia, local trade unions, NGO's, and universities remained largely dormant. Even though a "Movement against the FTAA" was established and began to coordinate actions against free hemispheric trade, Teivo Teivanen from the San Marcos University observed that in Peru the left-wing movement is still very weak and fragmented after the Fujimori regime in the 1990s eradicated not only the ideological roots of the terrorist groups like the *Shining Path,* but also the social base of left-wing parties and movements (OE Teivanen 2/10/04).

Regarding interaction patterns with the private sector, on the other hand, the Fujimori administration required a reliable coalition with business interlocutors to attain the sound implementation of market-oriented reforms. Therefore, the authoritarian leader, more than any other civilian force, prompted the business sector to participate in the new economic ruling. Key elements of this business friendly government style, according to Francisco Durand (1998), were the steady exchange with the National Confederation of Private Entrepreneurship Institutions (CONFIEP), the State President's continuous presence at the Annual Business Executives Conferences (CADE) and the appointment of entrepreneurs and business representatives as key officials in economic areas.

In the trade policy area, however, state-business relations turned out to be more conflictive and distant. Crucially, it was above all the local manufacturers associated to the National Industry Society (SNI) who opposed the flat rate concept pursued by the policy-makers of the Ministry of Economy and Finance. For Herbert Mulanovic, the SNI's Institutional Advisor, the technocratic and often dogmatic style of governance did not favour a collaborative climate with the industrial branches which saw themselves increasingly threatened by foreign competitors (BR 11/02/05).

In contrast, the relations with MITINCI were more fluid in general, according to Mulanovich, since its officials were usually more familiar with the problems faced by local manufacturers. Particularly, in recent years the office holders from MITINCI (and later from MINCETUR and the Production Ministry) entered into a strategic alliance with the SNI, the Exporters Associations (ADEX), and to a lesser extent, with the Lima Chamber of Commerce (CCL), and the Exporters Society (COMEX). Actions undertaken in February 2004 were paradigmatic of this situation. Faced by devastating popularity rates (below 10 percent at that time) President Alejandro Toledo decided to reorganise the Ministerial Cabinet. To avoid mandatory resignations to office, the head of MINCETUR, Alfredo Ferrero, called the leading business entities to back his administration (*El Comercio* 15/02/04). In the aftermath, Ferrero remained in his post, whereas Alfonso Velásquez, at that time President of ADEX, was appointed Minister of Production.

Those close personal ties were evidently reflected in the survey data from 2004. The surveyed people were asked: *Does the government closely coordinate with business associations in trade policy affairs, involving the conduction of international trade negotiations and the implementation of trade agreements? If not, in what sectors/issues can coordination gaps be identified?* More than 70 percent of the respondents considered state-business coordination as very or rather close. On the business side, practically without exception, the industry and export representatives made positive comments on the openness of MINCETUR's officials. Negative opinions stemmed mostly from certain sectors complaining of a lack of transparency, i.e. domestic market oriented agriculture, small manufacturers, regional chambers, and national laboratories. These chambers preferred direct contact with their corresponding sector Ministries of Agriculture and Health or tried to channel their concerns through the legislative powers.

Table 5.9: State-Business Coordination

	Experts (11)	State Officials (15)	Business (25)	Total (51)
very close	3	1	8	12 (26%)
rather close	6	7	8	21 (46%)
rather sporadic	1	4	5	10 (22%)
very sporadic	0	1	2	3 (6%)
no response	1	2	2	5

Despite the mostly close perceived coordination, the consultation mechanisms used by the MINCETUR were characterised as ad-hoc. While Pablo De la Flor (Vice-Minister) and Alfredo Ferrero (Minister) usually provided general overviews before and after each negotiation round, the head of (sub) areas frequently invited the business entities involved to meetings for consultation with the sectors and to coordinate positions among the entities. In this regard, responses revealed that areas such as agriculture, services and investment, coordinated by officials from the MINAG and the MEF were marked by a rather or very high degree of business openness. Moreover, during the US-AFTA talks the public-private exchange was facilitated by the Entrepreneurial Council of International Negotiations (CENI), an initiative born inside the business sector, as I shall expose in the next section.

Summary Independent Variable A1

In general, the institutional strength of Peru's state bureaucracy in the area of international trade policy affairs has been rather low, although intra-case variance could be noticed. Since 2002, the Ministry of Foreign Trade and Tourism (MINCETUR) has held the *responsibilities* in export related issues, hence trying to overcome inter-ministerial conflicts in this policy area. Regarding the variable dimension *resources*, the international trade policy expertise, mostly absent during the 1990s, was considerable strengthened by the creation of MINCETUR. With respect to *openness*, MINCETUR, in particular, maintains very close relations with the leading trade and industry chambers.

Box 5.3: Summary Independent Variable A1

Responsibilities	Resources	Openness
Set by the Ministry of Economy and Finance (MEF), in the 1990s trade policy responded strictly to unilateral adjustment policy logic, thus leaving little room for trade integration concerns. Since 2002, the Ministry of Foreign Trade and Tourism (MINCETUR) was created to define and coordinate all aspects related to the development of national exports. The division of labour in international trade policy among the numerous agencies involved remained complex though.	In the 1990s, the number of trade policy advisors with negotiation experience reduced to just a handful. As of 2002, a negotiation team was formed in the MINCETUR scope. Deficits remained regarding the lack of field experience on the part of young negotiators and the still scarce expertise in new trade issues.	Particularly the key officials of MINCETUR made international trade policy affairs – above all the FTAA and US-AFTA talks – popular within society. With regard to state-business coordination, the building of strategic alliances between MINCETUR officials and trade and industry entities has become a key element of policy making.

5.3 Organised Business: Between Solid and Fragile Rock

This section is structured in accordance with the variable dimensions of the Independent Variable A2. The first subsection, *Institutional Leadership*, analyses the domestic attempts to establish a widely recognised peak or "umbrella" association, capable of coordinating economic policies between the leading sectoral and regional representatives. It further describes the institutional mechanism aimed at the intermediation of trade interests among leading sectoral and regional representatives. The second subsection, *Organisational Strength,* makes an assessment of the professionalism involved in business advocacy, stressing the domestic pattern of financing, participatory behaviour, and in-house trade policy expertise. The last subsection summarises the results and provides an overview of the business representation pattern from 1985 to 2004.

Institutional Leadership

In "From Fragile Crystal to Solid Rock" (1995), Francisco Durand elucidates how Peru's entrepreneurship was able, after several failed attempts, to establish a multisectoral organisation in 1984 that increasingly acted as the single business spokesmen on the national level.[8] Box 5.4 highlights four reasons necessary to explain the institutional setting that allowed, in November 1984, the organisation of the National Confederation of Private Entrepreneurship Institutions (CONFIEP) integrating seven main sector associations from manufacturing, mining, fishing, export, commerce and construction.

---

[8] A first attempt to join business took place in 1974, when the SNI created a "United Front for the Defence of Private Property" to oppose the nationalisation of the fishing industry. Nonetheless, most associations did not dare challenge the authoritarian regime in search of a state-led economy and opted to be passive to avoid trouble, for example, having in mind the mandatory dissolution of the elite National Agrarian Society in the context of the agrarian reform implemented in 1969 (Durand 1995: 148). After General Juan Velasco left office in 1975, private sector entities continued to be divided although the government's was less hostile to capitalists. The Peruvian Union of Private Entrepreneurs (UEPP) created in 1977 by the trade and industry chambers, for example, ceased activities after six months. In this case, Durand argued (ibid.:149) that policy makers sought to exacerbate internal divisions by granting special favours to exporters and diversified business groups while seeking to isolate industrialists.

Box 5.4: The Four Reasons that Explain the Creation of CONFIEP

Return to Democracy	The adoption of a new Constitution in 1979 and the return to democracy in 1980 emphasised the right for free organisation and the search for concerted actions among the local business and labour sectors.
Personal Leadership	A generation of political business leaders, such as Jorge Calmet, Alfonso Bustamante or Arturo Woodman (known as *gremialistas*) fought for the creation and recognition of a formal peak organisation. Thereafter, the *gremialistas* attempted to institutionalise the policy dialogue with the government and to identify common positions beyond short-sighted sectoral needs.
Economic Crisis	Severe economic decline and increasing unemployment in 1983-84 urged the local business leaders to coordinate their actions so as pressure the government to insure predictable economic policies.
Tangible Advocacy Outcome	Three months prior to CONFIEP's creation, the coordinated action of the main sector associations prevented governmental plans from increasing taxes on credit transactions, i.e. the increase was only marginal (from 7 to 10, instead of 17 percent).

Source: own elaboration based on Durand 1995: 150-153

The breakthrough, related to the consolidation of a "solid business rock", occurred in 1987, however, when the CONFIEP membership managed to block the nationalisation of the banking sector. Prior to this, the populist governance style of the left-wing leader, Alan García, had marginalised formal business entities and maintained fluid relations "only with the big ones," in other words, with the country's largest multisectoral conglomerates, known as *grupos*.[9] As these informal channels proved to be more fruitful, for example, reaching individual tax stability contracts, the *grupos* that held important assets in the finance, manufacturing and commodity sectors were reluctant to bet their resources on the new official alliance, and thus, undermined CONFIEP's internal recognition.[10]

But the situation changed markedly at the time when Alan García announced the nationalisation of the banking sector in July 1987, which severely affected the basic principles of private entrepreneurship. Therefore, the most influential business sectors supported the

---

[9] For example, a widespread modification of tax incentives for economic sectors had been approved two days after Christmas 1985, without prior consultation. While business as a whole was negatively affected, foreign and large national companies were entitled to sign tax stability contracts with the government for a specific term.

[10] For example, CONFIEP faced certain competition levels with the Peruvian Institute of Business Administration (IPAE), comprised only by individual companies, and set forth a distinctive informal dialogue with the state. IPAE, founded in 1962, was also responsible for the organisation of the Annual Conference of Executives (CADE) that as of the late 1960's became the major business-government event of the year; see Durand 1985: 139-140.

CONFIEP in order to strengthen multisectoral coordination patterns. As a result, the state intervention in the banking sector could be mostly avoided and the umbrella organisation consolidated itself as an acknowledged business interlocutor in central economic policy areas. By 1988, CONFIEP had managed to notably expand its membership by increasing the number of affiliates from an initial 7 to 23 associated chambers (Durand 1995: 163-167).

By the time Alberto Fujimori came into office, the institutional leadership of CONFIEP favoured the establishment of efficient state-business relations. Hence, the umbrella organisation became the main supporter of the ongoing structural adjustment reforms. Although industrial sectors could no longer expect extensive subsidies, the associated entrepreneurship as a whole supported the wide-reaching liberal reforms embracing taxes, foreign trade, investment, labour regulations, and the privatisation of state owned companies.

The support went beyond economic reforms and involved affinity with the governmental fight against terrorism in particular, and in general the turn towards a "semi-authoritarian" ruling launched through the self-coup in April 1992.[11] Until the Fujimori regime collapsed in the midst of the political crisis in 2000, a majority group inside CONFIEP was convinced that hardliner policies inline with Chile's authoritarian experience were inevitable in order to overcome the prevalent structural lags of the local economy (Durand 1998; *Caretas* 04/04/02). The fluid state-business relations were underscored by numerous entrepreneurs holding key positions. For example, in January 1993, Diego Calmet, a business tycoon from the construction sector, CONFIEP President (1990-91) and early *gremialista,,* was appointed as Minister of Economy and Finance. Consequently, during the following six years Calmet ruled over the super agency and maintained tight connections with the CONFIEP authorities.

Calmet's long permanence in office (until May 1998), however, did not render harmonising effects on the internal composition of the peak entity. Throughout the second administration of Alberto Fujimori (1995-2000), clear conflict lines emerged between the "productive sectors" headed by the SNI, and the service oriented areas, i.e. banking, insurance, privatised public utilities, construction, and the national mining and fishery societies. The conflict stalled in March 1998 as the affiliates were not able to agree on the consensus oriented

---

[11] The political system enacted by Alberto Fujimori (1990-2000) converted Peru into a controversial "semi-authoritarian" regime. In April 1992, as President of the State, Fujimori faced opposition to his reform efforts, and dissolved the Parliament through an "auto-coup." The subsequent power shift inside Congress and the revised constitutional provisions enabled the implementation of profound economic reforms, as well as effectively dealing with terrorist movements. In any case, democratic checks and balances were increasingly abolished due to the presidential influence over the legislative and judicial branches and mass media, heading into a marked top down policy making, where policies reflected the presidential will and that of a handful of key technocrats in "super agencies" such as the Ministries of Economy and Finance, Presidency, Defense, and National Intelligence Service (Wise 2003: 233-287).

election system, thus, the group that lost power, composed by the SNI, ADEX and the Lima Chamber of Commerce, left the Executive Committee, and in August 1998 created its own Entrepreneurial Coordinator of Production and Trade (El Comercio 28/08/98; 25/09/98; 23/9/98). At CONFIEP's election in April 1999, inter-sectoral tensions were temporarily lowered since the rival alliance accepted the direction of Roque Benavides; President of the National Mining Association and Buenaventura, Peru's largest mining company. The definitive break-off occurred in April 2004 nonetheless. At that time, the SNI, ADEX and CCL no longer accepted the internal modus operandi and decided to disaffiliate. Box 5.5 underlines the four main factors involved in the inter-sectoral conflict initiated as of 1998.

Box 5.5: Factors that Explain the Division inside CONFIEP

Representation Pattern	When CONFIEP was created in 1984, among the seven founding members were the SNI, ADEX and CCL. In the following years, their leverage in the expanding Executive Committee drastically decreased considering that most new affiliates stemmed from services. Particularly, finance related branches increased their level of influence based on the banking association and on new members representing pension funds, insurance entities, and stock markets.
Pro or Against Fujimori	Past presidents from the "service-oriented side," such as Diego Calmet (90-91), Arturo Woodman (94-95), Jorge Picasso (96-97) and Manuel Sotomayor (98-99) were unconditional "*Fujimoristas*" because they enjoyed special treatment in tax matters, privatisation and state procurement affairs. Nevertheless, opposing leaders, such as Eduardo Farah (SNI), Manuel Yzaga (SNI) and Carlos Castro (ADEX) were political of the Fujimori regime, both from political and economic perspectives.
Economic Model	Beyond the personal level, the sectors most favoured by the liberalisation of foreign trade, constitutional guarantees for FDIs, strong local currency and privatisations were large scale companies in the mining, finance and public utilities sectors. The initial reform consensus began to be bitterly questioned as the economy stagnated as of 1998. Therefore, manufacturers and exporters vigorously protested and demanded the correction of the services and commodity friendly model.
Trade Policy	While the services and commodity sectors sustained the MEF plans to reach a low flat rate, industrialists and exporters fought for an escalated tariff structure similar to the CAN, enabling cheaper inputs and higher protection for domestic production.

Source: *El Comercio* 22/02/1998 and 13/03/1998; *Caretas* 05/04/2001 and 04/04/2002

The Intermediation of Trade Interests

One of the main conflict areas was the definition of trade policies. It is clear that as of 1998, CONFIEP no longer provided a space where economic sectors were able to coordinate their points of view. Apart from the never ending discussions related to tariff structures and the pros and cons of the prevailing economic model, the climate inside the peak entity deteriorated due to an increasing distrust among business leaders holding opposing political ties and private company interests.

On the other hand, the bustling regionalism both inside and outside Latin America persuaded trade and industry chambers to define appropriate institutional settings to respond to the challenging international scenarios. With regard to the ambitious FTAA process, it was the Lima Chamber of Commerce (CCL), being the country's largest and most traditional entity, which in 1998 gave life to the so-called FTAA-Peru Commission. Under the personal leadership of CCL-President, Samuel Gleiser, the FTAA-Peru Commission became a widely acknowledged forum where the Peruvian entrepreneurship underlined its affinity with the ongoing hemispheric integration project. The following three levels comprised the institution's action lines:

1) *Working Groups*: To monitor the evolution of free trade talks, nine working groups were created on the basis of negotiation issues such as market access, services, agriculture, investment, and intellectual property rights. Albeit that participation was not balanced within the nine working groups, the collaboration covered no less than 16 business chambers, four universities and four professional organisations of lawyers and engineers, among others (Gleiser 2003).

2) *General Assemblies*: By the time the FTAA experienced an impasse in 2004, the FTAA-Peru Commission had organised 25 General Assemblies. At these events the Working Groups presented the topics developed by them, thus facilitating the coordination of actions in the framework of Americas' Business Forum.[12] Furthermore, state officials had the opportunity to point out their points of view regarding ongoing talks (SO Honorio 8/07/04, OE Aroaz 23/02/04).

3) *FTAA Forum:* As of 2001, the Commission organised the Annual FTAA Forum as a platform to disseminate hemispheric projects in a broad public sphere, with extensive media presence and an increasing attendance of 300 persons in 2001, 500 in 2002 and

---

[12] The Americas Business Forum was organised prior to each Ministerial Conference. Business representatives from all over the hemisphere met in workshops and submitted recommendations to the official sector on the framework agreement.

700 in 2003, originating from the business and political spheres (Gleiser 2003; *Empresas & Negocios* 20/10/2003).

Despite the broad success in the diffusion and promotion of the hemispheric integration project, the leading entities from Lima saw the need to revise the coordination mechanisms before the forthcoming bilateral trade talks with the US. Two main problems were identified. The entities considered it important to professionalize the internal structure of the commission and to expand its underlying objectives, i.e. the institution requires the permanent support of a Technical Secretariat to organise the business participation in all possible negotiations in which Peru is involved.

The second problem concerned the overly prominent role of the Lima Chamber of Commerce, and above all, of its former President, Samuel Gleiser, who chaired the FTAA-Peru Commission. Consequently, the proposal of Gleiser to create the Entrepreneurial Commission of International Negotiations in September 2003 was first rejected by the industrial and exporting sectors (CENI 2003). After numerous anecdotes came to light with respect to the common Vanity Fair among local business leaders, in March 2004 the leading entities finally agreed on the creation of the Entrepreneurial Council for International Negotiations (CENI). Roque Benavides (president of CONFIEP 1999-2001 and successful mining entrepreneur) was appointed President and Political Speaker.

A comparison with the FTAA-Peru Commission is shown in Table 5.9, pointing to the principal organisational properties of the new CENI.

Table 5.9: Comparison of CENI and the FTAA-Peru Commission

	CENI	FTAA-Peru Commission
Members	25	16
Leadership	SNI, ADEX, COMEX, CCL	CCL
Absentees	CONFIEP, trade unions, civil society, universities (with the exception of the UP)	Defensive agrarian interests, small manufacturers, trade unions, civil society
Working Groups	8 main groups and 12 subgroups mainly in the areas of market access	9 main groups
Decision Making Bodies	Consensus oriented decision making in the scope of the *Multisectoral Council; Technical Secretary* summarises and filters proposals from working groups	Informal in the scope of *General Assemblies* and *Annual FTAA Forums*; creation of general proposals for presentation at the FTAA level emphasising policy dialogue
Technical Secretariat	Independent Technical Secretariat headed by César Peñaranda, high ranking economist; Remunerated personnel (2); Emphasis on "technical support "	As of December 2002, Silvia Seperack, Head of the Foreign Trade Division inside CCL was in charge; Non-remunerated personnel were hired; Emphasis on "coordination"
Scope	US-AFTA in 2004-05, subsequently other regional and multilateral forums	FTAA
Shortcomings	Lack of consensus; regular meetings only in market access, agriculture and state procurement	Lack of professional structures and rules; regular meetings only in the area of market access

Source: Peñaranda 2004; CENI 2004 a; b; BR Seperack BR 31/10/03; OE Cano 5/10/04

To a certain extent, CENI was able to overcome previous shortcomings in the coordination of business interests. Due to its remarkable multisectoral approach, the well equipped Technical Secretariat and the formal decision making structure, CENI became an acknowledged space in the course of the US-AFTA talks for coordination and the exchange of information. Nevertheless, at the time of writing, little progress had been made in surmounting the heterogeneity of private sector interests, or as a key official stated (Brandes 15/02/05); *"up to now, we have not been able to rely on sound business consensus."* Thereafter, the main obstacle for the efficient functioning of CENI was the institutional fragmentation that affected the coordination in each sector, as I shall outline below:

The National Agrarian Convention (CONVEAGRO): Founded in 1994, CONVEAGRO struggled from the outset due to the marked collective action problems inside the rural sector, considering the high number of peasant farmers and entities representing them. Though numerous passed efforts failed, CONVEAGRO has evolved in the past years into an important forum where small and medium sized peasant farmers can present their cases, and identify common strategies to defend home markets (OE Sueiro 14/12/04). During US-AFTA talks, representatives from 18 associated institutions, representing, among others, coffee, rice, cotton, sugar, maize, milk, and live stock producers participated in the weekly assemblies, holding lively debates on the perspectives and impacts of the ongoing trade talks. Therefore, CONVEAGRO became the main advocate for the defence of agrarian interests using varying lobby options, mainly through close links with Congress members and the Ministry of Agriculture. Nonetheless, participation in CENI was controversial. In December 2004, the leading rural entity suspended its membership since the positions related to phasing-out schemes and the local price band system contrasted with exporting and industrial sectors. Shortly after, however, CONVEAGRO rejoined CENI, mainly due to improved access to MINCETUR officials (BR Rebosio 14/07/04).

Association of Agro-Exporter Entities (AGAP): In contrast to the defensive rural concerns represented by CONVEAGRO, the AGAP has been trying, since January 2004, to unify the positions of a dozen rural organisations that represent exporters of grapes, lemons, asparagus, mangoes, *lúcuma*, onions, tomatoes, coffee and medicinal plants. According to the Managing Director, Alberto Blondet, (BR 16/07/04), the AGAP seeks the representation of the modern, outward oriented agrarian sector in a comprehensive way, and thus, aims to overcome individual lobby by firms or sectors. Nevertheless, the recently established advocacy group has been challenged to achieve higher internal and external recognition.

National Society of Foreign Trade (COMEXPERU): Beyond the recently founded AGAP, since 1989 Peruvian exporters have been divided into the Society of Exporters (later COMEXPERU or "COMEX") and the Exporters Association (ADEX). According to Patricia Teullet, Managing Director of COMEX (BR 07/07/04), *"our members left ADEX because the organisation promoted policies hostile to traditional exports."* Indeed, COMEX is considered as the large exporters' voice and acted as the executive branch of the national mining and fishery associations. Moreover, several big firms in the area of non-traditional agriculture and industrial goods are associated, and, when it became COMEXPERU from 1998, the entity also began to advocate in favour of importers' interests. In total, by 2003-04 the COMEX represented about 80 medium and large scale companies, accounting for 60 percent of exports and 40 percent of imports (SO Mathews 30/10/03; BR Teullet 07/07/04). Contrary to other chambers, COMEXPERU consequently followed an orthodox-liberal course sustained by economists such as Roberto Abusada and Fritz Du Bois from the Peruvian Institute of Economy (IPE), who acted as the principal advisors of economic reforms implemented by the MEF. In so doing, the entity's participation in the CENI scope has been controversial, as the intransigent liberal views often contrasted with more heterodox positions developed by local industry and agriculture.

Exporters Association (ADEX): The advocacy style of ADEX differed from COMEX. In searching for close ties with state departments from industry and trade, the chamber normally pushed for active polices such as fiscal incentives and other promotion facilities. Therefore, ADEX has become a prominent export promotion agency carrying out projects dedicated to the assistance of small and medium size exporters. With respect to the loggerheads maintained with COMEX, ADEX officials emphasised the former trajectory (founded in 1973) and the leading representation in the area of non-traditional exports (BR´s Ordoñez, Garcia Seminario 17/02/04). Nonetheless, the latter assertion must be questioned as both COMEX and AGAP represent non-traditional agro exporters, and the outward oriented textile and apparel industry has also been represented by the SNI (BR Reaño 16/02/04). In general terms, the influence of ADEX in the making of trade policies was limited in the past due to its intermittent participation, as an experienced key official observed (SO February 2005).

National Industry Society (SNI): The most influential policy maker in the private sector in general, and for the manufacturers in particular, was the "Society." Founded in 1896, and as of 1974 holding a Commission for Foreign Trade and Integration, the SNI was perceived as the local embodiment of the "protectionist club", with the power to influence state officials as regards subsidies and the imposition of measures to preserve the domestic market for the predominately medium or large sized industrialists (SO's Illescas; Sanchez 9/09/04). For example, in the US-AFTA talks, the national laboratories associated in ADIFAN severely opposed ALAFARPE, the association defending property rights of multinational companies. Nevertheless, the outward orientation of Peruvian manufacturers increased notably over the years, and hence, offensive interests raised its leverage inside the entity. Above all, the SNI Committee of Textiles, representing the companies exporting textiles to the US market, in recent years became the most influential organisation among the 46 sectoral committees associated in the SNI. However, Managing Director, Martín Reaño, admitted (BR 16/02/04) that even though about 90 percent of formal industry belongs to the Textile Committee, certain competition persists as most companies are likewise associated in ADEX and the companies in "Gamarra" (the most important industrial district for clothing and textiles manufacturers) have their own associations.

Lima Chamber of Commerce (CCL): The CCL, created in 1888, is the country's largest and most traditional entrepreneurial entity. In numerous occasions, the CCL authorities were responsible for private sector wide initiatives such as the creation of the FTAA-Peru Commission or policy proposals that facilitated foreign trade operations. Furthermore, the CCL has been the leading player in the provision of services and the organisation of seminars and events. In the recent negotiations held in the hemisphere, the chamber assumed certain leadership in the newer trade topics of services, investment and state procurement, informing local business of their importance of them through workshops and seminars or by coordinating activities in the scope of the CENI and the FTAA-Peru Commission (BR 31/10/03 Seperack). Notwithstanding the foregoing, the intermediation of trade policy concerns in the area of market access was inhibited by a very extensive membership covering roughly 4,000 companies in trade, services, and to a lesser extent, in industry.

Organisational Strength

Based on a survey with 29 business associations (selection), in this subsection I will shed light on aspects related to the organisational strength of private sector representatives, stressing the importance of diversified revenues, reliable payment of membership dues, active member participation, the existence of permanent staff and in-house trade policy expertise.

Diversification of Association Revenues: The majority of entities consulted were financed in 2004 exclusively by affiliation dues, and thus, suggested a somewhat low degree of diversification in local business organisations. Practically all the SNI committees and large company chambers from foreign trade (COMEX), fishery (SNP), mining and energy (SNMPE) and insurance (APESEG) reported that no other income was generated. Six chambers commented that additional funds constituted 10-40 percent, and a further 6 entities claimed to generate over 40 percent of their incomes from outside sources. Therein, the external income originated from the issuance of certificates of origin (CCL, ADEX and the SNI), promotion activities and service suppliers in general (ADEX, AGAP, CCL, Arequipa Chamber of

Commerce and PERUCAMARAS) and international donor projects (CONVEAGRO, and SME associations such as COMPYMEP and COPEI).

Table 5.11: What share of revenues originates from other than affiliation dues?

More than 40%	10-40%	0-10%	0%	No response
6 (22%)	6 (22%)	0 (0%)	15 (56%)	2

Predictability of Association Revenues: Concerning the prevailing paying habits, the results shown in Table 14 indicate that most entities depending strongly on affiliate dues had the capacity to collect these means. Out of this group, only the SNI Committees for cosmetics, vegetable oils, biscuits and cleaning agents admitted that certain irregularities occurred; that is only 50 to 75 percent of members regularly met the payment deadline. A similar situation was faced by chambers such as the AGAP representing agro exporters, SNI, ADEX and the Arequipa Chambers of Trade, Industry and Agriculture.

Table 5.12: What share of membership regularly meets the payment deadline?

80-100%	50-79%	20-49%	less than 20%	no response
12 (48%)	10 (40%)	0 (0%)	3 (12%)	4

In general, very few interviewees acknowledged wide-scale problems with regards to internal funding. Only the small scale organisations COMPYMEP, CONVEAGRO and the dairy livestock association FONGAL lamented the limited capacity to obligate associates to comply with their financial duties, considering that the chambers suffered from a disperse and informal membership composed of micro and small size firms. In the rural sector, funding problems were accentuated with the prohibition of mandatory contribution schemes, a result of the agrarian reform implemented under the Fujimori government, as Miguel Caillaux remarked (BR 14/07/04). To improve the entities' revenues, it has become quite common to search for economic support provided by international donor organisations. For example, in the case of CONVEAGRO, the insufficient payment by affiliates was compensated through contributions made by CEPES, an NGO dedicated to rural development which provided approximately 90 percent of the peak association's income in 2004.

Participatory Behaviour of Members/Business: Data relating to the participation of entrepreneurs in trade policy affairs provided a rather ambiguous picture. In no less than 17 chambers, responses indicated a rather or very active behaviour in the scope of internal decision making, whereas only seven chambers reported widespread passivity in connection with attendances at Board Meetings and the submission of proposals. On the other hand, by 2004, only one out of three entities held an internal body dedicated to foreign trade or integration affairs, such as in the case of the APESEG representing insurers, COMPYMEP, CCL, SNI, ADEX, Textile Committee, CONVEAGRO, AGAP and the Arequipa Chambers of Commerce and Agriculture. Consequently, two thirds of the answers provided referred to participation in the Board of Directors where a broad mix of topics was debated.

Table 5.13: Business/ member participation in trade policy

	Experts	State Officials	Total Experts + State Officials (25)	Business*(29)
very active	2	1	3 (14%)	5 (21%)
rather active	4	3	7 (32%)	12 (53%)
rather passive	3	9	12 (54%)	1 (4%)
very passive	0	0	0 (0%)	5 (21%)
no response	1	2	3	6

* Responses are referred to the behaviour of members inside the internal bodies of each chamber.

Moreover, the rather positive impressions gathered among business representatives contrasted in part with the observations collected among experts and state officials evaluating the behaviour of business in international trade policy affairs. In general, assessments made by state officials were more critical than those from experts. In the latter case, six out ten answers indicated very or rather active business behaviour, making reference to the private sector organisation in the scope of FTAA and AFTA talks. Moreover, two responses underscored the rent-seeking attitude, and thus, gave a negative connotation to active business participation. For the state officials consulted, the coordination efforts undertaken by means of the FTAA-PERU Commission and CENI were considered to be advances in local trade policy advocacy. However, beyond this general acknowledgment, no less than 9 out of 13 responses qualified the private sector as still rather passive with regard to attendance at convened meetings and the creation of policy proposals. On three occasions, the SNI representatives were exempted from general criticism, although their behaviour was associated with defensive lobbying strategies. Similar observations were made by a functionary from the Ministry of Agriculture, who recognised the recent efforts of CONVEAGRO in the defence of domestic markets.[13]

---

[13] Detailed information was provided by young MINCETUR official as regards formal consultations in negotiations on services undertaken in May/June 2002 (Paredes 21/02/04). Accordingly, out of the roughly 100 public and private entities consulted, only ten made concrete observations about the ongoing negotiations in the scope of FTAA

As outlined earlier, the launched US-AFTA talks suggested a turning point in the way local business encountered international trade policy affairs. Table 5.13 overviews the activities put forward in the scope of the Entrepreneurial Council on International Negotiations (CENI). Since the data provided covers the period up to December 2004, the list only encompasses the activities undertaken shortly after the completion of the 6th Negotiation Round in Tucson, Arizona.

Table 5.14: CENI Working Groups from May to December 2004

	Coordinating Entity	No. Meetings	No. of average participants	Entities/Companies Participating
Tariffs	SNI	27	15	1. SNI 2. ADEX, others: CCL, COMEX, Pacific University (UP)
Rules of Origin	SNI	9	8	1. SNI 2. ADEX, others: UP, CCL, COMEX
Textile and Clothing	SNI/ADEX	9	11	1. SNI 2. ADEX, others: COMEX, UP, Cotton Producers Association
Technical Obstacles	ADEX	8	7	1. ADEX 2. CCL, others: National Fishery Society, UP, COMEX
Safeguard	SNI	9	10	1. SNI, others: UP, ADEX, MINCETUR, CONVEAGRO
Customs Procedures	ADEX	6	5	1. ADEX, others: CCL; SNI; COMEX; UP; TALMA (airport services)
State Procurement and Investment	COMEX	9 by August	10	1. COMEX, others: CCL, SNI, UP, CONVEAGRO, Chambers of Construction and Banking
Agriculture/ Subsidies and Safeguards	CONVEAGRO	Weekly meetings	approx. 15	CONVEAGRO, SNI, COMEX, AGAP, poultry farming association

Source: CENI 2004b; BR Guillermo Rebosio14/07/2004 on the Working Group "Agriculture"

In general terms, the work inside the CENI was rather ambiguous. Even though the creation of the coordination mechanism was perceived as an important breakthrough, the participation in the working groups turned out to be fairly uneven and intermittent. For example,

and WTO. Among these, eight stemmed from public institutions, while the remaining two were submitted by the banking and insurance associations.

out of the 25 entities associated in the CENI, the organisations regularly attending meetings were usually limited to the SNI and its sector committees (representing close to 40 percent of total attendance), ADEX, COMEX, CONVEAGRO and CCL. Moreover, the strong presence of UP scholars, who participated on average with two-three persons, made the participation record seem higher than it actually was. In addition to the limited participation, activities beyond the traditional market access area were rather scarce. Even though 20 working groups were initially foreseen, the majority of them were either never put into practice, or carried out activities in an irregular manner (OE Cano 05/10/04). The main deficits were identified in newer topics. With the exception of the controversial sessions organised by COMEX on investment and state procurement, other topics such as financial service issues, electronic trade and telecommunications, trade in service in general, competition policies, labour and environment regulation were not addressed systematically within the scope of CENI.

Staff Size and Trade Expertise: The question of whether the CENI would be capable to overcome the limitations identified stands in close correlation with the disposition of the Peruvian entrepreneurs to strengthen the fairly modest internal structure of business organisations. Accordingly, the survey carried out in 2004 brought to light the fact that merely one third of the entities consulted had more than five employees, suggesting that local business organisations are sustained by a Managing Director and one or two administrative assistants. Middle range entities holding six to ten employees were COMEXPERU, SNI-Textile Committee, National Fishery Society and the Arequipa Rural Society SADA. Lastly, the top five were composed by SNI (60), ADEX (45), National Society of Mining & Energy (30), SNI Committee of Metal Mechanics (17, including the Centre of Industrial Development) and the Arequipa Chamber of Commerce and Industry (15). No detailed information was obtained in the Lima Chamber of Commerce, supposedly Peru's largest business chamber.

Table 5.15: What is the size of permanent staff?

more than 20	11-20	5-10	1-5	no response
3 (11%)	2 (7%)	4 (15%)	18 (67%)	2

This picture remains quite constant when the in-house trade policy expertise is analysed. While two organisations admitted that no one had really been observing what was going on in the policy field, the vast majority (21 out of 29 chambers) simply relied on the knowledge exhibited by the Managing Director. Conversely, in five entities one or more professionals monitored and analysed the evolution of international trade policy affairs; SNI, COMEX, CCL, ADEX, Arequipa Chamber of Commerce and CONVEAGRO.

Table 5.16: Who within the staff is monitoring and analysing trade policy affairs?

Think Thank (3 officials)	Trade Department (1-2)	Managing Director	None	no response
2 (7%)	3 (11%)	21 (75%)	2 (7%)	1

Against this background, the negative impressions gathered from experts and state officials were not surprising. Indeed, three quarters of the responses obtained qualified the level of technical expertise displayed in the business trade policy proposals submitted by Peru's private sector entities as rather or very low, emphasising moreover that knowledge existed merely in traditional market access areas but did not cover new topics in the area of international trade policy.

Table 5.17: How do you assess the technical level of business proposals submitted in the area of international trade policy?

	Experts (11)	State Officials (15)	Total (26)
very high	0	0	0 (0%)
rather high	3	2	5 (24%)
rather low	5	6	11 (52%)
very low	1	4	5 (24%)
no response	2	3	5

Special comments were generally related to the five principal chambers in the policy field. The most positive quotes referred to the SNI. Eduardo Brandes, key negotiator in the market access area since the late 1970s, recalled that although clashes with the SNI frequently occurred on the political level, the technical support provided by the SNI colleagues was steady, and thus, invaluable (SO 15/02/05). In the course of the 1980s, Brandes commented, the industrial leading association sent its functionaries abroad in order to advise the official team at the negotiation table. By 2003-04, SNI officials not only assumed informal advisory functions but also belonged to the negotiation team. Ramon Morante, as head of the Foreign Trade Department reported very proudly that within the FTAA talks he was the single business agent possessing an official status as negotiator (BR 29/10/03). In the US-AFTA talks, the former MITINCI bureaucrat entered the team as special advisor to the Production Minister, Alfonso Velásquez. Aside from Morante, the leading sectoral Committees of Textiles and Food

Processing were run by well trained trade experts, often appreciated by state authorities.[14] Lastly, the technical overhead of SNI Committees was equipped by the Institute of Economic and Social Studies (IEES), an in-house think-tank where three-four professionals carried out statistical and sectoral analysis.[15]

Furthermore, positive quotes also referred to the *COMEX* team, although its work has been more distant from the official negotiation team than the SNI's. The compact staff directed by Patricia Teullet, Vice-Minister of Economy 2001-02, consisted of three economists who participated actively in domestic trade policy making discussions. However, due to its modest budget resources, the representative of big exporters often depended on inputs from its strategic partner, i.e. the orthodox-liberal Peruvian Institute of Economy (IPE). The *Exporters Association (ADEX)* was recognised to a lesser extent for coherent policy analysis. The vast majority of its employees are usually involved in promotion activities supported by donor organisations. In the past, modest and unstable resources underlined the entity's dependence on voluntary contributions by associated entrepreneurs. Compared with the permanent presence of the SNI functionaries, the trade policy expertise displayed by ADEX staff has been intermittent. By 2004 though, the Economic Studies Department, with three employees, was directed by Carlos González, an economist holding a MA degree.

The *Lima Chamber of Commerce (CCL)* is considered to be the richest business entity and provider of a broad array of services, publications and events. However, the in-house trade policy expertise is limited. The Foreign Trade Department composed of half a dozen employees clearly focused on commercial operations, the provision of market data for members and the coordination of seminars to inform local traders on upcoming market challenges. Finally, a new actor in local trade policy debates was *CONVEAGRO*. The fact that the rural leading entity was converted into a widely recognised interlocutor was closely linked to the technical support provided by the Peruvian Centre of Social Studies (CEPES). Founded in 1976 and financed by diverse international donors, the NGO has specialised in rural development, carrying out projects to strengthen the articulation of agrarian interests. In 2004, CEPES shared office space with CONVEAGRO and permanently attended weekly Assembly meetings. By the time the US-AFTA talks began, CEPES-CONVEAGRO hired Guillermo Rebosio, an economist from the

---

[14] Martín Reaño, Managing Director from the Textile Committee, served in the past as governmental advisor in the area of rules of origin which became an increasingly fuzzy issue due to new complex mechanisms requiring mixed models in order to calculate the local content of exports in the scope of preferential trade regimes, among others.

[15] The IEES was deactivated during 2003 since its former head went over to UNCTAD in Geneva. In 2004, IEES was run by Javier Davila, professor in economy at the Lima University for 13 years and specialised in international commerce and the Asian-Pacific area.

Catholic University. Jointly with two other assistants, Rebosio began to work hand in hand with the Ministry of Agriculture in the evaluation and drafting of negotiation proposals.

Summary Independent Variable A2

This section points out the rather low institutional strength of business associations. Regarding the variable dimension *leadership*, the peak associations CONFIEP diminished as a reliable interlocutor of trade interests in the course of the 1990s. Lately, the main sectoral associations agreed on a multi-sectoral council in order to coordinate private sector concerns in the scope of the US-AFTA negotiations. The *organisation strength* of business associations is mostly absent, for the reasons outlined in Box 5.6.

Box 5.6: The Institutional Strength of Business Associations

Leadership	Peak Association	A reliable business interlocutor at the beginning of economic reforms, the CONFIEP capacity to intermediate among business sectors vanished as of 1998 due to the division of "productive" sectors that felt excluded from the economic model and benefited sectors related to services and commodities.
	Trade Policy Coordination	Although consensus building was limited, the private sector organisations were rather proactive regarding international trade policy affairs in establishing the "FTAA-Peru Commission" and the "Entrepreneurial Council of International Negotiations (CENI)" in 1998 and 2004, respectively.
Organisational Strength		Peru's business advocacy is weakly organised due to poorly diversified incomes and the lack of technical capacities in the trade integration area. Thus, the participation in the FTAA-Peru Commission and CENI working groups was intermittent and limited to a few officials of the leading trade and industry chambers.

5.4 Assessment

After examining one by one how the dependent and independent variables evolved during the period of analysis, in this final section I assess how, and to what extent, the pursuit of Peru's world market integration strategy can be explained by the two independent variables, or whether third variable influences became responsible for the mostly unsuccessful world market integration strategy.

But before stressing cause-effects links, I point out the main aspects which account for the way Peru pursued its integration into world markets. In the period from 1985 to 2004, the context of Peru's trade policy-making was marked by macroeconomic turmoil which occurred in the second half of the 1980s and the subsequent shift towards broad structural adjustment policies, as recommended by the Bretton Woods Institutions. On the political level, Peru's democratic consolidation initiated in 1980 became questioned by a semi-authoritarian style of governance assumed by Alberto Fujimori, State President from 1990 to 2001. These macroeconomic and political factors, embodied in variables C3 and C4, set the framework for domestic trade policy-making, as it had to adapt to the prevailing constraints and possibilities. On the other hand, several empirical puzzles related to Peru's approach to world market integration demand explanations which go beyond the influence of C3+4. The following two stand out in particular:

First, why did Peru not pursue a Multipolar Model from 1992, when the country decided to suspend its Andean Group membership? On the domestic level, at the beginning of the 1990s, there was a clear determination to pursue – as Chile did – the flat rate concept in combination with an individual bilateral trade integration strategy, as this was seen as more beneficial than being attached to the integration goals of Colombia and Venezuela, in particular. In the end, however, Peru returned to the CAN in 1997 and ended up applying seven different tariff lines instead of the initially pursued flat rate.

Second, why did Peru set forth a rather active trade policy in the ongoing decade, specifically as regards the strengthening of trade relations in the Western Hemisphere, the Pacific Area, with MERCOSUR, and the implementation of the National Export Strategy 2003-2013? Though the pursued Multipolar Model had yet to be consolidated in the period of analysis, the trade policy applied in recent years differed notably from the rather passive trade policy approach, i.e. only unilateral liberalisation, sustained in the 1990s.

In light of the posed questions, Table 5.17 sums up the value of the observed variables and the explanatory power each one possesses. Therefore, I will next explain when and how the values of variables changed over time, and how they influenced on the value of B.

Table 5.18: Explaining Peru's Rather Failed World Market Integration Strategy

Variable	Variable Dimension	Value (Variance 1985-2004)	Explaining Power for Policy Success/Failure (B)
A1: Institutional Strength of State Bureaucracy	Responsibilities	1985-2001: rather low 2002-2004: rather high	1985-2004: very high
	Resources	1985-1990: rather high 1991-2001: very low 2002-2004: rather high	1985-2004: rather high
	Openness	1985-1998: rather high 1999-2004: very high	1985-1998: rather low 1999-2004: very high
A2: Institutional Strength of Business Associations	Leadership	1985-2004: rather low	1985-2004: rather high
	Organisational Strength	1985-2004: very low	1985-2004: very high
C1: Heterogeneity Sectoral Preferences		1985-2004: rather high	1985-2004: rather low
C2: Heterogeneity Foreign Preferences		1985-2004: rather high	1985-2004: rather low
C3: Political Instability		2000-2001: very high	2000-2001: rather low
C4: Macroeconomic Instability		1989-1991: very high	1989-1991: very high

Institutional Strength of State Bureaucracy (A1)

According to Table 5.17, strong explanatory power can be ascribed to Variable A1; indeed the observed influence on the dependent variable was strong during the whole period of analysis. Above all, regarding the first question posed, the modifications inside the state bureaucracy that took place in the 1990s explain to a wide extent the incoherencies in the area of international trade policy.

Due to the public sector reforms implemented at the onset of the 1990s, specialised trade policy entities such as the Foreign Trade Institute (ICE) and the Ministry of Industry, Domestic Trade and Integration (MICITI) were dissolved (ICE) or drastically downsized (MICITI) in light of severe budget cuts affecting the central government. On the other hand, some key agencies, such as the Ministry of Economy and Finance (MEF), were greatly up-scaled. But the MEF staff, which became responsible for the structural adjustment reforms involving trade liberalisation, did not rely on traditional career bureaucrats, but was recruited from a group of special advisors close to the *Peruvian Institute of Economy (IPE),* a private think-tank based on orthodox-liberal standpoints.

This team, headed by economy minister Roberto Boloña, viewed trade policy as an instrument for the unilateral liberalisation of tariff and non-tariff barriers. Herewith, the application of uniform tariffs was perceived as modern since discretional policy-making could be avoided and the predictability of fiscal revenues increased. The aim of reaching a flat rate by the end of 1994, however, stood in contradiction with the intention of the Andean Group to establish a Common External Tariff (CET) that assumed an escalated structure with four tariff levels. Moreover, the intra-regional exchange of goods was unfavourable for Peru, as less than 10% of exports went to the Andean markets, whilst imports from Andean Group members were noticeably higher, causing permanent trade deficits from a Peruvian perspective.

As Boloña directly interfered in regional negotiations, in July 1992, Peru's suspension of the Andean Group membership was a coherent decision in mind of the ongoing unilateral trade policy. In the aftermath though, the coherence of the country's world market integration strategy couldn't be attained. Instead of pursuing a Multipolar Model, as was planned by Boloña's advisory team, from 1992 Peru perplexingly did not establish a flat rate, nor set forth an active bilateral negotiation strategy, and neither did it promote non-traditional exports.

In the 1990s, the special advisory staff inside the MEF (*resources*) focussed on unilateral trade reforms, whilst reciprocal forms of liberalisation played only a secondary role. Moreover, the *responsibilities* in the area of international trade policy were not clearly defined. For example, between 1991 and 1992 no state department was directly in charge of international negotiations in the scope of ALADI and the WTO. From October 1992, when the Ministry of Industry, Tourism, Integration and International Trade Negotiations (MITINCI) was created, the Peruvian government disposed again of an international trade policy branch. But the MITINCI was insufficiently staffed to implement active trade policies in the regional, extra-regional, and multilateral sphere (*resources*). Moreover, the few trade policy officials inside the MITINCI were divided into a group that supported the policy guidelines of the MEF (and thus the separation from the Andean Group), and another faction favouring the return to the Andean integration scheme.

The intra-governmental work became further intricate by the diplomatic staff inside the Ministry of External Affairs who sought, from the mid-1990s, a more protagonist role in international economic affairs (*responsibilities*). By then, the Peruvian diplomacy tried, together with parts of the MITINCI staff and local manufacturers, to enable Peru's return to the Andean Group, and thus, began stressing numerous inconveniences for definitive departure from the CAN, such as the displacement of its headquarters located in Lima, the difficulty in conducting common foreign affairs, the loss of privileged market access in the Andean markets, and the mandatory withdrawal from numerous shared institutions, i.e. the Andean Development Corporation (CAF), Latin American Reserve Fund (FAR), and technical assistance programs. Therefore, ias a result of *"one of the rare occasions of coordination between the Ministries of Foreign Affairs and the MITINCI, that the hardliners inside the MEF could be displaced"*, according to Luis Tello (2005: 118), who analysed the domestic power shift that took place by May-June 1997 when Peru returned to the Andean Group.

With the turn of the century, the institutional strength of the trade policy was significantly enhanced, explaining to a large degree the shifting approach to trade integration. Increasingly, the MITINCI staff focused on integration options in the Western Hemisphere and the APEC area. Above all, it was Alfredo Ferrero – Vice-Minister of International Negotiations and later Minister of Foreign Trade and Tourism – who managed to create domestic consensus to strengthen the development of national exports, especially to the US markets. Therefore, export-specific concerns gained increasing recognition among the public and private sector, making possible, in May 2002, the creation of well-doted trade policy staff inside the new Ministry of Foreign Trade and Tourism, MINCETUR (*responsibilities* and *resources*). In the aftermath, MINCETUR became the visible agency of the new proactive trade policy approach put forward from 2003, i.e. involvement in free trade talks with the US, comprehensive FTA with MERCOSUR, launched bilateral negotiations with Thailand, and the start of the first National Export Strategy based on 10-year objectives.

Whether this new trade policy approach will prove sustainable largely depends on the question of whether the mostly personalised style of governance leads into a major degree of institutionalisation of the trade policy-making. This is especially the case with respect to the high degree of *openness* that was maintained by Alfredo Ferrero. Under his direction, the government undertook multiple actions to make trade policy not only more transparent but also more popular within business, parliament and civil society. In particular, the close relations to local business factions became crucial to legitimise more active trade policies, mostly aimed at the US market.

The key officials from MINCETUR, therefore, built up strategic alliances with the National Industry Society (SNI) and the Exporters Associations (ADEX).

Institutional Strength of Business Associations (A2)

As indicated, the firm support of the leading industrial and export chambers – strongly encouraged by the export-oriented textile companies – was decisive to embark on the trade policy strategy that originated inside the MINCETUR department. Indeed, the Peruvian private sector behaved rather proactively as business coordination mechanisms were established in the scope of the FTAA-Peru Commission (1998-2003) and the Entrepreneurial Council of International Trade Negotiations (CENI), which joined business proposals during the free trade talks with the US, launched in May 2004. These institutional efforts had the effect of increasing awareness among local business regarding the upcoming challenges of the international trade agenda and facilitating dialogue with government authorities.

On the other hand, the institutional deficits of these initiatives have been widespread, and hence, put into question the sustainability of the pursued Multipolar approach that requires, among other tasks, the effective implementation of undertaken free trade agreements. By 2004, private sector organisations in Peru generally did not count on professional structures (*organisational strength*), i.e. most entities did not diversify their revenues, held small staff and did not permanently monitoring international trade policy affairs. Hence, the participation inside the CENI working groups was intermittent and focussed on traditional market access issues, while complex behind-the-border topics were mostly neglected. Moreover, 76 percent of surveyed experts and state officials qualified the technical level of trade policy proposals submitted by business entities as rather or very low.

With reference to previous periods, institutional deficits of local business associations negatively affected the coherent pursuit of international trade policy. In particular, the lack of concerted trade policy proposals (*leadership*) underscored Peru's difficulty to pursue coherent positions in the scope of the Andean Group. The peak entity CONFIEP, a strong business interlocutor of the structural adjustment reforms at the outset of the 1990s, lost its multisectoral coordination capacities towards the end of the decade, as opposing groups emerged inside the entity. On the one hand, services (mainly finance and public utilities) and commodity oriented sectors (mining and fishery) had benefited from the economic model in force, and hence, sustained the rationale of the Ministry of Economy and Finance, pursuing a flat rate model and individual forms of integration. On the other hand, the "productive group", favouring an escalated tariff structure and a return to the CAN, were represented by the three leading industry and trading chambers; SNI (manufacturers), ADEX (exporters), and CCL (chamber of commerce).

It is important to consider, nevertheless, that difficulties in coordinating trade policy interests went beyond the internal division of the CONFIEP, but also encompassed institutional fragmentation and the lack of solid trade policy proposals within the two groups, especially among manufacturers' and exporters' associations. Although the "productive group" petitioned for an escalated tariff system and the return to the CAN, there was no evidence of a comprehensive approach to world market integration either between the chambers composing the "productive group" or within each chamber. Instead of deeper commitments to pursue a Springboard Model, based on completing a common regional market, manufacturers were mainly concerned with uncertain market access conditions in the Andean markets and higher taxes on raw material and intermediate goods. In the aftermath, therefore, the "productive group" no longer acted as a firm advocate of the Andean integration process, for example by insisting on the convergence of external tariffs or the harmonisation of economic policies on the regional level.

Control Variables C1-C4

Assessing the influence of selected control variables C1-C4, disturbing effects were mostly kept under control in the Peruvian case.

Heterogeneity of Sectoral Preferences (C1): In general, trade policy interests among the private sector are relatively homogenous, especially since structural adjustment reforms were implemented in 1990-91, when maximum tariff rates came down to 25%. While the commodity sectors (mainly mining and fishery) traditionally have been outward-looking, the Peruvian manufacturing sector has strongly increased its export orientation, focussing principally on consumer goods (textiles, clothing, and foodstuff) and intermediates (plastic, chemicals, and various metals). Contrary to other South American countries such as Colombia, Brazil and Argentina, the fabrication of capital goods, normally inward-looking, is largely absent.

The main challenge for trade policy coordination was represented by the agriculture sector, thus far dominated by largely uncompetitive small scale production, for instance of maize, wheat, rice and sugar. Strikingly, however, the principal trade policy conflicts observed, above all in the scope of the CAN, where identified among manufacturers, which affected the coherence of Peru's world market integration. Hampered by collective action problems, the coordination of defensive rural concerns (in the scope of CONVEAGRO) first came into view when the free trade talks with the United States were envisaged. Nevertheless, the opposition organised inside CONVEAGRO, the main sectoral representative, did not posses the sufficient strength to avoid the conclusion of the free trade agreement, which was completed by the end of 2005.

Regarding the *Heterogeneity of Foreign Preferences (C2)*, Peru's decisions on trade policy matters had to take into account heterogeneous foreign preferences in the scope of the CAN, in particular. The goal of reaching a Customs Union on the Andean level reflected the interests of Colombia, and to a lesser extent, Venezuela. The multi-level or "escalated" tariff structure reflected their industrial policy preferences, enabling their manufacturers to expand their modest domestic markets in a familiar and less competitive environment. Therefore, Peru, which preferred a flat rate model, had two options. The first considered the definitive withdrawal from the CAN, so as to follow individual integration modes, and the second alternative required negotiating the Peruvian position within the Andean scope with perseverance and coherent technical arguments. Nonetheless, in the end, neither policy option was followed with the necessary determination.

Political Instability (C3): In Peru, the most noteworthy political crisis features can be linked to the government of Alberto Fujimori (disregarding the social unrest caused by the hyperinflation of the 1980s). In particular, the auto-coup initiated by Alberto Fujimori in April 1992 stands out, with the subsequent implementation of a semi-authoritarian regime by circumventing essential democratic checks of balances, and finally, the compulsory resignation of Fujimori in November 2000. Afterwards, Valentín Paniagua became transitory Head of State until July 2001, when Alejandro Toledo assumed the position as democratically elected State President for the period of 2001-06.

Nevertheless, the impact of these abrupt political shifts on Peru's trade policy was modest, for two main reasons. *Firstly,* the way trade policies were made under the Fujimori regime hardly differed from modes in the fully democratic regimes of the region, insofar as key players were found inside the executive power and the business sector. *Secondly,* the shift towards a more active trade policy approach was initiated at the end of the Fujimori regime. In 1999, Alfredo Ferrero (from November 2003 Minister of Foreign Trade and Tourism) assumed the position of Vice-Minister of Integration and International Trade Negotiations and began to pursue a dynamic Multipolar approach. Later on, Mr. Ferrero persisted in office under various ministers and state presidents, while at the same time, the new trade policy approach gained rising recognition among state and business actors.

Macroeconomic Instability (C4): After the macroeconomic turmoil witnessed in the second half of the 1980s, Peru experienced significant macroeconomic improvements. Compared with fiscal deficits of 9.4 and 7.5 percent of GDP in 1989 and 1990, and annual inflation rates of 2,775 and 7,650 percent in those years, the numbers registered in the aftermath were very favourable. Although annual budget deficits reached roughly 2 percent on average and until 1994 certain inflationary pressure remained at an annual variation rate of 139, 57, 39 and 31 percent, the Peruvian government was able to set stable grounds for economic prosperity involving the development of local exports.

5.5 References

Literature

Abusada, R., Illescas, J. and Taboada, S. (2001). *Integrando el Perú al Mundo*. Lima: Centro de Investigación de la Universidad del Pacífico/Instituto Peruano de Economía.

Arbués Pérez, Espinoza (2003). *Manual de Promoción de Exportaciones. Teoría, Política y Gestión.* Lima: Universidad de San Martín de Porres.

Boloña, Carlos (1993). *Cambio de Rumbo*. Lima: Instituto de Economía de Libre Mercado/Universidad San Ignacio de Loyola.

Boloña, Carlos and Javier Illescas (1997). *Políticas Arancelarias en el Perú 1980-1997*. Lima: Instituto de Economía de Libre Mercado/Universidad San Ignacio de Loyola.

Brenes, E., Emmons, W. and Madrigal, K. (2001). *Instituciones para la Competitividad en Colombia*. Reporte Benchmarking. Proyecto Andino de Competitividad (CAF)/ Instituto Centroamericano de Empresas (INCAE). Washington, DC: Georgetown University.

Camminati, J., Thorne, R. L. and Webb, R. (2005). *Antidumping Mechanisms and Safeguards in Peru*. Vol. 1. Policy Research Working Paper. World Bank.

CAN (2003). *Pespectivas de la Unión Aduanera Andina*. Documentos Informativos. October 2003. Lima: CAN General Secretariat.

CAN (2005). *Informe sobre el Estado de Situación del Programa de Liberación entre Perú y el Resto de Países de la Comunidad Andina*. August 2005. Lima: CAN General Secretariat.

Durand, Francisco (1995). "From Fragile Crystal to Solid Rock: The Formation and Consolidation of a   Business Peak Association in Perú" Pp.141-178 in *Business and Democracy in Latin America,* edited by Bartell, E. and Payne, L. Pittsburgh: University of Pittsburgh Press.

Durand, Francisco (1998). *The Transformation of Business-Government Relations. Under Fujimori.* Paper Presented to the XXI International Congress of the Latin American Studies Association- LASA. Chicago. September 24-26.

ECLAC (2003). *Latin American and the Caribbean in the World Economy. 2001-2002 Edition.* Santiago de Chile: International Trade and Integration Division.

FAO - Food and Agriculture Organization (2003). *WTO Agreement on Agriculture: The Implementation Experience - Developing Country Case Studies*. Santiago de Chile: Regional Office for Latin America and the Caribbean.

González Vigil, Fernando (2001). "La Política Comercial" Pp. 101-153 in *Factores Limitantes de la Inversión Extranjera en el Perú,* edited by Araoz, M., Bonifaz, J. Casas, C. and González Vigil, F. Lima: Centro de Investigaciones de la Universidad del Pacífico.

Niño Tarazona, Jaime Andrés (2003). *Elementos para el Diseño de una Estragia de Integración en el Sector Servicios para los Países de la Comunidad Andina en el Contexto de las*

Negociaciones del Alca y la Ronda de Doha de la OMC. University of Bogota/CAN General Secretariat.

Paredes, Carlos and Jeffrey Sachs (1991). *Peru's Path to Recovery: A Plan for Economic Stabilization and Growth.* The Brookings Institution.

Tello, Luis (2004). *El Perú en el Proceso de Integración Andina de 1992 a 1997.* Graduation Thesis in History. Universidad Nacional Mayor de San Marcos/CAN General Secretariat.

Wise, Carol (2003). *Reinventando el Estado: Estrategia Económica y Cambio Institucional en el Perú.* Lima: Centro de Investigaciones de la Universidad del Pacífico.

WTO (2000). *Trade Policy Review Peru.* Report by the WTO Secretariat. WT/TPR/S/69.

Other Documents

Araoz, Mercedes (2004). *Participación de la Sociedad Civil en el Proceso de Negociaciones del TLC con EE.UU. Pautas para el Diseño de un Esquema de Diálogo entre Sociedad Civil y el MINCETUR.* Preliminary Draft. Second Version. February 2004.

Caretas Journal (05/04/2001). "Luna de Hiel en CONFIEP."

Caretas Journal (04/04/2002). "5 de abril de 1992 El Autogolpe de Alí Baba."

CENI (2003). *Proyecto: Comisión Empresarial de Negociaciones Internacionales.* Confidential Paper. September 2003. Lima.

CENI (2004a). *Directory CENI – Executive Secretary.*

CENI (2004b). Minutes of Meetings from Working (Sub-) Groups "Tariffs", "Safeguards", "Textiles", "Technical Obstacles to Trade", "Rules of Origin", "Custom Procedures", "State Procurement and Investment."

DBLA (2005). *Economic Research. Latin American Database. Country Indicators from 1980 to 2004.*

De la Flor Belaúnde, Pablo (09/07/2004). *Balance de las Rondas de Negociación del TLC Peru-EE.UU. Jefe del Equipo Negociador para el TLC con EE.UU.* Vice-Ministry of Foreign Trade.

Empresas & Negocios (20/10/2003). "Durante III Foro Nacional ALCA: En la Recta Final hacia el ALCA."

El Comercio Newspaper (28/06/1997). "Gremios Satisfechos con Resultado de Negociación."

El Comercio Newspaper (22/02/1998). "Confiep debe dejar de Verse como un Gremio." Interview with Manuel Sotomayor.

El Comercio Newspaper (13/03/1998). "Con 21 votos, Manuel Sotomayor Alcanzó Presidencia de Confiep. SNI y ADEX se Retiran del Comité Ejecutivo."

El Comercio Newspaper (28/08/1998). "Coordinadora Empresarial Recoge el 95% de la Propuesta de la Confiep."

El Comercio Newspaper (25/09/1998). "Coordinadora Gremial se Reunirá para Moderar sus Propuestas."

El Comercio Journal (23/09/1998). "Coordinadora Gremial No Asistirá a la Reunión de Ministros con   CONFIEP."

El Comercio (15/02/2004)."Y, Ya sabes Quién se Queda en el Gabinete?"

General Office of Administration/MINCETUR (2004a). *Reseña Historica MITINCI desde el Año 1968.*

General Office of Administration/MINCETUR (2004b). *Planilla de Personal del Ministerio de Comercio Exterior y Turismo.*

Gleiser, Samuel (2003). *Costos y Beneficios del Proceso ALCA en el Caso Peruano.* Presentación de la Comisión ALCA/PERU. Lima. September 2003.

IDB (2002). *Foreign Trade Policy Development Program: PE-0219.*

La Gestión Newspaper (29/06/97). "Perú en el Grupo Andino: Se Acabó la incertidumbre."

La Gestión Newspaper (11/08/2005)."Pedro Pablo Kuczynski: No es Conveniente que Perú se Retire de la CAN."

La Gestión Newspaper (16/08/2005). Brief on FTA talks with Thailand.

La Gestión Newspaper (20/06/2002). "Presupuesto Comparado de Organismos de Promoción de Exportaciones Año 2000."

MINAG (2004). *Desarrollo de la Competitividad en el Perú.* Presentation by Dr. Juan Risi Carbone, General Director of Agrarian Promotion. June 2004.

MINCETUR (2003). *Perú: Plan Estratégico Nacional Exportadores (PENX) 2003-2013. Bases Estratégicas. Exportaciones: Motor del Desarrollo.* March 2003.

MINCETUR (2005a). *Monthly Bulletin of Foreign Trade.* No. 23. December 2005.

MINCETUR (2005b). *Cuadro Demostrativo de Remuneraciones y Beneficios por Niveles del MINCETUR.* Directorate of Human Resources.

Peñaranda, César (2004). *Presentación del Consejo Empresarial de Negociaciones Internacionales* (CENI). Secretario Técnico Ejecutivo. Lima. June 2004.

Prompex (2004). *Evolución de las Exportaciones y Tipo de Cambio.*

Interviews

OUTSIDE EXPERTS (OE)				
Date	Name	Type	Organisation	Function
30.10.2003 15.07.2004	González Vigil, Fernando	NEI Survey	Pacific University/ Research Centre CUIP	Professor of Economics
23.02.2004	Araoz, Mercedes	Survey	Pacific University/ Research Centre CUIP	Professor of Economics; Responsible for Civil Society Dialogue (IDB consultant)
24.02.2004	Larrazabal, Juán	NEI	General Secretariat CAN	International Functionary; Expert in ITN
27.02.2004	Mendez Chang, Elvira	Survey	Catholic University/ Faculty of Law	Director of Study Department
07.07.2004	Garcia, Jaime	Survey	Universidad de Lima/ Economics Department	Consultant; Ex-MITINCI official
08.07.2004	Peñaranda, Cesar	Survey	Málaga-Webb Consulting	Economist; CENI Executive Secretary; Ex-MEF advisor
13.07.2004	Davila, Javier	Survey	Institute of Economic and Social Studies IEES; Lima University	Professor in Economics; Head of IEES
14.07.2004	Tello, Mario	Survey	Catholic University/ Business Centre CENTRUM	Professor of Economics; International Consultant
14.07.2004	Rebosio, Guillermo	Survey	Peruvian Centre of Social Studies (CEPES)	Economist; Agriculture Policy Advisor
30.09.2004	Arredondo, Alberto	Survey	Institute for Development of Southern Peru (Pro Sur)	Economist; Consultant of Entrepreneurial Development
04.10.2004	Cornejo, Enrique	NEI	Lima University/ Department of Economics	Professor of Economics; APRA Economic Policy Advisor; Ex-ICE President
05.10.2004	Cano, Janet	NEI	Universidad de Lima; CENI	Professor of Economics; Assistant of CENI Executive Secretary
02.10.2004	Teivanen, Teivo	NEI	San Marcos University/ Master Program in Social Science	Professor of Political Science; Expert in Social Movements; Democracy and Global Transformation
09.02.2005	Mindreau, Manuel	Survey	Pacific University/ Research Centre CUIP	Professor of International Relations
09.02.2005	Lopez, Adolfo	NEI	General Secretariat CAN	International Functionary; Ex-Vice-Minister of Integration
11.02.2005	Morón, Eduardo	NEI	Pacific University/ Research Centre CUIP	Professor of Economics; Expert in State Reforms
11.02.2005	Tello, Luis	NEI	San Marcos University/ History Department	Researcher; Expert in Andean Integration

| 14.02.2005 | Campodónico, Humberto | NEI | San Marcos University/ Department of Economics | Professor/ International Trade and Globalization Affairs |
| 14.02.2005 | Sueiro, Ernesto | NEI | CEPES | Agriculture Policy Advisor |

STATE OFFICIALS (SO)

Date	Name	Type	Agency	Function
30.10.2003	Mathews, Juan Carlos	NEI	MINCETUR/Vice-Ministry of Foreign Trade (VICE)	National Director of Export Development
17.02.2004 21.02.2004 14.07.2004 15.02.2005	Paredes Castro, Ricardo	Survey, NEI	VICE	Trade Policy Advisor; Multilateral and Services Affairs
18.02.2004 10.02.2005	Elmore, Victoria	Survey NEI	VICE	National Director of Multilateral Affairs
24.02.2004	Romero, César	Survey	Ministry of Agriculture/ Planning Office of Agrarian Policy	Trade Policy Advisor; Agriculture Affairs
25.02.2004	Mesias, Luis	Survey	VICE	Trade Policy Advisor; Market Access
08.07.2004	Honorio, Liliana	Survey	VICE	FTAA Director
09.07.2004	Illescas, Javier	Survey	MEF/Vice-Ministry of Economy	General Director of International Economy, Competition and Private Investment
09.07.2004	Sanchez, Viviana	Survey	MEF/Vice-Ministry of Economy	Legal Advisor; Market Access Affairs
09.07.2004	García, Luis Alonso	Survey	INDECOPI	President of Intellectual Property Division
12.07.2004	Alfaro Espinosa, Silvia	Survey	External Affairs Ministry/ Undersecretariat of Economic Affairs and International Negotiations	Trade Diplomat; Market Access Affairs
12.07.2004	Paredes, Paul/ Gervasi, Ana	Survey	Undersecretariat of Economic Affairs and International Negotiations	Director of International Economy Department/ Policy Advisor in Agriculture Affairs
13.07.2004	Talavera, Karin/ Morales, Eduardo	Survey	PRODUCE/Vice-Ministry of Industry	Special Advisors of National Director and Vice-Minister of Industry
30.09.2004	Medina, Victor	Survey	MINCETUR/ Regional Office Arequipa	Regional Director of Foreign Trade and Tourism
01.10.2004	Butón, Denise	Survey	Arequipa Economic Development Department	Head of Department

14.02.2005	Franca, Paula	NEI	MINCETUR	Head of Human Resources Division
15.02.2005	Brandes, Eduardo	NEI	VICE	National Director of Regional Integration Division

BUSINESS REPRESENTATIVES (BR)

Date	Name	Type	Entity	Position
29.10.2003 19.02.2004	Morante, Ramon	NEI Survey	SNI	Head of Foreign Trade Department
31.10.2003 18.02.2004	Seperack, Silvia	NEI Survey	Lima Chamber of Comerse	Head of Foreign Trade Department; Coordinator FTAA Commission-Peru
16.02.2004 19.02.2004	Reaño, Martín	Survey, NEI	SNI-Committee of Textiles	Managing Director
17.02.2004	Ordoñez, José	NEI	ADEX	Area Manager of Agribusiness and Lumber
19.02.2004	Daly Arbulú, Alejandro	Survey	SNI-Committees (4) of Vegetable Oils, Wheat, Biscuits, Cleansing Agents and Cosmetics	Managing Director
24.02.2004	Larrea, Gilberto	Survey	CONVEAGRO	Technical Secretary
23.02.2004	Vigil Mattos, Jorge	Survey	National Fishery Society	Chief of Economic Office and Fishery Statistics
25.02.2004	Gamio, Pedro	Survey	ADEX-Textiles Comité	Director Textile Committee
26.02.2004	Mansur, Pedro	NEI	National Union of Textile Entrepreneurs	Managing Director
27.02.2004	Gómez, Raúl	Survey	National Society of Mining, Petroleum & Energy	Head of Administrative Department
06.07.2004	Gálvez, Alvaro	Survey	PERUCAMARAS	Trade Policy Advisor
06.07.2004	Tenorio, Luis	Survey	SNI-Committee of Metal Mechanics	Managing Director
07.07.2004	Fernández, Rómulo	Survey	COMPYMEP	President
07.07.2004	Teullet, Patricia	Survey	Foreign Trade Society of Peru – COMEXPERU	Managing Director
13.07.2004	Villalobos, Alvaro	Survey	SNI-ADIFAN	Managing Director
13.07.2004	Piskulich, Rolando	Survey	SNI-Committee of Dairy Industry (ADIL)	Managing Director
13.07.2004	Taipe, Luis	Survey	SNI-Committees of Glass, Ceramics, Lumber and Derivates, Alcoholic Beverage	Managing Director
13.07.2004	La Rosa, Carlos	Survey	SNI-COPEI	Managing Director
14.07.2004	Caillaux,	Survey	FONGAL – Conveagro	Trade Policy Advisor,

	Miguel			Agrarian Representative
16.07.2004	Blondet, Alberto	Survey	AGAP	Managing Director
	De Andrea, Raúl	Survey	Peruvian Association of Assurance Companies	Managing Director
29.09.2004	Novoa Málaga, Jorge	Survey	Arequipa Chamber of Industry and Commerce	Managing Director
30.09.2004	Zegarra del Carpio, Carlos	Survey	Arequipa Rural Society (SADA)	Board of Directors
01.10.2004	Cuzzi, Mario	Survey	Arequipa Association of Industrial District Companies (ADEPIA)	President
05.10.2004	González, Carlos Alberto	Survey	ADEX	Head of Economic Study Department
09.02.2005	Mulanovich, Herbert	NEI	SIN	Institutional Advisor
11.02.2005	Bonilla, Yolanda	NEI	SNI-Committee of Textiles	Administrative Assistant
01.07.2004	Villacorta, Rosa	Survey	SIN	Trade Policy Advisor

Selected Interview Partners

Adolfo López: Jurisprudent. Since the 1970s, Adolfo Lopéz's profession has been related to the Andean Integration process, first as a young functionary inside the Directorate of Integration in the scope of the Ministry of Industry and Trade, later as the Peruvian official inside the Assembly of the Cartagena Agreement (since 1997 General Secretariat of the Andean Community of Nations). In-between, he served as Vice-Ministry of Integration inside the Ministry of Industry, Tourism, Domestic Trade and Integration. However, the experience was rather short and covered the first eight month of the Alberto Fujimori Administration (July 1990 – March 1991). Currently, Adolfo Lopéz works as a Consultant of the CAN, heading the Informatics Unity inside the General Secretariat.

Victoria Elmore: Sociologist with a MA in Economic Planning. Together with Eduardo Brandes and Elva Rodriguez, Victoria Elmore belongs to the "Dinosaurian" inside MINCETUR. She entered the Ministry (by the Ministry of Trade) in 1977 as a policy advisor inside the Planning Office. After attending a two year postgraduate degree in France on International Economic Relations, in 1983 Elmore again became a trade policy advisor inside the Vice-Ministry of Trade (belonging first to the Ministry of Economy and later to the Ministry of Industry). Then, during the government of Alan García, she worked inside the newly created Institute of Foreign Trade as a specialist in export promotion and multilateral affairs. Later in the

1990s, she was transferred inside the MITINCI department and began directing the multilateral area, first in a rather informal manner in the scope of the Vice-ministry of Integration, and later, from 2000, as head of the National Directorate of Multilateral Affairs. Conversely to Eduardo Brandes, National Director of Integration, Victoria Elmore was more critical regarding the CAN, and hence, adopted the position sustained inside the Ministry of Economy and Finance.

Ramon Morante: In the 1980s, functionary of the Ministry of Industry and Trade; Ramon Morante later evolved in the 1990s into the Peruvian industry's principal trade policy advisor. Since the turn of the century, he has headed the SNI Department of Foreign Trade and represented the affiliated industrial branches in the most relevant international trade policy forums, above all the CAN and ALADI. Due to the close relation maintained with state officials inside MITINCI, and from 2002 MINCETUR, Ramon Morante has served in the past as advisor of the official negotiations team, i.e. in the scope of FTAA and US-AFTA talks.

6   Bolivia

Due to its central location within South America, one could be tempted to describe Bolivia as a potential engine for regional integration, especially if we consider the fact that the state is named after *Simon Bolívar*, who liberated the majority of the subcontinent at the beginning of the 19th century and crusaded for a unified South America. Yet, the integrative force of Bolivia is limited. Apart from its extensive area of 1,098,581 sq km^2 and its richness in natural resources, the country is sparsely populated with only 8.5 million habitants and exhibits a low per capita income of US$1,000 per year. This figure makes Bolivia poorer than any other South American nation. Furthermore, the scant physical integration inside Bolivia and the marked cultural disparities between the Andean highlands in the west and the tropical lowlands in the east have influenced the nation's possibilities to deepen its external economic relations.

Concerning the conceptual inputs for regional trade policy-making, however, the contribution of the poor Bolivian nation have been remarkable. Against the devastating hyperinflation in the aftermath of the debt crisis in Bolivia, reaching over 20,000 percent at its peak in 1985, the country became one of the earliest reformers in South America. Supported by Jeffrey Sachs' advisory team from Harvard, as of August 1985, Bolivia set forth a severe stabilisation program consisting of the application of a unified and market oriented exchange rate, the liberalisation of trade and capital accounts and harsh budget cuts. Therefore, inflation was brought under control within a few weeks, initiating a thus far unbroken phase of macroeconomic stability (see Morales/ Sachs 1990).

This chapter discusses the implications of this new economic policy on the world market integration strategy pursued by Bolivia from 1986 and 2004, and provides explanation for why the once visionary economic opening process failed, producing disrepair and social unrest among the Bolivian people. Accordingly, this chapter is structured along the following lines. The *first section* outlines the different policy areas making up the world market integration strategy (Dependent Variable B), i.e. unilateral trade regime, region and extra-regional integration, sector and export promotion. *Section two* enlightens the organisation of Bolivia's public sector in the trade policy area (Independent Variable A1), showing thus how the local bureaucracies were organised with respect to the conduction of international trade policy affairs during the period of analysis. Then, *section three* elucidates the institutional responses of the business sector on the same issue (Independent Variable A2). Based on section one to three, *section four* provides an assessment of the case, and explores the links between independent and dependent variables, and controls the possible influences of other variables (C1-4) on the B value.

6.1 The Failed Application of the Multipolar Model

This first section is structured in accordance with the different policy areas that make up the world market integration strategy (Dependent Variable B), i.e. unilateral trade regime, region and extra-regional integration, sectoral and export promotion policies. The last subsection summarises the results and provides an overview of the trade performance from 1985 to 2004.

Unilateral Trade Regime

The stabilisation plan set forth as of August 1985 by the Supreme Decree No. 21060 represented the end of state capitalism born out of the National Revolution of 1952. Instead of the state acting as controller of prices, provider and buyer of goods and services, lender of credits and subsidies, ruler of labour relations, etc., international market forces became the reference scheme. For Carlos Villegas from the State University UMSA, the essential innovation of the Decree 21060 was the introduction of a neoliberal economic ruling, even though the ruling primarily consisted of macroeconomic stabilisation actions to control inflation (OE 19/03/04). Thus, "export or die" were the words used by president Victor Paz Estensoro to persuade manufacturers that they should no longer be oriented to the small domestic market dominated by a handful of state-led firms, but look outwards for the abundant market opportunities abroad (OE Rodriguez 17/01/05). Enhanced capital inflows and cheaper capital goods were expected to provide the necessary inputs to accelerate the technical progress, and thus reduce the competitivity gaps when compared to foreign competitors (Zambrana 2002).

In this context, the trade policy measures adopted consisted of a rigorous dismantling of tariff and non-tariff barriers. By applying a uniform tariff of 20 percent and abolishing nearly all quantitative restrictions, new border policies became clear, in stark contrast to the previous heterodox and often discretional policies, such as the existence of multiple tariffs levels that reached 150 percent, import licenses and quotas (Zambrana 2002). Later, in 1990, tariffs were reduced to a uniform level of 10 percent, but excluded about 500 tariff items in the range of capital goods that were taxed by only 5 percent. In 2000, a further category for duty free imports was introduced in order to continue lowering the costs of capital goods for industrial development. By 2005, the arithmetical average rate applied was 8.2 percent, whereas 70 percent of all tariff lines applied the uniform rate of 10 percent (WTO 2005). Despite these modifications and exemptions from the flat rate model, tariffs in general were rather stable and enforced Bolivia's image as a transparent and reliable trading partner.

Against the conceptual turn of 1985, Bolivia soon envisaged the adherence to the world trade system as a means to consolidate its unilateral reform steps. Becoming a formal GATT member in 1989, the country's domestic policies were evidently brought in line with the guiding principles of the multilateral trading system. Hence, the WTO Secretariat Reports of 1993, 1999 and 2005 praised Bolivia as a model of autonomous liberalisation, highlighting the benefits of a 10 percent uniform tariff regime in terms of its predictability, transparency and promotion of an efficient allocation of resources. Special emphasis was furthermore placed on the prevention of trade distortions due to the removal of any outstanding sector-specific subsidies.[1]

In addition to low tariffs, Bolivia accentuated its salient "trade openness" by renouncing practically all trade defence measures, except for two interventions during 2002 and 2003 involving food products from Argentina and Peru.[2] Until 2005, domestic legislation had not considered any detailed trade defence mechanisms, and thus, made antidumping and safeguard actions rely on provisions signed in international agreements within the scope of the WTO or the CAN. Beyond the legal sphere, Bolivia has suffered severely from illegal imports, which accounted for an estimated 35 percent of total imports in 2002-03; i.e. US$600 million per year (Kreidler/ Rocha 2004: 51).[3] Therefore, the customs reform implemented in 1999, which cost the state US$35 million, failed to combat the structural constraints of contraband activities, such as rampant corruption in the customs authorities, extreme poverty in frontier areas and extensive and almost uncontrollable frontiers.

Regarding the market access for Bolivian products, both unilateral reforms and the GATT adherence entailed few tangible benefits. Since local exports consisted of a small group of primary and low processed goods for which international markets were either liberalised (e.g. mining products) or still distorted by subsidies and protectionist border measures (e.g. sugar, cotton and soybeans), the advantages provided by the Uruguay Round results were meagre.[4] Moreover, multilateral tariff reductions agreed on caused a general erosion of non reciprocal

---

[1] There is a significant gap between tariffs bound in the GATT (40 percent on practically all products) and effective applied tariffs; i.e. Bolivia could theoretically revise its open trade regime by raising tariffs up to 40 percent.
[2] Bolivia took countervailing measures against Peru on six elaborate food products because Peru denied the importation of Bolivian soy oil. Moreover, the country implemented safeguard measures against Argentina on the importation of wheat flour.
[3] Approximately 80 percent of consumer goods, 30 percent of intermediates, and 20 percent of capital goods are affected by contraband; see ibid: 44.
[4] For this reason Bolivia joined the Cairns Group in 1999.

tariff concessions made by developed countries in the scope of the Generalised System of Preferences (GSP).[5] Thus, Bolivia had clear incentives to consider regional preferential arrangements as a strategic option for gaining broader market access for its manufacturers.

Regional Integration

Strikingly, in the course of the 1990s the tiny Bolivian economy, along with Chile, evolved among Latin American countries as one of the most connected economies, at least from a legal perspective. Between 1990 and 1997, Bolivia was successful in signing comprehensive Free Trade Agreements (FTAs) with ten of the eleven ALADI states. Thus, in the following section I briefly sum up the negotiation pace undertaken by the Bolivian trade diplomacy.

Andean Community of Nations (CAN): During the period of state capitalism, the closest links on an international level were maintained with the Andean Group in which Bolivia was a founding member of the Cartagena Agreement of 1969. With the introduction of the New Economic Policy in 1985, Bolivia nevertheless neglected the integration scheme due to its strong association with the previously pursued ISI approach. Viewing policies such as the Sectoral Industrial Development Programs and the strongly selective treatment of foreign capitals, the accord signed in 1969 by Colombia, Venezuela, Chile, Peru, Ecuador, and Bolivia had been the fullest expression of "old regionalism" in Latin America, based on inward-oriented strategies (Devlin and Estevadeordal 2001: 24).

At the onset of 1990s, however, the objectives and modalities of Andean integration altered, becoming an interesting development tool for Bolivia's agriculture exports, particularly those originating from the tropical lowlands of eastern Bolivia. At this time, new guidelines were set by the Strategic Design in December 1989 when Bolivia, Colombia, Ecuador, Peru and Venezuela declared in Galapagos, Ecuador, their goal of accelerating intra-zone integration as well as becoming open towards extra-regional partners. In the "harmonising" context of economic liberalisation in the region, the group finally agreed in December 1991, through the Act of Barahona, on the complete removal of border restrictions and the formation of a CET by January 1992.

Although these deadlines were not fully met, the Andean Free Trade Area became a reality for Bolivia in February 1993. In the case of the announced CET, member countries decided in November 1994 on its implementation by January 1995. Andean Decision 370

---

[5] Nonetheless, the GSP conceded from the EU (known as the Andean GSP) and the US (Andean Trade Promotion and Drug Eradication Act or "ATPDEA") has been widened considerably in the last 15 years.

specified that the CET would contain four levels, i.e. 5, 10, 15, and 20 percent. To wide extents, this escalated tariff concept confirmed the "industry friendly" approach upheld by Colombia and Venezuela which was aimed at lowering costs for inputs and capital goods not produced locally, and providing higher protection for domestic production according to the degree of a products elaboration. Even so, from the outset of negotiations, the Bolivian authorities indicated their absent will to sacrifice the modern flat rate. Therefore, and for three main factors, Bolivia was granted exemption from applying the higher rates of 15 and 20 percent in order to maintain the principal national tariff of 10 percent on third world countries' imports.

1) *Small and Less Developed Country:* In the history of Latin American integration (the ALALC in 1960, Andean Pact 1969, ALADI in 1980) small and poor states like Ecuador and Bolivia had enjoyed a special status which enabled flexible and privileged treatment throughout integration issues; i.e. higher tariff preference, longer phasing-outs, less rigid rules of origin, etc.

2) *Landlocked Country:* Bolivia, as a landlocked country, and moreover, badly integrated in the regional transport system, causes low risks of serious CET perforations by means of cheaper imports via Bolivia.

3) *Trade Openness:* As described, in 1985 the country adopted a very open trade regime, and thus, didn't resist removing the remaining border restrictions for intra-zone imports.

At any rate, average tariffs among member states converged considerably due to the previous unilateral reforms, leaving Bolivia to stand out with its somewhat lower tariffs, as Table 6.1 shows.

Table 6.1: Andean Community Nominal Average Tariff 2001

CET	Bolivia	Colombia	Ecuador	Peru	Venezuela
13.6	9.6	11.6	11.2	11.6	11.9

Source: CAN General Secretariat

Despite this far-reaching convergence, discussions on the CET have so far uncovered severe conflicts among members. Accordingly, Peru also aimed for a flat rate model, but couldn't settle on the application of the above enlisted factors. Thus, Peru suspended its CAN membership between 1992 and 1997 and has since resisted the adoption of a harmonised CET as well as the complete removal of intra-zone trade restrictions; i.e. Bolivia used to suffer from the restricted entrance of soy and sugar products. As I outlined in the chapter on Peru, the incessant disagreements upheld between Peru and the CAN did much harm to the Andean integration process in general. Even though important institutional reforms were undertaken by the Trujillo Protocol in June 1997, by which the Andean Community of Nations was founded, the last years' experiences have shown that efforts aimed at establishing a common market enabling the free movement of goods, capital, services and people encounter clear limits in the Andean context.[6]

Concerning Bolivia's participation inside the CAN, the principal focus has traditionally been based upon improving and guaranteeing preferential market access for agricultural products from Bolivia's lowlands. The country has further benefited from the Andean Price Band System in force since 1995, by which the custom tariffs for up to 400 agricultural products have been variably adjusted according to the relation between domestic and world market prices. Bolivia, without applying the system, enjoyed higher protection, especially within the buyers' markets of Colombia and Venezuela.

Mexico: During the first government of Sánchez de Lozada (1993-97), Bolivia tried to foster economic integration with the NAFTA. But as the country did not feature on the Clinton administration's priority list, a FTA with ALADI member Mexico seemed to be a pragmatic step towards deeper hemispheric integration. Therefore, within the scope of ACE No. 31, in force since January 1995, the countries agreed not only on issues affecting the trade of goods, but also on commitments concerning new areas of services, state procurement, investment and intellectual property.[7] Regarding these behind the border measures, Bolivia was virtually overrun by Mexico's team of negotiators, who had accumulated expertise from the adherence to the NAFTA, as one negotiator remembered (SO De Rico 15/12/04). Bolivia maintained no offensive interests in these new areas, and thus, accepted the impositions with the hope of an expected export surge in manufactured goods, above all in tropical woods from the eastern lowlands. The total liberalisation of bilateral trade in goods had been planned for the beginning of 2009.

Common Market of the South (MERCOSUR): Since the mid-1980's, local diplomacy has been tempted by integration endeavours between Brazil and Argentina; first by the bilateral economic cooperation program, PICE, started in 1986, and later in March 1991, when the major economies in the region formed MERCOSUR together with Uruguay and Paraguay. For the

---

[6] The Trujillo Protocol introduced the Presidential Council and the Council of Foreign Ministers with decision-making responsibilities. Furthermore, the Protocol was aimed at reinforcing the internal cohesion of the Andean integration process by regrouping all its institutions under a new structure, the Andean Integration System (for details see www.comunidadandina.org.) With regards to the Andean Common Market, in May 1999 the member states assumed the commitment to create conditions for the free circulation of goods, the unimpeded movement of services, capital, and people in the sub region by 2005.

[7] In the case of services, specific commitments were reached in areas such as telecommunications, financial services, and professional services.

poor, landlocked Andean state, the principal foreign policy concern regarding the states forming the Rio Plata Basin was linked to the improvement of transport routes towards the Atlantic coast.[8] In the 1990s, expectations focussed on a waterway navigable from the tropical zones in the east (principally from *Puerto Suarez* in the Santa Cruz department) to the Atlantic ports of Argentina and Uruguay.[9] Regarding the regional trade flows, Bolivia was able to control trade deficits only due to natural gas exports to Argentina and (since 1999) to Brazil. Particularly, the competitive farming sector in the Southern Cone was perceived as a strong threat to local producers of wheat, soybean, dairy, meat, sugar and cotton. Conversely, the question of whether and to what extent Bolivian manufactures would take advantage of MERCOSUR's consumer markets (e.g. in textiles, leather, lumber and tropical fruits) was more uncertain.

But trade policy considerations played a minor role as of August 1993 because Bolivia's key officials inside the Foreign Affairs Ministry began working with enthusiasm on the idea that Bolivia could become the regional "hinge" between MERCOSUR and the CAN, or "Donna Flor and Her Two Husbands" according to the favoured metaphor of President Sánchez de Lozado (Sanjinés Avila 2004; Vol. II). As a consequence of intense diplomacy, in 1996 Bolivia became an Associate Member of MERCOSUR. Simultaneously, the country signed a comprehensive FTA with the trading block that replaced the previous, more limited, bilateral agreements maintained with each member state. The so-called ACE No. 36 covered all tariff lines and defined a general regime with progressive tariff reductions, starting at 30 percent in 1997 and reaching 100 percent by January 2006. Different groups of sensitive products were subject to specific schedules that will reach a zero tariff level within 15 to 18 years. In 2011, all exports towards MERCOSUR will be duty free, while in the case of Bolivia, tariffs on 28 items in the range of vegetable oil, sugar and wheat will be dismantled by 2014.

Evidentially, neither the members of MERCOSUR or CAN shared Bolivia's enthusiasm about its integrating role inside South America. The deliberations made by the Foreign Affairs Ministry evidently proved unrealistic, as former trade diplomats later admitted (OEs Tercero 18/01/05; Olmos 15/02/05). The CAN membership became displeased with this individual effort, given that the group had clear interests in envisaging joint free trade talks with the MERCOSUR (OE Larrazabal 08/02/05). For the Southern Cone states, Bolivia was neither a political nor an economic priority compared to Chile, who had previously negotiated a FTA with

---

[8] Since 1969, the country has been linked to the Rio Plata Basin by a multilateral treaty between Bolivia, Argentina, Brazil, Paraguay and Uruguay, aimed at the better use of common aquatic resources.

[9] By the mid-1990's, the states of the Rio Plata Basin moved into planning stages with the *Hidrovía* project, allowing ocean going vessels to make the 2000 mile trip from Argentinean and Uruguayan ports of the Atlantic to currently landlocked areas in Paraguay and Bolivia.

MERCOSUR.[10] Finally, local business (principally the threatened low-land farmers) sustained a strong advocacy against the wide-reaching approach (6.3), thus underlining the lack of justification for the perseverance exhibited by Bolivia's diplomacy. With respect to the content agreement signed in December 1996, several aspects have, in hindsight, provided particularly disappointing results for Bolivia.

1) *Small and Less Developed Country*: Compared to previous regional integration schemes, Bolivia renounced its Small and Less Developed Country status; i.e. market access concessions and trade disciplines were made on a reciprocal basis.

2) *Market Access*: MERCOSUR states showed a reluctance to open up their markets by setting long phasing-out chronograms, small import quotas for textiles and relatively severe rules of origin for industrial goods.[11] Numerous (phyto-) sanitary and customs measures later applied constrained the entrance of bananas, pineapples and tomatoes, among others.

3) *Powerless Observer:* Within the CAN-MERCOSUR negotiations that concluded in October 2004, Bolivia merely participated as an "observer". Thus, it was virtually powerless to prevent the erosion of market access preferences for soy products.[12]

4) *Waterway:* Even though the waterway project along the *Paraná* River received certain impulses in the scope of MERCOSUR, ACE No. 36 was limited to the removal of tariffs and did not encompass tangible commitments for physical integration towards the Atlantic.

Chile: Despite a preferential agreement agreed on in July 1993, in 2004 Chile was the only ALADI member without a FTA signed with Bolivia (disregarding Cuba). Although the original ACE No. 22, covering a limited preferential access for 200 Bolivian and 115 Chilean products, was gradually extended through several additional protocols, Bolivia refused Chile's request to enter into comprehensive free trade talks until the end of 2002 in light of the huge trade deficits registered. In the second government of Sánchez de Lozada, beginning in August 2002, the neighbours finally launched negotiations aimed at a far-reaching multi-issue agreement.

---

[10] For example, as the CET entered into force in 1995, MERCOSUR Resolution planned immediate negotiations only with Chile. Jorge Campbell (OE 08/06/04), by then Argentina's Chief Negotiator, confirmed that the talks with Bolivia were conducted because of Bolivia's insistence since initial, common negotiations with CAN were foreseen.
[11] After negotiations were closed in November 1996, Argentina insisted, for example, on a merely symbolic import quota of 27,000 t-shirts, one of the few products with market opportunities for Bolivia's manufacturers.
[12] For the regional perspectives of Bolivia's oleaginous sector; see Brenes, Madrigal y Montenegro 2001: 40-45.

By then, the offensive interests maintained by Bolivia's government moved away from market access issues towards the possibility of obtaining sovereign access to the Pacific coast in order to facilitate natural gas exports towards markets in Mexico and the US. However, the reestablishment of diplomatic relations with Chile, in combination with the commercial use of the huge natural gas reserves, turned out to be politically unviable. The relationship with Chile (formally interrupted since 1975) still encountered profound rejection among the Bolivian people as a result of the Pacific War, which cost Bolivia its only sovereign access to the coastline in 1904. Finally, a strong opposition comprised of labour, neighbourhood organisations and indigenous movements against the possible natural gas exports via Chilean ports ended, in October 2003, in violent struggles with military forces, provoking the necessary exile of Gonzalo Sánchez de Lozada. At that same time, the bilateral free trade talks ceased.

Extra-Regional Sphere

Strong opposition against further foreign trade commitments have hindered the country in the past years in its ability to continue the pursuit of a Multipolar Model in the extra-regional sphere. In any case, Bolivia's influence on trade integration outcomes was close to zero at this time as the country participated only as minor partner in the "mega negotiations" on the regional, hemispheric and multilateral levels started in 1998. As a result, Bolivia contributed very little to the bi-regional relations between the CAN and the EU, which had yet to pass pre-negotiation stages by 2005, and to the WTO Doha Development Round, which had not yet registered a major breakthrough, for example. More revealing from a domestic perspective, however, was Bolivia's recent participation inside the hemispheric sphere, and above all, within the US-AFTA talks.

Free Trade Area of the Americas (FTAA): With a 0.07 percent share of the hemisphere's GDP, Bolivia's leverage was insignificant in the FTAA negotiations formally launched in 1998. Hence, Bolivia could only adopt an observer's role in the key negotiations between the US and Brazil, those countries being the principal opponents on key issues such as intellectual property, agriculture, services and antidumping measures. Bolivia's offensive concerns focused on trade in agriculture and Special Treatment for Small and Less Developed States. According to the latter, Bolivia participated actively in the pertinent Declarations of Toronto, Buenos Aires and Quito (1999-2002), where related issues had been promoted and specified both in the framework of the CAN and FTAA.[13] Nevertheless, other potential offensive interests such as the legal protection

---

[13] According to Ana Maria Solares, Vice-Minister of International Economic Relations 1998-2002, Bolivia took over the leadership within CAN. In the FTAA sphere, Bolivia assumed the presidency of the FTAA Consultative

of the huge local biodiversity weren't pursued with sufficient perseverance, as a trade policy advisor from the local pharmaceutical industry observed (BR Dueñas 9/08/04). Finally, the new trade issues of services, state procurement, intellectual property, investment, labour and environmental standards, were not, or could not be, attended to by the limited Bolivian negotiation team (SO's De Rico 16/03/04; Alvarado 19/03/04; 5.2.2).

US-Andean Free Trade Agreement (US-AFTA): During 2004, the FTAA stalled because of a lack of space for the negotiation of key issues such as agriculture, antidumping, services, and intellectual property, and as a result, the Bush administration manifested its disposition to undergo bilateral trade talks with the Andean countries, after having completed Free Trade Agreements with Chile and the Common Market of Central America. Peru, Ecuador and Colombia took immediate advantage of this offer and entered into formal negotiations with the US in May 2004. At this time, Venezuela abstained due to the ideological quarrels put forth by President Hugo Chavez. On several occasions, the Bolivian government likewise declared its interest to join the talks, confirming the country's ambitions for deeper economic relations with the US since 1993 (Rodríguez 2003: 113).

Bolivia's recent interest in free trade with the US is explained mainly by the fact that since 1991 local exporters have enjoyed preferential access to the US market under the Andean Trade Preference Act (ATPA). In September 2002, ATPA was superseded by the Andean Trade Promotion and Drug Eradication Act (ATPDEA), renewing not only the tariff preferences until December 31, 2006 but also adding roughly 700 products to the previous list, including clothing, leather and wood manufactures, and jewellery. On this ground, the government argued that surging exports in these labour-intensive sectors would lose their preferences at the end of 2006, or at least, would face investment adverse uncertainty as regards an eventual superseding ATPDEA.

On the domestic level, though, the official free trade plans encountered strong opposition. Since 2002, oppositional forces have organised within the scope of the "Bolivian Movement against the FTAA Struggle". Coordinated by the Solon Foundation, a foreign financed NGO, the movement was composed of NGOs, labour, indigenous and small peasant groups, neighbourhood organisations, and state universities, and raised fundamental objections against the disruptive force of globalisation, best exemplified by the US's southwards expansion. Their intellectual leaders put emphasis on the impact of enhanced intellectual property rights, investment rules and services, arguing that the "latest generation" FTAs cement the existing

Group for Smaller Economies during 2001. The topic of technical assistance received special attention here in the scope of the Hemispheric Cooperation Program; see CADEX 2001, 35.

economic regime in favour of US interests (mainly those of installed multinationals, operating in services, pharmaceuticals, mining, hydrocarbons, etc.) in working as an intrinsic set of instruments to exploit Latin America by imposing US rules on the domestic legal framework.[14] Against this articulated social discontent, the government was hesitant in entering the talks as a formal party and attended the process merely as an observer. The US government was concerned about the social acceptance of the agreement and likewise opted to wait for more opportune moments for direct negotiations. In October 2005, both governments finally decided to handle the topic in 2006 (*La Razón* 13/10/05). The effectiveness by which oppositional forces have placed their arguments so far can mainly be explained by three factors:

1) *Organisational Linkages:* While "technical support" was provided by NGO's closely connected to the global anti-globalisation movement, the political mobilisations were implemented by traditional social actors such as labour, neighbourhood and indigenous organisations.

2) *Variety of Activities*: The movement made creative use of media, impacting videos, flyers and magazines, street protests and blockades, assemblies and workshops, and finally, presence in Parliament through the powerful Movement towards Socialism (MAS).

3) *Issue Linkages:* The protest against free trade was connected to other, even more polemic topics such as the eradication of coca cultivation, public water supply, natural gas reserves and the demand to enact a Constitutional Assembly process.

Export and Sector Promotion

For Gary Rodriguez (2004: 125), the New Economic Policy, in force as of 1985, had four central pillars: Planning, Subsidising, Protection and Promotion. Indeed, to enhance domestic competitiveness, in which Bolivia was ranked number 101 of 117 states (according to the WEF Global Competitiveness Report 2005-06), the governments of the Nationalist Revolution Movement party (MNR) paid exclusive attention to structural reforms. While the Victor Paz administration (1985-89) placed primary emphasis on deregulating the monetary and trade regime, Sánchez de Lozado (1993-97) linked reform power to the modernisation and disengagement of the state from its traditional economic activities, through a widespread

---

[14] The movement's intellectual leaders came from the state university UMSA or NGO's such as the Center for Rural Development Studies (CEDLA), Solon Foundation and the Bolivian Center for Information and Documentation (CEBID); see for example Instituto de Investigaciones Económicas – UMSA (2003).

capitalisation of public assets and autonomous, sector specific regulatory mechanisms, among other measures.[15]

As economic growth slowed down from 1998 onwards, and popular criticism of the "neoliberal achievements" increased, the official economic development approach began to alter somewhat. The most noteworthy attempt was embodied in the Bolivian System of Productivity and Competitiveness (SBPC) put into practice in November 2001 under the one year presidency of Jorge Quiroga, from the centre-right wing party Democratic Nationalist Action. Coordinated by the Productivity and Competitiveness Unit (UPC), the SBPC sought to counter the structural deficits faced by local industry in the range of a qualified work force, technology, economy of scale, and reliable and efficient public institutions, among others. Conceptual emphasis was put on the stimulation of supply chains, or vertical clusters, through sector agreements among stakeholders from the private, public and academic sectors. This act embraced Bolivia's potential export offer of soy, quinoa foods, textiles and clothing, leather, lumber and furniture, and jewellery.[16] However, the change of authorities in August 2002, coupled with high budget deficits and political and social instability (illustrated by two transitory governments between October 2003 and December 2005), strongly modified the institutional structure of the SBPC, hindering the effective implementation of the systemic approach to development.

With regard to export promotion facilities, official support was likewise perceived as generally insufficient by local manufacturers (Vaca Calderón/Soliz Salinas 2001: 117-130; CONEX 2004a-e). Nevertheless, a set of fiscal measures were envisaged in the Export Development and Taxation Law enacted in April 1993 by the Jaime Paz Zamora government from the Leftist Revolution Movement (MIR) (1989-93). Although modified on several occasions, the following mechanisms were still in force in 2005:

1) *The Tax Refund System*: The law introduced the principle of tax neutrality for export goods and services; i.e. indirect tax such as the Value Added Tax (VAT) and specific consumption tax (ICE) paid along the production process are reimbursed by so called Tax Refund Certificates (CEDEIM). However, export subsidies paid on non-traditional products were no longer granted from the moment the so-called CERTEX was abolished in August 1986. Complaints regarding the CEDEIM mechanism mostly concerned the

---

[15] See Larrazabal 2000. The major new regulations during the Sánchez de Lozada government were the Law on Banks and Financial Entities (1993), Capitalization Law (1994), Sectoral Regulatory System Law (1994), Electricity Law (1994), Telecommunication Law (1995), Central Bank Law (1995), Hydrocarbons Law (1996), Pension Law (1996), Mining Law (1997), Council of Judicature Law (1997), Ombudsman Law (1997), Stock Market Law (1998), Insurance Law (1998), and the Law on Concessions for Public Works in the Transport sector (1998).
[16] For detailed information, see UPC 2002 and Supreme Decree 26391 enacted on November 8, 2001.

arduous presentation of relevant fiscal or commercial invoices, implying several months delay on the return of paid taxes.[17]

2) *The Temporary Import Regime for Export Promotion (RITEX).* Under the current RITEX provisions, import duties and internal taxes are suspended for a maximum of 360 days for imports of raw materials and intermediate goods incorporated into a production process that makes products for export; i.e. for their production, processing, or assembly. In 2004, RITEX proved quite a popular option, enlisting 118 companies and exporting goods worth US$356 million, in comparison with 62 companies in 2001 with exports amounting to US$31 million (WTO 2005).

3) *Free and/or Industrial Zones.* These areas intended to encourage commercial activities and industrial development within a competitive environment by simplifying intermediations processes and broad tax exemptions. In 2005, 14 free or industrial zones held concessions whereby three of them were for pure commercial use. Nonetheless, their contribution to Bolivia's exports has been limited since they were poorly linked to other activities within their geographical zones.

Furthermore, official market assistance was poorly received by exporters. Since the inaction of the National Institute of Export Promotion (INPEX) in 1987, Bolivia's export promotion agency underwent numerous modifications, going through six different ministerial departments. Founded in 1997, the Promotion Centre of Bolivia (CEPROBOL), inside the Ministry of Foreign Affairs, was responsible in 2004 for the promotion of exports, foreign investment, and tourism. Nevertheless, to attend these broad fields CEPROBOL was designated only a marginal budget. According to calculations by the International Trade Centre (ITC), of the yearly budget of US$340,000 (2002) salaries accounted for 74% (ITC/BOL/61/80). The report concluded that CEPROBOL requires annual resources of approximately US$7 million to carry out its duties in an adequate manner.

---

[17] The critical voices gathered originated from the leading export entities such as CANEB and IBCE. Furthermore, former state officials like Adhemar Guzman, Vice-Minister for Exports 1998-2002, acknowledged ineffectiveness inside the system; Interview 21/01/05.

A cross-country analysis regarding official trade promotion expenditure in 2003 highlights yet further the local disregard for the importance of this area.[18]

Table 6.2: Official Trade Promotion Expenditure Compared (2003)

Country	Exports (X) US$ million	Promotion Expenditure (P)	% (P/X)	Principal Source
Mexico	166.424	188	0.11	State (*Bancomex*)
Spain	111.000	155	0.14	State
Portugal	23.312	51	0.22	State
Chile	18.425	25	0.14	State
Colombia	13.037	19	0.15	State (*Fideicomiso*)
Costa Rica	5.898	6	0.10	State *(ZOFRI)*
Bolivia	1.200	0,3	0.025	State

Source: Rodriguez 2004: 132

In the light of this absence of the State, private sector institutions such as the Bolivian Institute of Foreign Trade (IBCE), and national and regional export chambers have recently assumed a more protagonist role in the promotion of exports.[19] As a result, the awareness of the necessity to foster national export development has been growing. From the official side, concrete export facilitation measures were taken in April 2003, aiming to make better use of the preferential market access offered by the APTDEA system.[20] On the private sector side, the growing dissatisfaction was channelled in November 2001 into formulated guidelines with regard to a concerted National Export Strategy (6.2). Nevertheless, the fact that the requested strategy was not presented until May 2005 (the so-called ENEX 2005-15) highlights the domestic difficulties of following proactive export policies. It is very uncertain, though, whether and to what extent the far-reaching promotion policies sustained by the ENEX shall be implemented by the forthcoming government.

Summary Dependent Variable B

Bolivia's world market integration strategy pursued from 1985 to 2004 turned out to be an outright failure. The poor Andean country opened up its economy in 1985, and in the 1990s followed strongly outward-oriented regional trade diplomacy in undertaking comprehensive free trade commitments with the CAN, MERCOSUR, Mexico, and to a lesser extent, Chile. But as no

---

[18] As a matter of fact, Rodriguez made the international comparisons on the basis of countries that were rather famous for their efficient and well doted trade promotion facilities.
[19] In any case, most export promotion programs have been financed, at least in parts, by international donor agencies such as CAF, IDB, World Bank and bilateral donors.
[20] For example, exporters were permitted to duty free imports of complete industrial plants from abroad and to postpone the payment of the value added tax on imported capital goods. Finally, collective manufacturing facilities ("maquicentros") have been established in order to foster cooperation among small scale manufacturers.

export and sector-specific measures were adopted to develop potential export champions (bearing in mind the structural constraints of the local economy), the blind trade opening caused not only a poor trade performance with deep trade deficits, but also a strong domestic movement opposed to further trade liberalisation commitments in the extra-regional sphere. Therefore, the Multipolar Model could not be implemented effectively, putting into doubt future market access conditions for Bolivia's non-traditional exports, such as derivates of soy and textiles.

Box 6.1: Summary Dependent Variable B

Unilateral Trade Regime	Regional Integration	Extra-Regional Integration	Export Promotion	Sector Promotion
In 1985 trade liberalisation covering all tariff lines; adoption of "perforated" uniform tariff structure of 10 percent; 5% or duty free provisions for numerous capital goods. Rampant contraband.	1990-1997; Completion of FTAs with the MERCOSUR, CAN and Mexico. Against domestic protest, in 2003 free trade talks with Chile had to be cancelled. Strong trade deficits with regional partners.	Reaching a comprehensive FTA with the United States became an unviable endeavour due to discontent among social movements with the liberal outward-oriented strategy pursued.	From 1985, frequent modification of export promotion schemes and modest public resources for international market assistance avoided spurring non-traditional exports.	From 1985, Bolivia's economic policy was focussed on structural reforms, and the abolishment of significant sector-specific promotion.

From 1985 to 2004, Bolivia's trade performance was negative in quantitative as well as qualitative terms. Bearing in mind its share of world exports represented 0.07 percent in the 1970s (0.05 in 1980), the contribution of 0.025 percent in 2004 appears modest, despite an overall export growth from US$ 623 million to US$ 1918 million in the 1985-2004 period (DBLA 2005). Moreover, except for the trade surpluses registered in the scope of the CAN, the regional trade arrangements signed in the 1990s amplified existing trade deficits. Thus, annual trade deficits of about US$200 million on average represented a critical financial drain for the chronicle balance-of-payments deficit plagued US$8 billion economy.

Studying qualitative aspects, the initial dependence on mining exports, accounting for 62 percent, was lowered against the increased contribution of soy and hydrocarbons. Nonetheless, in 2004 close to 80 percent of export incomes still originated from mining, agriculture and energy commodities. Furthermore, the most salient non-traditional exports, such as soy products destined for the Andean markets, and textiles, jewellery and furniture sold in the United States, had an uncertain future. In light of ongoing free trade talks maintained by CAN members with MERCOSUR and the US, local soy farmers feared eroding tariff preferences would make soy production uncompetitive in Bolivia, given that exporters from Argentina, Brazil, Paraguay and the US have much cheaper transport costs. With respect to industrial manufacturers, at the end of 2004, it was unclear whether, and for how long, Bolivia's textiles and jewellery can further benefit from tariff preferences in the US market, as the ATPDEA preference scheme comes to a close in December 2006.

5.2 State Bureaucracy: The Unpredictable Trade Policy-Making Process

This section is structured along the following lines. The first subsection, *responsibilities,* exposes the division of labour in the conduct of international trade policy affairs, concerning the inter-ministerial coordination among the different departments involved. Subsection *resources* provides a description of how the trade policy team evolved over the last two decades with respect to staff size, technical expertise, and the application of civil service models. Subsection *openness* finally discusses consultation mechanism geared towards the business and civil society.

Responsibilities

Handling contradictory and fragmentary information was the main challenge when identifying the role of the various government departments involved in trade policy-making. Finally, however, with information gathered by the frequently modifying Laws of Executive Power Organisation (LOPE) and from a handful of open-minded key informants, it was possible to elaborate an historic reconstruction of the trade policy-making process inside the Bolivian State. Table 6.3 summarises the key features that have defined the institutional set up since the 1970s.

Table 6.3: Trade Policy-Making inside the Bolivian State 1972-2004

	Economic Policy	International Trade Policy	Inter-ministerial Coordination	Outstanding Features
1972 – 1986: The Rise and Decline of the SEGIN	Ministry of Planning and Coordination	General Secretariat of Integration (SEGIN)	CODEPLAN	Presidential support of the specialised SEGIN; Andean Group orientation
1986 – 1997: The Omission to Strengthen the Trade Policy Branch	Ministry of Finance	Ministry of Foreign Affairs	Super Ministries (from 1993)	From the mid-1990s, increasing involvement by the Ministry of Economic Development
1997 – 2003: Hopes and Despair with the MCEI	Ministry of Finance	Ministry of Foreign Trade and Investment (MCEI)/ Ministry of Foreign Affairs	CONAPES	Erection of a specialised trade policy branch; bureaucratic war between Foreign Affairs and MCEI
2003 and beyond: Towards a	Ministry of Finance	Ministry of Foreign Affairs/ Ministry of	CONAPES	Dissolution of MCEI; conflicts between

Foreign Affairs Model?		Economic Development		Ministries of Foreign Affairs and Economic Development

Source: Executive Power (Decree) Laws No. 10460 (1972); No. 1493 (1993); No. 1788 (1997); No. 2446 (2003)

The Rise and Decline of the SEGIN (1976-1986): Given the prominent regional integration attempts in the scope of the Andean Group launched in 1969, international trade policy affairs received strong attention during the government of Hugo Banzer (1971-1978), the authoritarian leader following a nationalist, state-led development strategy. Herein, the General Secretariat of Integration (SEGIN), which until 1976 had been a technical branch inside the Foreign Affairs Ministry, evolved into an independent agency that enjoyed a ministerial rank.

The SEGIN sought to bring domestic ISI policies in line with the industrial programming pursued inside the Andean Group.[21] Due to the conceptual importance of the Andean market, and the fact that the agency responded directly to the presidential office, the SEGIN officials held an influential voice inside the National Council of Economy and Planning (CODEPLAN) where economic policies were coordinated, planned and formulated.[22] Simultaneously, the Foreign Affairs Ministry lost competencies over international economic affairs, and the Ministry of Industry, Trade and Tourism acted as the agency in charge of the state administration of domestic and foreign trade.

Nevertheless, the combination of debt crises, deprived intra-regional trade and inflationary pressure caused the SEGIN to become an increasingly obsolete institution in the 1980s. In 1985, when the New Economic Policy was launched, the trade policy decision-making power was concentrated within an inter-ministerial team staffed by a small group of technocrats from the Ministries of Planning and Finance, advised by a Harvard team coordinated by Jeffrey Sachs.[23] Within this first reform stage the institutional leadership was still held inside the Planning Ministry led by Gonzalo Sánchez de Lozada (state president 1993-97 and 2002-03).

---

[21] According to Manuel Arana (SO 24/01/05), SEGIN obtained strong political backing by *Willy Vargas Vacaflor*, later General Secretary, who acted as Hugo Banzer's principal advisor in Foreign Affairs. At the end of the 1970s, SEGIN was denominated as the Ministry of Integration, even though this title was afterwards altered on several occasions.

[22] By the Decree Law of Administrative Structure of the Executive Power No. 10460 of 1972, CODEPLAN was ascribed a strategic role in the coordination and formulation of state-led development policies. The Council had first been directed by the Finance Minister and was composed of the Ministers of Transport, Communication and Civil Aeronautic; Industry, Trade and Tourism, Agriculture and Livestock Farming, Mining and Metal Industry, Energy and Hydrocarbons, and the Council's Secretary. Later on, the CODEPLAN was ruled by the Planning Ministry and began to also integrate the social policy area, originally attended by another council.

[23] Regarding the cooperation with the Harvard fellows, the principal nexus of the Bolivian side was Juan Careaga Osorio from the Finance Ministry. Thus, the increasing power of the Finance Ministry is closely linked to him, the "father of the stabilisation measures", who served as Minister from 1986 to 1988; see OE Zambrana 5/08/04.

This "institutionalised brain" of the Bolivian State disappeared later, however, as the new economic ruling no longer focused on 5-year state-led plans defining guidelines for fiscal policies and industrial production, but rather on the state's economic disengagement and fiscal discipline.[24] These priorities evidently favoured the role of the Finance Ministry as the principal economic policy-making institution.

The Omission to Strengthen the Trade Policy Branch (1987-1997): The SEGIN, at this point headed by a politician in his last career steps, became a "takeover candidate".[25] The possibility that the Foreign Affairs Ministry would regain the economic branch were thus high, especially since the Ministry of Industry, Trade and Tourism had also been plagued by the undertaken fiscal adjustments and the State's withdrawal from trade operations and industry planning. And indeed, the personal lobby of Guillermo Bedregal, then foreign affairs minister and influential MNR politician, as well as SEGIN staff interested in stable job environments, enabled the transfer into the Ministry of Foreign Affairs in 1987 (SO's Arana 24/01/05; De Rico 15/12/04).

Afterwards, the trade policy branch subsisted as the downgraded Undersecretary for Integration, subordinating its activities to the concerns of the leading political branch inside the foreign affairs department. Shortcomings became apparent at the outset of the 1990s when regional integration began gaining importance and Bolivia, as a new GATT member, entered into multilateral trade negotiations. Increasingly aware of the need to give pertinent institutional responses to the outward oriented policies, it was in July 1992 when the government of Jaime Paz Zamora sought to build up trade expertise through the creation of the Ministry of Exports and Economic Competitiveness (MECE). Under the young MIR deputy, Luis Fernando Campero, the enthusiastic MECE staff, which by then was inspired by Michael Porter's concept of competitiveness, aimed at pushing Bolivia's exports by measures such as the Unified Window, facilitating export paperwork, incorporating the National Institute of Export Promotion (INPEX), the establishment of free trade zones, and the reimbursement of paid import and domestic taxes, among other measures (OE Olmos 15/02/05; SO's Arana 24/01/05; Miranda 14/12/04). Though still under the responsibilities of the Foreign Affairs Ministry, the new export policy branch served, from this point, as the technical advisory body and provider of export development guidelines.

---

[24] In 1993, the Planning Ministry was finally relegated as a National Secretariat inside the Ministry of Sustainable Development and Environment, losing its influence on core economic issues and focusing instead on topics such as decentralisation and environmental policies.

[25] According to Helen de Rico (SO 15/12/04), the office holder in charge was anything but an expert on economic integration and stayed at home most of the time. Thus, he delegated all responsibilities to Ana Maria Solares, a young functionary who became a crucial official in the trade policy area towards the end of the 1990s.

The new drive inside the MECE vanished, though, after just one year, when Sanchez de Lozada entered the presidential office in August 1993. The former ministerial structure was abolished by the new Ministerial Law of the Executive Power (LOPE) No. 1493. The new underlying organisational logic emphasised the idea that economic policy-making was no longer based on sector-specific agencies but instead was part of a horizontal development concept. Therefore, the executive powers became concentrated in the Super Ministries that embraced the areas of Human Development, and Finance and Economic Development. The latter area hosted no less than six formal ministerial departments, and covered the National Secretariats of Industry and Trade, Finance, Energy and Hydrocarbons, Mining and Metal Industries, Transport, Agriculture and Livestock, Tourism, National Pension Funds, Capitalisation and Investment. However, the ambitious plans had to be revised in December 1994 when the areas of Economic Development and Finance were divided.[26]

Export concerns were only poorly attended inside the National Secretariat of Industry and Trade. Considering the envisaged structural reforms concerning the capitalisation of state owned firms and the implementation of an autonomous sectoral regulatory system, a proactive approach to developing exports enjoyed little support inside the Ministry of Economic Development (SO Montaña 14/12/04). Moreover, sound trade policy-making was hindered by increasing conflicts between the Ministries of Economic Development and Foreign Affairs for greater responsibilities in the area of international negotiations and trade promotion. In the latter case, office holders of the foreign affairs department requested that the promotion activities become part of the global diplomatic network, and hence, set up the Undersecretary of Economic Promotion. At the same time, the promotion authority INPEX depended on the Ministry of Economic Development in 1993. This superposition ended up in a struggle for scant available resources, jeopardising initial plans to expand official market assistance in important export markets (BR Fernandez 12/8/04).

Regarding the area of international trade policy affairs, it was the staff of the National Secretariat for Trade and Industry who began to assume a more protagonist role. In 1995, whilst in talks with MERCOSUR and Mexico the "singing voice" still belonged to the diplomatic cadre, this primacy was undermined by state secretary Douglas Ascarrunz in the scope of the CAN and FTAA.[27] This major involvement can be largely explained by the increased business

---

[26] Indeed, a senior official concluded that it eventually became impossible to control the political aspirations of the sectoral office holders (SO Montaña 14/12/04).
[27] Inside the CAN, one of the country's two official representations inside the Andean Commission came into the hands of the Secretary of Industry and Trade. Before, the Ministry of Foreign Affairs was the exclusive CAN representative. As regards the FTAA meetings, both Secretaries in charge, Douglas Ascarrunz and Mario Reyes,

pressure to counter-weigh the integration approach of foreign affairs minister, Antonio Aranibar Quiroga, and chief negotiator, Victor Rico; both from the left wing Free Bolivian Movement which, for four years, occupied the position of minority partner to the MNR government in the Ministry of Foreign Affairs. At this time, the farming-oriented Santa Cruz department lamented that when Bolivia signed a comprehensive FTA with MERCOSUR in December 1996, trade policies responded to the desires of Victor Rico and Antonio Aranibar to strengthen the political alliances with the emerging regional bloc in the Southern Cone (BR Rodríguez 27/07/04; OE Tercero 18/01/05). *"Since the doors of Rico were shut for our concerns, we sought to enter the office of the Trade and Industry Secretariat"*, concluded IBCE Managing Director, Gary Rodriguez (BR 27/07/04).

Hopes and Despair with the MCEI (1997 – 2003): Times changed from the moment the government of Hugo Banzer – a coalition between the right-wing ADN and the centre-left wing MIR – assumed the presidency in August 1997. The demands of national exporters for a better representation inside the state executive, lodged during the election campaign, were responded to by the new government through the installation of the new LOPE No. 1788. Supported by the IDB and other donors, the previous MECE concept (1992-93) was reborn within the newly established Ministry of the Foreign Trade and Investment (MCEI), which encompassed the four Vice-Ministries of Exports, Foreign Trade, Tourism, and Private Investments. The political standing of "export issues" was evidently augmented by the presence of the MCEI inside the newly founded National Council of Economic Policy (CONAPE) in charge of inter-ministerial coordination in the economic policy area.[28] A further up-scaling meant the incorporation of the new export promotion authority, CEPROBOL, and the removal of the promotion area inside the Ministry of Foreign Affairs.

But initial hopes embodied in the specialised agency soon encountered two major obstacles: (1) the lack of resources and (2) the struggles for competencies. Adhemar Guzman (OE 21/01/05), Vice-Minister of Exports from 1997-2002, recalled that from the outset, the agency did not have the necessary resources to execute its duties. *"Every year our budget got diminished by both general and sector-specific budget cuts dictated by the Ministry of Finance"*, concluding that *"even though official rhetoric favoured the development of exports, in practical terms trade issues were relegated since the political conjuncture, above all since 2000, has*

---

went out without prior coordination to represent the Bolivian State; see OE Larrazabal 8/02/05; SO Miranda 14/12/04.
[28] Since September 1997, CONAPE has been permanently composed of the Ministers of Foreign Trade and Investment, Agriculture, Economic Development, Finance, Presidency, and Sustainable Development and Planning. The Social and Economic Policies Analysis Unit (UDAPE) has operated as the advisory body of CONAPE.

focused on short-term economic emergency programs" (also OE Jurado 8/03/03, BR Arias 17/01/05).

Furthermore, the conflictive coexistence between the new export ministry and the foreign affairs department explained the increasing institutional deterioration of the MCEI. As this regard, the battle for competencies was apparent from the beginning, considering that the Vice-Ministry of Foreign Trade focused exclusively on international trade policy affairs and tried to bring in a new professional approach to the challenging multilateral and regional trade talks (OE Becerra 29/07/04). Consequently, business and state officials reported on the breakout of a "bureaucratic war", initiated between the two departments affecting all negotiation forums, ranging from the FTAA, CAN, and the WTO Development Round, to the extension of ATPA preferences and the deepening of the ALADI agreement with Chile (OE Guzman 21/01/05; BR's Fernandez 12/08/04; Rodríguez 20/07/04; SO De Rico 15/12/04). Although the Vice-Ministry of Foreign Trade was dissolved after eight months and incorporated into the Vice-Ministry for Exports, effective inter-ministerial relations were not ensured as MCEI office holders continued to argue for the need to handle foreign trade affairs within a specialised agency.

Towards a Foreign Affairs Model?(2003-04): The export agency's future became uncertain under the second presidential term of Sánchez de Lozada, beginning in August 2002.[29] By March 2003, the executive power had been reorganised under severe budget constraints, and the government decided to sacrifice the MCEI founded by the former administration. Together with the areas of industry, investment and domestic trade, LOPE No. 2446 assigned trade policy attributions to the wide-reaching Ministry of Economic Development, further comprised of the Vice-Ministries of Tourism, Urban Development, Culture, and Small Business. Under this regime, the Vice-Ministry of Industry, Commerce and Export (VICE) continued to hold the primary responsibilities with regard to the formulation and implementation of trade regimes and export promotion. In the area of international negotiations, the VICE was still expected to participate by providing technical support, but representation functions belonged exclusively to the Vice-Ministry of Foreign Economic Relations from the Foreign Affairs Ministry.

Although the new LOPE was expected to mitigate the inter-ministerial conflicts concerning Bolivia's participation in international forums, the survey carried out among 65 experts, state officials and business representatives from March to October 2004 still indicated a very ambiguous picture. The survey candidates were asked: *Inside the executive branch, is there*

---

[29] By August 2002, the Vice-Ministry of Exports had already been merged with the Vice-Ministry of Private Investment in order to save on budget resources. For ministerial reorganisation; see Supreme Decree No. 26772.

a clear division of labour in the conduction of international trade policy affairs? If not, in what areas can ambiguity be identified?

Table 6.4: Division of Labour in International Trade Policy Affairs

	Experts (15)	State Officials (14)	Business (36)	Total (65)
very clear	0	1	1	2 (4%)
rather clear	2	2	5	9 (17%)
rather unclear	4	7	21	32 (62%)
very unclear	4	2	3	9 (17%)
no response	5	2	6	13

In this regard, 80 percent of respondents perceived the division of labour as rather or very unclear. Of particular interest is the fact that the vast majority of state officials had problems in clearly identifying responsibilities. Additional statements highlighted the explicit or implicit way that the new institutional arrangement began to be questioned in October 2003, when Ana Maria Solares entered the VICE office. The accomplished but polemic trade diplomat had, on prior occasions, demonstrated her keenness to possess the "main voice", the latest of which being during the period of 1998-2002 when she was Chief Negotiator in the Foreign Affairs Ministry. Albeit on weaker legal grounds, Solares, as head of the VICE, sustained strong personal quarrels with Isaac Maidana, Vice-Minister of Foreign Economic Relations, in order to obtain a more prominent role inside international trade politics.

These disputes and the past erratic development inside the policy area also provoked very negative survey results in resonse to the following question: *Is their close inter-ministerial coordination among the departments involved in International trade policy affairs? If not, in what areas can coordination gaps be identified?* Along the three categories, survey data indicated strong coordination deficits, with the relation between the Ministries of Economic Development and Foreign Affairs receiving most criticism. Moreover, several diplomats from the foreign affairs department, traditionally in charge of domestic consultations before important international trade policy events, lamented the weak contributions made by sectoral departments from agriculture, industry, transport, communication, and health, etc.

Table 6.5: Inter-ministerial Trade Policy Coordination

	Experts (15)	State Officials (14)	Business (36)	Total (65)
very close	0	0	0	0 (0%)
Rather close	0	3	2	5 (10%)
Rather sporadic	4	9	19	32 (63%)
very sporadic	5	1	8	14 (27%)
no response	6	1	7	14

In an act that took all sectors by surprise, in May 2004 Carlos Mesa, transitory president between October 2003 and June 2005, took the decision within CONAPE to ascribe the responsibility for coordinating the upcoming US-AFTA talks to the Ministry of Economic Development, whilst the regional and multilateral forums were maintained inside the Ministry of Foreign Affairs.[30] An alleged solution to the confused situation between the two principal trade policy areas was found in September 2004, when the staff of the Foreign Affairs Ministry "compensated" for their limited influence over the supposedly prestige-laden US-AFTA talks by receiving control of the promotion authority, CEPROBOL, embodied in the Supreme Decree 27732. The greatly desired incorporation of CEPROBOL into the global diplomatic network was expected to represent a watershed in the way the Bolivian State promotes local products, and thus, put an end to the destructive "back and forth" relationship that had occurred in past decades. Moreover, in the same month Ana Maria Solares resigned from her post as Vice-Ministry of Commerce, Exports and Industry in light of broad criticism against her person.

It remains uncertain whether the new institutional arrangement proves sustainable or not, however. The role of VICE role appeared, by the end of 2004, to be at its weakest point. To date, the US-AFTA coordination, in which Bolivia participated as an observer, implied only social unrest and the absorption of scant resources. With respect to the agency's major task, the formulation, coordination and implementation of a national export strategy that will lead to the creation of jobs in non-traditional, manufacturing branches, the current attributions are insufficient. Since the execution of export promotion passed over to the foreign affairs department, the VICE is only responsible for the formulation of promotion regimes; i.e. setting legal frameworks for export support and technical assistance. Whenever tax concessions are involved – and this is nearly always the case – policy formulation is carried out jointly with the Finance Minister, giving the latter the primary responsibility. The Finance Ministry is further in charge of fiscal policy, and thus embraces competencies regarding the defining of the national tariff structure, absorbing another crucial area in the development of local exports.[31]

Resources

From the mid-1980s, when the SEGIN staff transferred to the Ministry of Foreign Affairs, the teams in charge of international trade policy affairs became minority players struggling for

---

[30] For example, on July 4, 2004, the influential Santa Cruz Export Chamber (CADEX) published a letter in the Sunday Edition of La Razón, Bolivia's principal newspaper, directed to Carlos Mesa in which the presidential decision had been described as without reason, misleading and causing further incoherencies in the trade policy formulation.

[31] The Ministry of Finance likewise supervises the National Customs Service.

recognition inside the bureaucratic structures. Even so, much of the negotiation skills that remained have their roots in the SEGIN created in the 1970s. Though comments provided by former SEGIN officials were often vague and influenced by certain nostalgia, the interviewees pointed at an autonomous agency composed of 40 to 60 well-trained experts recruited by rather meritocratic selection procedures (OE Tercero 18/01/05; SO's Arana 24/01/05; De Rico 15/12/04).[32] In stark contrast to current trends, the majority of officials had not studied law, but were trained as specialists in integration, relevant industrial or rural sectors. The team was staffed by young professionals between 30 and 35 years of age, several of which later held important public positions in trade related areas.[33]

As the SEGIN transferred to the Ministry of Foreign Affairs in 1987, the new Undersecretariat of Integration failed to adapt to the upcoming regional and multilateral challenges.[34] While technical requirements ascended due to the proliferation of trade forums and topics, the internal structure of the responsible agency altered little, espite its changing denomination.[35] As previously mentioned, both attempts undertaken to respond to the changed international setting (in 1992 and 1997 by establishing the MECE and MCEI, respectively), whilst only faint-hearted in nature bearing in mind the modestly disbursed budget resources compared to other more traditional ministries, were rejected by the subsequent[36].

Moreover, the founded "export ministries" produced several counter-productive effects. *Firstly,* the competing ministries focused more on the bureaucratic wars on the domestic level than on the conquest of external markets. *Secondly,* as the number of talented, experienced experts was small, key negotiators changed their original ministry on different occasions, and hence, avoided building up essential institutional memory.[37] *Thirdly,* local business was often left confused as to with whom to coordinate wit on certain topics, as I shall elucidate in section three.

---

[32] Nevertheless, there were no indications that civil service exams had been applied in a strict sense.

[33] Examples are Helen de Rico, Giovanna Miranda, Javier Jiménez, Hugo Ferrufino, Francisco Terceros, Víctor Rico and Ana Maria Solares. Most of these people later took on a diplomatic career path.

[34] In the Uruguay Round, for example, Bolivia concluded as an observer since the last two years of negotiations in Geneva were assisted by only one young diplomat. Rosa Chavez commented that from 1989-91 the delegation in Geneva consisted originally of four diplomats, but that she later remained as the single representative; SO 17/03/04.

[35] Later denominations were the National Secretariat of International Economic Relations (1993-97), the Vice-Ministry of International Economic Relations (1998-04), and the Vice-Ministry of Economic Relations and Foreign Trade in 2004.

[36] According to the Ministry of Finance and Economic Development (1993; 2001), MECE's budged in 1993 totaled 2.6 million *Bolivianos* (about US$650,000) making it smaller than any other ministry's budget except the Ministry of Hydrocarbons with 2.5 million *Bolivianos*. In 2002, the MCEI's financial means were much bigger with roughly US$4.5 million but still were the second smallest budget (the Ministry of Justice had the smallest at its disposal).

[37] For example, the first Vice-Minister of Foreign Trade inside MCEI, Vincent Gomés Garcia, previously worked in the Foreign Affairs Ministry. By the time Gomés transferred, he hired several key Foreign Affairs diplomats.

The survey data collected in 2004 confirmed the difficulties in forming a team soundly prepared to face the increased international challenges. The surveyed people were asked: *Is the official team in charge of international trade policy affairs adequately staffed in order to comply with the technical requirements of modern international trade policy affairs (staff size, talent and experience)? If not, in what areas/issues can limitations be found?*

Table 6.6: Trade Policy Staff

	Experts (15)	State Officials (14)	Business (36)	Total (65)
very adequate	0	1	0	1 (2%)
Rather adequate	1	1	6	8 (15%)
Rather inadequate	4	7	18	29 (55%)
very inadequate	6	4	5	15 (28%)
no response	4	1	7	12

Only 9 out of a total of 53 responses considered the official cadre as rather adequate. Strikingly, 11 out of 14 consulted state officials perceived their capacities as insufficient to handle the technical requirements of ongoing free trade talks. In asking in what areas/issues can limitations be found, the commonly stated answers were, *"our negotiators are only generalists, not specialists, as regards involved topics"*, *"the size of the staff is small and only three or four negotiators are really accomplished"*, *"the team composition has been discontinuous and biased by party influence"*, and *"negotiators do not sufficiently consider the realities of the economic sectors"*.

According to the ministerial structures upheld in 2004, negotiation expertise was found in the following agencies. Inside the *Ministry of Foreign Affairs and Worship,* the weight of the Vice-Ministry of Foreign Economic Relations as the "economic branch" has clearly been lesser, with just two general directorates, when compared with the eight offices inside the "political branch" (Vice-Ministry of Foreign Relations and Worship).[38] Inside the economic branch, each general directorate was integrated by 18 officials, wherein 15-20 diplomats were dedicated to the trade negotiation forums of MERCOSUR, Chile, Mexico, CAN, FTAA and the WTO. In March 2004, the officials involved in these areas served inside the General Directorate of Integration made up by the Directorates of South American Integration, Hemispheric Integration, and Multilateral Affairs.[39] While each area was monitored by three to four professionals, the different topics involved were not handled by specialists but required "orchestra negotiators" monitoring

---

[38] The total number of career diplomats accounted for about 230 officials in 2004.
[39] The other area had been called "General Direction for Economic Negotiations" and consisted of the Direction for Integration and Regional Cooperation, Economic Promotion and Economic Relations, monitoring the Amazon Cooperation/ La Plata Basin, Export Promotion, and Technical Assistance.

four to five issues simultaneously (SO Invernizzi 18/03/03). Nonetheless, *"in order to conduct negotiations adequately we should settle on about 36 specialised functionaries, two for each topic"*, calculated Julio Alvarado, General Director of Integration (SO 19/03/04).

Compared to other state departments, diplomatic career officials enjoy a stable working environment. Together with the Finance Ministry and the Central Bank, the foreign affairs department is considered to be the most prestige-laden agency, since t is only in these offices that recruitment systems and civil services careers have been implemented properly. Therefore, the National Diplomatic Career Scale responds to a special labour regime, ruled by Law No. 1444 and deriving regulations which set norms as regards entrance, qualifying systems, career paths, upgrading regimes, service abroad, and social security. Consequently, all diplomats must complete two years of training inside the Diplomatic Academy Rafael Bustillo. Several features enlisted below, however, undermined the necessary strength of the trade policy branch.

> *Generalist:* The academy's curriculum focussed on the training of "generalists" prepared to do all possible tasks within the diplomatic world, while specialists mastering the complex technical issues involved in current trade talks have not been trained sufficiently.

> *Rotations:* As in most foreign policy agencies, the stability and expertise of the local staff is undermined by the positional career changes that take place, on average, every three to four years.

> *Low Salaries:* While the salaries paid domestically normally bare few economic incentives, most functionaries are enthusiastic to serve in foreign embassies or to be contracted by international donor agencies for special consulting services in order to gain salaries in excess of US$1,500 per month.

To face these deficits, the Vice-Ministry for Foreign Economic Affairs promoted the creation of the International Trade Negotiation Unit (UNCI), financed by an IDB loan of US$5 million (BO-0212). The UNCI is aimed at coordinating negotiation policies and strategies and participating in trade talks, directing the technical aspects of negotiations to the various international forums. The project, first rejected in June 2003 inside CONAPE, was finally approved in December 2004 and enabled a pre-selection of 32 area experts via a public invitation procedure. However, by the end of 2005, the UNCI had yet to be put into force.

Ministry of Economic Development (MDE): In May 2004, the MDE holding the Vice-Ministries of Industry, Commerce and Exports (VICE), Tourism, Urban Development, Culture and Small Scale Business was comprised of 340 functionaries. The VICE employed 34 persons, including senior, technical and administrative staff. If the areas of Industrial Development, Domestic Trade and Private Investment are discounted, the number of foreign trade related officials shrank down to one dozen and consisted of the vice-minister, three special advisors, the General Director of Commerce and Exports, the Director of Exports, and six officials inside the Directorate of Exports (MDE 2004a). Hence, the limited staff seriously questioned the capacity to provide technical negotiation support.

Likewise, since its creation the former MCEI suffered from regular budget cuts (OE Guzman 21/01/05). In 2002, of an approved budget of 48 million *Bolivianos* (approx. US$6 million), merely 33 million were disbursed, lowering the "trade area" resources inside the Vice-Ministry of Exports from 4.9 to 3.8 million *Bolivianos*. Later, in August 2002, means had to be shared with the "private investment area" inside the newly established Vice-Ministry of Export and Private Investment. As the MCEI disappeared in March 2003, the new VICE was compelled to operate with scant resources of 3.5 million *Bolivianos* from the former industry office, reducing the trade policy staff by about 50 percent compared to 2002.[40]

Beyond financial constraints, officials faced uncertainty due to the continuous replacement of office holders. Since the creation of the MCEI in August 1997, the foreign policy area outside the Foreign Affairs Ministry underwent the following personal changes.

Table 6.7: Office Holders from 1997 to 2005

Period	Office Holders	Presidency
08/1997 – 06/1999	Jorge Crespo (MCEI)	Hugo Banzer, AND
06/1999 – 10/2000	Carlos Saavedra Bruno (MCEI)	Hugo Banzer, AND
10/2000 – 07/2002	Claudio Mansilla (MCEI)	Banzer (- 07/2001); Jorge Quiroga
07/2002 – 03/2003	Juan Carlos Virreira (MCEI)	Gonzalo Sanchez de Lozada, MNR
03/2003 – 10/2003	Luis Fernando Peredo (VICE)	Gonzalo Sanchez de Lozada, MNR
10/2003 – 08/2004	Ana María Solares Gaite (VICE)	Carlos Mesa Quisbert, independent
10/2004	Juan Carlos Iturri (VICE)	Carlos Mesa Quisbert, independent
10/2004 – 02/2005	Carlos Tadic (VICE)	Carlos Mesa Quisbert, independent
Since 02/2005	Gonzalo Molina Sardan (VICE)	Carlos Mesa Quisbert, independent

---

[40] In 2004 and 2005, the VICE budget was reduced again, ending up at 2.5 million *Bolivianos* (US$300,000) in 2005. Therefore, several functionaries such as Helen Rico, Giovanna Miranda and Gustavo Invernizzi transferred to the Foreign Affairs Ministry in 2003; see Sigma-Ministry of Finance 2001-05; SO Invernizzi 18/03/04.

The political and financial instability maintained since 1997 hindered the strengthening of civil service provisions embodied in the Civil Servant Statute of 1999.[41] Requirements regarding the transparent recruitment and upgrading regimes became almost obsolete; i.e. both the designation and the ascendance of functionaries relied mostly on informal allies.[42] Therefore, stable bureaucratic careers were almost entirely absent, being limited to lower-ranked administrative staff.[43] Moreover, the upper reaches covering General Directors and Vice-Ministers weren't covered by the Civil Servant Statute, and thus, remained politically appointed. In this volatile environment, the MCEI/VICE personnel likewise suffered frequent changes, i.e. positions were occupied for less than one year on average. Finally, the most experienced professionals hold little interest in occupying senior positions since these are perceived merely as useful career steps towards a consultant position financed by international donor agencies or private sector entities.[44]

Ministry of Finance: Inside the Finance Ministry, responsible for defining the national tariff structure, the "tariffs and integration area" inside the Vice-Ministry of Tax Policy was noticeably downsized in the past years, and consisted of only four officials by August 2004. What stands out, however, is that the remaining functionaries passed meritocratic civil service exams and were part of the administrative career (SO; K. Rico 13/08/04). The Finance Ministry is further in charge of negotiation issues related to sate procurement. In this respect, since 2004 Bolivia pursued the policy to favour small domestic suppliers of goods and services by implementing the Buy Bolivian Act. But during 2004, the team inside the General Directorate of Administrative System – financed by the World Bank – likewise suffered significant reductions, and consequently, just one single functionary was monitoring the ongoing trade talks in 2004 (BR De Los Angeles 9/08/04).

Ministry of Agriculture and Small Farming Affairs: The participation of the Agriculture Ministry in international negotiations has traditionally been insufficient, considering that local farming is responsible for approximately 15 percent of the GDP. Thus, an institutional reform launched during 2001 sought to streamline the ministry which was traditionally dominated by party politics. Accordingly, the office holder then in charge commented that the personnel were

---

[41] By Law No. 2027 the Hugo Banzer administration sought to perfect the initial steps towards more transparent public administration embodied in the Law of Integrated System of Financial Administration and Governmental Control (SAFCO) from 1991.

[42] According to the Ministry's Director of Human Resources, about 90 percent of the selected personnel is related to personal recommendation; see Interviews 10/08/04 and 24/01/05.

[43] Out of 340 employees inside the Ministry, only 19 had a permanent career status. Furthermore, administrative careers in chief areas are largely unattractive for top officials since salaries do not surpass the US$1,100 ceiling.

[44] According to the Supreme Decree No. 27327 of January 31, 2004, salaries of Special Advisors cannot exceed the salaries received by a General Director (18,900 *Bolivianos* or US$2400). However, short-term consulting, specific projects, or studies weren't covered by this provision (Art. 9/ II). For salary data; see MDE 2004b.

reduced from 300 to 108, but of these, 85 had been selected through a transparent and meritocratic recruitment mechanism (OE Nuñez 10/08/04). In the trade policy area, the Walter Nuñez administration created a "Unit for International Negotiations" integrated by well trained economists, whereas previously only one official attended international agriculture talks (SO Jimenez 9/08/04). Nonetheless, under later office holders, the department was downgraded anew and left with only one professional monitoring ongoing trade talks during the period of 2003-04.[45]

The Analysing Unit for Economic and Social Policy (UDAPE): The think-tank established in 1983, and initially financed by the USAID agency, became a prestigious advisory board monitoring the implementation of the economic liberalisation efforts. The team used to be composed of selected, well-trained collaborators who minimally held a MA degree. Towards the end of the 1990s, however, the agency's excellence began to deteriorate as party politics increasingly came into view and the think-tank transferred from the Finance Ministry to the presidential office, ending up inside the Ministry of Economic Development as the Technical Secretariat of CONAPE. The fact that out of roughly 30 area experts only one had been devoted to the "External Sector" certainly underlines the agency's priority on macroeconomic policy (SO Zambrana 5/08/04).

Other Agencies: The number of institutions involved since the trade agenda in both the multilateral and regional sphere was established became broader. In the scope of the Inter-Institutional Working Group where affected governmental areas have been regularly convened by the Foreign Affairs Ministry, the following state agencies were invited in February 2004 to collaborate in the FTAA, CAN, MERCOSUR, and the WTO: Vice-Ministries of Justice; Tax Policy; Natural Resources and Environmental Policy; Health; Agriculture and Livestock Farming; Science and Technology; National Customs Authority, SENASA responsible for (phyto-) sanitary regulation, SENAPI in charge of intellectual property rights and sectoral regulatory bodies for telecommunications, banking, and the standard organisation IBNORCA and OBA.

In May 2004, as the AFTA Bureau inside the Ministry of Economic Development began coordinating Bolivia's observation within these trade talks, 29 public agencies monitored the area of market access, textiles, agriculture, rules of origin, safeguards, (phyto-) sanitary measures, technical obstacles, services, financial services, telecommunications, electronic commerce, state procurement, intellectual property rights, competition policy, labour and

---

[45] In August 2004, the Ministry was about to hire four trade experts according to the chief of area; see SO Jimenez 9/08/04.

environment regulation, institutional affairs, and dispute settlement and cooperation (MDE 2004c). However, most of the agencies that specialised in these topics did not possess explicit negotiation expertise and were often poorly informed of the potential impacts of ongoing talks, as a confidential key official report commented (Ministry of Foreign Affairs; April 2004)

Openness

The erratic institutional development which took place inside the executive branch also marked the modes of interaction towards business. In simplified terms, three different governance-styles could be observed in the last two decades:

1) *Insulated Technocratic Style*: When the New Economic Policy was designed in 1985, the group of involved actors were limited to a handful of policy makers inside the Ministries of Planning and Finance. As several officials originated from private sector organisations, the incorporation of business views occurred inside the government. On the contrary, formal business associations were practically excluded from important trade policy decisions such as the GATT adherence (BR Gastelu 20/01/05).

2) *Informative Reunions:* Since the late 1980s, the Foreign Affairs Ministry has been convening state and business entities in the scope of the Inter-Institutional Working Group, inviting them to learn about situations presented within the framework of the regional and multilateral trade regimes (SO's De Rico 16/03/04; Chavez 17/03/04). Usually, the entities considered are: the Bolivian Confederation of Private Entrepreneurship, the Departmental Federations of Private Entrepreneurship, and the national entities of industry, commerce, exports, banking, mining, farming, assurance, pharmaceutical, oleaginous, forestry, and construction sectors.

3) *State-Business Collaboration:* The conviction that the making of trade policy should be an endeavour shared by state and business developed relatively late in Bolivia. The most ambitious attempt to date in this regard has been the National Export Council (CONEX), which was launched as an integral part of the Export Development and Taxation Law No. 148 enacted by the Jaime Paz Zamora administration in April 1993. According to article 24, the public-private advisory body is in charge of proposing and evaluating policies, programs, and strategies to promote the country's export development.

From the outset, however, the implementation of CONEX became arduous and struggled to achieve recognition among involved actors. Table 6.8 sums up both attempts undertaken by the governments of Gonzalo Sánchez de Lozada (1994) and Hugo Banzer (1998) to revive the CONEX by regulating its activities.

Table 6.8: CONEX Regulations 1994 and 1998

Legal Base	Supreme Decree 23822, July 1994	Supreme Decree 25023, April 1998
Focus	Development of non-traditional exports, excluding mining and hydrocarbons by trade promotion facilities, market assistance, trade defence, export incentive mechanisms, international trade negotiations, and industrial policies.	Development of value added exports by trade promotion facilities, export incentive mechanisms, international trade negotiations.
Functions	Recommend, suggest, propose and assess policies, strategies, guidelines and programs.	Recommend, suggest, propose and assess policies, strategies, guidelines and programs.
Presidency	National Secretary for Industry and Trade (MDE)	Minister of Foreign Trade and Investment (MCEI)
Internal Commissions	1. Foreign Economic Promotions (coordinated by Foreign Affairs) 2. Integration (Foreign Affairs) 3. Foreign Trade Development (MDE) 4. Productive Development (MDE)	On ad-hoc basis
Permanent Governmental Members	National Secretaries of Foreign Economic Relations, Agriculture and Livestock, and Finance	Vice-Ministers of Exports, Foreign Trade; Agriculture, Foreign Economic Relations, and Fiscal Policy
Permanent Business Members	CANEB, CNI, CNC; CEPB only in extraordinary cases; Presidents participate in plenary reunions; Managing Directors in internal commissions	CANEB; Associations of Mining and Hydrocarbon if considered necessary by permanent members
No. Reunions	Regular monthly meetings and more frequent if considered necessary	Regular monthly meetings and more frequent if considered necessary

In general, the 1994 decree contained more detailed provisions, such as the exclusive focus on non-traditional exports and the establishment of internal commissions with designated responsibilities. Therein, export development was conceptualised not only as an exclusive mix of trade policies, but it also involved accompanying industrial policies in which the Ministry of Economic Development took over the leadership. Compared to the second CONEX version, this distinction is best explained by the fact that, between 1993 and 1997, the trade and industry areas were paired together inside the Ministry of Economic Development, while the Foreign Affairs Ministry occupied the major responsibilities in the areas of international negotiations and export promotion. Conversely, in 1998, CONEX primarily concerned the preferences of the MCEI officials and National Chamber of Exporters (CANEB), the latter being the private organisation that most pushed for the creation of the MCEI. From 1998, the Vice-Ministry of Foreign Economic Affairs became one of only five invited vice-ministries which did not hold any specific competencies. Regarding the incorporation of business, the CANEB was assigned a representative monopoly without exhibiting the features of a valid interlocutor (6.3).[46]

In the end, both CONEX versions were poorly implemented.[47] As a permanent coordination channel, CONEX only operated from October 2000 to July 2002 when Claudio Mansilla directed the MCEI. Mansilla, as former CANEB president and soy exporter from Santa Cruz, enjoyed a "natural" closeness to business. Therefore, CONEX convened on a monthly basis during 2001, and followed a clear working agenda ending with a set of "Guidelines for a National Export Development Strategy" handed over to the State President Jorge Quiroga at the First National Export Convention in November 2001 (Guidelines 2001; BR Cabrera 13/12/04). Afterwards, CONEX entered an impasse of two years and was first revived in May 2004, then sustained by the idea to complete the National Export Strategy (ENEX).

But despite this revival which enabled six plenary reunions in 2004 and the formulation of "ENEX 2005-2015", the prospective for an efficient coordination pattern remained adverse. The council's destiny has depended thus far on the frequently alternating office holders who each maintained different approaches of communicating with the private sector. Furthermore, the Foreign Affairs Ministry, as the responsible agency for export promotion and trade negotiations, generally participated only faint-heartedly, since other governmental areas presided over the institution. Finally, the limitation of having only CANEB at the round table reduced the scope of policy deliberation, often being considered as a mechanism to enhance particular company interests instead of coordinating enlightened policies that favour Bolivia's insertion into the world market. Therefore, CONEX could not offer adequate space for consultations in international trade policy affairs, but instead had to delegate this coordination activity to the umbrella organisation, CEPB, where most economic sectors have traditionally assisted (6.3).

---

[46] The formal consideration of the mining and hydrocarbon sector did not concern CANEB because those entities are exclusively focused on traditional export products.

[47] According to key informants, CONEX did not launch reunions before 1998, when the second regulating Supreme Decree was signed (SO Chavez 17/03/04; BR Arias 17/01/05). Adhemar Guzman (OE 21/01/05) specified however, that between 1993 and 1998, CONEX operated only in a sporadic manner.

Studying the survey data, the responses gathered in 2004 indicated that the consultation channels offered by the government were deficient. The survey candidates were asked: *Does the government closely coordinate with business associations in trade policy affairs, involving the conduction of international trade negotiations and the implementation of trade agreements? If not, in what sectors/issues can coordination gaps be identified?* As can be seen below, two thirds of the consulted entities considered the relations to be rather sporadic concerning trade policy affairs. Even though principal export sectors acknowledged the openness exhibited by most officials as of 1997, the ongoing inter-ministerial conflicts and the instability inside the state executive hindered the establishment of solid working relations.[48] Contrary to business, experts and state officials perceived the coordination between state-business as very or rather close. In the case of experts though, most views referred to privileged informal channels offered to large scale mining and farming elites in the lowlands, and thus, insinuated forms of business capture.

Table 6.9: State-Business Coordination

	Experts (15)	State Officials (14)	Business (36)	Total (65)
very close	1	3	1	5 (9%)
rather close	6	5	7	18 (34%)
only sporadic	3	4	22	29 (55%)
very sporadic	0	0	1	1 (2%)
no response	5	2	5	12

Concerning transparency measures put forward to inform on international trade policy affairs, business responses replicated the prior results to wide extents. Even though consulted chambers recognised the official communication efforts, most of them saw information as insufficient or inopportune, as it was either "too late" or "imprecise." Expert views provided a different picture. While a majority perceived state-business channels as close, seven of nine responding experts qualified the governmental efforts to lighten up trade policy affairs as insufficient. The apparent contradiction can be explained by fact that several experts associated with civil society organisations like CEDLA, UMSA and the Solon Foundation made critical objections regarding the lack of transparency towards society in a broad sense.

---

[48] Officials like Ana Maria Solares, Hugo Mansilla and Isaac Maidana maintained very close relations with CANEB, CAMEX, CADEX and IBCE. An IBCE representative reported that after having suffered from sporadic relations in 1993-97, since 1997, MCEI and Foreign Affairs started to compete for privileged channels with the private actors.

Table 6.10: Transparency in International Trade Policy Affairs

	Experts (15)	Business (36)	Total (51)
very transparent	0	1	1 (2%)
rather transparent	2	10	12 (29%)
rather non-transparent	5	21	26 (62%)
very non-transparent	2	1	3 (7%)
No response	6	3	9

These critical assessments contrasted with the increasing attempts to explain and legitimise the daily work inside the public sector. Above all, in the final years of the study the local diplomacy tried to counter common views such as *"our diplomats negotiate for their own purpose"* or *"they like to appear in the diplomatic world without caring for domestic need"*, thus giving the impression of an insulated, self-preserving diplomacy. Against this, the Vice-Ministry of Foreign Economic Affairs organised numerous public events during 2003-04, often in coordination with private entities such as the IBCE, in order to outline the official position with regard to ongoing FTAA talks, the deepening of relations with Chile and Peru, and the (possible) impacts of the WTO Development Round and the US preference scheme, APTDEA.

Previously unseen efforts were made during the US-AFTA negotiations launched in May 2004. The US-AFTA Bureau sought direct contact with organisations of small business, peasants, mining workers, indigenous groups, and thus, incorporated some of the sectors previously excluded from trade policy-making (SO Alvarado 16/12/04). Furthermore, the Bureau published a range of documents (such as impact studies, brochures, and newsletters) which sought to make society aware of the pros and cons of an eventual US-AFTA agreement.

To some extent, this new openness was confirmed by the survey data, as 29 out of the 35 responses indicated that transparency was enhanced compared with the 1990s, when Bolivia negotiated various regional trade agreements. Only four business representatives and two experts openly denied any improvement. An annalist from CEDLA objected that the information channels opened by the government were only due to the increased pressure originating from the "Bolivian Movement against the FTAA Struggle," arguing that the official sector remained uninterested in establishing true relations, but instead aimed to establish better public relations. Alberto Zelada, a diplomat and expert in international economic law, responded (OE 10/08/04), *"It remains our task, indeed, to better incorporate civil society into the decision-making, but we don't know them and have little idea who they are representing; in contrast, we have identified the business sectors very well."*

Summary Independent Variable A1

In general, the institutional strength of Bolivia's state bureaucracy in the area of international trade policy affairs has been very low during the whole period of analysis, as resumed in Box 6.2. In particular, the creation of "export ministries" on two occasions caused only struggles for *responsibilities* and left unmet hopes and consternation among exporters. Regarding the variable dimension *resources*, the trade policy staff in charge of international trade policy affairs has been inadequate to deal with the technical requirements involved in regional and multilateral trade policy. In the variable dimension "openness", I showed that interaction patterns with business and civil society have been unstable, therein negatively affected by the erratic institutional development inside the state bureaucracy.

Box 6.2: Summary Independent Variable A1

Responsibilities	Resources	Openness
The creation of "export ministries" in 1992 and 1997 put into question the prevailing Foreign Affairs Model. However, forthcoming governments held other priorities and hindered the consolidation of a specialised agency that deals with export concerns, embracing promotion, regulation and market access negotiations.	Despite far-reaching commitments undertaken in the regional and multi-lateral sphere, until 2004 the official negotiation team had been inadequately staff (small number, lack of specialists) in order to comply with the international requirements involved in international trade policy affairs.	Although trade policy officials sought close ties with business, above all since 1997, unclear responsibilities hindered close business-state collaboration. Furthermore, recent attempts to initiate a stable dialogue with civil society failed as a result of the fundamental critics regarding the ongoing free trade talks with the US.

6.3 The Regional Division of Business Advocacy

This section is structured in accordance with the variable dimensions of the Independent Variable A2. The first subsection, *Institutional Leadership*, analyses the domestic attempts to establish a widely recognised peak or "umbrella" association, capable of coordinating economic policies between the leading sectoral and regional representatives. It further describes the institutional mechanism aimed at the intermediation of trade interests among leading sectoral and regional representatives. The second subsection, *Organisation Strength*, makes an assessment of the professionalism involved in business advocacy, stressing the domestic pattern of financing, participatory behaviour, and in-house trade policy expertise. The last subsection summarises the results and provides an overview of the business representation pattern from 1985 to 2004.

Institutional Leadership

In Bolivia, the process of forming business entities is still fairly young compared to other countries in the region, where the leading institutions were created in the 19th century (Conaghan/Malloy 1994; Mansilla 1994; Sanjinés Avila 2004). On the domestic level, the only chamber founded in this century was the La Paz Chamber of Commerce, erected in 1890 (becoming later the National Chamber of Commerce). A few decades later, traders from Santa Cruz (1913) and Cochabamba (1922) likewise decided on common representative structures. The industry associations did not emerge before the 1930s, with the National Industry Chamber (CNI) in 1931 and the Departmental Chambers of Cochabamba (1938) and Santa Cruz (1947). Regarding branch organisations, the majority of the entities from forestry, agriculture, and manufacturing began the organisational process in the period between 1960 and 1980, with the exception of the previously created mining, pharmaceutical and banking associations.

Given this relatively delayed institutional building process, the establishment of the multisectoral Confederation of Private Entrepreneurship of Bolivia (CEPB) in 1962 can be seen as athe first timid trial to raise and coordinate the private sector's voice in the context of a distinct state-led development model maintained from 1952 to 1985, wherein the leading companies in the mining, hydrocarbons, banking, and manufacturing sectors were state owned.[49] Therefore, the New Economic Policy enacted in August 1985 converted the CEPB into the privileged civilian partner of the government of Victor Paz Estenssoro. Several functionaries

---

[49] The Bolivian Mining Corporation (COMIBOL) accounted for 60 percent of exports and the oil company YPFB 80 percent of the domestic production of oil and natural gas. Furthermore, most of the banking system was state owned by the Rural, Mining and State Banks. Through the Bolivian Development Corporation (CBF), the state also controlled the manufacture of glass, textiles, cement, dairy products, oils, and sugar.

associated with the CEPB took over strategic state executive positions, with Fernando Illanes assuming the role of Ambassador in Washington, and Fernando Romero and Roland MacLean becoming top policy makers inside the Ministries of Planning and Finance. Hence, the peak entity assumed a key role inside the private sector and society in general, setting forth a proactive liberal agenda covering mainly fiscal, investment and labour policies. Moreover, in promoting the acceleration of structural reforms by claiming the privatisation of state owned companies, the ambitious business agenda even began to contrast with the slower reform pace upheld by the public sector until 1993.

Within the private sector, the leadership was increased by a fast institutional expansion during the presidency of Carlos Calvo (1989-1992), augmenting the affiliates from 20 to 32 associated organisations. For example, the Eastern Chamber of Agriculture and the Chamber of Hydrocarbons - two influential entities from the eastern lowlands – joined the peak association (Sanjinés Ávila 2004, vol. II: 167-210).

From an institutional perspective, the fast growth of the peak association nevertheless proved to be unsustainable, since the national business representation structures have been marked by the phenomena of "overrepresentation". Indeed, considering a GDP of US$8 million and the informal economy reaching up to 60-70 percent, Bolivia would appear to have more chambers than large-scale companies. This institutional disorder can best be exemplified by the CEPB's internal structure in which four, often overlapping, member categories can be identified.

Box 6.3: The Four Overlapping Member Categories inside the CEPB

Departmental Peak Associations	Departmental Federations of Private Entrepreneurship which are composed of regional sector chambers from industry and commerce, among others.
National Chambers composed of Firms, and Regional and Sectoral Entities	The National Chambers of Industry and Commerce are characterised by a membership of regional chambers from industry and commerce, national branch organisations and firms located in La Paz. Although individual firms are formally associated inside the La Paz Chambers of Industry and Commerce, their financial contributions sustain the national chambers since their premises and staff are identical to their regional organisations.

National Chambers Representing Departmental Entities	The National Chambers of Exporters (CANEB), Construction (CBC), and Banking (ASOBAN) contain special arrangements. While CANEB and CPC represent only their regional chambers and not firms, ASOBAN represents private banks and used to likewise hold regional subsidiaries.
National Chambers Representing Firms	The national branch organisations integrated entirely by individual firms are the chambers of hydrocarbons, pharmaceuticals, assurances, mining, etc.

The varying logics of medium and large company representation (disregarding the marked institutional fragmentation among small and micro business associations) caused business organisations to permanently struggle for internal (among firms) and external (among state authorities) recognition. A clear example can be found in the situation of the brewery sector where three companies represent close to 100 percent of the domestic market. These firms are associated in the National Brewery Chamber (CABOFACE), created in 1996. CABOFACE, in turn, holds an affiliation inside the CEPB and the National and Chambers of Industry and Commerce. The breweries are further individually associated inside the Departmental Chambers of Industry and Commerce, and hence, supported the operation of the National Chambers as the contributions of sectoral and regional chambers are marginal.

Beyond the overlapping memberships, the CEPB's role as leader of the national *bourgeoisie* received a serious setback as a consequence of the privatisation of state owned firms and the creation of the private pension funds system under the government of Sánchez de Lozado (1993-97). The fact that Bolivia's capitalists, coordinated by the peak association, followed these reforms as mere observers – considering that all companies came under Bolivian ownership – was clear evidence for many of the persistent risk adversity among national entrepreneurs.[50] Even though the CEPB complained to state authorities that local companies were mainly shut out of the bidding procedures, the transnationalisation of domestic assets hindered the CEPB in the aftermath in its ability to spread the powerful properties of private business. Moreover, in the context of a stagnating economy and a growingly tense political climate from 1998, the institutional fragmentation inside the national private sector came increasingly into view.

Nevertheless, the principal dividing forces had regional grounds. With increasing potency, the business entities from the department of Santa Cruz began to openly question the legitimacy of the national organisations located in the capital city La Paz. Regarding the CEPB's

---

[50] Even the former CEPB General Secretary, Augusto Estívariz (1993-1996), admitted that local entrepreneurs lacked sufficient aggressiveness; see Sanjinés Ávila 2004, vol. II: 289 and personal interview BR 12/12/04.

decision-making structure, for example, the factions from Santa Cruz argued that the economic importance of their agro-industrial, service and hydrocarbon sectors were by no means considered and pointed to their under representation inside the Directing Council.[51] To underline this distortion, the powerful Santa Cruz Chamber of Industry, Commerce, Services and Tourism evidenced its regional contribution to the nation's welfare in 2002 by measures of its in-house Centre for Bolivian Economy (CAINCO 2003).

➢ *GDP Share:* The Santa Cruz GDP share increased from 26.8 in 1990 to 30.6 percent, whereas the La Paz contribution decreased from 25.9 to 23.1 percent.

➢ *Exports:* While Santa Cruz provided 50.7 percent of exports (from 35.2 in 1999), La Paz was only responsible for 13.8 percent of exports. Furthermore, 67.1 percent of Santa Cruz exports were classed as non-traditional.

➢ *FDI:* Seventy-five percent of FDIs went to Santa Cruz or their southern neighbour Tarija, with the latter accounting for more than 80 percent of all natural gas and oil reserves.

Until 2000, initiating regional rivalries had been covered by the unremitting "Santa Cruz Presidencies" of Carlos Rechezal (1994-1996) and Jose Luis Camacho (1996-2000). The picture changed under the new presidency of Ernest Calvo (2001-2003) when the breakout of the regional conflict became inevitable. To analyse the clash, which came to a climax at the end of 2003 through the disaffiliation of the Santa Cruz and Tarija related chambers, at least four conflictive features ought to be taken into account:[52]

1) *Tax Policy:* By the end of 2003, the natural gas and oil exporting Departments of Santa Cruz and Tarija had rejected governmental plans to increase taxes on hydrocarbon production and banking transactions, whereas CEPB authorities supported the project of State President Carlos Mesa.

2) *Regional Autonomy:* The Santa Cruz business elites assumed a leading force in the forceful struggle for greater regional autonomy witnessed in the final years of the study. Therein, it is an open secret that regional entities, such as CAINCO in particular, strongly backed the Department's Civic Committee in charge of the political battle.

3) *Idiosyncrasy:* The *cambas,* i.e. people of Santa Cruz decent, consider themselves to be dynamic, risk-loving entrepreneurs, always ready to do business, whereas they describe

[51] Since each member had been represented by two members inside the governing body and the Santa Cruz region enjoyed only a direct representation by 4 out of 30 chambers, the nominal representation of Santa Cruz used to be rather weak compared to its economic contribution.
[52] The pertinent chambers were the Federations of Private Entrepreneurship from Santa Cruz and Tarija, the National Chambers of Forestry and Hydrocarbon and the Eastern Chamber of Agriculture. Besides, departmental sector chambers withdrew their national associations, such as CAINCO from the National Chamber of Commerce and the Santa Cruz Chamber of Construction from the National Chamber of Construction.

the *collas* from La Paz as conservative and risk adverse. For the *collas*, however, the *cambas* are just lucky as they rarely face protesting labour, neighbourhood and indigenous groups. Moreover, they qualified them as unserious since *cambas'* companies keep double-entry accounts, and therefore, are rarely registered in the local stock market.

4) *Economic Structure*: While the lowland producers have been interested in preserving the domestic market for their agriculture and forestry products, La Paz has sought cheaper prime materials for its food processing and furniture industry. Such conflicts were increasingly difficult to handle in the trade policy scope, as I demonstrate in the next subsection.

The Intermediation of Trade Interests

The business advocacy in the area of trade policy not only replicates the fragmented pattern identified preciously, but builds a paradigmatic case for the dilemma faced by national business. To identify internal divisions, manifold regional, sectoral, and institutional aspects need to be considered. The principal weakness, however, concerns the lack of reliable national institutions capable of articulating either offensive or defensive interests concerning Bolivia's insertion into world markets. Box 6.4 sums up the major shortcomings of the main national chambers involved in trade policy affairs.

Box 6.4: The Shortcomings of National Trade Policy Advocates

National Chamber of Commerce CNC (Foundation 1890)	• Heterogeneous, overlapping membership (sectors, regions, firms) • Representation of importers' interests mainly • La Paz oriented (local firms sustains CNC)
National Chamber of Industry CNI (1931)	• Heterogeneous, overlapping membership • La Paz oriented (local firms sustains CNI) • Weak trade policy branch
CEPB (1962)	• Heterogeneous, overlapping membership • Internal division between La Paz and Santa Cruz • Weak trade policy branch
National Chamber of Exporters CANEB (1983)	• Dependence on Santa Cruz Chamber of Exporters (CADEX) • Individual advocacy of La Paz Chamber of Exporters (CAMEX) • Weak trade policy branch
Bolivian Institute of Foreign Trade IBCE (1986)	• Representation in La Paz only since 2004 • Considered as a representative from the Santa Cruz Department

A common feature to all the national chambers is the regional division between La Paz and Santa Cruz, which has increased in the recent times of social unrest and distinctive articulations of regional autonomy movements. Subsequently, I will present the adverse grounds for national trade policy intermediation and the accentuating misbalance as regards regional advocacy power.

The Failed National Coordination: Noteworthy efforts for national consensus building were set forth inside the CEPB in 1992 when the Commission of Integration and Foreign Trade was put into force. Key informant reports described the commission as a technical advisory body in which meetings took place twice per month and which enjoyed wide recognition among members' delegates (SO Arana 24/01/05; BR's Gastelu 20/01/05 and Rodríguez 20/07/04; 17/01/05). The Commission benefited at the beginning from the prestige-laden presidencies of Carlos Iturralde and Adalberto Violand, both former CEPB presidents and high-ranked diplomats, and the fact that Manuel Arana, as secretary, provided sound expertise due to his career inside the SEGIN, Andean Group and CAF.[53] Moreover, between 1994 and 2000, the CEPB was presided over for the first time by entrepreneurs from Santa Cruz, and thus, raised the entity's acceptance in the economically boosting lowland region.

Over the years, however, the business factions from La Paz perceived an increasing misbalance in the internal decision-making. While, for the Santa Cruz entities, the Commission of Integration and Foreign Trade provided a useful forum to place their sectoral concerns, the La Paz chambers behaved rather passively in ongoing talks with the CAN, MERCOSUR, Chile and Mexico. As a consequence, on countless occasions the lowland region was able to demonstrate its superior business advocacy, and hence, managed to make use of the limited negotiation capacities of state authorities. Accordingly, a Bolivian official serving for the CAN General Secretariat in Lima stated that, in the past, his government pursued a single issue agenda inside the CAN and pointed at efforts undertaken to guarantee and preserve the Andean markets for soy products (OE Larrazabal 08/02/05). As local exports regularly faced safeguard or discriminatory measures applied by Colombia, Venezuela and Peru, intensive diplomacy in the CAN scope became necessary to obtain and control preferential market access conditions.[54] Furthermore, Bolivia had to repeatedly insist on their Andean partners' prompt application of the Common

---

[53] Carlos Iturralde was formally Foreign Affairs Minister and Violand served as Ambassador to Chile in the 1970s.
[54] In 2002, for example, Colombia imposed safeguard measures of 29 percent tariffs on vegetable oils from the Andean partners; see CAN Resolution 671. Other measures applied by Colombia were related to a differential VAT treatment according the value added on imported products. For recent restrictions taken by Venezuela during 2005, the principal buyer's market, see *El Nuevo Día* 18/08/2005 or IBCE publication *Comercio Exterior*, March 2005.

External Tariff for soy products (15-20 percent) and the Andean Price Band System, which in combination guaranteed higher tariff preferences in the case of low world market prices.[55]

While chambers from La Paz did not oppose the search for market access for soy and other lowland products like sugar, cotton and lumber, discussions became more conflictive when Santa Cruz sought to protect its local production. For example, the food processing industry in La Paz showed little comprehension to the idea that commodities such as wheat, sugar, and milk should enjoy a more protectionist treatment by means of non-tariff barriers or longer phasing-out schemes than value added products like wheat flour or dairy products (BR's Fernandez 12/08/04; Gastelu 20/01/05). One case that provoked particular debate concerned the lumber imports from Chile, where the domestic forestry located in Santa Cruz was able to convince authorities to avoid preferential access in the ACE No. 22 scope at the expense of the export oriented furniture companies in La Paz. Manuel Arana reported (SO 24/01/05) that arduous internal work was required towards the end of the 1990s to find a solution accepted by both the Bolivian Forestry Chamber and furniture factories represented by George Satt, the then President of the La Paz Chamber of Exporters and owner of the leading export company directed towards the US market. Nevertheless, the adaptation of the domestic lumber sector to the requirements of furniture production seemed unviable and the Bolivian Forestry Chamber located in Santa Cruz continued to insist on the existing protection margin.

For the CEPB, the failure to coordinate in such occasions meant a serious setback in its pretension to intermediate among regional positions. Consequently, between 2000 and 2003, the Foreign Trade Commission held no regular meetings, and it was only during 2004, when Bolivia entered the US-AFTA talks as an observer, that these were revived. These discrepancies were reflected inside the CANEB, as the national representative of non-traditional exports. Against the rising internal leverage of the Santa Cruz Export Chamber (CADEX), which was owed to the strong growth of soy exports in the 1990s, the weakened La Paz Export Chamber (CAMEX) headed by George Satt demonstrated, in the internal election of 1998, its unwillingness to accept the decision power assigned to CADEX.[56] Thus, the CAMEX disaffiliated from the CANEB and

---

[55] The purpose of this system, in force since February 1995, is to stabilise domestic prices for palm oil, soybean oil, rice, sugar, barley, milk, corn, soybeans, wheat, chicken, and pork, among others. Thus, when the international bench mark price falls below a predetermined minimum level, member countries will apply a variable-rate surcharge on imports of such products, over and above the CET. Likewise, when the international bench mark price rises above a certain ceiling, the member countries will lower the normal tariff rate to reduce the import cost of the staple.
[56] According to the articles of the associations from 1991, when La Paz was the principal exporter, a 60 percent share of exports implied the assignment of a 42 percent of votes by the elections of the chamber's Directorate.

individually pursued its regional interests for six years, although the entity continued to share the same two-floor building with the CANEB.[57]

The Rise of Santa Cruz: The bargaining power of Santa Cruz inside national chambers and before state agencies has been closely linked to the institutional responses given concerning the regional and multilateral challenges on the horizon from the outset of the 1990s. By this point, Santa Cruz, more than any other department, began to define its trade policy interests and to achieve a high degree of inter-institutional coordination. In order to explain the coherence of Santa Cruz's lobbying it is pertinent to point out the distinctive social cohesion among local elites, enrooted in four centuries of insularity and disconnection from the country's economic and political centres (Waldmann 2001). Yet, another crucial explanation concerns the state-led development strategies implemented in the second half of the 20th century which produced a significant awakening of the tropical lowlands. Inspired by the so-called Bohan Report carried out by US diplomat Merwin L. Bohan in the 1940s, it was public agencies such as the Bolivian Development Corporation that used the vast majority of public investments for the development of the isolated eastern parts of the country, through the construction of roads and railways from La Paz and Cochabamba, and the preparation of large scale agriculture soils.

The creation of the Santa Cruz oriented Bolivian Institute of Foreign Trade (IBCE) in March 1986 represented a perfect match between local social cohesion and state support.[58] Francisco Tercero (OE 18/01/05), IBCE's first Managing Director, recalled that the idea of creating an institution specialising in export issues emerged during the Convention "Santa Cruz in 2000" organised in 1985 by the state-ruled regional Development Corporation, CORDECRUZ. Later, in 1986, CORDECRUZ facilitated a start-up capital of US$20,000, half of the initial investment, and further made available a group of experts that designed the organisational setting together with the leading entities from industry, trade, agriculture and forestry. During the first years of its existence, IBCE focused, together with the also recently created CADEX, on working streams related to (1) the analysis and capacity building of exporters in the range of customs and tax procedures, (2) trade promotion by providing technical assistance and participating in trade fairs in neighbouring countries, and last but not least (3), improved physical access to the Paraguay-Paraná waterway through the Tamengo Channel, so as

---

[57] Finally, in 2004, CANEB succeeded in incorporating CAMEX. But its involvement has been hesitant so far because the La Paz chamber still resists paying its monthly affiliation rate of US$500.

[58] Obviously, the national denomination was questioned by the La Paz entities, and thus, required first a Minister of Trade, Industry and Tourism from the Santa Cruz Department, Freddy Teodovich Ortiz, until the name was accepted in 1988 by the Supreme Resolution No. 204442.

to carry local products towards the Atlantic ports in Uruguay and Argentina (OE Tercero 18/01/05; IBCE 1997).

Analytical skills in trade integration have mainly been built up since 1990. Under the coordination of Gary Rodriguez, Technical Manager from 1986 to 1996 and Managing Director from 1996, the IBCE assumed a regional "gate keeping" role before, during, and after trade negotiation rounds. Furthermore, the five associated chambers from industry and trade (CAINCO), forestry (CFB), customs agents, agriculture (CAO), exports (CADEX), and the invited Federation of Private Entrepreneurship, created in 1993 the Santa Cruz Monitoring Committee for International Trade Negotiations. From this point on, the IBCE coordinated monitoring committee evolved into a technical body where regional entities defined common positions and brought together relevant sector information (BR Cirbián 25/03/04). Rodriguez reported (BR 27/07/04) that, initially, the chambers' officials would meet twice a month on average, yet later the meetings were organised on a more and more informal, ad-hoc basis. As mutual trust grew among the members, Rodriguez stated, *"I started to carry out consultation through e-mail, and if nobody objected to my propositions, I presented my technical points of view in the framework of the CEPB and before the state authorities."* Due to this institutional mechanism, the participating of Santa Cruz inside the CEPB was permanent and unified, despite the breath-taking trip from the tropical lowlands to the capital city at 3600 metres. In 1994, IBCE, as a non-CEPB member, became an "invited institution" inside the Commission of Foreign Trade and Integration, and hence, was able to set the meetings' rhythm and the contents as regards ongoing regional integration.[59]

Uncoordinated Voices from La Paz: By the time Bolivia entered free trade talks with Mexico and MERCOSUR, the national chambers CNI, CNC, and CANEB also recognised the necessity for better inter-institutional coordination. Therefore, in 1993, the three entities formed a National Council of Industry and Trade, denominated COINCI, to submit "national" business proposals to the authorities on solid technical grounds, according to Julio Olmos, at that time COINCI Executive Secretary (OE 15/02/05). In hindsight, however, to delimit the council's purpose as the one taken over by the CEPB's Commission of Foreign Trade and Integration is puzzling as the secretaries of both institutions claimed *"the unification of national business interests"* (Arana 24/01/05; Olmos 15/02/2005).

---

[59] Important guidelines were defined in the study "Bolivia in the Context of Latin American Integration: The Vision of the Exporting Sector from Santa Cruz," carried out in 1993 by IBCE and CADEX. The 140-page document handed over to Antonio Araníbar (Foreign Affair Minister from 1993-97) made recommendations for giving priority to CAN and not MERCOSUR, to lessen the time-costing bureaucracy by implementing trade agreements, and to insist on the Special and Differential Treatment foreseen in the ALADI scope.

Instead, the creation of COINCI was considered an attempt by the chambers of La Paz to counter-weigh the concerted positions attained by Santa Cruz. Nevertheless, in the aftermath of MERCOSUR talks, the involved chambers could no longer agree on the body's modus operandi. Simultaneously, the regional asymmetries regarding the trade policy advocacy widened as Santa Cruz was the only department that permanently sent representatives to negotiation rounds overseas. Therefore, in 2000, the La Paz chambers undertook a new effort to better local coordination by creating the Foreign Trade Unit, this time in the ambit of the La Paz Federation of Private Entrepreneurship.[60] After several meetings among delegates of the CNI, CNC, CAMEX and the Departmental Chamber of Custom Agents, however, the project was once again abandoned. The new failure was in part related to the appointment of CAMEX leader, Bruno Guissani, as President of the National Customs Authorities, who took over the initiative in this enterprise. Nonetheless, at least two more factors must be highlighted to shed enlightenment on the lack of collective action.

1) *Rivalry:* In particular, the National Chambers of Industry and Commerce, as the country's most traditional entities, have maintained a relationship marked by envy and suspicion concerning the internal and external recognition among La Paz's major companies and state authorities. In the event of COINCI, in which the Executive Secretariat was hosted within the CNC, the industrialists saw the shared institution captured by the importing sectors grouped in the CNC.[61]

2) *Financial Commitment:* The associated members have proved unwilling to pay costs related to technical staff and travels necessary for accompanying the official negotiation team.[62]

Given the failed attempts in La Paz, it was the IBCE from Santa Cruz that sought from 2004 to convert its Bolivian denomination into a program full of content. Therefore, the IBCE established a regional office in the capital city that aimed at improving technical support inside the CEPB Commission of Foreign Trade and Integration, recovering the sound intermediation of national exporters' interests. Nonetheless, the project supported by the Swiss State Secretariat of Economic Affairs (SECO) has to be considered as a long-term investment in the still contending

---

[60] Cochabamba, the third important Department economically (mainly dedicated to the export of fruits), managed, prior to La Paz, to establish a Foreign Trade Unit under the Federation of Private Entrepreneurship, yet without having permanent presence in trade talks. Though loosely organised, the Unit was still operating in 2004.

[61] With regard to MERCOSUR negotiations, importers tended to be more in favour of a fast opening up of the economy, while the industrialists sustained (albeit timid and partial) Santa Cruz's critical standpoints regarding the official attempts to sign a complete FTA; see *Diario Hoy* 27/02/97; OE Olmos 15/02/05; BR Fernandez 12/08/2004.

[62] IBCE was mostly present with Gary Rodriguez and Carlos Roca. Further representatives came from the farming entity CAO, and especially from the "National" Association of Oleaginous and Wheat Producers (ANAPO).

regional antagonism. Even though Soraya Fernandez, as Managing Director of the La Paz office, has showd a clear willingness to better articulate exportation views from the highlands (for example by the analysis of regional offers in the range of textiles, jewellery, alpaca clothing, leather wear, etc.), IBCE's physical presence is likely to arouse certain suspicion, at least initially, with the La Paz dominated organisations.[63]

Organisational Strength

Based on a survey with 36 business associations (see Appendix) his subsection I will shed light on aspects related to the organisational strength of private sector representatives, stressing the importance of diversified revenues, reliable payment of membership dues, active member participation, the existence of permanent staff and in-house trade policy expertise.

Diversification of Association Revenues: Bolivian business chambers tend to diversify their revenues, and consequently, reduce their dependency on affiliation dues. Fifty percent of given answers indicated that, in 2004, more than 40 percent of entities' incomes were generated by mechanisms such as the provision of services, rent of office spaces, the management of collective funds, or donor agency contributions. On the contrary, less than one third of entities reported that revenues relied entirely on the payment of affiliation dues (e.g. national associations representing mining, pharmaceuticals, banking, telecommunications and breweries).

Table 6.11: What share of revenues originates from other than affiliation dues?

More than 40%	10-40%	0-10%	0%	No Response
17 (50%)	4 (12%)	3 (9%)	10 (29%)	2

The sustainability of additional funding wasn't always clarified in the survey, however. Mainly among small scale business chambers like the FEBOPI, departmental CADEPIA's and the CIOEC, an almost complete dependence on contributions made by donor agencies seemed to be rather common. Conversely, interesting examples of diversified revenues were identified inside the *CEPB* and its *Departmental Federations*. In this example, incomes depended between 60-70 percent on means provided by INFOCAL, an associated foundation dedicated to the industrial and vocational training of workers and financed by firms' voluntary contributions of one percent of salary volume. Even though the peak entity suffered from a painful shrinking of these incomes in recent years, INFOCAL funds remained essential, considering that member

---

[63] Therefore, IBCE has regularly participated within the scope of the CEPB Commission of Foreign Trade and Integration and has therein assumed the role of Technical Secretariat. In formal terms, however, IBCE staff was compelled to attend using the name of CANEB due to the ongoing division between Santa Cruz and La Paz.

quotas of the 30 members, ranging from US$250 to $1500, appeared too modest to sustain a professional lobby organisation.

Nearly without exception, chambers from Santa Cruz enjoyed strongly diversified incomes. Carlos Rojas (BR 23/07/04), President of the *National Association of Oleaginous and Wheat Producers (ANAPO)*, proudly explained that US$250,000 of annual incomes, representing roughly 30 percent, was related to a buyer's arrangement between ANAPO and GRAVETAL, one of the leading companies dedicated to the transformation and exportation of soy. As GRAVETAL is closely located to the Brazilian border, and thus, interested in soy imports from Brazil by means of the Temporary Admission Regime, the company offered guaranteed prices and volumes to local producers as long as ANAPO used its advocacy power for the maintenance of this regime. This deal allowed ANAPO not only to charge 50 cents per sold tonne, but also to oblige the remaining exporting companies to pay a similar value.[64]

Although affected by recent income losses due to mismanagement and a general decline suffered by the farming sector, during the 1990s the influential *Oriental Chamber of Agriculture (CAO)* was able to base its revenues on similar incomes generated by the affiliated membership (US$200,000), the organisation of Bolivia's biggest Trade Fair "EXPOCRUZ" (US$200,000), and the administration of the Central Storehouse of Farming Equipments (ACAP) (US$150,000), according to CAO's former Managing Director, Walter Nuñez 1989-98 (OE 10/08/04; also BR Arano 24/03/04). With regard to the *Santa Cruz Chamber of Industry, Commerce, Services and Tourism (CAINCO)*, Operating Manager Mario Cirbián (BR 25/03/04) indicated that due to serious efforts to capture more external funds made in the 1990s, nowadays the chamber offers business an impressive array of services, in which SICOMEX stands out by providing permanent information to importers from the customs areas. According to Cirbián, the incomes generated by external funds were responsible, therefore, for 60 percent of total revenues.

Predictability of Association Revenues: Local associations clearly face problems in persuading their members to comply with their financial duties. Even though consulted functionaries were reluctant to make accurate information available, the survey data from 2004 highlighted that the prompt payment of members' dues was rather unusual, since 50 percent of memberships did not meet payment deadlines regularly. In general terms, large scale entities from banks, insurances, breweries, mining, forestry and leading trade organisations like the IBCE and CAINCO had fewer problems in this respect than entities of small scale farmers or manufacturers. Nonetheless, several "big company advocates" such as the CEPB, CANEB, CNI

---

[64] Further revenues in the amount of US$100,000 originated from the utilities of the entity's seeds plant, created in 1985. Finally, ANAPO ran several projects of technical assistance financed by international donor organisations such as *PROTRIGO* from USAID and Food Safety-PASA sponsored by the European Union.

and ANAPO also encountered uncertainties as regards the capture of dues. The widespread local efforts to maintain external funding are thus comprehensive.

Table 6.12: What share of membership regularly meets the payment deadline?

80-100%	50-79%	20-49%	less than 20%	No response
12 (35%)	5 (15%)	11 (39%)	6 (21%)	2

Participatory Behaviour of Members/Business: When consulting on the properties of internal trade decision-making, two thirds of the entities qualified their members' participation as rather or very active, pointing at the frequent presence in meetings and, to a lesser extent, the submission of proposals. Yet, the validity of data seemed rather modest since the responses were often aimed at casting a positive light on their own members. Moreover, in only 7 out of 23 chambers which indicated an active participation, did the organisation hold a commission related to foreign trade and/or integration affairs: IBCE, CIFABOL (pharmaceuticals), ASOBAN (banks), ABA (insurance), CNC and the Cochabamba Chambers of Industry and Exports. In total, twelve entities maintained an issue related commission in 2004.

Table 6.13: Business/ member participation in trade policy affairs

	Experts	State Officials	Total Experts + State Officials (29)	*Business*(36)
very active	0	2	2 (9%)	*12 (36%)*
rather active	2	3	5 (22%)	*12 (36%)*
rather passive	4	6	10 (43%)	*6 (19%)*
very passive	4	2	6 (26%)	*3 (9%)*
no response	5	1	6	*3*

* Responses are referred to the behaviour of members inside the internal bodies of each chamber.

Furthermore, the data provided by business contrasted with the observations collected from experts and state officials concerning the behaviour of business entities in international trade policy affairs. Sixteen out of the 23 responses suggested a very or rather passive behaviour. The most positive remarks concerned the agro-industrial lobbies from Santa Cruz. On eight occasions, five state officials and three experts made explicit reference to the eye-catching presence of the IBCE and the five associated members. With respect to the negative quotes, many answers highlighted the business participation in general. Several specific comments considered the segment of small scale business, yet, leading organisations like the National Chamber of Industry received official criticism for barely taking part in ongoing trade negotiations (SO's R. Chavez 17/03/04; Velázquez 9/08/04; Zambrana 5/08/04).

Staff Size and Trade Expertise: Many private sector organisations in Bolivia maintain a large staff base compared with corresponding entities in Argentina and Peru. By 2004, in 44 percent of the chambers the number of employees was higher than ten, compared to 18 percent in Argentina and Peru. Evidently, the staff size was closely associated to activities going beyond lobbying and concerned the chambers search for strengthening its institutional position by offering a broad range of selective goods, i.e. customs services, (phyto-) sanitary controls, technical assistance, data, trade missions and fairs, collective seller, or buyers arrangements, etc.

Table 6.14: What is the size of permanent staff?

more than 20	11-20	5-10	1-5	no response
7 (22%)	9 (22%)	6 (17%)	14 (39%)	0

Given this service providing approach, the number of employees is not necessarily linked to the extent of trade policy advocacy. Table 6.15 gives a brief overview.

Table 6.15: Bolivia Top Ten Business' Entity Administrations

Rank	Name	Staff	Location	Outstanding Properties
1	FEGASACRUZ (Santa Cruz livestock federation)	86	Santa Cruz	Technical assistance, slaughterhouse, banking and trade facilities, etc.
2	CNC	60	La Paz	Unit of Custom Services
3	CNI	50	La Paz	Centre of Sustainable Technology Promotion (CPTS)
3	CAINCO	50	Santa Cruz	Wide range of business services, impressive CAINCO Tower with Convention Center
5	ANAPO	32	Santa Cruz	Technical assistance provisions
6	CIOEC (Coordinator for Small peasant Units)	30	La Paz and regions	Technical assistance for small peasants; 90 percent financed by international donors
7	CADECO (Cochabamba Chamber of Commerce)	21	Cochabamba	Wide range of business services
8	IBCE	18	Santa Cruz	Trade promotion and analysis
9	CAMEX	17	La Paz	Trade data and promotion
10	CADEX	15	Santa Cruz	Trade data and promotion

Even though the ranking notified several modifications, the leadership of Santa Cruz's entities was repeated when asking how many employees monitor trade policy affairs. Export promotion facilities excluded, one third of the consulted chambers had experts observing the outcomes of trade talks in 2004. In general, most of these entities, such as the CADEX, CAINCO, ANAPO, the Cochabamba Chambers of Industry, Exports and Commerce, CIFABOL (pharmaceutical industry), CAMEX, CEPB and CIOEC, had at their disposal one trade policy specialist and one assistant. The single organisation holding a technical department with three ore more employees was the IBCE. Altogether, the trade policy branch at that time consisted of seven persons from General Management (one), the Technical Division (four), and the La Paz quarter (two). Furthermore, most Santa Cruz chambers, such as CAINCO, the Forestry Chamber, CAO, and FEGASACRUZ, indicated that they often relied on IBCE's expertise, commonly calling it their "technical branch".

Table 6.16: Who within the staff is monitoring and analysing trade policy affairs?

think thank (3 officials)	Trade Department (1-2)	Managing Director	none	no response
1 (3%)	11 (31%)	12 (34%)	11 (31%)	0

Conversely, the trade policy advisory units of the national chambers were rather modest or absent. For budget reasons, the *CEPB* maintains a modest technical staff that only encompasses the Directors of the Economic, Institutional and Legal Divisions. Only temporarily, from March 2003 to September 2004, did the peak association count on a Foreign Trade Director who supported the technical work inside the Foreign Trade Commission. Later, the position remained vacant due to a lack of financial resources. A similar situation was faced by the *CNI* at the end of 2003, when the person responsible for foreign trade was no longer replaced. In any case, taking into account the fact that the national industry representative decided, in 1997, to establish an area of foreign trade (financed by means of an IDB trade promotion project), highlights the modest importance ascribed to this policy field. Finally, *CANEB*, an allegedly responsible national entity for export concerns, was also forced to reduce technical staff for budget reasons. Excluding the trade promotion area which runs externally financed projects, the administrative structure only contained the positions of an Executive Director and an Administrative Assistant in 2004.

The modest in-house expertise upheld by most entities was confirmed by the impressions gathered among experts and state officials. Eighteen out of 21 given answers considered the technical level of business policy proposals submitted by business entities in the area of international trade policy as very or rather low.

Table 6.17: How do you assess the technical level of business proposals submitted in the area of international trade policy?

	Experts (15)	State Officials (14)	Total (29)
very high	0	1	1 (5%)
rather high	2	0	2 (10%)
rather low	4	8	12 (57%)
very low	4	2	6 (28%)
no response	5	3	8

The quotes either indicated that entities where short of accomplished experts and/or that contributions normally did not go beyond the particular interests of a small group of companies dominating the chambers. Closely interrelated with the observations made regarding the participative behaviour, nine comments (five state officials and four experts) excluded technical work undertaken by the IBCE staff from the general criticism.

Summary Independent Variable A2

This section indicates a low institutional strength of business associations, especially of those representing national business concerns. Regarding the variable dimension *leadership*, the lack of multi-sectoral coordination capacity stands out, negatively affecting the intermediation of economy and trade related policies before the government. The *organisation strength* of national business associations is largely deficient, although regional differences needs to be considered, as Box 6.5 point out.

Box 6.5: Summary Independent Variable A2

Leadership	Peak Association	The leadership that the peak entity CEPB enjoyed at the beginning of the New Economic Policy decreased in light of the growing regional division between business factions from La Paz, the capital city located in the highlands, and the private sector from Santa Cruz, the most important economic centre in Bolivia's lowlands. By the end of 2003, the Santa Cruz related organisations decided to disaffiliate from the CEPB.
	Trade Policy Coordination	The trade policy advocacy has been marked by the lack of reliable national intermediating institutions and the regional discrepancies regarding the high degree of inter-institutional coordination among Santa Cruz entities and the largely disorganised entities in La Paz.
Organisational Strength		Based on the provision of services and other funding activities, Bolivia's business administrations are relatively big. The organisational strength of the Santa Cruz entities was eye-catching, which through the solid trade policy branch of IBCE maintained a clear advantage over the inadequately staffed national and departmental organisations in La Paz.

6.4 Assessment

After examining separately the evolution of the dependent and independent variables over the period of analysis, in this final section, I assess how, and to what extent, Bolivia's failed world market integration strategy was effectively caused by the explanatory variables A1+2, or whether third variable influences became responsible for the observed policy failure.

Before stressing the posed hypothesis, however, I point out the main aspects of Bolivia's pursuit of world market integration. In 1985, in light of a scenario of hyperinflation, the country embarked on a strategy based on liberal structural adjustment policies. In the ongoing decade, this market-led model that characterised Bolivia's approach to world market integration came under increasing pressure. As well as a radical opposition from social movements against free trade, fiscal constraints and political crisis strongly hampered the concerted search among domestic actors for sound trade policy-making. Therefore, when analysing Bolivia's world market integration strategy in the last two decades, these macroeconomic and political turbulences need to be considered. Conversely, several empirical puzzles cannot simply be linked to Control Variable C3+4, but require the examination of the selected independent variables.

First, from 1985 to 1997, why did Bolivia undertake, on the regional and multilateral sphere, more trade policy commitments than any other country in South America (except Chile)? Generally, these free trade arrangements neither entailed positive effects on the development of exports nor caused a significant surge of foreign investments. Instead, the agreements signed in the regional sphere, above all, caused strong trade deficits, and hence, negatively affected the balance of payment and the domestic market access of local products.

Second, why did Bolivia choose not to implement coherent export promotion schemes in order to foster non-traditional exports in the range of industrial and agricultural manufactures, thus spurring sales in markets where preferential access had been negotiated? With meagre results, the National Council of Exports (CONEX) established in 1993 was in charge of concerting policy guidelines and instruments aimed at strengthening the national export development.

Third, why did Bolivia participate in the US-AFTA negotiations only as an observer, considering the necessity to consolidate preferential market access conditions for Bolivia's non-traditional exports, for which the US market represents the main destination? In fact, by the end of this study, it was highly uncertain whether, and for what duration, the US preference scheme for Andean countries, ATPDEA, will be extended.

Forth, how can the successful consolidation of the Andean markets for Bolivia's oleaginous products be explained? While in general Bolivia suffered from huge trade deficits, since the 1990s, increasing soy exports to Colombia, Venezuela, Ecuador, and Peru became responsible for regular trade surpluses in the scope of the CAN.

In the light of these empirical puzzles, Table 6.18 sums up the value of the observed variables and the explanatory power each one possesses. Therefore, I will next outline when and how the values of variables changed over time and how they influenced on the value of B.

Table 6.18: Explaining Bolivia's Failed World Market Integration Strategy

Variable	Variable Dimension	Value (Variance 1985-2004)	Explaining Power for Policy Success/Failure
A1: Institutional	Responsibilities	1985-2004: very low	1985-2004: very high
Strength of State	Resources	1985-2004: very low	1985-2004: rather high
Bureaucracy	Openness	1985-1992: rather low	1985-1992: rather low
		1993-1997: very low	1993-1997: very high
		1998-2004: rather high	1998-2004: rather low
A2: Institutional	Leadership	1985-1997: rather high	1985-1997: rather low
Strength of Business		1998-2004: very low	1998-2004: very high
Associations	Organisational Strength	1985-2004: rather low*	1985-2004: rather high
C1: Heterogeneity Sectoral Preferences		1985-2004: rather low	1985-2004: very low
C2: Heterogeneity Foreign Preferences		1985-2004: rather low	1985-2004: rather low
C3: Political Instability		2000-2004: very high	2003-2004: rather high
C4: Macroeconomic Instability		1997-2003: rather high	1997-2003: rather high

* High in the case of exporters from Santa Cruz, having strong influence on B.

Institutional Strength of State Bureaucracy (A1)

According to Table 6.18, strong explanatory power can mainly be ascribed to Variable A1. Between 1985 and 2004, no clear organisational model for the international trade policy area could be consolidated. In particular, the Foreign Affairs Model was broadly questioned by the private sector because the limited economic branch inside the foreign affairs department could not adequately respond to their concerns and the technical requirements involved in ongoing regional and multilateral challenges *(resources)*.

Moreover, the trade policy drawn up inside the Ministry of Foreign Affairs was developed at a distance from domestic business *(openness)*. Especially, from 1993 to 1997, when Bolivia undertook far-reaching commitments of reciprocal liberalisation with the MERCOSUR and Mexico, the private sector organisations felt shut out of trade policy-making. Hence, Bolivia's international trade policy did not reflect the preferences and possibilities of economic sectors, but relied, above all in the case of the MERCOSUR agreement, on the keenness of the leading diplomats to strengthen the political alliances with the emerging regional bloc in the Southern Cone, who suggested that Bolivia could become a regional hinge between the CAN and MERCOSUR.

Given the widespread distrust of the local trade diplomacy, the business sector sought to empower the trade policy staff outside the Ministry of Foreign Affairs. But the stronger involvement of the staff from the Secretariat of Industry and Trade (1993-97), and the Ministry of Foreign Trade (established in 1997 and dissolved in 2003), primarily caused inter-ministerial struggles for *responsibilities* in the areas of international trade policy and export promotion. Above all, the personal quarrels between key trade policy officials hampered the development of export development strategies, as the emphasis was placed more on inter-ministerial disputes than on improving market access conditions abroad.

For example, together with the Export Development and Taxation Law, in April 1993 the Bolivian government launched the National Export Council (CONEX), which was aimed at building an institutionalised public-private mechanism for concerting proactive policies that foster national exports. But in the aftermath, effective work inside the CONEX was not viable due to the unclear *responsibilities* within the executive branch. In this regard, the reluctance of the Foreign Affairs Ministry to acknowledge the legitimacy of the institution (which was headed by the Ministry of Economic Development and later by the Ministry of Foreign Trade and Investment) stood out.

In the period 2003-2004, as political instability increased and free trade talks with the United States became a concrete option for Bolivia, the institutional deficits of the trade policy branch were abundant considering the ongoing inter-ministerial conflicts and the deteriorating budget resources. As a result, the Bolivian government lacked the necessary authority to convince the population, principally the growing opposition to free trade maintained by social movements, of the benefits of furthering trade liberalisation commitments with the United States.

To a certain extent, previous trade policy failures committed by the government, i.e. opening up the economy without prior consultation and strengthening of economic sectors, influenced negatively on the credibility of governmental attempts to outline the positive impacts anticipated from freer trade with the US.

Institutional Strength of Business Associations (A2)

The failure to open up the economy without undertaking complementary measures aimed at increasing the competitiveness of domestic sectors can hardly be associated with the behaviour of local business associations. Therefore, the unilateral opening of the economy of the mid-1980s was designed by a small inter-ministerial staff inside the Ministries of Planning and Finance, without noteworthy participation of the leading peak and sectoral organisations. Moreover, in the 1990s, it was the private sector organisations, above all the business entities from Santa Cruz, which broadly rejected the wide-reaching liberalisation commitments undertaken by the MERCOSUR agreement in December 1996.

On the other hand, the absence of strong national coordination mechanism in the trade policy area entailed strong counter-productive effects on the development of coherent export promotion schemes. For example, the inter-ministerial conflicts in the scope of CONEX were largely confirmed by the lack of recognised business interlocutors. The National Chamber of Exporters (CANEB), which at one point claimed a monopoly for the private sector representation, had not only been characterised by a precarious administrative structure without holding significant in-house trade policy expertise *(organisational strength)* but increasingly suffered from the internal division between the regional chambers from Santa Cruz and La Paz, respectively *(institutional strength)*. In fact, the chamber from La Paz disaffiliated in 1998, before returning in 2004. Similar conflict patterns were also observable in other national entities, such as the peak association CEPB and the national chamber of industry CNI.

In general, the institutional strength of trade policy advocacy exhibited by the private sector in Santa Cruz was notably higher than in the capital city La Paz. The presence of the business think thank IBCE, which facilitated a high degree of inter-institutional coordination among Santa Cruz entities and a permanent monitoring of international trade policy affairs, largely accounts for the rather successful consolidation of the Andean markets for agricultural products from the lowlands, above all soy exports, which represented 25% of national exports in 2004. In close coordination with Bolivia's official negotiation team, the IBCE staff undertook permanent efforts to guarantee and preserve the Andean markets for soy products. As local exports regularly faced safeguard or discriminatory measures applied by Colombia, Venezuela and Peru, intensive diplomacy in the CAN scope became necessary to obtain and control preferential market access conditions.[65] Furthermore, Bolivia had to repeatedly insist on their Andean partners' prompt application of the Common External Tariff for soy products (15-20 percent) and the Andean Price Band System, which in combination guaranteed higher tariff preferences in the case of low world market prices.[66]

Control Variables C1-C4

Assessing the influence of selected control variables C1-C4, certain disturbing effects on the value of B were observed regarding C3 and C4.

Political Instability (C3): After numerous alternating military regimes and the return to democracy (1982-85) accompanied by economic and social turmoil, from 1985 Bolivia entered a longer phase of political stability that enabled five democratic governments to conclude their terms properly (1985-2002). Increasing political instability began to appear towards the end of the 1990s, nonetheless. Several polemic topics, such as the eradication of coca plants, the engagement of multinational companies in public water supply, possible natural gas exports towards the US via Chilean ports, and the US-AFTA talks, led to a series of social protest and street blockades from workers, indigenous and neighbourhood organisations. Massive riots finally provoked the compulsory retreat of State President Sánchez de Lozada in October 2003. In the aftermath, the transitory presidency of Carlos Mesa (until June 2005) likewise operated on highly unstable grounds, making the political agenda dependent on popular demands such as the referendums which concerned the use of natural gas resources and the convocation of the Constitution Assembly.

Studying the effects on B, the governance crisis experienced, above all, from 2003, subordinated concerns on long-term oriented trade policies. On the other hand, it can be argued that the strong opposition by civil society movements did not primarily jeopardise the ongoing world market integration strategy, for example in struggling against the free trade talks with the

---

[65] In 2002, for example, Colombia imposed safeguard measures of 29 percent tariffs on vegetable oils from the Andean partners; see CAN Resolution 671. Other measures applied by Colombia were related to a differential VAT treatment according the value added on imported products. For recent restrictions taken by Venezuela during 2005, the principal buyer's market, see *El Nuevo Día* 18/08/2005 or IBCE publication *Comercio Exterior*; March 2005.

[66] The purpose of this system, in force since February 1995, is to stabilise domestic prices for palm oil, soybean oil, rice, sugar, barley, milk, corn, soybeans, wheat, chicken, and pork, among others. Thus, when the international bench mark price falls below a predetermined minimum level, member countries will apply a variable-rate surcharge on imports of such products, over and above the CET. Likewise, when the international bench mark price rises above a certain ceiling, the member countries will lower the normal tariff rate to reduce the import cost of the staple.

US, but has to be seen as a reaction to the failed process of economic opening, in which domestic constraints had not been adequately considered.

Regarding the *macroeconomic instability (C4)*, after experiencing rampant hyperinflation in the mid-1980s, Bolivia was able to control inflationary pressure during the whole period of analysis. From 1997 to 2004, however, the Bolivian State suffered under high budget deficits of 3 percent and beyond. Between 2001 and 2004, the corresponding rate even moved between 6 and 9 percent, and thus, offered a deprived panorama for the expansion of sector-specific and export promotion facilities, an indispensable element of the Multipolar Model (B).

Studying the *sectoral preferences (C1)*, heterogeneous interests were mostly observed along the regional lines, i.e. while the lowland producers from Santa Cruz have been interested in preserving the domestic market for their agriculture and forestry products, La Paz has sought cheaper prime materials for its food processing and furniture industry. Nevertheless, since the highest tariff rate applied by the Bolivian government does not exceed 10%, the presence of strong multisectoral business organisations should have allowed for the reconciliation of these opposing sectoral views.

Preferences of others countries (C2): Bolivia's trade policy has been virtually unaffected by other countries, disregarding specific market access restrictions for various agricultural goods and industrial manufactures. In general, the country has been widely granted with a special and differentiated treatment. For example, Bolivia recieved, in contrast to Peru, exemption from the Andean CET (not applying the higher tariff levels of 15 and 20%). Although rather opposed to by the CAN membership, moreover, Bolivia pursued a Multipolar strategy in negotiating a bilateral FTA with the MERCOSUR.

6.5 References

Literature

Arano, Lorgio and Gary Rodríguez (2003). *Análisis del Comercio Exterior de Bolivia y Aprovechamiento de Acuerdos Preferenciales.* Santa Cruz de la Sierra: IBCE/SECO/Universidad Sur.

CAN (2005). *Informe sobre el Estado de Situación del Programa de Liberación entre Perú y el Resto de Países de la Comunidad Andina.* August 2005. Lima: CAN General Secretariat.

Conaghan, Catherine and James Malloy (1994). *Unsettling Statecraft. Democracy and Neoliberalism in the Central Andes.* London: University of Pittsburgh Press.

Brenes, E., Madrigal, K. and Montenegro, D. (2001). *El Cluster de la Soja en Bolivia: Diagnóstico Competitivo y Recomendaciones Estratégicas.* Proyecto Andino de Competitividad (CAF)/Instituto Centroamericano de Empresas (INCAE).

Devlin, Robert and Antoni Estevadeordal (2001). *What's New in the New Regionalism in the Americas?.* Working Paper 6. Washington DC: Inter-American Development Bank.

IBCE/CADEX (1993). *Bolivia en el Contexto de la Integración Latinoamericana: La Visión del Sector Exportador Cruceño.* Santa Cruz de la Sierra.

Instituto de Investigaciones Económicas-UMSA (2003). *¿ALCA?.* Dinámica Económica. No. 12.

Kreidler, Alfonso and Antonio Rocha (2004). *El Contrabando en Bolivia. Una visión Heterodoxa.* Santa Cruz de la Sierra: IBCE/ SECO.

Larrazabal, Córdova et. al (2000). *Ajuste Estructural y Desarrollo Productivo en Bolivia.* La Paz: Centro de Estudios para el Desarrollo Laboral y Agrario (CEDLA).

Mansilla, Hugo C. F. (1994). *La Empresa Privada Boliviana y el Proceso de Democratización.* La Paz: Fundación Milenio.

Morales, Juan A. and Jeffry Sachs (1990). "Bolivia's Economic Crisis" Pp.157-268 in *Developing Countries' Debt and Economic Performance, Vol. 2,* edited by Sachs J. Chicago: The University of Chicago Press.

Niño Tarazona, Jaime Andrés (2003). *Elementos para el Diseño de una Estrategia del Integración en el Sector Servicios para los Países de la Comunidad Andina en el Contexto de las Negociaciones del ALCA y la Ronda Doha de la OMC.* Universidad de Bogotá/ CAN General Secretariat.

Rodriguez, Gary (2004). *Apertura Económica y Exportaciones en Bolivia: El Papel del Estado (1980- 2003).* Santa Cruz de la Sierra: IBCE/ SECO/ Universidad Autónoma Gabriel Rene Moreno.

Sanjinés Avila, Ricardo (2004). *Los Empresarios en la Historia. Biografía de la Empresa Privada Boliviana.* Volume I.- III. La Paz: CEPB.

UPC (2002). Sistema Boliviano de Productividad y Competitividad -SBPC- (2002). *Estado de Situación de la Competitividad en Bolivia.* La Paz: Unidad de Productividad y Competitividad.

Vaca Calderón, Patricia and Sául Antonio Soliz Salinas (2001*). La Inserción de Productos Manufacturados Bolivianos en el Mercado Mundial. Factores de Estabilidad e Inestabilidad.* La Paz: CEDLA.

Waldmann, Adrian (2001). "Geschichte, Wirtschaft und Identität in Santa Cruz de la Sierra: Soy Camba, y qué ?" in *Bolivien: Das verkannte Land*, edited by Sevilla, R. and Benavides A. Bad Honnef: Horlemann.

WTO (1999). *Trade Policy Review Bolivia. Report by the WTO Secretariat.* WT/TPR/S/57.

WTO (2005). *Trade Policy Review Bolivia. Report by the WTO Secretariat.* WT/TPR/S/154.

Zambrana Calvimonte, Humberto (2002). *La Apertura Externa en Bolivia.* La Paz: Unidad de Análisis de Políticas Sociales y Económicas (UDAPE).

Other Documents

CADEX (2001). "Evaluación y Perspectiva de la Participación Boliviana en el ALCA" by Ana Maria Solares, Pp.34-35 in *Foro ALCA-Bolivia. Necesidad de una Visión Estratégica Compartida.* Santa Cruz de la Sierra.

CAINCO (2003). *El Aporte de Santa Cruz a Bolivia. Santa Cruz Ratifica su Liderazgo Productivo y Competitivo en Bolivia.* Santa Cruz de la Sierra: CEBEC.

Comercio Exterior Journal (March 2005). Santa Cruz: Situación Actual y Perspectivas de la Oferta Exportable. No. 130. Santa Cruz de la Sierra: IBCE.

Comercio Exterior Journal (April 2005). La Paz: Situación Actual y Perspectivas de la Oferta Exportable. No. 131. Santa Cruz de la Sierra: IBCE.

CONEX (2004a-e). *Actas de la 1ª, 2ª, 3ª, 4ª, 5ª Reunión Ordinaria del Consejo Nacional de Exportaciones* "CONEX". 11/05/04; 4/08/04; 31/08/04; 5/11/04; 14/12/04.

DBLA (2005). *Economic Research. Latin American Database. Country Indicators from 1980 to 2004.*

Diario Hoy Newspaper (27/02/97). "CNI: la Industria Boliviana entrará en desventaja al MERCOSUR".

El Deber Newspaper (03/08/95). "Posición del CEPB. No debe Precipitarse la Negociación con el MERCOSUR."

El Nuevo Día Newspaper (18/08/05). "Las Medidas que Venezuela aplica a las Exportaciones de Soya Boliviana dejarán Grandes Pérdidas Económicas y de Empleo."

"Guidelines for a National Export Development Strategy" (2001). *Primer Convención Nacional de Exportadores*, November 26, 2001. Cochabamba: CANEB/ Vice-Ministry of Exports/ SECO.

IBCE (1997). *Memoria Institucional del IBCE. 12 años al Servicio de Bolivia. 1986-1997.* Santa Cruz de la Sierra.

INE-UDAPE-IBCE (2003). *Compendio Estadístico de Comercio Exterior: Bolivia 1980-2002.* La Paz.

INE-UDAPE-IBCE (2004). *Anuario Estadístico de Exportaciones – Bolivia 2003.* La Paz.

Jornada Newspaper (14/12/04). "Conflictos Sociales se Profundizarán el 2005 por Ingreso al TLC."

La Estrella del Oriente Newspaper (27/11/96). "Di Tella No Sabe si es Chiste. Critican a Empresarios Argentinos por Temor a competir con Bolivia."

La Razón Newspaper (09/03/97). "Empresarios: Bolivia Encaró una Negociación Desigual con el MERCOSUR."

La Razón Newspaper (04/07/04). Letter Directed to State President Carlos Mesa from the Santa Cruz Chamber of Exporters.

La Razón Newspaper (13/10/05). Postponement of FTA talks with the US for 2006.

MDE (2004a). *Personograma Despacho del Ministro de Desarrollo Económico.*

MDE (2004b). *Planilla Presupuestaria.* Vice-Ministry of Industry, Commerce and Exports.

MDE (2004c). *Participación de Bolivia en las Negociaciones del TLC con EE.UU.*

Ministry of Finance and Economic Development (1993). *Estado de Ejecución Presupuestaria de Gastos de la Administración Central por Entidades y Fuentes de Financiamiento.* Secretary of Finance.

SIGMA (2001-2005). *Estadísticas de Presupuesto y Ejecución por Entidad-Dirección Administrativa-Unidad Ejecutora.* Sistema Integrado de Gestión y Modernización Administrativa.

VICE (2004). *Boletin Estadistico, Enero-Diciembre 2004.* General Directorate of Foreign Trade.

VREI (2004). *Reunión Informativa Negociaciones Comerciales* (OMC-ALCA-CAN-MERCOSUR). Circular VREI-DIH-C-090/2004-02-13.

Interviews

OUTSIDE EXPERTS (OE)				
Date	Name	Type	Organization	Function
08.03.2003	Jurado, Wilfredo	NEI	International Trade Center (UNCTAD/WTO)	International Consultant; Export Development
16.03.2004	Pérez, Abraham	Survey	UMSA/ Institute for Economic Studies	Professor of Economics
18.03.2004	Chavez, Gonzalo	Survey	Catholic University/ Master Program for Development	Professor of Economics and Development Studies
18.03.2004	Mercado, Alejandro	Survey	Catholic University/ Institute of Socio-Economic Research (IISEC)	Economists; Director IISEC
18.03.2004	Peredo, Luis Fernando	Survey	British Department of International Cooperation (DIFID)	Consultant; Ex-Vice-Minister of Exports
19.03.2004	Villegas, Carlos	Survey, NEI	UMSA-CIDES/ Master Program on Development Science	Economist; Director CIDES
23.03.2004	Gutiérez, Osvaldo	Survey	National Council of Economists of Bolivia	President; Policy Advisor of State and Business Entities
19.03.2004	Castillo Simbrón, Max	Survey	Bolivian Association of International Political Economy	President; Ex-UMSA Professor in International Law
20.07.2004	Garcia, Luis Fernando	Survey	Private University of Bolivia, Santa Cruz	Professor of Economics
22.03.2004 20.07.2004 27.07.2004 17.01.2005	*Rodríguez, Gary (Selected Interview Partner)*	*Survey, NEI*	*IBCE; University NUR/ Master on International Trade*	*IBCE Managing Director; Professor of International Trade*
08.06.2004	Campbell, Jorge	NEI	IMCG Consulting	Consultant; Argentinean Chief Negotiator 1994-1999
22.07.2004	Serrate, Guillermo	Survey	Autonomous University „Gabriel Rene Moreno"/ Department of Economics	Director; Rural Development Studies
24.07.2004	Escobar, Emilio Javier	Survey	Autonomous University „Gabriel Rene Moreno"/ Department of Economy	Professor of Economics; Expert in International Economy
29.07.2004	Becerra, Marco	NEI	Cochabamba Chamber of Customs Agents	Managing Director; Ex-MCEI Official
04.08.2004	Vaca Calderón, Patricia	Survey	Study Center of Labor and Rural Development (CEDLA)	Economist, Expert in Foreign Trade and Economic Policy
10.08.2004	Zelada, Alberto	Survey, NEI	Andean University Simón Bolívar/ Master on International Economic Law	Legal Expert in Foreign Economic Relations; Ex-Director UDAPEX
10.08.2004	Nuñez, Walter	Survey	Bolivian Competitiveness in Commerce and Business (BCCN)	USAID Contractor; Ex-Minister of Agriculture and CAO Managing Director
10.08.2004	Rojas Ulo, Edwin	Survey	UMSA-CIDES/ Master Program on Development	Professor of Economics; Expert in Industrial Policy

			Science	and Public Investment
13.08.2004	Kruse, Thomas	Survey	Study Centre of Labour and Rural Development (CEDLA)	Expert in International Economy
18.01.2005	Tercero, Francisco	NEI	Santa Cruz Department Authorities	Director Productive Development; EX-Trade Diplomat and Managing Director of IBCE and CADEX
21.01.2005	Guzman, Adhemar	NEI	PCAB-Andean Community of Nations	International Consultant; Ex-Vice-Minister of Exports
08.02.2005	Larrazabal, Juan	NEI	Andean Community of Nations	International Functionary; Ex-Bolivian Trade Diplomat
15.02.2005	Olmos, Julio	NEI	Andean Community of Nations	International Functionary, Ex- Business Trade Policy Advisor

STATE OFFICIALS (SO)

Date	Name	Type	Agency	Function
16.03.2004 11.08.2004	Otálora, Carmen	Survey, NEI	Ministry of Foreign Affairs/ Vice-Ministry of International Economic Relations (VREI)	Trade Diplomat; ALADI and Market Access Affairs
16.03.2004 15.12.2004	*De Rico, Helen (Selected Interview Partner)*	*Survey, NEI*	*VREI*	*Director of Hemispheric Affairs; Ex-SEGIN and MCEI Official*
17.03.2004 02.08.2004	Chavez, Rosa	Survey, NEI	MDE/Vice-Ministry of Industry, Commerce and Exports (VICE)	General Secretary CONEX; Trade Diplomat
18.03.2004	Invernizzi, Gustavo	Survey	VREI	Trade Diplomat; Advisor in the Vice-Ministerial Office
19.03.2004 14.12.2004	Montaña, José	Survey, NEI	VICE	Trade Policy Advisor in the Vice-Ministerial Office
19.03.2004 16.12.2004	Alvagardo, Julio	Survey	VREI	General Director of Integration; Coordinator of the US-AFTA talks
05.08.2004	Chambi, Irina	Survey	MDE/Vice-Ministry of Micro and Small Scale Producers	Policy Advisor; SME Trade Promotion
05.08.2004	Peñaranda, Marco	Survey	MDE/Vice-Ministry of Micro and Small Scale Producers	Advisor in the Vice-Ministerial Office
05.08.2004	Zambrana, Humberto	Survey, NEI	MDE/UDAPE	UDAPE Annalist; Area "External Sector"
09.08.2004	Velázquez, Paola	Survey	VICE	Policy Advisor; Foreign Trade and Statistics Affairs
09.08.2004	Jimenez, Andrés	Survey	Ministry of Agriculture	Director of Agriculture Markets
10.08.2004 24.01.2005	Cortez, Juan Carlos	NEI	MDE	Director of Human Resources

12.08.2004	Torres, William	Survey	Ministry of Foreign Affairs/UDAPEX	Director UDAPEX
13.08.2004	De Rico, Katerine	Survey	Ministry of Finance/ Vice-Ministry of Tax Policy	Chief of Area "Tariffs and Integration"
14.12.2004	Miranda, Giovanna	NEI	VREI	Trade Diplomat since the 1980s
17.12.2004	Rodriguez, Zandra	NEI	VREI	Director of South American Integration
24.01.2005	*Arana, Manuel (Selected Interview Partner)*	*NEI*	*VICE*	*General Director of Industry*

BUSINESS REPRESENTATIVES (BR)

Date	Name	Type	Entity	Function
15.03.2004 05.08.2004 12.08.2004	*Fernandez, Soraya (Selected Interview Partner)*	*Survey NEI*	*IBCE-La Paz Representation*	*Managing Director*
16.03.2004	Pardo, Luis	Survey	CNI	Sub-Managing Director
17.03.2004	Quiroga Patiño, José	Survey	La Paz Federation of Private Entrepreneurship	Sub-Managing Director
23.03.2004	Menacho, Carlos	Survey	CADEX	Sub-Managing Director
23.03.2004	Bowles, Arturo	Survey	Bolivian Forestry Chamber (CFB)	Managing Director
24.03.2004	Arano, Lorgio	Survey	IBCE	Head of Trade Policy Advisory Unit
24.03.2004	Nogales, Walter	Survey	Santa Cruz Chamber of Small Scale Industry (CADEPIA)	President
25.03.2004	Cirbián, Mario	Survey	CAINCO	Sub-Managing Director
26.03.2004	Antelo, Juan Armando	Survey	Eastern Chamber of Agriculture	President
26.03.2004	Kempff, Julio	Survey	Santa Cruz Federation of Private Entrepreneurship	Managing Director
23.07.2004	Zabala, Rolando/ Rojas, Carlos	Survey, NEI	ANAPO	Managing Director/President
26.07.2004	Cirbián, Luis Alfredo	Survey	Santa Cruz Federation of Livestock Farming (FEGASACRUZ)	Annalist Planning Department
26.07.2004	Cardona, Gregorio	Survey	Association of Vegetable and Fruit Producers (ASOHFRUT)	Vice-President
28.07.2004	Barrios, Juan Carlos	Survey	Association of Beans Producers (ASOPROF)	Managing Director
28.07.2004	Cortéz, Mamerto	Survey	National Association of Maize, Sorghum, Beans and sunflower (PROMASOR)	Managing Director
29.07.2004	Loayza, Jimena	Survey	Cochabamba Chamber of Exporters (CADEXCO)	Managing Director

29.07.2004	Grájeda, Nathalie	Survey	Cochabamba Chamber of Industry	Trade Policy Advisor
29.07.2004	Avila, Richard Alvarez	Survey	Cochabamba Chamber of Commerce and Services	Managing Director
30.07.2004	Candia, Ramiro	Survey	Cochabamba Chamber of Small Scale Industry (CADEPIA)	General Coordinator
30.07.2004	Lujan, Ronny	Survey	Bolivian Federation of Small Scale Industry (FEBOPI)	President
02.08.2004	Endara, José	Survey	CNC	Head of Foreign Trade Department
02.08.2004	Mendoza, José	Survey	Bolivian Chamber of Automobiles	Assistant
03.08.2004	Uriona, Hugo	Survey	National Association of Medium Sized Mining	General Secretary
03.08.2004	Collao, Katya	Survey	Association of Micro Finance Entities (ASOFIN)	Economic Policy Advisor
03.08.2004 12.12.2004	Estivariz, Augusto	Survey, NEI	Bolivian Chamber of Brewery (CABOFACE)	Legal Advisor; former CEPB General Secretary
03.08.2004	Abvanad, Ana	Survey	Bolivian Chamber of Telecommunication (CATELBO)	Assistant
03.08.2004	Arduz, Fernando	Survey	Bolivian Chamber of Electricity (CBE)	Managing Director
03.08.2004	Ramos, Maria Luisa	Survey	Coordinator of Small Scale Farming Unit Organizations of Bolivia (CIOEC)	Annalist of Agrarian Policy
05.08.2004	Rojas, Ronald	Survey	CEPB	Director of Foreign Trade
05.08.2004	Kuhn, José	Survey	CAMEX	Managing Director
05.08.2004	Balcazar, Ana Carola	Survey	CANEB	Managing Director
09.08.2004	Dueñas, Erika	Survey	Chamber of the Bolivian Pharmaceutical Industry (CIFABOL)	Managing Director
09.08.2004	De los Angeles, María	NEI	CIFABOL	Legal Advisor
09.08.2004	Carpio Díaz, Gonzalo	Survey	CADEPIA – La Paz	Managing Director
11.08.2004	Baudoin, Carlos	Survey	Bolivian Association of Assurances (ABA)	Managing Director
09.08.2004	Custer, Elisabeth	Survey	Bolivian Association of Private Banks (ASOBAN)	Economic Policy Advisor
11.08.2004	Hinojosa, Javier	Survey	Chamber of Construction (CADECO)	Managing Director
13.12.2004	Glover Paz	NEI	CANEB	President
13.12.2004	Cabrera, Cecilia	NEI	IBCE – La Paz	Trade Policy Advisor; Ex-MCEI Official
20.01.2005	Gastelu, Max	NEI	CEPB	Director of Institutional Affairs; Ex-Trade Diplomat

Selected Interview Partners

Arana, Manuel: Economic Professor at the Catholic University. Manuel Arana started his career as a trade diplomat in the 1970s as a Bolivian functionary inside the Andean Group. Between 1976 and 1982, Arana worked inside the General Secretariat of Integration (SEGIN) as one of the country's principal negotiators within the ongoing regional integration, ALALC, ALADI and Andean Group. Later he worked for the Andean Development Corporation CAF until 1986. In the last 20 years, Manuel Arana was occupied as a university professor in economics and an economic policy advisor for several business and state institutions, standing out in his position as Chief of the Economic Department inside the peak association CEPB during the 1990s and as General Director of Industry within the 2003-04 period.

De Rico, Helen: Economist. In 1983, Helen De Rico became a trade policy advisor inside SEGIN. In 1987, the SEGIN staff was incorporated into the Ministry of Foreign Affairs. During the government of Gonzalo Sanchez de Lozada (1993-97), she worked inside the Secretariat of Industry and Trade in charge of international trade policy affairs. Within the following administration of Hugo Banzer (1997-2002), Helen De Rico became part of the erected Ministry of Foreign Trade and Investment, again attending the area of international negotiations. By 2003, she returned to the Ministry of Foreign Affairs and has been heading the Hemispheric Division inside the General Directorate of Integration, thus, becoming Bolivia's principal negotiator within the FTAA talks.

Fernandez, Soraya: Trade Policy Advisor. Soraya Fernandez worked between 1986 and 1988 first as a junior official inside the Foreign Trade Division of the Ministry of Industry and Trade. In the following nine years, she became part of the established Export Promotion Authority, INPEX. From 1997 to 2003, Soraya Fernandez headed the Foreign Trade Department in the National Chamber of Industry. Finally, as of April 2004, she started to establish a business trade policy branch in La Paz within the scope of the Bolivian Institute of Foreign Trade. Therefore, Fernandez assumed the Technical Secretariat position inside the Foreign Trade Commission of the peak association CEPB.

Rodríguez, Gary: Economist with an MA in International Commerce from the Autonomous University "Gabriel René Moreno," and author of the book, *Economic Opening and Exports in Bolivia: The Role of State (1980-2003).* Gary Rodríguez has worked for the Bolivian Institute of Foreign Trade since its creation in 1986, first as of Head of the Technical Division, and as of 1996 as its Managing Director. In the last 15 years, he has therefore evolved as the principal trade policy advisor of Bolivia's private sector, and particularly of the Santa Cruz Department.

7   Conclusions

Since the mid-1980s, the patterns of world market integration have transformed significantly, and therein, have particularly challenged the capabilities of development nations. Given a general tendency towards trade liberalisation, and the inclusion of developing nations into multilateral and regional trade regulatory frameworks, the essence of trade policy-making no longer refers to the level of national tariffs, but to the need for permanent coordination among a broad set of policy areas, covering both border and behind-the-border measures, parallel negotiations on different international levels, and the complex incorporation of trade agreements into national laws. For the purpose of this study, therefore, a successful world market integration strategy has been conceptualised as a *"high degree of coherence reached by implementing a particular set of trade related policies that developing countries adopt within a context of gradual liberalisation of the global economy and a shift of trade policy-making towards regional and multilateral levels, considering to what extent essential principals, policies, and objectives of the selected strategy have been put into practice and maintained over the period of analysis (1985 to 2004)."*

However, existing theories on trade policy mainly focus on the preferences of domestic actors, and refer to the redistributive character of trade policies that are manifested at given moments. In this respect, International Political Economy literature conceives trade decisions as conflict management among economic sectors that face dramatic changes in the rules that govern their markets (Milner 1988; Hillman 1989; Frieden 1991; Rodrik 1995; Hiscox 2002). Based on sectoral approaches, the outcomes of such processes are explained by analysing the political behaviour of export-oriented industries that favour liberalisation, and respectively, the import-competing sector that is affected by reform steps.

But this traditional view on the "politics of trade reforms" needs to be complemented in light of the current challenges of world market integration. Particularly, in this thesis I examined the effects of institutions involved in the domestic policy-making process, that is, formal and informal rules which shape the behaviour of collective actors, analysing to what extent these factors favour, or hinder, the success of world market integration strategies. In this regard, the study focused on the state bureaucracy and business associations. The analysis of the complex internal structures of the state bureaucracy, defined as the executive branch in charge of trade policy, proved particularly revealing due to its central position in the conduction of international trade policy affairs, considering that in developing countries the involvement of the legislative branch is often very limited. Conversely, business associations, i.e. trade and industrial chambers, and peak and sectoral organisations, are not only expected to assume the task of intermediating among the economic sectors affected by trade policy rules, but should also have key trade data at their disposal, such as growth perspectives, consumer trends, technological innovation, fiscal and labour regulations, sanitary rules and technical obstacles. In light of these institutional imperatives, this book has sought to find answers to the following research question: *How, and to what extent, does the success of world market integration strategies in developing countries depend on the institutional strength of state bureaucracies and business associations?*

In analysing institutional factors of state bureaucracies and business associations, I draw mostly on existing theoretical Neo-Institutionalism insights, such as Schmitter and Streeck (1999) and Peter Evans (1995). Accordingly, the institutional strength of collective actors (parties, interest groups, etc.) relies on stable and predictable rules and norms which govern interactions among actors. But unlike individuals acting in particular social contexts, the behaviour of collective actors is determined by the internal structural constraints of involved organisations. Hence, the outcome of collective action cannot be seen as the simple aggregate of individual preferences, but as a result of several factors influencing, or filtering, collective actors' interests, such as internal decision-making procedures, the number of actors involved, common resources and principals.

Regarding the collective action of entrepreneurs, the institutional strength of business associations is related to the complicated, intermediary position between two independent and resourceful actors – firms on one side, and state authorities on the other. So as not to be overlooked, a business association is obliged to insert itself into the direct exchange of market actors and state authorities, by offering a service at a beneficial price or quality, according to the neocorporatist logic sustained by Schmitter and Streeck (1999: 19). Therefore, the *institutional strength of business associations* is defined as the capacity of organisations that represent private sector interests – i.e. trade and industrial chambers, business councils, peak entities, farmers organisations, entities representing specific sectors or branches – to effectively intermediate the often opposing preferences within the private sector, and simultaneously, to maintain close relations with state authorities.

In the case of state bureaucracies, institutional strength concerns the structures and norms that determine the work inside the executive branch and the way other non-state actors, especially business agents, are incorporated into the trade policy-policy making process. With this, it is indicated that the behaviour of bureaucrats is not simply guided by an obvious, clearly defined "public interest", but by the outcome of multifaceted interaction patterns with other state and non-state actors.

Bearing in mind the rampant corruption and rent-seeking behaviour commonly found in developing countries, Peter Evans' concept of Embedded Autonomy (1995) combines the strength of bureaucratic structures with two seemingly opposing features: *First,* a high degree of autonomy, or insulation, of policy makers from societal pressure, in order to reduce rent-seeking opportunities. *Second,* bureaucrats require the capacity to maintain fluent relations with the business sector through channels that allow the permanent negotiation and monitoring of economic goals and policies, in order to fine-tune and adapt public policies to the possibilities of economic sectors responsible for efficient strategy/policy implementation. In this study, the notion of Embedded Autonomy was adapted to the underlying context and objectives. Hence, *the institutional strength of state bureaucracy* was conceptualised as an executive branch, wherein the responsibilities, as regards the conduction of international trade policy affairs, are clearly perceived, the trade policy staff are adequately doted, and finally, a degree of openness is sustained towards business and non-business regarding their incorporation into the trade policy-making process.

Regarding the effects of the institutional strength of state and business organisations on the outcome of trade policy-making, the analytical framework developed in this book was built upon the following *test hypothesis*: *The success of world market integration strategies in developing countries (Dependent Variable B) depends on the institutional strength of state bureaucracies (Independent Variable A1) and business associations (Independent Variable A2).*

As mentioned, a successful world market integration strategy is conceptualised as a "high degree of coherence reached by implementing a particular set of trade related policies that developing countries adopt within a context of gradual liberalisation of the global economy and a shift of trade policy making towards regional and multilateral levels, considering to what extent essential principals, policies, and objectives of the selected strategy have been put into practice and maintained over the period of analysis (1985 to 2004)." The measurement of the degree of coherence took as reference two idealistic modes of world market integration, which were both pursued in South America in the given time period: the Multipolar Model, based on the creation of a dense network of bilateral free trade agreements in- and outside the region, and the Springboard Model, which focuses on deeper forms of regional integration so as to establish a common regional market and a customs union (see Table 2). It was further assumed – but not analysed in this study – that a coherently implemented world market integration strategy contributes to improve the trade performance of a country, and finally, to achieve the goal of economic growth and, simultaneously, poverty reduction.

To mitigate such disturbing influences as economy, culture, geography and politics, the focus of this study was narrowed down to South American countries, thus ensuring *similar background conditions* between the cases. Moreover, the countries selected – Argentina, Bolivia, Chile and Peru – held in common their traditional dependence on commodity exports (and thus had clear incentives to foster diversification), as well as the implementation of far-reaching market reforms coupled with the transition from authoritarian to democratic rules, which both took place during the last two decades. Other case selection criteria were *extreme values on the study variable* and *varia*nce both in-case and between cases, and *the access to data*. Despite this, to ensure that the value of B was not caused by a factor other than A1+2, I controlled the influence of another four variables; *Heterogeneity of Sectoral Preferences (C1)*, *Heterogeneity of Foreign Preferences (C2)*, *Political Instability (C3)*, *Macroeconomic Instability (C4)*.

The propositions of the analytical framework were investigated by means of case studies derived from one developing region: Since the 1980s, South America has become a paradigmatic case in order to understand the modern challenges of world market integration. South American States not only embarked upon wide-reaching market reforms (mainly as a consequence of the debt crisis of the 1980s) and adhered to the WTO system, but made intensive use of reciprocal forms of liberalisation. Regarding this latter point, countries' involvement in regional liberalisation schemes became especially widespread. In this respect, both the customs union agreements of the Common Market of the South, or "MERCOSUR" (Brazil, Argentina, Paraguay, and Uruguay) and the Andean Group (Colombia, Peru, Venezuela, Bolivia, and Ecuador) stand out, as do numerous bilateral preferential trade agreements, both between Latin American countries, and with trading partners in Europe, North America, and Asia. But despite this general tendency towards economic liberalisation, and a major integration into regional and multilateral regulatory schemes, there is significant variance regarding the policy success of each country.

Case Study 1: Chile went through several different stages during the process of adopting an exemplary Multipolar Model. Military leaders (Chile maintained an authoritarian regime from 1973 to 1989) can take credit for putting in practice the so-called "flat rate" regime and the wide-reaching export promotion schemes that were implemented as of 1985. But the cornerstone of the current trade policy was launched under democratic ruling, i.e. it was in the 1990s when the Southern Cone State evolved into a world wide pioneer of New Regionalism. Inside Latin America, Chile's trade integration advanced more than in any other country, through the signing of bilateral Free Trade Agreements (FTAs) with practically every Latin American State. Later, from 1996, emphasis was placed on strengthening extra-regional ties. Through so-called "latest generation" FTAs, involving a broad range of new trade topics, with North American, European and Asian countries, the small emerging economy became an attractive partner in trade and investments for the big players of the world economy. As a result of these combined efforts, Chile registered impressive export growth rates as well as a significant export diversification based on non-traditional export champions, such as lumber, cellulose products, fruits, vegetables, salmon, wines and various manufactured goods.

Case Study 2: Argentina's strategy for world market integration was far less successful than that of its neighbour country. Although responsible for an innovative, proactive Integration Programme for Economic Cooperation (PICE) with Brazil (1986-1989), this approach, which aimed to gradually search for industrial complementarities in specific sectors, received major revision from 1990 onwards. Aside from far-reaching unilateral trade reforms, the MERCOSUR, founded in March 1991, took on a universal and automatic liberalisation approach (rather than a gradual, sector-specific one), by setting a four year timeframe for full liberalisation, and thus favouring the fast expansion of intra-zone trade in sectors where Argentina enjoyed comparative advantages, such as petrochemicals and food processing.

In the aftermath, however, a coherent implementation of this world market integration strategy based on the MERCOSUR became undermined by several factors. *First,* the goal of establishing a common regional market and a customs union (in line with the Springboard Model), which demanded common external trade policies and the harmonisation of behind-the-border measures, stood in contradiction to Argentina's economic policy. Hence, the implementation of the regional integration objectives stagnated, as Argentina and the other member states failed to assume the MERCOSUR as a reference scheme for unilateral policy-making. In general, the observable lack of intra-MERCOSUR cohesion, and a loss of international credibility, hindered the group's ability to act as a powerful trading block, both inside and outside Latin America. For example, virtually all external negotiations launched became deadlocked. *Second,* several permanent and temporary exceptions from the liberal trade regime persisted. Furthermore, the fact that such protectionist measures were applied in an uncoordinated, ad-hoc manner underlined the high unpredictability of domestic trade policies and the lack of clarity related to the strategy for each sectors' world market integration. *Third,* while sector-specific policies were absent (except for the automotive regime), official export promotion facilities suffered from the combination of frequent modifications, modest resources and a high degree of institutional fragmentation.

Case Study 3: In 1991, Peru implemented far-reaching market reforms, in which trade liberalisation was a cornerstone. In a strategy strongly influenced by the Chilean experience, the country sought to adopt a "modern" flat rate tariff, and to define individual forms of trade integration by leaving the Andean Group (later Andean Community of Nations - CAN) where members pursued a Common External Tariff (CET) based on a four-tier structure. Nevertheless, the desired policy goals failed to materialise. Rather than setting forth vigorous bilateral trade diplomacy, in 1997 Peru returned to the CAN without making any clear commitment to comply with the ongoing Andean integration process. In fact, the controversies on the Common External Tariff (CET) had yet to be resolved by the end of the period of analysis. Furthermore, the flat rate model pursued by Peru has not been reached thus far, and indeed, as of 2002 Peru has been applying seven different tariff lines.

By the beginning of the new millennium Peru had attained certain policy success, nonetheless, discerning significant progress in assuming a Multipolar Model. The country set forth a rather active trade policy, combining the strengthening of trade relations with the US, the Pacific Area, and MERCOSUR, with the implementation of the National Export Strategy 2003-2013. Though the pursued model had not been consolidated at the time of writing, the trade policy applied in the final years of th study period differed notably from the passive and incoherent trade policy sustained in the 1990s.

Case Study 4: The Bolivian experience can be considered an outright failure. The impoverished, landlocked Andean country opened up its economy in 1985, abandoning such policies as tariff ceilings, price regulations and subsidies, and became one of the earliest reformers in Latin America. Later, during the 1990s Bolivia signed several far-reaching trade arrangements in the multilateral, and above all, regional spheres. The FTAs signed with the CAN (itself being a CAN member), MERCOSUR, and Mexico were of particular importance.

But since no significant support schemes for exporters were put into practice, such as market assistance, fiscal incentives or sector-specific measures, the enhanced market access opportunities remained largely unexploited. In light of the massive structural shortcomings faced by the local entrepreneurship (market size, infrastructure, technology, etc.), the distinctive liberal trade regime primarily caused large trade deficits. In recent years, the market-led, outward-looking strategy became drastically opposed to by civil society actors, such as indigenous groups, workers, NGOs and state universities. Above all, the government's intention to strengthen trade relations with the US caused major domestic social unrest. Furthermore, the blind search for "trade openness" was responsible, along with other factors, for the increasing destabilisation of the political system, which began to materialise as of the year 2000.

In this final chapter of the book I summarise and compare the results of the empirical case studies, proceeding as follows. In the first part, I show how, when and to what extent the policy failure/success observed in the four countries from 1985 to 2004 was caused by the Institutional Strength of State Bureaucracy (the Independent Variable A1). In the second part, the explanatory power of the Independent Variable A2, the Institutional Strength of Business Associations, will be discussed. In the third part, I discuss whether, and to what extent, third variable influences, represented by C1-C4, became responsible for the values of B. In the final part, all the variable influences are presented for comparative purposes.

Studying Table 7.1, the empirical results suggest that A1 exhibits a high explanatory power throughout all of the cases and periods of analysis, becoming in several occasion the key factor that accounts for the observed intra-case variances. In general, the relevance of the variable dimensions *Responsibilities* (division of labour and inter-ministerial coordination) and *Openness* (state-business coordination and transparency) seem slightly higher than *Resources* (trade policy staff).

Table 7.1: The Institutional Strength of State Bureaucracy (A1)

		Chile	Argentina	Peru	Bolivia
Value of A1	Responsi-bilities	85-94: rather low 95-04: very high	85-87: rather high 88-04: rather low	85-01: rather low 02-04: rather high	85-04: very low
	Resources	85-94: rather low 95-04: rather high	85-04: rather high	85-90: rather high 91-01: very low 02-04: rather high	85-04: very low
	Openness	85-04: very high	85-89: rather high 90-95: very low 96-04: rather high	85-98: rather high 99-04: very high	85-92: rather low 93-97: very low 98-04: rather high
Effect on B (Policy Failure/ Success)	Responsi-bilities	85-94: rather high 95-04: very high	85-04: very high	85-04: very high	85-04: very high
	Resources	85-04: rather high	85-88: rather high	85-04: rather high	85-04: rather high
	Openness	85-04: very high	85-89: rather low 90-95: rather high 96-04: rather low	85-98: rather low 99-04: very high	85-92: rather low 93-97: very high 98-04: rather low

In *Chile,* the emergence of a broadly accepted Foreign Affairs Model (*responsibilities*) as of 1995, embodied in the institutional strengthening of the General Directorate of International Economic Affairs (DIRECON), proved to be decisive for the successful Multipolar approach to world market integration. Prior to this, international trade policy affairs policies had generally lacked coherence. During the military regime, the DIRECON – created in 1979 – was only theoretically in charge of international trade policy affairs. In practice, the export-oriented strategy launched in 1985 was based on unilateral tariff reductions and far-reaching export promotion schemes, as the *Chicago Boys* inside the Ministry of Finance conceived trade policy to be merely a unilateral tool, that is, something that must be liberalised regardless of what may occur in country A, B or C.

Thus, putting an end to this orthodox, "ivory-tower" attitude was the real achievement of democratic policy-makers. They understood that successful world market integration goes beyond coherent, predictable, business-friendly domestic policies, by demanding an accurate analysis of what is needed domestically, and what can be obtained externally. In this regard, the democratic government that took office in 1990 did not only aim to preserve the trade policy of its authoritarian predecessor (e.g. by maintaining the "flat rate regime") but also to complement efforts in extending market access opportunities through preferential trade agreements with a wide array of global economies, thereby attaining a paradigmatic Multipolar Model.

In the first democratic government (1990-94), however, the Ministries of Finance, Economy, and Foreign Affairs sustained different trade integration goals, and thus, created a struggle for competencies. While the department of economy pursued the development of value-added exports by strengthening relations with Latin American markets (above all with the emerging MERCOSUR), the finance department paid greater attention to a possible adherence with the NAFTA, as this option was seen as an opportunity to "cement" previous unilateral liberalisation. Finally, the foreign affairs department, at this time still rather weak, considered deepening trade relations with the Andean and Southern Cone states as an appropriate way to restore good neighbourhood in the region.

During the second government of the centre-left coalition *Concertación* (1995-2000), the different state departments involved decided to strengthen the DIRECON office, converting it into the leading international trade policy branch (a process which included a strong up-scaling of trade policy officials; *resources*), in order to encounter the rising challenges of regional and multilateral forces. As a result, inter-ministerial coordination improved, as the division of labour was clearly set, i.e. the Ministry of Finance remained in charge of tariff policy, investment measures, and financial services; the Ministry of Agriculture was responsible for negotiations on agricultural trade; and the Ministry of Economy served as an advisory unit on intellectual property rights, sector-oriented regulatory issues and technical trade obstacles.

Inside the Ministry of Foreign Affairs, the DIRECON enjoyed a distinct autonomous status, especially with regards budget spending and the appointment of officials. Thus, without significant interference from the political branch, the engagement of this economic policy agency could be exclusively focussed on improving market access conditions for export industries, both by means of negotiating preferential trade agreements in- and outside the region, and through the market assistance activities in the scope of the export promotion authority *Prochile*, which itself forms part of the DIRECON office. In fact, from 1995 the DIRECON office began to spur international trade talks across the globe, becoming a pioneer in South America by signing comprehensive FTAs with Canada, the United States, the European Union, Korea, Singapore, and China.

Another crucial factor of A1 that strongly influenced the Dependent Variable B was the high degree of *openness* to business. Indeed, the establishment of close working relations with business entities, above all with the Society of Manufacturing Promotion (SOFOFA), is one of the essential factors that helps us to understand appropriately why, and how, Chile pursued the Multipolar approach to world market integration. In keeping with the tradition of the military regime, which in the aftermath of the debt crisis in 1982-83 opened steady participation channels with organised business sectors, the systematic incorporation of business views has been a key element, particularly for the DIRECON. There are two main reasons for this: First, the ambitious trade agenda set forth required the private sector to contribute with its "decentralised intelligence" from markets, through the provision of information on trade obstacles, investment perspectives, and market trends. Second, the SOFOFA became a strategic partner for the DIRECON inside the business sector, as it strongly shared the principals and objective of the Multipolar Model, thus providing firm domestic coalitions and disseminating the properties of trade policy among local sectors.

Regarding the influence of A1 in the case of *Argentina,* the explanatory power was mostly concentrated in the variable dimension *responsibilities*. In fact, the local "partnership model" in which the Ministry of Economy defines "what" has to be negotiated in trade policy affairs, and the Ministry of Foreign Affairs decides "how" to implement those inputs on the international level, remained unclear during practically the entire period of analysis, negatively affecting the development of international trade policies.

In 1986-87, the Secretariat of Industry and Foreign Trade (SICE), part of the Ministry of Economy, took over the clear responsibility of designing the innovative PICE approach, whilst the Foreign Affairs Ministry launched the initial talks and assumed the overall coordination of this first substantial integration step with Brazil since the return to democracy in 1983. The previous merger of the areas of "trade" and "industry" inside a single state secretariat (a precondition set by Roberto Lavagna when taking office) was moreover crucial to explain the sectoral approach to integration that combined export promotion with industrial policies. By then, the technical work inside the SICE was strongly supported by the Foreign Trade Service, a specialised cadre of career trade diplomats inside the Ministry of Economy (*resources*). Furthermore, the staff in charge of the different sectoral negotiations maintained close working relations with the private sector (*openness*). Hence, the state bureaucracy exhibited apparently adequate institutional structures for successful trade integration initiatives. On the side of the private sector, however, such conditions were lacking, as I later expose.

In the aftermath, however, the institutional strength of the executive branch declined, helping explain, to a wide extent, the subsequent failures in the country's world market integration strategy. In particular, effective inter-ministerial coordination could no longer be ensured in the light of an unclear division of labour for the conduction of international trade policy affairs. Instead, the course of action became strongly dependent on personalised decisions and undermined the institutional role of state bureaucracy as a whole (*responsibilities, resources, and openness*).

Specifically, Domingo Cavallo, Minister of Foreign Affairs (1989-90) and Minister of Economy (1991-1996), defined – being advised by a group of personal advisors from the orthodox-liberal think tank Mediterranean Foundation – the scope of economic reforms and trade liberalisations. The integration scheme embodied in the MERCOSUR treaty of 1991 can also be seen as a reflection of the policy style sustained by Cavallo's economic advisory team, which aimed at a fast expansion of intra-regional trade and the attraction of foreign investment. These new rules favoured the steel, petrochemicals, foods, and automobiles industries, where large companies dominated, whilst small scale manufacturers, especially in the range of capital goods, suffered due to the lack of industrial policies, increased import competition and overvaluation of the local currency.

Contrary to the PICE process, private sector organisations were almost entirely excluded from the key decisions regarding the institutional set-up of MERCOSUR (*openness*). The adoption of the Customs Union by December 1994, which contradicted both current and, indeed, future national policies, came to be seen as a concession to Brazil, in order to avoid deteriorating bilateral relations (the goal of reaching the CET was yet to be defined in 1991). Evidently, the concession made by Carlos Menem was opposed by the economy minister (who favoured a free trade zone), although Mr. Cavallo (then as foreign affairs minister) supported the decision in March 1991, when the Asunción Treaty was signed and the goal of reaching a CET by 1995 was set, as Jorge Campbell, chief negotiator within the Ministry of Affairs (1994-99) explained.[1]

---

[1] Anecdotically, Campbell reported that Cavallo called, only ten days prior to the *Ouro Preto* Protocol, for a meeting with Menem and Di Tella in order to put arguments on the table in favour of a simple FTA, which was too late to retract. Later on, Cavallo remained the Customs Union's major adversary. By March 2001, when he was again

From 1995, the ambitious goals set in the scope of MERCOSUR – which required the harmonisation of trade, macroeconomic, sectoral, and fiscal policies – overstrained the institutional capacities of the local bureaucracy. In particular, the trade policy staff within the Ministry of Economy experienced a steady decline after the Foreign Trade Service transferred to the Ministry of Foreign Affairs in 1993, with continued budget cuts taking place as of 1996 *(resources)*.

Given the decline in the capacity of the Ministry of Economy to monitor, and technically support, the international trade policy, the trade policy branch inside the Foreign Affairs Ministry increasingly assumed the role of defining both policy guidelines, and the implementation of negotiation strategies on the MERCOSUR and extra-regional level. Effectively, however, these far-reaching *responsibilities* weren't fully assumed before 2002 because of a range of internal constraints, such as the difficulties of incorporating the Foreign Trade Service into the traditional diplomatic career scale, and the weak leadership of the office holders in charge between 1999 and 2001 *(resources)*.

It was not until the period of 2002-04, under chief negotiator Martin Redrado, that the Ministry of Foreign Affairs assumed almost full *responsibility* – although opposed in parts by the Ministry of Economy – and was able to put forward an ambitious Multipolar Model, initiating and planning numerous negotiations in the regional and extra-regional sphere. Moreover, Mr. Redrado insisted on a marked involvement of the private sector, and revived the Centre of International Economy (CEI) in order to convince a broad public, with technical arguments, of the pursued Multipolar strategy *(openness)*.

By the end of 2004, however, it was still unclear whether the proactive Multipolar strategy could be successfully implemented, for two main reasons: First, a lack of intra-MERCOSUR cohesion persisted by 2004, and thus, the conclusion of initiated and planned free trade talks was highly uncertain. Between 1995 and 2004, when Chile and Mexico rapidly expanded trade relations towards (extra-) regional areas, the negotiations launched by MERCOSUR mostly deadlocked. Second, although state-business coordination was much more intense in 2004 than in the first half of the 1990s, the business sector still faced similar institutional deficits.

---

appointed Minister of Economy, the dynamic but unpredictable technocrat openly threatened to downgrade MERCOSUR to a FTA.

In **Peru,** the empirical results suggest a high explanatory power for Variable A1 regarding the key aspects of the country's world market integration. Above all, the Peruvian government's incoherent attitude towards the Andean integration process is strongly associated with the modifications inside the state bureaucracy that took place in the 1990s. Due to the public sector reforms implemented in 1990-91, specialised trade policy entities such as the Foreign Trade Institute (ICE) and the Ministry of Industry, Domestic Trade and Integration (MICITI) were dissolved (ICE) or drastically downsized (MICITI) in light of severe budget cuts affecting the central government. On the other hand, some key agencies such as the Ministry of Economy and Finance (MEF) were greatly up-scaled. But the MEF staff, which became responsible for the structural adjustment reforms involving trade liberalisation, did not rely on traditional career bureaucrats, recruiting instead from a group of special advisors close to the *Peruvian Institute of Economy (IPE),* a private think-tank based on orthodox-liberal standpoints. As a result, the pattern of policy-making strongly resembled market reforms implemented in Argentina under the guidance of Mr. Cavallo's advisory team.

The team, headed by economy minister Roberto Boloña, considered trade policy in essence as an instrument for the unilateral liberalisation of tariff and non-tariff barriers, as did the *Chicago Boys* in Chile's authoritarian regime. Herewith, the application of uniform tariffs was perceived as modern, since discretional policy-making could be avoided, and the predictability of fiscal revenues increased. The aim of reaching a flat rate by the end of 1994, however, stood in contradiction with the intention of the Andean Group, of which Peru was a member, to establish a Common External Tariff (CET) that assumed an escalated structure with four tariff levels. Moreover, the intra-regional exchange of goods was traditionally unfavourable for Peru, as less than 10% of exports went to the Andean markets, whilst imports from Andean Group members were noticeably higher, causing permanent trade deficits from a Peruvian perspective.

As economy minister Boloña directly interfered in negotiations on the Andean level, in July 1992, Peru's suspension of the Andean Group membership was a coherent decision in mind of the ongoing unilateral trade policy. In the aftermath, however, the coherence of the country's world market integration strategy could not be attained. Instead of pursuing a Multipolar Model, as had been planned by Mr. Boloña's advisory team, from 1992 Peru failed to establish a flat rate, nor did it set forth an active bilateral negotiation strategy, and neither promoted non-traditional exports.

In the 1990s, the special advisory staff inside the MEF (*resources*) focussed on unilateral trade reforms, whilst reciprocal forms of liberalisation played only a secondary role. Moreover, the *responsibilities* in the area of international trade policy were not clearly defined. Between 1991 and 1992, there was, incredibly, no state department in charge of international negotiations in the scope of ALADI and the WTO. From October 1992, when the Ministry of Industry, Tourism, Integration and International Trade Negotiations (MITINCI) was created, the Peruvian government disposed again of an international trade policy branch. But the MITINCI was not sufficiently staffed to implement active trade policies in the regional, extra-regional, and multilateral spheres (*resources*). Moreover, the few trade policy officials inside the MITINCI were divided into a group that supported the policy guidelines of the MEF (and thus the separation from the Andean Group), and another that favoured the return to the Andean integration scheme.

The intra-governmental work became further complicated by the diplomatic staff inside the Ministry of External Affairs who sought, from the mid-1990s, a more protagonist role in international economic affairs (*responsibilities*). At this point, the Peruvian diplomacy attempted, together with parts of the MITINCI staff and local manufacturers, to facilitate Peru's return to the Andean Group, and thus, began stressing numerous inconveniences of a definitive departure from the CAN, such as the displacement of its headquarters located in Lima, the impossibility to conduct common foreign affairs, the loss of privileged market access in the Andean markets, and the mandatory withdrawal from numerous shared institutions, such as the Andean Development Corporation (CAF), Latin American Reserve Fund (FAR), and technical assistance programs. Therefore, it was due to *"one of the rare occasions of coordination between the Ministries of Foreign Affairs and the MITINCI, that the hardliners inside the MEF could be displaced"*, according to Luis Tello (2004: 118), who analysed the domestic power shift that took place in May-June 1997, when Peru returned to the Andean Group.

In the ongoing decade, the institutional strength of the trade policy branch was significantly enhanced, thus explaining, to a large degree, the shifting approach to trade integration. Increasingly, the MITINCI staff focused on integration options in the Western Hemisphere and the APEC area. Above all, it was Alfredo Ferrero – Vice-Minister of International Negotiations and later Minister of Foreign Trade and Tourism – who managed to create domestic consensus to strengthen the development of national exports, especially to the US markets. Therefore, export-specific concerns gained increasing recognition among the public and private sector, making possible, in May 2002, the creation of a well-doted trade policy staff within the new Ministry of Foreign Trade and Tourism, MINCETUR (*responsibilities* and *resources*). As a result,, MINCETUR became the leading agency in the new proactive multipolar approach put forward from 2003, i.e. involvement in free trade talks with the US, comprehensive FTA with MERCOSUR, the launching of bilateral negotiations with Thailand, and the start of the first National Export Strategy, based on 10-year objectives.

Similarly to Argentina, the question of whether this new trade policy approach, strongly based on the Multipolar Model, will prove to be sustainable or not, largely depends on the question of whether the mostly personalised style of governance will lead to a greater degree of institutionalisation of the trade policy-making. This is especially the case with respect to the high degree of *openness* that was maintained by Alfredo Ferrero. Under his direction, the government undertook multiple actions to make trade policy not only more transparent, but also more popular within business, parliament and civil society. In particular, the close relations with local business factions became crucial to legitimise more active trade policies, mostly aimed at the US market. The key officials from MINCETUR, therefore, built up strategic alliances with the National Industry Society (SNI) and the Exporters Associations (ADEX).

In *Bolivia,* the empirical results suggest that the state bureaucracy variable (A1) is the principal cause for the outright failure of its world market integration strategy. To a greater extent than in any other country observed, Bolivia's world market integration was negatively affected by the fact that no clear organisational model for the international trade policy area could be consolidated between 1985 and 2004. In particular, the Foreign Affairs Model was broadly questioned by the private sector because the limited economic branch inside the foreign affairs department failed to adequately respond to their concerns and the technical requirements involved in ongoing regional and multilateral challenges *(resources).*

Moreover, the trade policy drawn up inside the Ministry of Foreign Affairs was handled in isolation from domestic businesses *(openness)*. Particularly, from 1993 to 1997, when Bolivia undertook far-reaching commitments of reciprocal liberalisation with the MERCOSUR and Mexico, the private sector organisations felt shut out of trade policy-making. Hence, Bolivia's international trade policy did not reflect the preferences and possibilities of economic sectors, but relied, above all in the case of the MERCOSUR agreement, on the keenness of the leading diplomats to strengthen the political alliances with the emerging regional bloc in the Southern Cone, pretending that Bolivia could become a regional hinge between the CAN and MERCOSUR.

Given the widespread distrust of the local trade diplomacy, the business sector sought to "empower" the trade policy staff outside the Ministry of Foreign Affairs. But unlike the successful creation of the MINCETUR in Peru ("Foreign Affairs Model"), in Bolivia the stronger involvement of the staff from the Secretariat of Industry and Trade (1993-97), and the Ministry of Foreign Trade (established in 1997 and dissolved in 2003), primarily caused inter-ministerial struggles for *responsibilities* in the areas of international trade policy and export promotion. Above all, the personal quarrels between key trade policy officials hampered the development of export development strategies, as the emphasis was placed more on inter-ministerial disputes than on improving market access conditions abroad.

For example, coupled with the Export Development and Taxation Law, in April 1993 the Bolivian government launched the National Export Council (CONEX), which aimed to build an institutionalised public-private mechanism to concert proactive policies that would foster national exports. But in the aftermath, effective work inside the CONEX never became viable due to the unclear *responsibilities* within the executive branch. In this regard, the reluctance of the Foreign Affairs Ministry to acknowledge the legitimacy of the institution (which was headed by the Ministry of Economic Development and later by the Ministry of Foreign Trade and Investment) is particularly prominent.

In the period 2003-2004, as political instability increased and free trade talks with the United States became a concrete option for Bolivia, the institutional deficits of the trade policy branch became very apparent, considering the ongoing inter-ministerial conflicts and the deteriorating budget resources. As a result, the Bolivian government lacked the capacity to convince the population (principally the growing opposition to free trade maintained by social movements) of the benefits of furthering trade liberalisation commitments with the United States. To a certain extent, previous trade policy failures committed by the public sector, i.e. opening up the economy without prior consultation and strengthening of economic sectors, influenced negatively on the credibility of governmental attempts to outline the expected positive impacts from freer trade with the US.

Regarding the influence of the second explanatory variable, the Institutional Strength of Business Associations (A2), the empirical results suggest a mostly high influence on the success of world market integration strategies, often strengthening the effects of the state bureaucracy variable on the value of B.

Table 7.2: The Institutional Strength of Business Associations (A2)

		Chile	Argentina	Peru	Bolivia
Value of A2	Leadership	85-04: very high	1985-2004: very low	85-04: rather low	85-97: rather high 98-04: very low
	Organi-sational Strength	85-94: rather high 95-04: very high	1985-2004: very low	85-04: very low	85-04: rather low*
Effect on B	Leadership	**85-04: very high**	**85-04: very high**	85-04: rather high	85-97: rather low 98-04: very high
(Policy Failure/ Success)	Organi-sational Strength	85-94: rather high 95-04: very high	**85-04: very high**	85-04: rather high	85-04: rather high

Above all, in *Chile* the explanatory power of A1 is strongly linked to the effects of A2. In fact, the effective incorporation of entrepreneurs into the development of the Multipolar Model required strong interlocutors inside the private sector. Specifically, the leadership of the multisectoral organisation CPC, a business-wide recognised entity in coordinating sectoral positions was crucial for Chile's international trade policy until the mid-1990s. By this point, the CPC had become responsible for organising the private sector in preparation for the possible adherence to the NAFTA treaty. For instance, by carrying out exhaustive impact assessments regarding such an integration step, the CPC managed to channel and articulate the strong interest among the local entrepreneurship, and herewith, signaled to the Chilean and US government the marked preposition to face this challenge. Thus, the CPC played a similar role to that adopted by the Mexican business council CCE, which Schneider (1997) qualified as decisive in explaining Mexico's entrance into the NAFTA.[2]

From 1994 to 1996, moreover, the leadership of CPC was crucial for the harmonisation of opposing sectoral views during the controversial negotiations with the MERCOSUR. While the

---

[2] But contrary to Mexico, the US government however decided later to leave Chile and other Latin American countries out of the NAFTA, and to launch the FTAA initiative embracing the whole Western Hemisphere.

industrial and service related sectors favoured far-reaching economic integration (albeit a full membership was rejected due to the customs unions concept), the CPC authorities placed special emphasis on the defensive concerns of local farmers, in order to balance the inter-sectoral interests. Supporting the free trade agreement in general terms, the umbrella organisation stressed the potential liberalisation costs for farmers, and thus, supported the claims of the National Society of Agriculture (SNA) for far-reaching compensation measures and long phasing-out schemes. As a result, the agreement with MERCOSUR became viable despite strong heterogeneous interests among domestic sectors.

In the second, and more dynamic, stage from the mid-1990s, the schemes of business intermediation underwent significant changes. The variable dimension *organisation strength* attained more relevance because sectoral associations increased their protagonism. As previously pointed out, the SOFOFA became the privileged interlocutor of the DIRECON office, not only because of its leadership among export-oriented branches, but especially due to its collaborative behaviour in supporting trade policy officials through the permanent monitoring of foreign markets and accomplished technical proposals. For this purpose, the SOFOFA hired two former trade diplomats to build up an Area of Foreign Trade and International Economic Relations as of 1995, when negotiations with MERCOSUR and Canada where underway, attaining herewith state-of-the-art trade policy advisory skills. Aside from the SOFOFA, other sectoral entities from agriculture (SNA) and services (Santiago Chamber of Commerce) likewise increased their trade policy skills in order to facilitate an efficient exchange with state authorities.

In sum, the manner in which Chile pursued its integration into world markets assumed a neocorporatistic flavour, considering the close state-business collaboration pattern. Aimed at improving its capacity to coordinate public policies – in this case international trade policies – the Chilean government was interested in establishing close and stable relations with particular business associations, wherein strong leadership and organisation strength were the most important selection criteria. In general, such policy-making patterns are criticised for their lack of inclusiveness, because they imply "representation monopoly", leaving little room for minority actors or groups facing collective action problems.

In Chile's trade policy, indeed, several actors' preferences have been reflected scarcely. In this respect, prominent examples include the segment of import-competing small scale manufacturers, workers and other members of the civil society, all of which suffer from a widespread fragmentation of their interests. In parts, the centre-left coalition *Concertación,* in power since the transition to democracy in 1990, sought to compensate such asymmetries, for instance by providing technical assistance and subsidised loans to small manufacturers to enhance their competitiveness.[3] Regarding the participation of civil society, the government made widespread efforts to foster dialogue with a broad range of society actors on international trade policy affairs. To date, however, free trade critical civil society organisations have largely felt excluded from the world market integration strategy in force.

Contrary to the Chilean example, in *Argentina* close state-business interactions were absent during the period of analysis, mostly due to the institutional deficits of organised business, which hampered the coherent implementation of trade policies. Differing from the key sectoral associations in Chile, such as the SOFOFA, SNA, or the Santiago Chamber of Commerce, in Argentina, stable working relations between state and business entities has been negatively affected by the *organisational weakness* of the key business entities, generally as a result of unreliable revenues, the passive behaviour of entrepreneurs and weak trade policy advisory units, as chapter four exposed in detail.

With respect to the particular sequences of world market integration, *organisational weakness* usually appeared in combination with a lack of *leadership* within the key associations. In 1986-87, significant progress in the sectoral negotiations with Brazil in the PICE scope was avoided by the lack of intermediation capacity of the national manufacturers association UIA. Rather than coordinating between export-oriented and import-competing sectors, defining effective compensation measures for threatened sectors (as Chile's CPC did in the negotiations with MERCOSUR), the UIA authorities were an unreliable interlocutor for the government. Therefore, sectors and individual companies pursued their mostly protectionist interests outside the UIA institutions, and in so doing, limited the state officials' room for negotiations.

In the 1990s, the UIA and seven other leading sectoral associations were organised in the scope of the G-8 alliance. Contrary to previous decades, the private sector demonstrated unity and supported the ongoing economic reforms launched by Mr. Cavallo. But beyond a general business consensus, which was largely based on the conviction that liberalisation was needed to control inflationary pressure, the leading business organisations did not develop detailed and

---

[3] Chile strengthened its framework dedicated to improving the competitiveness of SMEs, increasing expenditures from 0.34 to 0.93 percent of the GDP between 1990 and 1999 (Ministry of Economy 2000).

concerted policy proposals regarding the MERCOSUR. Instead, the attitude towards this regional integration schemes depended on short-term interests affecting the particular sectors.

For example, the behaviour of local business on the CET issue has been described as passive in comparison with Brazil, where the private sector provided permanent advice to its diplomacy during negotiations; indeed before Ouro Preto, no domestic policy debate really took into account the long-term impacts of a common trade policy regime (Botto 2004; Bouzas and Pagnotta 2003; Da Motta Veiga 2002). Initial criticism expressed against the CET, principally by powerful industries such as food processing, steel, and chemicals, disappeared in the light of the impressive Brazilian import growth that took place from the beginning of 1994 (a consequence of Brazil's macroeconomic stabilisation plan *"Real"*).

From 2002 to 2004, when the Argentinean government began to pursue an ambitious external trade agenda, a strategy denominated "Multipolar" by chief negotiator Martin Redrado, the participation of business associations was generally faint-hearted or disperse. Contrary to the 1990s, a multisectoral coordination mechanism no longer existed. Moreover, the UIA, the leading industrial entity, suffered from internal divisions, since several sectors, such as steel, metalworking, and textiles, built up their own "Industrialist Group", undermining the *leadership* of the "official UIA". Moreover, trade policies set forth by the UIA were focussed almost exclusively on the claim for an institutionalised safeguard mechanism inside the MERCOSUR, in order to protect local industries from the threatening import surges originating in Brazil.

The business support for Mr. Redrado's (chief negotiator) Multipolar strategy was limited almost exclusively to the branches related to booming agriculture commodities. From an institutional perspective, the creation of the Institute for International Agriculture Negotiations (INAI), in 1999, can be seen as the first timid attempt by local farmers to overcome the fragmentation among rural representatives, and the lack of professional advocacy structures. After the failed WTO Ministerial in Seattle, and backed by chambers representing cereals and oleaginous crops, INAI began to serve as a steady technical counterpart for the Secretariat of Agriculture and the Ministry of Foreign Affairs within the agriculture talks on the regional and multilateral sphere. Although market access conditions could not be improved fundamentally within the period of 1999-2004, the enhanced public-private coordination efforts gave lead to a stronger international presence of the Argentinean government in this crucial policy area.

In *Peru*, the firm support of the leading industrial and export chambers, in this case strongly encouraged by export-oriented textiles, clothing and agriculture (asparagus, mangoes, and grapes) was decisive to the trade policy strategy embarked upon inside the MINCETUR department as of 2002. Indeed, the Peruvian private sector behaved rather pro-actively, as business coordination mechanisms were established in the scope of the FTAA-Peru Commission (1998-2003) and the Entrepreneurial Council of International Trade Negotiations (CENI), which joined business proposals during the free trade talks with the US launched in May 2004. These institutional efforts had the effect of raising awareness among local business regarding the upcoming challenges of the international trade agenda, and facilitating the dialog with government authorities.

On the other hand, the institutional deficits of those initiatives have been widespread, and hence, put into question the sustainability of the pursued Multipolar approach that required, among other tasks, the effective implementation of the undertaken free trade agreements. By 2004, as in Argentina, Peruvian private sector organisations generally did not count on any professional structures (*organisational strength*), i.e. most entities showed no signs of diversifying their revenues, held small staff bases and did not permanently monitor international trade policy affairs. Hence, the participation inside the CENI working groups was intermittent, and focussed on traditional market access issues, while complex behind-the-border topics were largely neglected. Moreover, 76 percent of surveyed experts and state officials qualified the technical level of trade policy proposals submitted by business entities as rather or very low.

With reference to previous periods, the institutional deficits of the local business associations negatively affected the coherent pursuit of the international trade policy. In particular, the lack of concerted trade policy proposals (*leadership*) underscored Peru's difficulty to pursue coherent positions in the scope of the Andean Group. The peak entity CONFIEP, a strong business interlocutor of the structural adjustment reforms at the outset of the 1990s, lost its multisectoral coordination capacities towards the end of the decade, as opposing groups emerged from within the organisation. On the one hand, the services (mainly finance and public utilities) and commodity oriented sectors (mining and fishery) had been favoured by the economic model in force, and hence, sustained the rationale of the Ministry of Economy and Finance that pursued a flat rate model and individual forms of integration. On the other hand, the "productive group" who favoured an escalated tariff structure and a return to the CAN, were represented by the three leading industry and trading chambers; SNI (manufacturers), ADEX (exporters), and CCL (Chamber of Commerce).

It is important to consider, nevertheless, that difficulties in coordinating trade policy interests went beyond the internal division of the CONFIEP, by also encompassing institutional fragmentation and the lack of solid trade policy proposals within the two groups, especially among manufacturers' and exporters' associations. Although the "productive group" vied for an escalated tariff and the return to the CAN, there was not a comprehensive approach to world market integration either among the chambers composing the "productive group", or inside each of the teams. Instead of deeper commitments to pursue a Springboard Model, based on completing a common regional market, manufacturers were mainly concerned with uncertain market access conditions in the Andean markets, and higher taxes on raw material and intermediate goods. Therefore, in the aftermath, the "productive group" no longer acted as a firm advocate of the Andean integration process, for example by insisting on the convergence of external tariffs or the harmonisation of economic policies on the regional level.

In light of the extremely negative effects of the state bureaucracy variable (A1), in *Bolivia* the explanatory power of the business association variable is rather limited. Particularly, the failure to open up the economy without undertaking complementary measures aimed at increasing the competitiveness of domestic sectors can hardly be associated with the behavior of local business entities. Therefore, the unilateral opening of the economy in the mid-1980s was designed by a small, inter-ministerial, staff inside the Ministries of Planning and Finance, without noteworthy participation of the leading peak and sectoral organisations. Moreover, in the 1990s, it was the private sector organisations, especially the business entities from Santa Cruz, which broadly rejected the wide-reaching liberalisation commitments undertaken by the MERCOSUR agreement in December 1996.

On the other hand, the absence of strong national coordination mechanisms in the trade policy area entailed strong counter-productive effects on the development of coherent export promotion schemes. For example, the inter-ministerial conflicts in the scope of CONEX were largely confirmed by the lack of recognised business interlocutors. The National Chamber of Exporters (CANEB), which at one time claimed a monopoly for the private sector representation, not only had been characterised by a precarious administrative structure, without holding significant in-house trade policy expertise (*organisational strength*), but increasingly suffered from the internal division between the regional chambers from Santa Cruz and La Paz, respectively *(institutional strength)*. In fact, the chamber from La Paz disaffiliated in 1998, before returning again in 2004. Similar conflict patterns were observable also in other national entities, such as the peak association CEPB and the National Chamber of Industry CNI.

In general, the institutional strength of trade policy advocacy exhibited by the private sector in Santa Cruz was notably higher than in the capital city La Paz. The presence of the business think-tank IBCE, which facilitated a high degree of inter-institutional coordination among entities in Santa Cruz, and a permanent monitoring of international trade policy affairs, largely explains the rather successful consolidation of the Andean markets for agricultural products from the lowlands, above all soy exports which represented 25% of national exports in 2004. In close coordination with Bolivia's official negotiation team, the IBCE staff undertook permanent efforts to guarantee and preserve the Andean markets for soy products. As local exports regularly encountered safeguard, or discriminatory, measures applied by Colombia, Venezuela and Peru, intensive diplomacy in the CAN scope became necessary to obtain and control preferential market access conditions.[4] Furthermore, Bolivia had to repeatedly insist on their Andean partners' prompt application of the Common External Tariff for soy products (15-20 percent) and the Andean Price Band System, which in combination guaranteed higher tariff preferences in the case of low world market prices.[5]

---

[4] In 2002, for example, Colombia imposed safeguard measures of 29 percent tariffs on vegetable oils from the Andean partners; see CAN Resolution 671. Other measures applied by Colombia were related to a differential VAT treatment according the value added on imported products. For recent restrictions taken by Venezuela during 2005, the principal buyer's market, see *El Nuevo Día* 18/08/2005 or IBCE publication *Comercio Exterior*; March 2005.

[5] The purpose of this system, in force since February 1995, is to stabilise domestic prices for palm oil, soybean oil, rice, sugar, barley, milk, corn, soybeans, wheat, chicken, and pork, among others. Thus, when the international bench mark price falls below a predetermined minimum level, member countries will apply a variable-rate surcharge on imports of such products, over and above the CET. Likewise, when the international bench mark price rises above a certain ceiling, the member countries will lower the normal tariff rate to reduce the import cost of the staple.

Regarding disturbing influences on the value of B, Table 7.3 indicates the existence of several factors which at times entailed effects on the pursuit of world market integration strategies, often in negative terms.

Table 7.3: Control Variable C1-C4

		Chile	Peru	Argentina	Bolivia
Value of C1-C4	Heterogeneity Sectoral Preferences (C1)	85-04: rather high	85-04: rather high	85-04: rather high	85-04: rather low
	Heterogeneity Foreign Preferences (C2)	85-04: rather high	85-04: rather high	85-04: rather high	85-04: rather low
	Political Instability (C3)	85-04: very low	00-01: very high	01-02: very high	00-04: very high
	Macroeconomic Instability (C4)	85-04: very low	89-91: very high	88-90: very high 00-02: very high	97-03: rather high
Effect on B (Policy Failure/ Success)	Heterogeneity Sectoral Preferences (C1)	85-04: rather low	85-04: rather low	85-04: rather low	85-04: very low
	Heterogeneity Foreign Preferences (C2)	85-04: rather low	85-04: rather low	95-04: rather low	85-04: rather low
	Political Instability (C3)	85-04: rather low	00-01: rather low	01-02: rather high	03-04: rather high
	Macroeconomic Instability (C4)	85-04: rather low	89-91: very high	88-90: very high 00-02: very high	97-03: rather high

The influences of the selected control variables C1-C4 were mostly kept under control in the case of *Chile*. Studying the *sectoral preferences (C1)* involved, however, one is tempted to argue that the successful development of the export-oriented strategy was made possible by the small and homogenous private sector that survived the drastic reforms undertaken from the 1970s (see Bartell 1995; Montero 1990). But this argument appears to loose validity when the large number of signed free trade agreements is brought in line with the marked protectionist attitude of the influential farming elites organised inside the National Society of Agriculture (SNA). Hence, the coherent implementation of particular trade policies might be favoured by the rather homogenous, export-oriented preferences of local manufacturers (e.g. compared to the more heterogeneous industry in Argentina), but strongly opposed to by farming sectors vulnerable to free trade (e.g. compared to the homogenous, export-oriented preferences of Argentinean farmers).

Regarding the *heterogeneity of foreign preferences (C2)*, only once was Chile seriously restricted in its pursuit of a Multipolar Model. In the 1990s, Chile appeared to be ready to undertake a comprehensive NAFTA-style agreement with the United States. But for reasons not related to Chile, this step could not be accomplished before 2003. Thus, the course of action was influenced, but not the essence of Chile's approach to world market integration. On the regional level, Chile circumvented heterogeneous preferences by opting for a Multipolar Model rather than a Springboard approach, where strong economic policy coordination among neighbour countries would have been needed.

Finally, Chile did not suffer from any *political (C3)* or *macroeconomic (C4) instability* during the period of analysis, in stark contrast to most other South American countries. As mentioned, during the period of analysis, Chile passed from authoritarian to democratic rule. But the concerted method of administering this process avoided the emergence of political crisis or drastic changes in the making of economic policy. On the contrary, the stable environment was strongly conducive to coherent trade policy making, and explains, to some extent, the successful implementation of the world market integration strategy. Compared to the strong influences of A1 and A2, the positive effects of C3 and C4 were rather low.

In the ***Argentinean*** case, however, the control of influences on the B-value derived from C1-C4 was more difficult than in Chile, especially regarding C2, C3 and C4. With respect to the former (*heterogeneity of foreign preferences)*, the sensitive agricultural issue caused notable difficulties in the free trade talks with the US, EU, CAN, and Mexico, considering that Argentina, together with Brazil, is one of the world's largest foodstuff producers. On the other hand, problems linked to heterogeneous agriculture interests became, in parts, compensated by the attractive consumer markets offered by the emerging trading block; indeed, from 1995 North American, European and Asian countries demonstrated clear interests in deepening trade relations with MERCOSUR states. Moreover, other FTAs such as between Chile-Canada, Chile-EU and Australia-US, indicated the possibility of excluding certain tariff items from reciprocal liberalisation, or defining special phasing-out schemes for sensitive products.

Therefore, the main factor for the deadlocked talks was the poor implementation of the internal agenda of MERCOSUR, especially the harmonisation of economic policies, and opposing interests between Argentina and Brazil. For example, Brazil's defensive concerns in new behind the border issues contrasted with the far-reaching liberalisation commitment of Argentina (key issues in the FTAA and MERCOSUR-EU negotiations).

Within the MERCOSUR, integration progress depended strongly on Brazil assuming a clear agenda-setting role. Therefore, failures in regional integration can be largely explained by Brazil's reluctance to limit its national policy-making autonomy, widespread protectionist measures against intra-zone imports, and its unwillingness to provide necessary funds to face structural asymmetries among members. It is important to note, however, that Argentina confirmed the absent commitment among members for deeper regional integration, considering the lack of incorporation of communitarian norms into national law, and the repeated entry barriers for intra-zone imports. As indicated, Chile, on the other hand, mistrusted from the onset the possibility of coordinated liberalisation efforts on the regional level, and hence, decided to set forth independent forms of trade integration, thus rejecting the MERCOSUR's Customs Union.

Regarding the effects of control variable C4 *(macroeconomic instability)*, throughout the 1980s, Argentina suffered from strong inflationary pressure, a shortage of foreign capital, and high fiscal deficits, explaining in parts the decline of the sectoral PICE approach in 1988-89. Later, the introduction of the Currency Board in 1991, and the economic stabilisation in Brazil by 1994, provided favorable grounds for the expansion of intra-regional trade and the consolidation of MEROCOSUR. This integration friendly context was again interrupted by Brazil's abrupt currency devaluation in January 1999, and Argentina's breakdown of the Currency Board in January 2002. During this period, Argentina faced macroeconomic turbulences due to its growing foreign debt, and fiscal deficits of between 3.4 and 5.4 percent of GDP. The period from 2003 to 2004 was again encouraging for regional integration in the context of low inflation and a comparable evolution of exchange rates between Argentina and Brazil.

In conclusion, in the last 20 years trade relations in the Southern Cone were largely influenced by macroeconomic factors. On the other hand, it can be argued that successful regional integration policies were not hindered primarily by macroeconomic variables, but by the scant advances made during the "golden times" of MERCOSUR (particularly 1994-98 and 2003-04) in which no solid base was built to encounter more unstable circumstances. In these periods, practically no progress was noticeable regarding the harmonisation of trade and economic policies, such as the convergence of the CET, (phyto-) sanitary measures, and the liberalisation of services. Furthermore, in times of macroeconomic stability, it was largely the development of coherent unilateral policies on export promotion and sectoral development, which supported the ongoing world market integration process.

In accordance with macroeconomic turmoil, *political instability (C3)* was registered in 1989-1990 and 2001-02. In the latter occasion, the combination of an unemployment rate beyond 20 percent, the four-year recession and the rampant fiscal and debt crises, caused the compulsory resignation of State President Fernando de la Rúa. Strikingly, the stabilisation of the economy and political system took place within 2002. As indicated under *macroeconomic instability*, the instability registered in 1989-90 and 2001-02 both resulted in a backlash, principally for the ongoing trade integration endeavors with Brazil. Conversely, the country's behaviour in the times in between didn't provide significant evidence that coherent trade policies had been implemented.

With respect to the *heterogeneity of sectoral preferences (C1)*, in the past the private sector was often divided into export-oriented agriculture and inward-looking industry. This heterogeneity appears to explain the failed attempt to create a business-wide coordination pattern, such as the establishment of a strong peak association. But as of 1990, when economic reforms were implemented, this explanation appears to become increasingly invalid. *First,* many manufacturing sectors became export-oriented and peak tariffs came down to 22 percent, disregarding the automotive regime maintained in the MERCOSUR. *Second,* intra-sectoral division became as widespread as inter-sectoral differences. While the rather homogenous rural interests are represented by no less than four peak entities, and several branch organisations lobbying outside these institutions, the manufacturers' association UIA was unable to coordinate a wide range of existing common interests among local manufacturers, a fact that became particularly evident with the economic opening in the 1990s. Therefore, the main problem of domestic business advocacy has institutional roots, and is not the result of extremely heterogeneous preferences.

In the case of **Peru,** disturbing influences from C1-C4 were mostly kept under control. However, some specific comments must be made on the *heterogeneity of sectoral preferences (C1).* In general, trade policy interests among the Peruvian private sector are relatively homogenous, especially since the structural adjustment reforms implemented in 1990-91, when maximum tariff rates came down to 25%. While the commodity sectors (mainly mining and fishery) have traditionally been outward-looking, Peruvian manufacturing has strongly increased its export orientation, focussing principally on consumer goods (textiles, clothing, and foodstuffs) and intermediates (plastic, chemicals, and various metals). Contrary to other South American countries such as Colombia, Brazil and Argentina, the fabrication of capital goods, normally inward-looking, is largely absent.

The main challenge for trade policy coordination was represented by the agricultural sector, thus far dominated by the largely uncompetitive, small scale, production of, for instance, maize, wheat, rice and sugarcane. Strikingly, however, the principal trade policy conflicts observed, above all in the scope of the CAN, where identified among manufacturers, affecting the coherence of Peru's world market integration. Hampered by collective action problems, the coordination of defensive rural concerns first came into view in the build up to the free trade talks with the United States. Nonetheless, the opposition that organised within CONVEAGRO, the main sectoral representative, lacked the sufficient power to avoid the conclusion of the free trade agreement, which had been approved by the end of 2005.

Regarding control variable C2, Peru's decisions on trade policy matters had to take into account heterogeneous foreign preferences in the scope of the CAN, particularly. The goal of reaching a Customs Union on the Andean level reflected the interests of Colombia, and to a lesser extent, Venezuela. The multi-level, or "escalated", tariff structure reflected their industrial policy preferences, enabling their manufacturers to expand the modest home market in a familiar and less competitive environment. Therefore, Peru, which preferred a flat rate model, had two options. Whilst the first considered the definitive withdrawal from the CAN, and the implementation of individual integration modes, the second alternative required negotiating the Peruvian position within the Andean scope with perseverance and coherent technical arguments. Nonetheless, by the end of the study period, neither policy option had been followed with the necessary determination.

Regarding the control variable C3 (*political instability*), the most noteworthy events were linked to the government of Alberto Fujimori (disregarding the social unrest caused by the hyperinflation of the 1980s). The auto-coup initiated by Alberto Fujimori in April 1992 stands out, with the subsequent implementation of a semi-authoritarian regime by circumventing essential democratic checks of balances, and finally, the compulsory resignation of Fujimori in November 2000. Afterwards, Valentín Paniagua became transitory Head of State until July 2001, when Alejandro Toledo assumed the Presidency for the period of 2001-06.

Nevertheless, the impact of these abrupt political shifts on Peru's trade policy was modest, for two main reasons. *Firstly,* the way in which trade policies were designed under the Fujimori regime differed very little from the methods used in the full democratic regimes of the region, insofar as key players were found both inside the executive power and the business sector. *Secondly,* the shift towards a more active trade policy approach was initiated at the end of the Fujimori regime. In 1999, Alfredo Ferrero (as of November 2003 Minister of Foreign Trade and Tourism) assumed the position of Vice-Minister of Integration and International Trade Negotiations, and began to pursue a dynamic Multipolar approach. Later on, Mr. Ferrero persisted in office under various ministers and state presidents, while at the same time, the new trade policy approach gained rising recognition among state and business actors.

Finally, with respect to *C4 (macroeconomic instability),* the effects on B were modest after macroeconomic turmoil was left behind from 1991. Compared with fiscal deficits of 9.4 and 7.5 percent of GDP in 1989 and 1990, and annual inflation rates of 2,775 and 7,650 percent in the same years, the figures registered in the aftermath were very favourable indeed. Although annual budget deficits reached roughly 2 percent on average, and until 1994 certain inflationary pressure remained at an annual variation rate of 139, 57, 39 and 31 percent, the Peruvian government was able to set stable grounds for economic prosperity, involving the development of local exports.

As was the case in Argentina, the ***Bolivian*** study implied a relatively difficult control of disturbing influences on B, especially taking into account the rather strong effects of C3 (political instability) and C4 (macroeconomic instability). After numerous alternating military regimes and the return to democracy (1982-85), accompanied by economic and social turmoil, from 1985 Bolivia entered a longer phase of political stability that enabled five democratic governments to properly conclude their terms (1985-2002). Increasing political instability came into view towards the end of the 1990s, nonetheless. Several controversial topics, such as the eradication of coca plants, the engagement of the multinational companies in public water supply, possible natural gas exports towards the US via Chilean ports, and the US-AFTA talks, led to a series of social protests and street blockades by workers, and indigenous and neighbourhood organisations. Massive riots finally provoked the compulsory retreat of State President Sánchez de Lozada in October 2003. In the aftermath, the transitory presidency of Carlos Mesa (until June 2005) like-wise operated on highly unstable grounds, whereby the political agenda became dependent on popular demands such as the referendums concerning the use of natural gas resources and the convocation of the Constitutional Assembly.

Studying the effects on B, the governance crisis experienced, above all from 2003, subordinated concerns on long-term oriented trade policies. On the other hand, it can be argued that the strong opposition by civil society movements did not primarily jeopardise the ongoing world market integration strategy, for example in struggling against the free trade talks with the US, but has to be seen as a reaction to the failed process of economic opening, in which domestic constraints had not been adequately considered.

Regarding the *macroeconomic development (C4)*, after experiencing rampant hyperinflation in mid-1980s, Bolivia was able to control inflationary pressure during the whole period of analysis. From 1997 to 2004, however, the Bolivian State suffered from high budget deficits of 3 percent and beyond. Between 2001 and 2004, the corresponding rate even moved between 6 and 9 percent, and thus, offered a deprived panorama for the expansion of sector-specific and export promotion facilities, an indispensable element of the Multipolar Model (B).

Studying the *sectoral preferences (C1)*, heterogeneous interests were mostly observed along the regional lines. While the lowland producers from Santa Cruz were interested in preserving the domestic market for their agriculture and forestry products, La Paz sought cheaper prime materials for its food processing and furniture industries. At any rate, given that the highest tariff rate applied by the Bolivian government does not exceed 10%, the presence of strong multisectoral business organisations should have allowed for the reconciliation of these opposing sectoral views. Finally, with regard to the *heterogeneous foreign preferences (C2)*, Bolivia's trade policy was only minimally affected by other countries, disregarding specific market access restrictions for various agricultural goods and industrial manufactures. In general, the country had been widely granted with a special and differentiated treatment. For example, Bolivia was allowed, in contrast to Peru, to be exempted from the Andean CET (not applying the two higher tariff levels of 15 and 20%). Moreover, although the CAN membership generally opposed such a policy, Bolivia pursued a Multipolar Model in negotiating a bilateral FTA with the MERCOSUR.

The following Table 7.4 summarises the results of the empirical analysis, and depicts the factors that had the strongest influence on the outcomes to be explained, in each of the five year periods of the study.

Table 7.4: Synopsis of Factors Affecting the Trade Policy Success/Failure

		1985-89	1990-94	1995-1999	2000-2004
Chile		B: partial success (export support scheme and flat rate model)	B: partial success (export Promotion, flat rate model, NAFTA preparation)	B: success (implementation of multipolar model)	B: success (consolidation of multipolar model)
		institutional strength of the Ministry of Finance (A1) and CPC (A2)	institutional strength of the Ministry of Finance (A1) and CPC (A2)	institutional strength of DIRECON (A1) and SOFOFA (A2)	institutional strength of DIRECON (A1) and SOFOFA (A2)
Argentina		B: partial success (innovative PICE approach)	B: partial failure (inconsistence between MERCOSUR and unilateral trade policy)	B: partial failure (modest implementation of MERCOSUR; discretionary unilateral trade policy)	B: partial failure (modest implementation of MERCOSUR; discretionary unilateral trade policy)
		institutional strength of SICE (A1)	personalised governance style of Mr. Cavallo (A1); weak UIA institutions and multisectoral coordination (A2)	unclear partnership model (A1), institutional weakness of UIA and multisectoral coordination (A2)	unclear partnership model (A1), institutional weakness of UIA and multisectoral coordination (A2), macroeconomic turmoil (C4)
Peru		B: failure (strongly discretionary trade policy)	B: partial failure (largely absent international trade policy)	B:Failure (largely absent international trade policy, unclear strategy inside the CAN)	B: partial success (launch of multipolar strategy; fostering exports to the US market)
		macroeconomic turmoil (C4), inter-agency conflicts between ICE and MITICI (A1); organisational weakness of business advocacy (A2)	dominance of the MEF team, weak role of MITINCI (A1); organisational weakness of business advocacy (A2)	unclear division of labour between MEF, MITINCI, and Foreign Affairs Ministry (A1); weak business organisation, deficient (multi-)sectoral coordination (A2)	strengthening of MINCETUR under personal leadership of Mr. Ferrero incorporating business entities (A1)
Bolivia		B: partial failure (lack of export and sector-specific support schemes)	B: partial failure (lack of export and sector-specific support schemes)	B: Failure (bilateral FTA with MERCOSUR, lack of export and sector-specific support schemes)	B: Failure (failed US-AFTA talks; lack of export and sector-specific support schemes)
		Dominance of the Ministry of Finance, weak role of the Ministry of Industry, Trade and Tourism (A1)	failed creation of "export ministry", inter-ministerial struggles between Ministries of Economic Development and Foreign Affairs (A1)	Inter-ministerial struggles between Ministries of Foreign Affairs and Economic Development, and later with "export ministry" MCEI (A1)	abolishment of MCEI, inter-ministerial struggles between Ministries of Foreign Affairs and Economic Development (A1), fiscal debts (C4) and political crisis (C3)

In conclusion, the study of institutional factors involved in the domestic trade policy-making process has proved to be extremely enlightening. It has aided in the understanding of the problems faced by developing countries when taking on the modern challenges of world market integration processes, even though in some cases, above all in Bolivia and Argentina, it was at times rather difficult to isolate the assumed cause-effects links. The analytical focus on executive branches and business organisations was warranted, given the abundant observations already made on the deficient involvement of legislators and civil society actors in trade policy-making, herein often causing the general lack of democratic legitimacy of world market integration processes.

Concentrating on the degree of coherence reached in pursuing world market integration strategies, I was able to demonstrate, by means of the four country studies carried out in South America, that trade policy success depends, to a large extent, on the institutional strength of state bureaucracy and business associations. With respect to the independent variable A1, I proved that a clear division of labour in the conduction of international trade policy affairs, which was achieved in Chile from 1995 (and to some extent in Peru from 2002), became crucial to successfully encounter ongoing trade policy challenges, considering the permanent linkages among a broad set of policy areas that cover both border and behind-the-border measures, parallel negotiations on different international levels, and the complex incorporation of trade agreements into national laws. On the other hand, it was also shown that the failure to consolidate a particular organisational model in Bolivia and Argentina hindered the implementation of successful trade policies during the period of analysis.

Disregarding whether there was a single (or "pilot") agency in charge of international trade policy affairs (such as the DIRECON in Chile) or not, the empirical results suggest the importance of relying on an effective inter-ministerial coordination pattern involving broad parts of the executive branch. Although the official negotiation team can provide valuable input, or even guidelines, for development strategies, it should act primarily as an "implementing agency", converting policy proposals originated from domestic policy agencies into feasible responses on the international level. This close involvement, for example, of the Ministries of Industry, Agriculture, or Labour, becomes decisive for the effective application of trade agreements on the national level, i.e. when the official negotiation team is no longer the responsible actor. However, the existence of burdensome coordination mechanism inside the state bureaucracy, the lack of awareness regarding the implications of international trade arrangements on the side of domestic policy oriented state agencies, and in particular, inter-ministerial struggles, often limited the effective compliance with the corresponding tasks.

Furthermore, the *openness to business*, in combination with clear-cut responsibilities, was highlighted as an essential component for successful world market integration strategies. In Chile and, to a lesser extent, in Peru, the establishment of close working relations with business entities is essential when understanding appropriately why, and how, these countries succeeded in pursuing a particular approach to world market integration. In line with corporatist views, trade policy-makers had clear incentives for a systematic incorporation of business views, for two main reasons: *First,* the ambitious trade agenda set forth required the private sector to contribute with its "decentralised intelligence" from markets, through the provision of information on trade obstacles, investment perspectives, and market trends. *Second,* policy-makers needed strategic partners inside the business sector which shared the principals and objectives of a particular trade policy approach, thus providing firm domestic coalitions and disseminating the properties of trade policy among local sectors.

With regard to the variable dimension *resources,* the effects on B were less obvious, considering that variances between the cases (especially between Chile, Argentina and Peru) were smaller than with respect to *responsibilities and openness.* Even though the Chilean State had an internationally recognised negotiation team at its disposal, the principal distinction was related to the vast negotiations experiences in the extra-regional sphere (e.g. with US, Canada and EU), which helped the mainly young negotiators become familiar with state-of-the-art international trade policy affairs. Conversely, the implementation of a stable and well trained bureaucratic staff, in line with Max Weber's writings, was absent in all observed countries (contrary to the development states in East Asia; Evans 1995).[6]

Given the shift towards market-led development strategies that took place in every one of the four examined South American States in the last two decades, conversely, the organisational features of the private sector were more decisive than in the export-led growth strategies in East Asia, where the State assumed the role of planning the modes of industrial and trade development. Regarding the effects of the independent variable A2, therefore, the empirical results indicated that the (in-) effective organisation of business interests was in most cases a key factor in explaining the observed policy success/failure.

---

[6] Thus far, in South America two mechanisms permitted the circumventing of generally limited career perspectives inside the public administration: (1) well doted temporary contracts for trade policy advisor, often sustained by international donors, or (2) the diplomatic career status. The former modus (predominately applied in Peru and Chile) inhibited the formation of a coherently organised bureaucratic body, which is supposed to enable an effective implementation and administration of undertaken foreign trade commitments in a long term perspective. On the other hand, the diplomatic career (prevailing in Argentina and Bolivia) offered a high degree of stability and institutional commitment by state officials, but has been accompanied by diplomatic training favouring the "generalist type" instead of required area experts, and absent incentives to serve for longer periods inside domestic trade policy offices.

Specifically, the existence of broadly recognised business entities (*leadership*) with the capacity to reconcile opposing business interests, and to develop concerted private sector proposals, became crucial for the coherent implementation of world market integration strategies. Most strikingly, in the cases of Argentina and Chile, I was able to demonstrate that the absence and existence, respectively, of broadly recognised peak and sectoral associations largely explains the policy failure (in Argentina and to a slightly lesser extent in Peru and Bolivia) and success (in Chile). While Chile's business entities provided firm coalitions in favour of particular integration steps, Argentina's business entities generally failed to create consensus around common goals. As a consequence, Chile's policy-makers could work upon clear mandates both within domestic and international policy-making processes, enabling the pursuit of coherent trade policies. Conversely, Argentina's key officials suffered from wobbly business proposals that were based on heterodox sector- and company-specific demands, mostly responding to short-term needs rather than long-term oriented sector strategies.

Often combined with the amount of *leadership,* the degree of *organisational strength* of the business associations, in the sense of professional administrative structures, became another important element when understanding whether, and how, the countries were (un) able to manage the modern requirements of international trade policy affairs. Although effects were mostly inferred in general terms by interviewed key actors, the existence of trade policy advisors in charge of monitoring and analysing negotiations and foreign market developments, the active involvement of associated companies, and stable and diversified revenues, can be considered as essential so as to detect, and adequately assess, market opportunities, and to put forward the sound technical arguments required in international trade negotiations.

In general, this study has contributed to the understanding of whether, and how, institutional factors on the domestic level determine the success of world market integration strategies pursued by developing countries, and hence, provided practical insights on attempts aimed at the effective institutional strengthening of trade policy-making. On the other hand, further research is required regarding the question of how the institutional strength of state bureaucracy and business associations is acquired. In this regard, the empirical observations clearly indicated noteworthy explanatory power related to the ongoing multilateral and regional integration forces. Specifically, in Chile and Peru, a clear tendency for institutional strengthening could be observed in the context of wide-reaching free trade agreements with industrialised countries, especially with the United States. Nevertheless, more systematised work is needed to confirm such effects of international trade policy affairs on the institutional development at the domestic policy-making level.

8 References

Amsden, Alice (1989). *Asia's Next Giant: South Korea and Late Industrialization*. New York/ Oxford: Oxford University Press.

Amsden, Alice (2001). *The Rise of the Rest: Challenges to the West from Late Industrializing Countries*. New York/ Oxford: Oxford University Press.

Arrow, Kenneth J. (1974). *The Limits of Organization*. New York: Norton.

Atteslander, Peter (1995). *Methoden der Empirischen Sozialforschung*. 8th Edition. Berlin: de Gruyter.

Bartell, Ernst (1995). "Perceptions by Business Leaders and the Transition to Democracy in Chile" Pp.49-104 in *Business and Democracy in Latin America,* edited by Bartell, E. and Payne, L. Pittsburgh: University of Pittsburgh Press.

Bhagwati, Jagdish (1992). *Regionalism and Multilateralism*. The World Economy 15:535-555.

Botto, Mercedes (2004). *The Impact of New Regionalism on Trade Policy Making: The Case of MERCOSUR and the FTAA in Southern Countries*. Draft Version. Buenos Aires: FLACSO.

Bouzas, Roberto and Emiliano Pagnotta (2003). *Dilemas de la Política Comercial Argentina*. Buenos Aires: Universidad de San Andrés/ Siglo XXI Editores/ Fundación Osde.

Buchanan, J.M., Tollison, R.D. and Tullock, G. (1980*). Toward a Theory of the Rent-Seeking Society*. Collage Station: Texas A&M University Press.

Bulmer-Thomas, Victor (1994). *The Economic History of Latin America since Independence*. Cambridge Latin American Studies. Vol. 77. New York: Cambridge University Press.

Burki, Shahid Javed and Guillermo Perry (1998). "Beyond the Washington Consensus: Institutions Matter." *World Bank Latin American and Caribbean Studies*. Washington, D.C.

Czada, Roland (1994). "Konjunkturen des Korporatismus: Zur Geschichte eines Paradigmenwechsels in der Verbändeforschung" Pp.37-64 in *Verbände und Staat,* edited by Wolfgang Streeck. PSV Sonderheft 25. Opladen.

Da Motta Veiga, Pedro Luis (2002). "Trade Policy Making in Brazil: Transition Path" in *The Trade Policy-Making Process. Level One of the Two Levels Game*. Occasional Paper 13, edited by Ostry, S. Buenos Aires: IDB/Munk Center.

Devlin, Robert and Antoni Estevadeordal (2001). *What's New in the New Regionalism in the Americas?*. Working Paper 6. Institute for the Integration of Latin America and the Caribbean/ Integration Trade and Hemispheric Issues Division/ Statistics and Quantitative Analysis Unit. Washington, DC:IDB.

Diamond, L., Hartlyn, J., Linz, J. and Lipset, S. M. (1997). *Democracy in Developing Countries: Latin America.* London: Boulder.

Dollar, David and Aart Kraay (2001). "Trade, Growth and Poverty" in *Finance and Development Magazine of the International Monetary Fund.* Vol. 38: 3.

Dollar, David and Aart Kraay (2003). *Institutions, Trade, and Growth: Revisiting the Evidence.* Policy Research Working Paper Series 3004. The World Bank.

ECLAC (2002). The Chilean Strategy of Trade Liberalization and Market Access. Santiago de Chile: International Trade and Integration Division.

Edwards, Sebastian (1995). *Crisis and Reform in Latin America: From Despair to Hop.* New York/ Oxford: Oxford University Press.

Edwards, Sebastian (1998), Openness, Productivity and Growth: What Do We Really Know?, Economic Journal,108, 383-398.

Evans, P., Jacobson, H. and Putman, R. (1993). *Double-Edged Diplomacy: International Bargaining and Domestic Politics.* Berkeley: University of California Press.

Evans, Peter (1995). *Embedded Autonomy: States and Industrial Transformation.* Princeton: University of Princeton Press.

Evans, Peter (1997). "State Structures, Government-Business Relations and Economic Transformation" Pp.63-87 in *Business and the State in Developing Countries*, edited by Schneider and Maxfield Ithaca: Cornell University Press.

Evans, Peter and James Rauch (1999). "Bureaucracy and Growth: A Cross-National Analysis of the Effects of 'Weberian' State Structures on Economic Growth" in *American Sociological Review.* Vol. 64, 5: 748-765.

Fields, Karl J. (1995). *Enterprise and the State in South Korea and Taiwan.* Ithaca: Cornell University Press.

Frankel, Jeffrey A. and David Romer (1999). "Does Trade Cause Growth?" in *American Economic Review.* American Economic Association Vol. 89: 379-399.

Frieden, Jeffry A. (1991). *Debt, Development, and Democracy: Modern Political Economy in Latin America, 1965-1985.* Princeton: Princeton University Press.

Fukuyama, Francis (1995). *Trust: The Social Virtues and the Creation of Prosperity.* New York: Free Press.

Gourevitch, Peter (1986). *Politics in Hard Times.* Ithaca: Cornell University Press.

Graham, C. and Naím Moisés (1998). "The Political Economy of Institutional Reform in Latin America" Pp.321-362 in *Beyond Tradeoffs: Market Reform and Equitable Growth in Latin America,* edited by Birdsall, G. and Sabot. Washington, D.C.: IDB/Brookings Institution Press.

Hillman, Ayre (1982). Declining Industries and Political-Support Protectionist Motives. American Economic Review 72. 1180-1187.

Hillman, Ayre L. (1989). *The Political Economy of Protection*. Chur: Hardwood Academic Publishers.

Hirschmann, Albert O. (1971). "The Political Economy of Import Substituting Industrialization in Latin America" Vol. 3 in *A Bias for Hope: Essays Development and Latin America*. New Haven: Yale University Press.

Hiscox, Michael J. (2002). *International Trade and Political Conflict: Commerce, Coalitions, and Mobility*. Princeton: Princeton University Press.

Hoekman, Bernhard (2001). *Strengthening the Global Trade Architecture for Development: The Post Doha Agenda*. Washington, DC: World Bank Working Paper.

Jackson, John H. (1997). *The World Trading System. Law and Policy of International Economic Relations*. Second Edition. Cambridge: Massachusetts Institute of Technology.

Johnson, Chalmers A. (1982). *MITI and the Japanese Miracle*. Stanford: Stanford University Press.

Jordana, Jacint and Carles Ramió (2002). *Diseños Institucionales y Gestión de la Política Comercial Exterior en América Latina*. Occasional Paper 15. Buenos Aires: INTAL/IDB.

Katzenstein, Peter J. (1989). *Small States in World Markets. Industrial Policy in Europe*. Ithaca- London: Cornell University Press.

Kostecki, Michael M. (2002). *Business Advocacy and Trade Policy-making: How to the Business Community in Developing Countries Can Benefit from the Doha Development Round?*. Geneva: International Trade Centre.

Kraus, Peter A.(1999). "Assoziationen und Interessenrepräsentation in neuen Demokratien" Pp.23-43 in *Systemwechsel 4: Die Rolle von Verbänden im Transformationsprozess*, edited by Merkel, W. and Sandschneider, E. Opladen: Leske+Budrich.

Krueger, Anne (1974). "The Political Economy of a Rent Seeking Society" in *American Economic Review*. Vol. 64, 3: 291-303.

Lawrence, Robert (1996). *Regionalism, Multilateralism and Deeper Integration*. Washington, D.C.: The Brookings Institution.

Lengyel, Miguel F. and Vivianne Ventura-Dias (2004). *Trade Policy Reforms in Latin America - Multilateral Rules and Domestic Institutions*. New York: Palgrave Macmillan.

Loser, Claudio and Martine Guerguil (1999). "Trade and Trade Reform in Latin America and the Caribbean in the 1990s" in *Journal of Applied Economics*. Vol. II, 1: 61-96.

Mainwaring, Scott and Matthew Soberg Shugart (1997). *Presidentialism and Democracy in Latin America.* New York: Cambridge University Press.

Maxfield, Silvia and Benjamin Ross Schneider (1997). *Business and the State in Developing Countries.* Ithaca-New York: Cornell University Press.

Mendez, José Luis (1999). "Estudio Introductorio" Pp. 7-61 in *La Política de la Burocracia,* edited by Guy Peters, B. Mexico D.F.: Fondo de Cultura Económica.

Merkel ,Wolfgang and Eberhard Sandschneider (1999). *Systemwechsel 4. Die Rolle von Verbänden im Transformationsprozess.* Opladen: Leske+Budrich.

Merkel, Wolfgang and Hans-Jürgen Puhle (1999). *Von der Diktatur zur Demokratie. Transformation, Erfolgsbedingungen, Entwicklungspfade.* Opladen: Leske + Budrich.

Milner, Helen (1988). *Resisting Protectionism.* Princeton: Princeton University Press.

Milner, Helen R. (1997). *Interests, Institutions and Information.* Princeton: Princeton University Press.

Montero, Casassus (1990). "La Evolución del Empresariado Chileno. Surge un Nuevo Actor?" Pp. 91-122 in *Colección Estudios CIEPLAN.* No. 30. Santiago de Chile.

Nef, Jorge (2003). "Public Administration and Public Sector Reform in Latin America" Pp.523-535 in *Handbook in Public Administration,* edited by Peters and Pierre. London: Sage Publications.

North, Douglas. C. (1990). *Institutions, Institutional Change and Economic Performance.* Cambridge: Cambridge University Press.

O'Donnell, Guillermo (1973). *Modernization and Bureaucratic-Authoritarianism: Studies in South American Politics.* Berkeley: Institute for International Studies.

Offe, Claus and Helmut Wiesenthal (1980). „Two Logics of Collective Actions: Theoretical Notes on Social Class and Organisational Form" in: *Political Power and Social Theory* 1980/1, 62-115.

Olson, Mancur (1982). *The Rise and Decline of Nations: Economic Stagflation, and Social Rigidities.* New Haven: Yale University Press.

Ostry, Silvia (2002). *The Trade Policy-Making Process: Level One of the Two Level Game: Country Studies in the Western Hemisphere.* Buenos Aires: IDB/Munk Center.

Porras, José Ignacio (2003). *La Estrategia Chilena de Acuerdos Comerciales: Un Análisis Político.* Santiago de Chile: CEPAL/ECLAC.

Prats, José. 2000. *Reforma del Estado y Desarrollo Humano en América Latina.* Quórum: Revista de Pensamiento Iberoamericano.

Putnam, Robert (1993a). "Diplomacy and Domestic Politics: The Logic of Two-Level Games" Pp. 427-460 in *Double-Edged Diplomacy: International Bargaining and Domestic Politics*, edited by Evans, P., Jacobson, H. and Putnam, R. Berkeley: University of California Press.

Putnam, Robert (1993b). *Making Democracy Work*. Princeton, NJ: Princeton University Press.

Redrado, Martin (2003). *Exportar para Crecer*. Buenos Aires: Editorial Planeta.

Redrado, Martin and Hernán Lacunza (2004). *A New Approach to Trade Development in Latin America*. Occasional Paper 2. Buenos Aires: INTAL/IDB.

Robin, Christian (2001). *Kollektives Unternehmerhandeln im Prozess der demokratischen Konsolidierung Lateinamerikas vor dem Hintergrund einer liberalen Wirtschaftsordnung. Eine vergleichende Fallstudie der politischen Regime Argentiniens und Chile in den 90er Jahren*. MA Thesis in Political Science. University of Zurich.

Rogowski, Ronald (1989). *Commerce and Coalitions*. Princeton, NJ: Princeton University Press.

Rodrik, Dani (1995). Political Economy of Trade Policy, in G. Grossman and K. Rogoff. Pp.1457-1494 in *Handbook of International Economics 3*. Amsterdam: Elsevier.

Rodrik, Dani (1999). *The New Global Economy and the Developing Countries: Making Openness Work*. Washington, DC: Policy Essay, Vol.24.

Rodrik, Dani (2000a). *Trade Policy and Economic Growth: A Skeptic's Guide to the Cross-National Evidence*.

Rodrik, Dani (2000b). *Trade Policy Reform as Institutional Reform*. Working Paper. Harvard University.

Sachs, Jeffrey and Andrew Warner (1995). "Economic Reform and the Process of Economic Integration" in *Brookings Papers of Economic Activity*, 1:1-95.

Sachs, Jeffrey and Wing Thye Woo (2000). "Understanding China's Economic Performance." *Journal of Policy Reform*. Vol. 4, Issue 1. 2000.

Saéz, Sebastián (2005). *Trade Policy Making in Latin America: A Compared Analysis*. Santiago de Chile: International Trade and Integration Division.

Sangmeister, Hartmut (1999). "Der MERCOSUR – eine Zwischenstufe der Globalisierung?" in *Lateinamerika: Analysen, Daten, Dokumentation*. Hamburg, 16: 78-92.

Schmitter, Philippe C, and Wolfgang Streeck (1999). *The Organization of Business Interests: Studying in the Associative Action of Business in Advanced Industrial Societies*. Discussion Paper. Köln: Max Plank Institut für Gesellschaftsforschung.

Schneider, Ben Ross (1997). "Big Business and the Politics of Economic Reform: Confidence and Concertation in Brazil and Mexico" Pp. 191-215 in *Business and the State in*

Developing Countries, edited by Maxfield and Schneider. Ithaca -London: Cornell University Press.

Schubert, Klaus (1995). "Pluralismus versus Korporatismus" Pp. 407-423 in *Politische Theorien. Lexikon der Politik Band 1*, edited by Nohlen, D. and Schultze, R.O. München: Beck.

Silva, Verónica (2001). Estrategia y Agenda Comercial Chilena en los Años Noventa. Santiago de Chile: CEPAL/ECLAC.

Srinivasan, T.N. (1999). *Developing Countries in the World Trade System: From GATT, 1947, to the Third Ministerial Meeting of WTO*. CT Economic Grow Center. New Haven: Yale University.

Tello, Luis (2004). *El Perú en el Proceso de Integración Andina de 1992 a 1997*. Graduation Thesis in History. Lima: Universidad Nacional Mayor de San Marcos/CAN General Secretariat.

Thorp, Rosemary and Francisco Durand. (1997). "A Historical View of Business-State Relations: Colombia, Peru and Venezuela Compared" Pp.216-237 in *Business and Politics*, edited by Schneider, B. and Maxfield, S. Cambridge: Cambridge University Press.

Van Evera, Stephan (1997). *Guide to Methods for Students of Political Science*. Ithaca-London: Cornell University Press.

Wade, Robert. (1990). *Governing the Market: Economic Theory and the Role of Government in East Asian Industrialization*. Princeton, N.J.: Princeton University Press.

Weaver, Kent and Bert Rockman (1993). Do Institutions Matter?. Washington, D.C.: The Brookings Institution.

Williamson, John (1990). *Latin American Adjustment: How much has happened?*. Washington D.C.: Institute for International Economics.

Winters, Alan (1996). *Regionalism versus Multilateralism*. Discussion Papers No. 1525. London: Center for Economic Policy Research.

Wood, Adrian (1997). "Openness and Wage Inequality in Developing Countries: The Latin American Challenge to East Asian Conventional Wisdom", The World Bank Economic Review, vol. 11, 33-57.

World Bank Development Report (2002). *Building Institutions for Markets*. New York: Oxford University Press.

World Trade Organization (2004). *Regionalism: friends or rivals?* <http: //www.wto.org>.

Yin, Robert K. (1998). "The Abridged Version of Case Study Research. Design and Method." Pp.229-259 in *Handbook of Allied Social Research Methods Chapter 8,* edited by Bickman, L. and Roq, D.J. Thousand Oaks. London United Kingdom: Sage Publication.

9   APPENDIX

Table 9.1: Profile of Business Entities Surveyed

	Total Entities	Geographical Focus	Sectoral Focus	Key Features
Argentina	58	Buenos Aires (capital city)	50% Industry 25% Agriculture 25% Trade and Services	Strongly diversified business representation structure, i.e. firms channel interests via branch organisations
Bolivia	36	La Paz (capital city)/ Santa Cruz	30% Industry 20% Agriculture 50% Trade and Services	Division of economic power between La Paz and Santa Cruz; Importance of peak entities
Peru	29	Lima (capital city)	50% Industry 25% Agriculture 25% Trade and Services	Importance of peak entities located in Lima
Chile	5	Santiago de Chile (capital city)	Multisectoral (1), Industry (2), Agriculture (1), Trade (1).	Importance of peak entities

Table 9.2: Questionnaire Business Associations (February – October 2004)

Objective	Analysis of Business Associations in Argentina, Bolivia, Peru and Chile, placing emphasis on business entities' participation in international trade policy affairs. Additionally, the survey evaluates the perceptions of business actors regarding the organisation of the state executive branch and the coordination mechanism between public and private sectors in the conduction of current international trade negotiations on the bilateral, regional and multilateral level.
Organisation Name	
Sector	
Year of foundation	
Name of surveyed person	
Position and length of time in that position	
Telephone/E-Mail	
Date	

1) What is the profile of your associates?

□ mainly businesses	□ only businesses	□ mainly chambers	□ only chambers

2) How representative is the entity? (with regards the sectors revenue)

□ 80-100%	□ 50-79%	□ 20-49%	□ 0-19%

3) Are there any other entities that represent the sector, or a part of the sector?

□ We are the only representative of the sector.	□ We are the main representative.	□ There is a certain institutional fragmentation within the sector.	□ The sector suffers from elevated institutional fragmentation.

4) How diversified are the organisations revenues?

□ The revenues originate exclusively from its members.	□ The members' contributions constitute more than 90% of revenues.	□ Between 10 and 40% of revenues are obtained through activities and services.	□ More than 40% of revenues are obtained through activities and services.

5) What share of membership regularly meets the deadline for membership fees?

□ 80 -100%	□ 50-79%	□ 20-49%	□ less than 20%

6) Which internal body is responsible for international trade policy affairs?

☐ There are specific commissions for international trade negotiations and for foreign trade.	☐ There is a foreign trade commission that also handles international trade negotiations.	☐ The commission or executive board places great importance on international trade policy affairs.	☐ International trade policy affairs are not a priority within the entity.

7) How do you evaluate members' participation in the scope of internal bodies responsible for international trade policy affairs?

☐ very active	☐ rather active	☐ rather passive	☐ very passive

8) Is there any permanent staff in charge of international trade policy affairs?

☐ There is a Centre of Economic Studies with three or more technicians.	☐ There is a foreign affairs department or management with 1-2 technicians.	☐ The executive Director is an expert in this issue and/or we have external assessors specifically for this issue.	☐ International trade policy affairs are not a priority issue for the permanent staff.

9) Has the organisation carried out impact studies regarding concluded or ongoing international trade negotiations?

☐ Technical studies were carried out for particular trade negotiations/integration processes (ALCA, WTO, MERCOSUR, etc.)	☐ A general technical study on the trade negotiations has been elaborated.	☐ Studies were carried out in conjunction with other entities on a wider sector.	☐ No such studies were carried out.

10) Hoy many employees work permanently (minimum 50% dedication) **for the organisation?**

Size of the administrative body:	Size of the technical body:	Total number of employees:

11) In your opinion, does the government take adequate measures to ensure transparency concerning advances and possible impacts of ongoing international trade negotiations?

☐ Yes, absolutely	☐ On the whole, yes	☐ On the whole, no	☐ Absolutely not

12) Bearing this in mind, can improvements be noted in the last ten years?

☐ Yes, there has been a great improvement.	☐ Yes, there has been a slight	☐ No, it has worsened slightly.	☐ No, it has clearly worsened.

	improvement.		

13) Does the government closely coordinate with business associations in trade policy affairs, involving the conduction of trade negotiations and the implementation of trade agreements? If not, in what sectors/issues can coordination gaps be identified?

□ Yes, very closely.	□ Yes, rather closely.	□ No, coordination is only sporadic.	□ No, there is practically no coordination.

Comments:

14) Inside the executive branch, is there a clear division of labour in the conduction of international trade policy affairs? If not, in what areas can ambiguity be identified?

□ Yes, it's very clear.	□ Yes, it's quite clear.	□ No, it's quite unclear.	□ No, it's very unclear.

Comments:

15) Is their close inter-ministerial coordination among the departments involved in international trade policy affairs? If not, in what areas can coordination gaps be identified?

□ Yes, it's very close.	□ Yes, it's rather close.	□ No, it's quite sporadic.	□ No, it's very sporadic.

Comments:

16) Is the official team in charge of international trade policy affairs adequately staffed in order to comply with the technical requirements of modern trade negotiations (staff size, talent and experience)? If not, in what areas/issues can limitations be found?

□ very adequate	□ rather adequate	□ rather inadequate	□ very inadequate

Comments:

17) In your opinion, does the government carry out adequate impact assessment regarding the benefits and costs of international trade agreements? If not, in what areas/issues can limitations be found?

□ Yes, definitely	□ It's generally appropriate	□ It's generally inappropriate	□ No, definitely not

Comments:

Table 9.3: Questionnaire Outside Experts (February – October 2004)

Objective	Survey of the perceptions of outside experts in the areas of Foreign Trade and Economic Integration regarding the institutional features of trade policy-making processes in four Latin American countries. Particular importance is given to the organisation of the state executive branch and business sector in the conduction of current international trade negotiations on the bilateral, regional and multilateral level.
Name of surveyed Expert	
Institution	
Area of Investigation/ Work	
Telephone/E-Mail	
Date	

1) Inside the executive branch, is there a clear division of labour in the conduction of international trade policy affairs? If not, in what areas can ambiguity be identified?

□ Yes, it's very clear.	□ Yes, it's quite clear.	□ No, it's quite unclear.	□ No, it's very unclear.

Comments:

2) Is their close inter-ministerial coordination among the departments involved in international trade policy affairs? If not, in what areas can coordination gaps be identified?

□ Yes, it's very close.	□ Yes, it's rather close.	□ No, it's rather sporadic.	□ No, it's very sporadic.

Comments:

3) Is there a shared vision between the foreign affairs and economic agencies regarding the country's world market integration strategy?

□ Yes, absolutely.	□ It is generally shared.	□ There are many divergences.	□ No, absolutely not.

Comments:

4) In your opinion, does the government carry out adequate impact assessment regarding the benefits and costs of international trade agreements? If not, in what

areas/issues can limitations be found?			
□ Yes, definitely.	□ It's generally appropriate.	□ It's generally inappropriate.	□ No, definitely not.

Comments:

5) In your opinion, does the government take adequate measures to ensure transparency concerning advances and possible impacts of ongoing international trade negotiations?

□ Yes, absolutely	□ On the whole, yes.	□ On the whole, No.	□ Absolutely not.

Comments:

6) Bearing this in mind, can improvements be noted in the last ten years?

□ Yes, there has been a great improvement.	□ Yes, there has been a slight improvement.	□ No, it has worsened slightly.	□ No, it has clearly worsened.

Comments:

7) Does the government closely coordinate with business associations in trade policy affairs, involving the conduction of international trade negotiations and the implementation of trade agreements? If not, in what sectors/issues can coordination gaps be identified? (Comments)

□ Yes, very closely.	□ Yes, rather closely.	□ No, coordination is only sporadic.	□ No, there is practically no coordination.

Comments:

8) Is the official team in charge of international trade policy affairs adequately staffed in order to comply with the technical requirements of modern trade negotiations (staff size, talent and experience)? If not, in what areas/issues can limitations be found?

□ Yes, very adequate.	□ Yes, rather adequate.	□ No, rather inadequate.	□ No, very inadequate.

Comments:

9) How do you qualify the business behaviour in international trade policy affairs?

□ very active	□ rather active	□ rather passive	□ very passive

Comments:

10) In light of the ongoing international trade negotiations, does the government implement policy measures to prepare local sectors for the challenges ahead, so as to take advantage of the future trade agreements?

□ Yes, absolutely.	□ Yes, measures are generally adequate.	□ No, there is little activity in this regard.	□ No, absolutely not.

Comments:

11) How do you assess the technical level of business proposals submitted in the area of international trade policy?

□ very high	□ rather high	□ rather low	□ very low

Comments:

12) How would you consider the role played by NGOs within the process of world market integration?

□ Very efficient, the NGOs nourish the public debate in an influential way.	□ Rather efficient, NGO contributions are rather influential.	□ Rather inefficient, their contributions are not very relevant.	□ Very inefficient, NGOs have very little influence in this debate

Comments:

13) How would you qualify the contribution of the academic sector within the process of world market integration?

□ Excellent, the universities nourish the public debate with the necessary inputs.	□ Rather good, the universities generally assume the importance of this process.	□ Rather poor, the academic sector generally doesn't comply with its corresponding role.	□ Very poor, the universities are absent from the debate.

Comments:

Table 9.4: Questionnaire State Officials (February – October 2004)

Objective	Survey of the perceptions of civil service employees from the international trade policy related areas (economic integration, trade negotiations, and foreign trade) regarding the institutional features of trade policy-making processes in four Latin American countries. Particular importance is given to the organisation of the state executive branch and business sector in the conduction of current international trade negotiations on the bilateral, regional and multilateral level.
Name of surveyed State Official	
Department/ agency	
Position	
Telephone/E-Mail	
Date	

1) Description of competencies of the state department/agency

2) Institutional record (since servant entered the agency)

3) Staff size
Size of the permanent technical body:
Total number of staff:
Special advisors (external staff):

4) Labour (salary structure, social security, recruitment system, staff rotation, etc.)

5) Inside the state executive branch, is there a clear division of labour in the conduction of international trade policy affairs? If not, in what areas can ambiguity be identified?

□ Yes, it's very clear.	□ Yes, it's quite clear.	□ No, it's quite unclear.	□ No, it's very unclear.
Comments:			

6) Is their close inter-ministerial coordination among the departments involved in international trade policy affairs? If not, in what areas can coordination gaps be identified?

□ Yes, it's very close.	□ Yes, it's rather close.	□ No, it's rather sporadic.	□ No, it's very sporadic.

Comments:

7) Is there a shared vision between the foreign affairs and economic agencies regarding the country's world market integration strategy?

□ Yes, absolutely.	□ It is generally shared.	□ There are many divergences.	□ No, absolutely not.

Comments:

8) In your opinion, does the government carry out adequate impact assessment regarding the benefits and costs of international trade agreements? If not, in what areas/issues can limitations be found?

□ Yes, definitely.	□ It's generally appropriate.	□ It's generally inappropriate.	□ No, definitely not.

Comments:

9) Is there close coordination between state and business actors in trade policy affairs, involving the conduction of international trade negotiations and the implementation of trade agreements? If not, in what sectors/issues can coordination gaps be identified?

□ Yes, very closely.	□ Yes, rather closely.	□ No, coordination is only sporadic.	□ No, there is practically no coordination.

Comments:

10) Is the official team in charge of international trade policy affairs adequately staffed in order to comply with the technical requirements of modern trade negotiations (staff size, talent and experience)? If not, in what areas/issues can limitations be found?

□ Yes, very adequate.	□ Yes, rather adequate.	□ No, rather inadequate.	□ No, rather very inadequate.

Comments:

11) How do you qualify the business behaviour in international trade policy affairs?

□ very active	□ rather active	□ rather passive	□ very passive

Comments:

12) In light of the ongoing international trade negotiations, does the government implement policy measures to prepare local sectors for the challenges ahead, so as to take advantage of the future trade agreements?

□ Yes, absolutely.	□ Yes, measures are generally adequate.	□ No, there is little activity in this regard.	□ No, absolutely not.

Comments:

13) How do you assess the technical level of business proposals submitted in the area of international trade policy?

□ very high	□ rather high	□ rather low	□ very low

Comments:

14) How would you consider the role played by NGOs within the process of world market integration?

□ Very efficient, the NGOs nourish the public debate in an influential way.	□ Rather efficient, NGO contributions are rather influential.	□ Rather inefficient, their contributions are not very relevant.	□ Very inefficient, NGOs have very little influence in this debate

Comments:

15) How would you qualify the contribution of the academic sector within the process of world market integration?

□ Excellent, the universities nourish the public debate with the necessary inputs.	□ Rather good, the universities generally assume the importance of this process.	□ Rather poor, the academic sector generally doesn't comply with its corresponding role.	□ Very poor, the universities are absent from the debate.

Comments:

Curriculum Vitae

Christian Robin was born on 7 November 1975 in Uznach, Canton St. Gallen. He went to elementary and secondary school in Rapperswil-Jona and graduated from High School in Wattwil *(Maturität Typus E – Wirtschaft, Kantonsschule Wattwil)* in 1996.

In the fall of 1996 Christian Robin enrolled at the Faculty of Arts of the University of Zürich in Political Sciences, Social and Economic History, and Media and received a Masters Degree (Lizentiat) in June 2002. Between 2003 and 2006 he carried out field research in Latin America as doctoral candidate of the Centre for International and Comparative Studies (CIS) Zurich and worked for the Swiss State Secretariat for Economic Affairs (SECO) in the scope of the Trade Cooperation Programmes in Bolivia and Peru.

Christian Robin submitted his doctoral thesis in International Political Economy in February 2006. He is currently working and living in Berne.

0 1341 1273849 4

LaVergne, TN USA
30 March 2010
177579LV00004B/37/P

9 783838 101019